Y0-DXC-927

ADMINISTRATIVE SYSTEMS ABROAD

Revised Edition

Edited by

Krishna K. Tummala

UNIVERSITY
PRESS OF
AMERICA

LANHAM • NEW YORK • LONDON

Copyright © 1982 by

University Press of America,™ Inc.

4720 Boston Way
Lanham, MD 20706

3 Henrietta Street
London WC2E 8LU England

TO

ANU & SUREN

AND ALL OTHERS

BELIEVING IN A WORLD

OTHER THAN THE ONE

THEY LIVE IN

ACKNOWLEDGEMENTS

In bringing this volume out, I had incurred many debts. Germination of this work took place with my participation in successive Third World Conferences, held at the University of Nebraska at Omaha. My thanks are due to the organizers, H. Carl Camp and Joon-Gun Chung for providing the forum and the occasion for me to be a chairman, panelist and discussant.

I am very grateful to Gerald Caiden for his constant encouragement and for suggesting the names of some of the specialists. Caiden, Robert LaPorte, Jr., and David Rosenbloom have been sources of inspiration and support in this and other academic endeavors of mine. My academic friendship with Mohabbat Khan and Jon S. T. Quah have been fruitful. Garth N. Jones has been a good friend. But for each of the contributors, this work would not have been; I gratefully acknowledge my deep sense of appreciation to all.

I am greatly indebted to Fred W. Riggs who had generously provided the Epilogue, in spite of his rather busy schedule and my last minute request. The volume is only richer by his contribution.

I am thankful to the Regents of the University of California for permitting me to incorporate some of the material on China which is pulled out of an article by Maria Chan Morgan that was published in Asian Survey 21, No. 2 (December 1981), pp. 1223-1236.

I appreciate the support given to me by Richard L. Haines and Ken Weaver, past and current Chairmen of my Department, respectively, and thank Bob Taylor for his help in preparing the map.

Chris Peterson had labored as my research assistant and also diligently typed most of the manuscript. Kim Marshall and Lucille Pope had helped complete the typing. The Departmental Secretaries, Cathy Johnson and Nancy Poole have always been helpful.

My thanks are due to James E. Lyons, Vice President and Managing Editor, University Press of America, for his help in an early publication.

As always, most part of what all I accomplished belongs to Pramila.

MAP SHOWING THE COUNTRIES COVERED IN THIS VOLUME

MEXICO
GAUTEMALA
COLOMBIA
VENEZUELA
BRAZIL
ARGENTINA

USSR
TURKEY
ISRAEL
PAKISTAN
NIGERIA
CHINA
INDIA
BANGLADESH
INDONESIA
PHILIPPINES

0   1000   2000 miles

Bogge hemisphere equal area projection

Table of Contents

CHAPTER I

PROLOGUE

Krishna K. Tummala

Comparative administration as an academic discipline, never enjoyed the same currency that comparative
politics did. In fact, these two fields have largely
been separate.[1] Since 1960, with the formation of the
Comparative Administration Group (CAG) under the aegis
of Fred W. Riggs, comparative administration found its
place in the sun. But in 1973, the CAG ceased to exist
independently.[2] During this time however, quite a bit
of publication out-put was seen.[3] Yet the subject is
considered to be "floundering", and the the prospects
not bright. [4] That this was largely a "self-imposed
failure" due to unattainable goals was argued by Robert
T. Golwmbiewski.[5] There was also the lack of conceptual
clarity; "dissensus prevailed".[6] This however, does
not mean that the subject is either dead, or of no
interest.

The extended meaning of 'comparative administration' as "the generalized or global framework for
thinking about problems," is of considerable interest
and importance considering the shrinkage of the world
and its interdependence.[7] This view is further sustained by the Global 2000 and Global Future: Time to Act
reports, which not only are the first attempts by a
national government but also provide a framework of
concerted action.[8] Renewed academic interest in this
area is also seen lately. The National Association
of Schools of Public Affairs and Administration (NASPAA)
in its revised Guidelines and Standards recommends that
the common curriculum for Masters Degree in Public
Affairs/Administration shall "provide each student with
a basic understanding of the environment of public policy..." And the term "environment" was broadly interpreted to include International and Comparative Administration components.[9]

In a recent survey, nearly one half (41) of the
respondents (79) claimed to have a course on these lines,
and yet another quarter of them indicated plans to
strengthen this area.[10] Yet, in terms of reading/
reference material, there is not much readily avaialble.
The one major American journal that dealt with this
area, Journal of Comparative Administration, folded in

1

1974 after a short life of five years.[11] Perhaps, the one best book is by Ferrel Heady.[12] Last year just another appeared on the Asian Administrative systems from Kuala Lumpur.[13]

This volume deals with the Third World Countries (LDCs - Less Developed Countries, as they are currently known). It avoids the term 'comparative' in order not to get into methodological issues therein. The word "system" in the title ought not to be taken as a reflection of the approach of this book. However, it does to an extent follow the bureaucratic model as it provides a more manageable framework.[14] The book neither starts with a preconceived theory or paradigm; nor does it end with one, newly developed. The work in essence has a more modest purpose in that it attempts to fill in a gap in existing literature by providing information on many of the systems of the LDCs in one comprehensive volume. If in the process this were to help others to come up with a bureaucratic paradigm for LDCs, it will have served more than its purpose.

Bureaucracies, as the fourth branch of government, were originally conceived in instrumental terms. But soon enough they found themselves not only entrenched but also indispensable. The power they have come to exercise in the modern days was long recognized, and nearly half a century ago two titles appeared reflecting these concerns: Lord Hewart's <u>New Despotism</u> in 1929, and C. K. Allen's <u>Bureaucracy Triumphant</u> in 1931. And there has been no dearth of critical literature since then. Yet, modern state is an administrative state and as Gerald Caiden in the frontispiece shows, the ideology of administrative state has universally been accepted.

Bureaucracies in the LDCs have a crucial role to play. A considerable ratio of the national elite is drawn into this group, and the administrative system provides a channel for upward mobility to several. Besides, it is also true that the public sector, as the employer of last resort, provides the major source of employment. Bureaucracies not only represent but also mediate interests.[15] In addition, the "New Public Administration" advocates social concern and activism, contradicting the traditional policy/administration dichotomy.[16] This is further buttressed by the ideological concerns that place a great deal of trust in social intervention in human affairs which leads to a large public sector within the context of

development. All this leads to two important considerations: administrative capability and political control.
Administrative capability, according to a study by the
United Nations Organization, is a function of three
variables: performance, structure and environment.[17]

The large size, advantage of expertise possessed,
the permanent nature of the positions occupied, alongside the more or less monolithic nature of the bureaucracies pose the more important problem of control by
the political representatives of the people. Even in
the United States, some argued that the decline of
Tammany Hall led to the loss of party control.[18] In
addition to the abundance of critical literature
showing and criticizing bureaucracies for having become self-centered and uncontrollable, a few even
suggested collusion with the private bureaucracies,
thus breeding oligarchies.[19]

There is also the adaptation problem. Most of
the administrative systems are inherited in that the
majority of the LDCs are former colonies. How to mould
these to native political, social and economic situations is of paramount importance. Thus nativising the
service, the need to increase quantity and to improve
quality of performance, rationalization of the procedures and the exercise of political control alongside
normative concerns come to be of significance. And
these nations expend a great deal of energy on administrative reform which is almost in the nature of a cult.
However, most of the effort unfortunately is spent in
tinkering with administration without a linkage to
political, social and economic factors resulting in
"reform ritualism and inoccuous incrementalism,"
where rhetorical enthusiasm outstrips capability and
implementation.[20]

The nations covered here are from Asia, Africa,
Latin America and the Middle East. While the majority
of them are from Asia, and are former British colonies,
at least two (Nigeria and Philippines) are trying to
shape their administrative systems on the American
model. As to the political systems, they range from
the largest working democracy (Indian) to the largest
totalitarianism (China). Majority are inspired by
the Fabian socialist or socialist thinking and a few
are of capitalist persuasion. While some spend as
much as a third of their budgets on defense (Israel)
others spend most of theirs on services. Put together,
although all these nations occupy less than ten per

cent of the earth physically, they support nearly half of the global population. Thus an attempt has been made here to provide a variety of sources and experiences. And to obviate the common problem of lack of coherence inherent in most edited volumes, and to ensure certain uniformity of purpose and of format, each of the papers was specially written for this volume keeping the following in view:

i.   A very brief structural overview within the cultural context;

ii. Concept of 'merit' and attempts to politicize or depoliticize the bureaucracy;

iii. Efforts at rationalization and motivation (i.e., making the bureaucracy a better instrument);

iv. Bureaucratic role in the developmental process, policymaking and politics in general; and

v.   Control mechanisms (in terms of balance between the elected/appointed, legislative/ executive bodies and the bureaucracy.)

Thus, the following chapters deal with a macro-level analysis and are also ecological in the treatment of subject matter.

Footnotes

[1] Dwight Waldo, "Public Administration," in Marian
D. Irish, ed., Political Science: Advances of the Discipline, Englewood Cliffs, NJ: Prentice Hall, 1968, p.
182. For a critical assessment of comparative administration as an area of discipline, see the introduction
in Ferrel Heady, Public Administration: A Comparative
Perspective, 2nd ed., New York: Marcel Dekker, Inc.,
1979.

[2] The CAG was merged in 1973 into the Section on
International and Comparative Administration (SICA),
within the American Society for Public Administration.

[3] Without naming several names, who are too numerous to list here, Duke University publications deserve
mention. Also see the highly critical review essay of
these works by Garth N. Jones, "Frontiersmen in Search
of 'Lost Horizon': The State of Development Administration in the 1960's," Public Administration Review (PAR)
36, No. 1 (January-February 1976), pp. 99-110.

[4] See Lee Sigelman, "In Search of Comparative
Administration," PAR 36, No. 6 (November-December 1976),
p. 625. Also, Heady, op. cit., p. 31.

[5] Robert T. Golembiewski, Public Administration as
a Developing Discipline: Part I, Perspectives on Past
and Present, New York: Marcel Dekker, Inc., 1977,
pp. 142-149.

[6] See Fred Riggs' introduction in his edited,
Frontiers of Development Administration, Durham, North
Carolina: Duke University Press, 1970, pp. 3-37. As
a matter of fact, no clear distinction was made between
'comparative' and 'development' administrations. If
these terms were not used synonymously, they were
certainly inter-changeable. And all Duke University
publications contained in their titles, 'Development'
or 'Developmental', and not 'Comparative'.

[7] To Riggs, "Comparative administration" has two
other meanings. For some it connotes "foreign", and
for others, it is "methodology". See his, "The Group
and the Movement: Notes on Comparative and Development
Administration," PAR 36, No. 6 (November-December 1976),
p. 652.

[8]The Global 2000 Report to the President: Entering the Twenty First Century, and Global Future: Time to Act. Submitted to President Jimmy Carter in 1980 and 1981 respectively: Both are prepared by the Council on Environmental Quality. Washington, DC: Government Printing Press, 1980, 1981.

[9]Discussion of NASPAA Revised Guidelines and Standards, Annual Meeting, Lexington, KY, October 17, 1981.

[10]Survey conducted by Robert H. Manley of Seton Hall University, South Orange, NJ. Personal communication, November 1981. It should however be noted that that survey was among the members of NASPAA. It is quite likely that as part of the comparative politics curriculum, many more departments of Political Science may be providing these courses. Even among the survey sample, in 2/3 of the programs, students could choose offerings in this area as electives.

[11]This journal merged and became Administration & Soceity in 1974, thus reflecting a diffused focus. There is no other major journal in this area in the United States. See James S. Bowman and Sami G. Hajjar, "The Literature of American Public Administration: Its Contents and Contributors," PAR 38, No. 2 (March-April 1978), pp. 156-165.

[12]Heady, op. cit.

[13]Amara Raksasatya & Heinrich Siendentopf, eds., Asian Civil Services: Developments and Trends, Kuala Lumpur: Asian and Pacific Development Administration Centre, in cooperation with Konrad Adenauer Stiftung, 1980.

[14]See Jon S. Jun, "Renewing the Study of Comparative Administration: Some Reflections on the Current Possibilities," PAR 36, No. 6 (November-December 1976), p. 643.

[15]This was long argued in the United States by Pendleton Herring in his Pulbic Administration and the Pulbic Interest, New York: McGraw Hill, 1936.

[16]See Frank Marini, ed., <u>Toward a New Public Administration: The Minnowbrook Perspective</u>, and its companion volume, Dwight Waldo, ed., <u>Public Administration in a Time of Turbulence</u>, Scranton: Chandler Publishing Company, 1971.

[17]<u>Appraising Administrative Capability for Development</u>, New York: United Nations Organization, ST/TAO/M/46.

[18]Theodore J. Lowi, "Machine Politics--Old and New," <u>Public Interest</u> 9 (Fall 1967), pp. 83-92.

[19]Lowi, <u>The End of Liberalism: Ideology, Policy and the Crisis of Public Authority</u>, New York: Norton & Company, Inc., 1969, and John Kenneth Galbraith, <u>Economics and the Pulbic Purpose</u>, Boston: Houghton Mifflin Company, 1973.

[20]Krishna K. Tummala, <u>The Ambiguity of Ideology and Administrative Reform,</u> New Delhi: Allied Publishers Private Limited, 1979, p. 25. Similar conclusion was reached earlier by Albert O. Hirschman, <u>Journeys Towards Progress</u>, New York: The Twentieth Century Fund, 1963.

CHAPTER II

COMPARATIVE BUREAUCRACY

Gerald E. Caiden

Because of the many variables involved, the possible permutation of administrative systems is certainly large and seemingly endless as we learn more about them. As humanity strives to perfect its social systems, their study, dating back at least to Aristotle, is enticing. What can we discover of lasting value when we compare and contrast the different combinations? If we want stability, what can the ancient empires of Rome, China and Zimbabwe which lasted hundreds of years teach us? If we seek ruthless efficiency, we might better study the Spartans, the Spanish colonialists and the Third Reich. History provides fascinating material for those who would like to unravel the secrets of past successes and failures or who need evidence to support their hypotheses about the fall of civilizations. Alas, historical studies are expensive to undertake, rarely complete (depending on imaginative reconstruction) and of limited value to the contemporary world.

If study of contemporary administration systems is preferred, different challenges confront us. The events reviewed are too fresh for us to see them in their proper perspective. They are still unfolding; we cannot forecast what will eventuate. As we are part of the events themselves, we cannot be impartial. Our lenses are distorted by our values, predisposition and objectives, even by our perceived career prospects or fears for our personal safety. How many of us are willing to expose corrupt practices or destroy legal fictions or contradict the prevailing myths of the time? Even if we could overcome our personal predicaments and as a community of scholars agree on what constitutes truth, we still have to solve the problem of arranging what we know into understandable and meaningful patterns that not only satisfy our intellectual curiosity but also provide guidelines for action. The field of administration sets a high premium on utility or useful knowledge. We study administrative systems less for their own sake, more to improve them, to correct their deficiencies and to build on their strengths. Here again, what we consider to be good or bad is quite subjective; we can never get far away from personal convictions and idiosyncracies that, cloaked in technical language, may be difficult to discern, especially if they coincide with our own.

With this warning in mind, we are fortunate we can take so much in the contemporary world for granted. We do not have to rediscover the wheel. Our administrative heritage has a rich tradition embodied in our institutions, laws, practices and norms. What makes the contemporary world so different is the rise of an international order of sovereign nation-states which has raised government to higher forms of art, thanks largely to the bureaucratization of social organizations and the virtual universal acceptance of the ideology of the administrative state. While bureaucracy and activist government are hardly new, in combination and hitched to modern order and of all social institutions, they are probably the most impactful. Over the past two centuries, they have made deep inroads in what used to be the exclusive domains of the family, religion and business enterprise. Indeed, this century has seen the propagation of totalitarian ideas that deify the bureaucratic state and argue for its supremacy over other social institutions. Be that as it may, there is no doubt that the bureaucratic state had been in the recent decades the preferred instrument for societal development in many countries of varying political persuasions around the world as this collection of country studies well illustrates.

Preference For the Bureaucratic State

When we look more closely at this preferred instrument of societal development, we find that it does hold out advantages over other possible alternatives, not so much because it is inherently virtuous (it is not!) but because the others are more defective. Whereas they are selective and discriminatory, it is universal and all encompassing. Whereas they are voluntary and avoidable, it is compulsory and inescapable. Whereas they tend to be self-serving and uncontrollable, it can be held responsible and accountable. It promises more equal access to public goods and services that are prone to narrow monopolization by the privileged. It promises to protect, guarantee and enforce basic human rights even against its own agents. It promises to mobilize the collective resources of society to advance the common welfare. As a matter of record, it has performed exceptionally well in the circumstances but like

9

so many other human devices, it has been used wrongly
and badly, it has done immense harm and evil in the
wrong hands, and it suffers inherent deficiencies and
defects, what we now recognize as bureaupathologies, a
self-explanatory term if ever there was one. It is a
double-edged weapon that has to be carefully handled,
whose use has to be carefully controlled, and whose
limitations have to be carefully defined.

For these reasons, it is necessary for us to look
closely at some of the prevailing expectations that have
strengthened the bureaucratic state. Three in particular stand out. They are: (1) in the absence of sufficient initiative and enterprise being demonstrated by
other social institutions, the administrative state
should fill the vacuum and if necessary, take the lead;
(2) in assuming this leadership role, the state or public bureaucracy should be reshaped and if necessary,
reconstructed not only to provide encouragement and
inspiration to the community but to undertake productive
and efficacious activities to advance the general welfare; and (3) in delivering this wider range of public
goods and services, the public servants who staff the
public bureaucracy should keep abreast of advances in
the state of the art and adopt the best arrangements
and practices known. These are reasonable expectations.
We know that other social institutions cannot rise to
the occasion every time and they are not capable or adequately equipped to meet rising public demands. The
bureaucratic state is uniquely capable in some ways of
detecting changes in public attitudes, of defining
societal shortcomings, or spotting opportunities, and
of anticipating threats and dangers. This is not to say
that other institutions cannot do these things, only
that for other reasons they cannot move quick enough on
a sufficient scale. Whereas other institutions have
failed to exhibit initiative and enterprise in many
Third World countries, the government has been forced
by their default to call upon the bureaucratic state to
lead.

In pursuit of the new roles expected of them, governments have recognized the need to reshape their
machinery and revamp the public service. They have embarked with mixed success on elaborate administrative
reform campaigns, reorganizing structures, revising
laws, overhauling procedures, enlarging public services,
and institutionalizing reform agencies. They have
sought international technical assistance and they have

trained new cadres of public officials and emphasized professionalism. They have experimented with innovative delivery systems and been receptive to new ideas. Indeed, many breakthroughs in modern administrative technology have been achieved in the public sector first.

Not surprisingly, the bulk of literature on development administration addresses itself to strengthening the bureaucratic state, to reforming the public bureaucracy, and to encouraging the growth of a new profession of development administrators, that is, a new class of public servants capable of planning and executing development initiatives. Much international effort has gone to designing the machinery of government not only in new states where the need was obvious, but also in old states where traditional arrangements had not been adapted to modern requirements. Particular emphasis has been placed on educating and training public servants to design new procedures for themselves and in general to act as their own administrative reformers. One obstacle that has to be overcome is the public personnel system itself which does not attract top talent into public service, does not stress creative and enterprising abilities, does not allow creative and enterprising public servants to show initiative, and does not encourage or support administrative reform efforts. Even self-styled merit systems have failed to overcome traditional sins of inertia, red-tape, procrastination, insensitivity, bias, lack of initiative, mediocrity, sloth, lack of challenge, low productivity, insufficient incentives, and corruption, all which have damaged the reputation of the public sector, reduced government performance and perpetuated barriers between the public bureaucracy and the public.

The failure of administrative reform to transform bureaucratic ethos has been accompanied by misgivings about the whole process of enlarging the political arena, aggrandizing government, bureaucratizing the delivery of public goods and services and entrusting development prospects to bureaucrats. The deliberate speeding up of the process in new states by international technical assistance programs, fashionable in the 1950's and 1960's, stressed bureaucratic development at the expense of political development. Thus countries which had never really experienced self rule before, found that independence merely transferred rule from one set of bureaucrats to another, from colonial

11

administrators to indigenous elitists who perpetuated
or imitated authoritarian (if often paternalistic) administrative reforms. Further, the burgeoning public
bureaucracy stiffled or handicapped other forms of
developmental initiative. Thus a vicious circle was
created--weak non-bureaucratic initiatives led to stress
on bureaucratic initiatives which weakened non-bureaucratic initiatives ad inifinitum. Modernization became
lopsided. The state and its attributes took on the
appearance of contemporary chic but much of the remainder, especially those out of range of the capital
city and regional agencies, stayed where they were.
Often, the growing gap between them and the political
instability generated could only be handled by authoritarian means.

The Inadequacies of Public Bureaucracy

If bureaucratic aggrandizement had guaranteed
satisfactory performance, lopsided modernization might
have been bearable. But it did not. It did not even
guarantee any kind of performance, not where the public
bureaucracy has served itself first and others not at
all. The world had witnessed the deterioration of several countries under bureaucratic rule. In some, dome-
setic agencies are so incompetent and corrupt, that outside agencies have to be employed to get anything done
at all. In others, the bureaucracy, overwhelmed by
social predicaments, has virtually given up, maintaining a holding action with occasional flashes of initiative largely for public relations purposes. Its pes-
simism and cynicism infect the whole society--few
believe that the public bureaucracy is capable of
handling anything competently, that government performance (or output) is so inadequate, stress is placed
upon resources or inputs (or rather obtaining more
resources) irrespective that existing resources are
misused, and on changing the administrative system
without changing bureaucratic attitudes that put self-
service before public service.

Altogether, too much emphasis is placed on means
rather than ends, form rather than substance, processes
rather than results, understandably so if the public
bureaucracy has given up on effective performance. It
is easier to deal with the manipulation of means than
the attainment of ends. It sounds so professional, and
much less political. It fits in well with the tunnel

12

vision of bureaucracy. It gives the appearance of doing something effective when little is actually being accomplished--it is activity without action. It is impressive until one looks through the ritual to examine the results. The public does not see government any different. They do not feel uplifted appreciably by bureaucratic rule. They hardly discern any improvement in the quantity or quality of public goods and services. The political leaders (where not members of the bureaucratic elite) still complain that they cannot get anything done and they remain as suspicious as ever of the bureaucracy on which they are dependent simply for lack of alternatives. Even administratively, there is little to show. Much heralded draft legislation is never passed or if it is passed, is not implemented, or if implemented, is selectively applied to perpetuate the status quo. Reorganization often ends in hopeless confusion and tacit continuation of the status quo ante. Newly injected talent is sidelined or deprived of power or resources. Corruption persists. In short, administrative reform is much of a charade, a diversion, not taken too seriously by the old hands, but considered useful enough to occupy the Young Turks and quite fashionable.

In brief, the bureaucratic state in many countries has not quite worked out as its early advocates hoped it would. Far from encouraging development, it has been obstructive. Far from improving government performance, it has been incompetent. Far from nurturing a new class of progressive development administrators, it has perpetuated a reactionary authoritarian elite. But this has been the worst side. Elsewhere, it has scored remarkable successes. It has been the vanguard of development efforts and it has fostered alternative developing initiatives. Indeed, where the colonialists walked out leaving virtually no developmental activities in progress, it has brought the country through hard times intact and if not flourishing certainly transformed from the previous condition. It has improved governmental performance. Though accurate measures are still lacking, its impact can readily be seen in extending government into the hinterland, providing basic public goods and services where none existed before, expanding public enterprises, establishing social welfare services on a national basis, revamping the taxation system, and generally improving the quality of traditional public services such as postal deliveries, customs clearance, licensing and public record keeping.

It has opened public service to all and in the process
encouraged if not a new class of development administrators, certainly a new cadre of competent, devoted,
professional public servants dedicated to national
development.

Shaping the Bureaucratic Ethos

These contrasts, sometimes geographically in close
proximity on the continents of Africa, Asia, and Latin
America, if not within Europe and North America as well,
direct attention at the causes and consequences. How
can it be that in this country the bureaucratic state
has been a failure while in that country it appears to
have succeeded? What can or should be done in a country
where the bureaucratic state seems dysfunctional to make
it functional? What can countries learn from one another? Can the successful practices of one country be
adopted by another with the same results? If not, why
not? These timeless questions need to be reexamined in
every generation. The answers will never be the same,
simply because circumstances never repeat themselves
identically.

Before any answer is attempted, it is useful to
remind ourselves of certain perennial factors. First,
all states, expecially new states, need a strong central
government apparatus to rule effectively, minimally
defense forces, police, a legal system, and administrative services. Second, all states have been experiencing pressures to increase government responsibilities
and as a result the public sector has tended to expand
as governments find that they have to provide public
goods and services through their own agents. Attempts
to reverse or halt the growth of the bureaucratic state
have so far failed although they may have slowed down
the rate of growth. Third, all states have to adjust
on a regular basis their machinery of government to
accomodate themselves to environmental changes and to
incorporate advances in the state of the art. So far
this process has emphasized public enterpreneurial
activities over regulatory activities and administrative
values have been shifting from efficiency considerations
to effectiveness measures. Fourth, all states have to
guard against dysfunctional tendencies in the public
bureaucracy, such as isolation, unconcern with the public, excessive privilege, self-aggrandizement and trans-
position of objectives, and to tackle bureaupathologies
before they imperil government itself. Fifth, perhaps

never before has public administration, its developmental aspects and the quality of the public servants who staff its activities, been so important.

All the countries studied in this book, despite some disillusionment with bureaucratic performance, still strongly believe and depend on statism, on the patrimonial state, on public bureaucracies to reshape society, to transform social institutions, to speed up modernization and to develop their potentialities. To this extent, they are all bureaucratic states in which senior public servants still see themselves and are seen by outsiders as a guardian class, that is, custodians of social ideals dedicated to the common good and advancement of the public interest who have to educate, guide and lead the rest of society. In practice, they act more as a caste bureaucracy than a guardian bureaucracy because with a few notable exceptions, the senior public servants are a closed elite recruited from the same restricted social class, usually upper crust, that monopolizes public life to protect that status quo generally and its own special interests when threatened, thus careful to preserve its status and privileges and tending in its conduct of public affairs to be antiquarian, formalistic and heavy handed.[1]

Because senior public officials tend to be aloof, independent, snobbish and self-perpetuating, competing elites attempt to control them usually by some form of politicization to make them subordinate, accountable, responsive and sensitive to the changing moods of the masses who distrust and despise them. But recurrent politicization merely panicks them into passivity and merely leavens the public bureaucracy with technically incompetent, undisciplined, inexperienced, rapacious if loyal partisans. Bureaucratic behavior has not changed; it remains aggrandizing, conservative, exploitive, self-centered, fragmented, legalistic, irrational, corrupt, and inept from a developmental perspective. In short, independence, the replacement of foreign administrators with local people, the expansion of the public sector, and the multiplication of public agencies, periodic reorganizations of the machinery of government, and the strengthening of constitutional, political, legal and economic controls over the public bureaucracy, have not altered the fundamentals of bureaucratism. Not surprisingly, in all of them the bureaucratic state is seen as a necessary evil and there is little reason to believe that elsewhere the situation is much different.

Obviously, there are factors at work which inhibit the transformation of the bureaucratic state into something that idealists of social engineering would prefer and that other classes, perhaps even the bureaucrats themselves, would find more acceptable. Amongst these factors, three external to the public bureaucracy and three internal seem to be crucial. As regards external factors, scarcity influences social behavior in general and bureaucratic behavior in particular. As there is not enough to go round even for subsistence for large numbers of people, there is intense competition to secure some share of what is available and to protect it from being taken away by others. This forces a selfish frame of mind whereby self-service is disguised by lip service to the public or general interest. Public office is used to gain, protect and enlarge one's personal interests. The public bureaucracy is exploitive, aggrandizing, self-serving, privileged, corrupt, underemployed, wasteful from a societal viewpoint.

Heterogeneity reinforces competition and rivalry as the different social groups struggle for available resources. National unity is only surface thin. Otherwise ascription is all. Established elites try to dominate major social institutions, among which the public bureaucracy is probably the key institution. They are continually being challenged by upward mobile groups who also see the public bureaucracy as a key institution to infiltrate, dominate and control. Rarely is the public bureaucracy representative of the wider society. Some groups--usually urban, prosperous, educated and well connected--are over-represented while others are clearly shut out and cannot identify with public institutions and consider themselves discriminated against in access to public resources. Within the public bureaucracy, group ascription largely determines career prospects and manifests itself in discriminatory patron-client relations in administrative style.

Scarcity and heterogeneity contribute to instability. Several of the countries considered here have experienced war and persistent external threats to national integrity. Others have gone through civil wars and communal riots which have left lasting social scars. Government weaknesses have brought about several changes of regime, numerous coups and attempted coups, and periodic purges of the public bureaucracy. Instability promotes safety first, prudence, care, and hesitation to undertake risks. Public servants have to look at the immediate rather than to the future. There has to be quick returns, visible projects, show pieces to reassure the public that government works and the public bureaucracy is well-meaning, useful and effective. This may not lead to the best use of public resources and it may well promote rapaciousness on the part of the insecure and inertia on the part of the secure.

The internal inhibitions would principally include elitism. Senior public servants are elitists or assume elitist attitudes toward the public and their subordinates. In most countries, they are privileged. They are a select inbred group. They are an identifiable, experienced, knowledgeable class. But they are also isolated or they separate themselves from other classes and they live exceptional lives. They look down on other public servants who, along with the masses, they distrust. They arrogate to themselves power and authority and fail to delegate. As a result they are overworked, they deal with too much detail, they cause bottlenecks, and their efforts result in uneven development of governmental programs. The whole governmental apparatus tends to be highly centralized, with policy-making confined to fairly select groups, which look upon the bureaucratic state as an instrument for sharing spoils if not downright self-enrichment. Rank oriented, hierarchial behavior predominates with deference expected.

A second inhibition is not so much rapid growth or size as such, although they too present problems, but fragmentation of the public bureaucracy into separate and distinct fiefdoms. Divisions, once made, tend to stick and the lines are protected. Consequently, one part of the public bureaucracy may not know what any other is doing. Cooperation between different parts is difficult to achieve, a problem further compounded by the hiving off of public enterprises and the existence of large numbers of autonomous agencies which act as if development was an administrative not a political issue. The personalization of authority at the top is accompanied by excessive legalism, redtape and defensiveness down the line as the overlords insist on loyalty and obedience. Consequently, administrative standards and performance are uneven, standardization is rare. Across the board there is lack of rationality and reliability and difficulty in adhering to priorities.

Finally, widespread _inertia_ prevails. Despite every effort to move the bureaucracy in a different direction, it rarely changes. Numerous reform commissions have attempted to transform the public bureaucracy without success. Their reports have not been implemented or implemented so selectively as to reinforce rather than change the status quo. Form alters but the same behavior persists. The only reforms that are adopted are those which the bureaucratic elite wants, usually of a self-serving variety, or which the autocratic leaders have imposed by force on the reluctant bureaucracy. From a bureaucratic viewpoint, there are few incentives to innovate. For many bureaucrats, public administration is administration _of_ the public, not administration _for_ the public.

None of these particular factors is likely to change in the foreseeable future. It is not surprising, then, that outside observers are somewhat pessimistic about prospects for improvement. Changes there will be, but short of a revolutionary situation or downright disaster, nothing fundamental will significantly alter. Rival elites lack the experience, competence and inside knowledge of the bureaucratic elite which knows that it is indispensable if governments are to deliver anything at all. However badly they may perform by foreign standards, there is nothing better domestically and given the circumstances under which they operate they feel that they do well just to hold the line. They have no experience of anything different and they cannot envisage any sudden change for the better in their circumstances.

Facing the Future

Is the future prospect so bleak? No doubt things could and should be better. But then the same is probably true of every country. The studies presented in this volume read familiar to anyone who is acquainted with nineteenth century bureaucracies in the then developing countries. They were also called upon to bear a burden beyond their capacity. They were also maintaining outmoded administrative arrangements that ill-suited governmental purposes. They were also suffering from bureaupathologic behavior. They were also short on experienced, qualified and public spirited staff. Yet they were able to transform themselves, admittedly after a great deal of public protest, administrative reform effort and internal self-revitalization over three succeeding generations of public officials. Contemporary public bureaucracies start from a much better position, having their experience to draw upon and the advances in administrative technology that are currently available.

If left alone, things could deteriorate and they have done during the difficult transition period not yet completed from a colonial-style bureaucracy to a development-style bureaucracy. But often appearances deceive. What may appear to be deterioration from the outside may well hide a slow but important transformation inside. Several country studies do point to significant features of lasting dimensions. First is that the blame is not wholly internal. Apart from world events which have adversely affected individual countries more than others and specific events which have singled out certain victims, poor countries without oil and other natural resources in high international demand have been battling hard in the past twenty years just to stay in place. Foreign and international aid have failed to redress trade and balance of payments deficits. To their credit, the public bureaucracies of the poor countries have artfully kept their countries from regressing. They have begun to master the intricacies of international relations to their advantage and presumably in the future they will make a better showing.

A second factor in their favor is that they have realized that foreign models are unreliable. For years they were persuaded to follow models of development that had worked (in different circumstances) for the rich countries, and aping rich countries' elites, senior public officials rather fancied themselves as a mandarin class that would speed up modernization. The models proved unreliable. Realization dawned on the bureaucrats that they would have to tailor their own development and modernization schemes to fit indigenous conditions. They have begun to question not just the models thrust on them by foreigners but also to question the assumptions behind those models and their goals. They have found them wanting in many respects and they are no longer timid to reject them outright and to substitute their own. They reject much academic writing (by scholars from rich countries) as being irrelevant, recognize foreign aid for what it largely is namely, Cold War rivalry that has its uses but also its snares, and see through none too subtle attempts at cultural imperialism. All this is probably for the better although their countries are so weak that they themselves are also carried along by external pressures to embrace an international order that is to their permanent disadvantage and leaves them even more dependent on decisions made beyond their influences. To master their own destiny, they know they have to sacrifice the short term gains of playing to somebody else's rules for the more permanent gains of playing to their own rules.

A third factor is that despite administrative deficiencies, government in poor countries has not collapsed. On the contrary, it has been extended geographically beyond major cities into more desolate and isolated regions where it never really functioned before. Furthermore, the range and variety of public goods and services has grown quite significantly, including a large number that had previously been unknown and whose delivery is much more complicated and demanding. In attempting to deliver quite sophisticated public services with traditional administrative mechanisms, bad mistakes were made and horror stories about them are legion. But at least the attempt was made and has not been abandoned. Instead the embarrassment of failure has spurred the public bureacracy to avoid repetition and to study the parameters of feasibility, perhaps even to be less ambitious, less hasty, less impatient. They know they have to do better. But they also know they are not going to get much help from outside. In many cases foreign delivery of public goods and services is unacceptable while private sector delivery is too unreliable, too discriminatory, too uneven, and too exploitive. Traditional ways cannot do the job but they can be incorporated into new delivery systems of copartnership and coproduction. Unfortunately, mass illiteracy still remains a handicap as does immature political leadership. In short, there is no ready alternative to improving bureaucratic performance, even if this means that bureaucratic development continues to outdistance political development in many poor countries and without effective competing political elites (or countervailing forces) the public bureaucracy rarely responds to public complaints.

The country studies in this volume point to an agenda for improvement.

1. A change of heart is needed in the public

bureaucracy. Public officials should cease their self-serving behavior and become true public servants, i.e., servants of the public. They should end their exploitation of public office and their parasitism. They should weed out the unfit and incompetent. Like born-again Christians, virtue not avarice should be their guide. Such moral revolution should come from within.

2. The new morality should lead to the suppression of corruption and "bureaucratic rot." As long as corruption is institutionalized, there can be little hope for administrative improvement. The ethic transformation has to be reinforced by institutional arrangements that penalize corrupt behavior.

3. Rationality should be strengthened as an organizational value. The Weberian model of bureaucracy has advantages over the personalized systems for developing countries. It stresses universalism over particularism, achievement over ascription, reliability over instability, equity over discrimination, evenhandedness over prejudice. Development prospects would be enhanced if public administration were refashioned on these lines.

4. Existing proposals for administrative reform should be implemented. Numerous reform commissions and other bodies of inquiry have labored in vain to suggest ways and means to improve administrative arrangements. Their recommendations should be acted upon for they are eminently suitable and based on the best available thinking.

5. The bureaucratic elite should be unified and professionalized by deemphasizing the generalist principle and incorporating top level specialists and professionals, strenthening administrative capabilities through education and training in administrative sciences, devising integrative mechanisms, and generally standardizing the conditions of employment in the public sector.

6. The image and style of the public

bureaucracy should be transformed to emphasize
dedication to social goals, identification
with the aspirations of the public, advancement of the state of the art, and personal
integrity.

These are all worthy items for serious consideration.
If followed, they should indeed reduce bureaupathologies and enhance administrative performance.

They will not solve the political problems of any
society. Indeed continued reliance on a dominant
public bureaucracy may only lead to a further institutional asymmetry, further aggrandizement of the public
bureaucracy at the expense of other social institutions,
and further bureaupathologies as the administrative
state over-extends itself. If, as Fred Riggs argues,
development involves increasing ability to make collective decisions, a more efficient administration of
development may not require strengthening the public
bureaucracy so much as the emergence of extra-
bureaucratic institutions capable of taking some of the
burden off the bureaucracy and imposing responsibility
on bureaucrats, the selection of administrative tech-
nologies than institutionalize changes that enable
public agencies to serve public bureaucracies more
effectively, and the establishment of a balance of
power between bureaucracies and their extra-bureaucratic
institutions.[2] After all, as the contributors to
this volume imply, good government is more than good
administration.

Footnotes

1. F.M. Marx, _The Administrative State_, Chicago: The University of Chicago Press, 1957, pp. 54-72.

2. F.W. Riggs, "Bureaucracy and Development Administration," _Philippine Journal of Public Administration_ 25, No. 2, (April 1977), pp. 105-122.

CHAPTER III

THE ADMINISTRATIVE SYSTEM OF ISRAEL

David H. Rosenbloom
&
Gregory S. Mahler

The Israeli administrative system is exceedingly
complex and central to the nation's political, economic,
and social life. By western standards, the nation is
thoroughly bureaucratized. The average citizen is
highly dependent upon the national administrative system for many services and necessities. These range
from securing housing, education, and employment to
obtaining drivers' licenses and telephones. Indeed, the
citizenry perceives the bureaucracy to be a potent and
intrusive force in daily life. Similarly, the economy
is heavily regulated and influenced by the bureaucracy,
which has been enmeshed in Israeli efforts at economic
development. The administrative system is also an integral part of the Israeli political process generally.
Ruling coalitions have long made use of bureaucratic
positions and ministry budgets to force alliances. Yet,
despite its centrality--or perhaps because of it--the
Israeli national bureaucracy remains a highly problem-
atic feature of the political system.

Structure and Personnel[1]

Structurally, the Israeli bureaucracy is similar
to administrative systems elsewhere. It is hierarchical
and departmental. During the first 25 years of statehood (1948-1973), the bureaucracy grew to consist of 21
Ministries. The most important of these are the Ministries of Defence, Foreign Affairs, Finance, Education,
and Labour. Together, they have consistently controlled
about 90 percent of the national budget. Most of the
remaining ministries have parallels in other nations,
but some are exceptional. Among the latter are a Ministry of Absorption, which deals with immigration; a
Ministry of Police, having not only normal police functions, but also a heavy responsibility for maintaining
security along the nation's permeable borders; and, the
Ministry of Religious Affairs, which has no counterpart
in more secular states and which has been a major bene-
ficiary of coalition politics.

The bureaucracy also witnessed rapid growth in

terms of personnel. In the first quarter century after its inception, the administrative system quadrupled the number of its employees to a total of about 57,000. Expansion was especially great in the Ministries of Finance, Labour, Health, Commerce and Industry, and Communication. Like the bureaucracy generally, the personnel system is rather fragmented. There are several systems, but about 85 percent of all <u>administrative</u> personnel are grouped under a uniform schedule of 20 grades. The hierarchical nature of the system is evident from the concentration of employees in the lower and middle levels. Less than 10 percent are in the top five grades, which have a great deal of responsibility for policy development and implementation. Occupationally, the largest single group is engaged in clerical work, followed by technicians, maintenance workers, and social welfare and health service workers. About 10 percent of the personnel are supervisors and professionals. The average civil servant has a high school degree, but less than 20 percent have completed a higher education.

Throughout its history, staffing the bureaucracy with competent personnel has been a severe problem for Israel. At the outset, the nation's political and ideological outlook displayed an anti-professional strain. As Leonard Rein once observed: "By and large, Israel's founding fathers were schooled in the doctrine of agrarian socialism, they were ideologically opposed to the hierarchic implications of professionalism. They believed that good will and hard work could conquer all. They themselves had successfully practiced egalitarian voluntarism."[2] Consequently, in the early days of settlement and statehood, there was a prevailing attitude among potential administrative leaders that "we did not come to Palestine to be clerks."[3]

The lack of professionally trained and highly motivated public personnel has contributed to pronounced inefficiencies in program implementation and service delivery. This situation has been compounded by two additional factors. First, until 1959, the personnel system was highly politicized. In that year, the development of a merit-based civil service became a professed national objective. By that time, the state had been successfully established, the crush of new immigrants had abated, a more technological and less generalist outlook was emerging throughout several segments of the society, the major political parties shared a greater degree of institutionalization and were better able to mobilise popular support with less reliance on administrative patronage, and, finally, some of the earlier distaste for British methods had worn off. However, the process of civil service reform has been uneven and patronage, or protectzia, in the form of political connections remains an important means of personal advancement within the civil service.[4]

It is important to emphasize that politicization was not confined solely to personnel matters, but rather whole Ministries were taken over or "colonised" by one political party or another. As a result, administrative "services were performed chiefly for the party faithful."[5] Therefore, to an extent, one's housing and employment were related to one's political allegiance and connections. As these tendencies progressed, "certain ministries became hardly distinguishable from party cells."[6] Even today, tendencies along these lines remain.

A second aspect of the personnel system detracting from professionalism and motivation has been the heavy reliance placed on collective bargaining in establishing working conditions. Salaries and a host of other personnel arrangements are largely determined by agreement between the Israeli Civil Service Commission, employee unions, and the Histadrut (General Federation of Labour). Unionization is almost complete and labor relations tend to follow the "syndicalist" pattern of Western Europe.[7] Strikes are common and personnel turnover has been a persistent problem.

Largely as a result of these elements, in 1956 the general condition of the Israeli bureaucracy was appropriately summarized in the following words:

> The Civil Service exhibited much of the malaise common to new or inexperienced Administrations; a concentration of work at the top levels and a lack of proper delegation and decentralization, poor organization with responsibilities badly allocated or ill-defined, a general lack of adequate directives and instructions for the execution of the work, indifferent supervision, poor office methods and physical working conditions, a tendency to start projects before

26

previous ones had been properly carried
through and consolidated; indifferent
treatment of the public and a lack of
leadership and esprit de corps.[8]

Although somewhat overstated today, in essence this
indictment must still stand. Despite efforts at modernization and depoliticization, "one must not lose sight
of the fact that these rules are not applied in practice; promotions are controlled at the top by the politicians and at the bottom by the unions. The experts
who devised the system and who believe in it have no
power at all to insure the operation."[9] In large part,
as this outlook suggests, a primary complexity of the
Israeli bureaucracy is a pronounced gap between formal
bureaucratic structure and actual administrative process.

Process

Israel, as Gerald Caiden cogently observes, is a
nation without even the semblance of a coherent administrative culture or traditon.[10] There was very little
to build upon when Israel became an independent nation,
and the establishment of an administrative culture
stressing rationality, efficiency, and other modern organizational concepts has remained elusive. Nor has
the Israeli bureaucracy been noted for promoting equity.
Administration of Palestine under the Turks and the
British was haphazard and often ineffectual. Although
the Jewish community enjoyed a substantial measure of
autonomy and self-governance, its experience was insufficient to provide for successful administrative practice after independence. Jews who worked in the public
service under British Mandatory Administration were
looked upon with disfavor; the Zionist leaders and revolutionaries were unsuited to the new administrative
tasks at hand:

> Above all, the State lacked good civil-
> ian organizers. . . . Many of the lead-
> ing business men, soldiers, and politi-
> cians were muddlers when it came to or-
> ganizing an office of a staff. . . .
> The old guard that did yeoman service as
> Zionist organization emissaries, as
> presidents of local Zionist groups, and
> collectors of funds and propagators of
> propaganda, were seen to have outgrown

27

their usefulness. As in all revolutions, the old revolutionaries, the born rebels and propagandists, became a liability once their cause had triumphed.[11]

Indeed, even a full decade after independence, a member of the dominant political party announced in the national legislature that "it is still not clear to us[12] what is the desirable image for our civil service." Nor was it thought that Israel could "simply copy other countries."[13]

Although an administrative culture is currently developing in Israel, it still consists of several diverse and often mutually incompatible strands, as Caiden observes. He points to four main administrative subcultures.[14] The first is the "indigenous Middle Eastern style." Here, "business is transacted at a regal pace, in a charmingly courteous, if exasperating, fashion." Deference to authority, status, and rank are combined with bureaucratic officiousness and the need for bargaining skills. By and large, "it is a bargaining rather than a bureaucratic posture."

The second legacy is from the British. It "... lingers in important areas of national government, despite attempts to reduce its influence in the early days of the state." Caiden views it as a "no-nonsense, orderly, condescending, bureaucratic approach, with little room for bargaining, local initiative, or disruption." It is most prevalent in the legal system and police organization, although traces of this tradition can be found elsewhere as well.

In addition to these legacies are two traditions which are more closely related to Jewish circumstances. In Caiden's words,

> The third strand is composed of traditions brought by Jewish immigrants from their countries of origin, as varied as the contents of a spicery. Paranoiac ghetto attitudes mingle with dynamic, cosmopolitan, liberal entrepreneurship. Efficient, dogmatic, Central European bureaucrats work alongside contemplative philosophers unused to standardization and impersonal legal-rational authority. These variations are contained within a

framework of bureaucratization, professionalism, functional requirements and
clientele pressures. While in time they
lost some of their sharpness, they do
create a continuing problem in cooperation
and coordination. Occasionally, under
pressure, they explode into conflict.

Finally, there is the tradition of the <u>vatiquim</u>, or
old-timers and their offspring. This consists of a
"variety of styles related to position, experience, education, age, political ideology, and personal ambitions." In general, however, this tradition relies on
the pragmatic feel of things, confidential and in-group
decision-making, and personal or political connections.
Here, bargaining is tolerated as a necessary evil and
frequently relied upon, although with some distaste.

The net result of these cultural strands is inconsistency, incoherence, and not a small measure of inefficiency. Some offices approach the Weberian ideal
type bureaucracy: rules, formalization, specialization,
hierarchy, impersonality, and merit based neutrality
are the order of business. Others, however, are better
likened to an "oriental bazaar." Here, virtually everything is bargainable. Rules exist, but are largely ignored; impersonality is out of the question. The client
seeks to strike the best deal possible. Pleading is
often highly personalized, appealing to the bureaucrat's
sense of humanity. The administrative culture enables
the bureaucrat to bargain over the application and interpretation of rules, thereby both enhancing and dim-
inishing bureaucratic authority at once. Exceptions
are common, and deals once struck, must often be re-
negotiated at some later stage. In many offices of this
nature there is virtually no technological sophistica-
tion--the shoe box replaces the file and computer as a
storage mechanism, and even the telephone is useless.
Interaction is extremely time-consuming and red tape
abounds. Indeed, a survey of Israeli citizens found
that "wasted time" and "being sent from one clerk to
another" were the factors that were found most disturbing when interacting with the bureaucracy.[15]

The absense of a clear-cut, agreed upon administrative culture raises additional problems as well. Among
the most important of these are (1) the inability of
the civil service to develop a favorable public image
and self-image, and (2) the continuing practice of

treating the administrative system as an adjunct of the partisan coalition process. It is to these matters that we now turn.

Image and Self-Image

Israelis, it often seems, have an endless supply of tales of stupidity, inefficiency, and woe perpetrated by the national bureaucracy. Although such anecdotal information is often colorfully revealing, the image of the Israeli bureaucracy is more cogently portrayed by summarizing the findings of a systematic study of it. In Bureaucratic Culture: Citizens and Administrators in Israel, Nachmias and Rosenbloom reached the following conclusions based upon the results of a survey of the Israeli population: As a whole, Israeli citizens report that the bureaucracy has a considerable impact on their daily lives, that it is of high salience to them, and that they interact with it frequently. They also feel that it has a considerable impact on national development, social integration, and democracy, although less so with regard to the latter. Nevertheless, Israelis are overwhelmingly negative in their characterization of the bureaucracy's impact in these areas. Indeed, at least 60 percent of the public gave its activities a negative rating in each of these areas, and "extremely negative" ratings were several times more frequent than "extremely positive" ones. The average Israeli also tends to consider civil servants to be relatively dishonest, unpleasant, inefficient, passive, slow, and unstable. Israelis also feel that successfully influencing the course of the bureaucracy is unlikely. This partly explains why less than 20 percent of the public has ever attempted to influence the bureaucracy, despite its pervasiveness and strong impact upon their daily lives. Nor do Israelis attach great prestige to civil service employment. In sum, Israelis find their national bureaucracy and its employees to be undesirable features of the political community, which have a considerable, yet largely unfavorable, influence upon their society.

As might be expected from the lack of a coherent administrative culture, the public is not uniform in its image of the Israeli administrative system. Some are far more negative than others. Most important in this respect, approximately 30 percent hold such a negative image that they are so poorly adjusted to the bureaucratization of public life as to be unable to enjoy fully the benefits of citizenship. This segment believes that the bureaucracy is too complex to be understood readily and that it is unfair. They tend to view it as an unwelcome and threatening force in the political community and do not feel as able as other citizens to interact successfully with it. The remainder of the public is more amenable to bureaucratization, but only a minority can be categorized as basically supportive of the national administrative system.

The difficulties inherent in the public's generally negative image of the Israeli bureaucracy are compounded by civil servants' self-images. Nachmias and Rosenbloom also surveyed Israeli bureaucrats. By and large, they found that the average Israeli bureaucrat is considerably more sanguine than the public with respect to his or her orientations toward the national administrative system. On the whole, the civil servants tended to attribute to the bureaucracy a greater impact on the daily life of the nation. They also felt that it has had a greater impact on national development, the maintenance of democracy, and especially on the promotion of social integration. Moreover, the bureaucrats were far more positive in their characterization of the bureaucracy's impact in these areas. This was particularly true in the higher ranks of the civil service. They also considered bureaucrats to be considerably more honest, pleasant, efficient, active, and stable than did the general public. Nevertheless, civil servants' self-image is somewhat more negative than positive. Relatedly, a large proportion of the bureaucrats expressed a desire to be employed outside the national bureaucracy. Their propensity to leave its ranks is associated with a sense of powerlessness and frustration with politicization of the civil service. Thus, in general, the Israeli civil servant is more supportive of the bureaucracy and its personnel than is the typical member of the general public, but nevertheless bureaucrats' characterization of the administrative system is largely unfavorable.

As is the case among the public, some bureaucrats are far more favorable than others in their image of the Israeli administrative system. About 35 percent of the bureaucrats believe that the personnel system is not merit oriented. As a whole, these civil servants are the most critical of the bureaucracy. Those who share this perception and seek to render service to the community consider the bureaucracy to be an obstacle.

They hold the most negative image of the civil service
among the bureaucrats. They see it as largely repressive, ineffectual, and inefficient. Similar perceptions
are reflected among those bureaucrats sharing the same
general view of the personnel system, but being inner-
oriented rather than community oriented in their outlook. Put simply, they do not view the bureaucracy as
an effective instrument for anything more than dispen-
sing patronage and providing political connections.
The remaining bureaucrats, on the other hand, tend to
be more sanguine in their general image of the Israeli
administrative system.

It is evident that the Israeli bureaucracy suffers
many shortcomings from the perspectives of administrative theory and practice. It has failed to develop an
effective administrative practice. It has failed to
develop an effective administrative culture and is characterized by widespread inefficiencies. It is almost
as disorganized as organized. Its personnel are not
highly regarded. Indeed, civil servants' self-image is
largely negative. Nor has the national administrative
system been widely perceived as effectively promoting
democratic government and social equity. Many of the
factors contributing to this general condition have
already been identified and reviewed. One, however,
and an overriding one at that--politicization--deserves
more extended analysis.

The Politics of Administration

Bureaucratic structures and bureaucratic hierarchies are terribly important in the contemporary Israeli
political system. Ministries, the heads of the governmental bureaucracies, are important in the governmental
system as "rewards" to be doled out in the process of
forming political coalitions, which are central in the
daily operation of Israeli government.

Never in Israel's history has a single political
party received a majority of seats in the Knesset, Israel's parliament. Because of this fact, it has been
necessary after every election in Israel's history to
have a government coalition formed--a number of political parties pooling their relative strength (in this
case Knesset seats) in order to build a majority. This
coalition-formation process is directly related to the
visible structure of Israeli bureaucracy, because one
of the more obvious signs of the coalition-formation

process is the distribution of ministries.

It is interesting to examine the relationship between the party members of government coalitions and the "payoffs" they receive for joining the coalition. There are, broadly speaking, two types of "payoffs" available to political parties in return for their joining a coalition. First, parties may demand certain policy payoffs, such as demanding that the new government pass a specific piece of legislation that has been advocated by that political party. Second, parties may demand bureaucratic or positional payoffs, such as demanding that they receive two or three specific Ministries--and thereby bureaucratic and policymaking infrastructures--in exchange for their support in the coalition. The former payoffs will not be the focus of attention here; it is to the latter that we turn our attention.

After every election since independence, until 1977, the Mapai party formed the basis of the government in Israel. There has never been in Israel what Valerie Herman and John Pope have called a "majority situation", that is, one in which the party organizing the government has more than 50 percent of the seats in parliament. Israel has always been an illustration of a "minority situation, majority government," one in which a party with less than a majority of parliamentary seats joins with other minority parties to form a majority government.[16] This situation has resulted in coalitions being formed not only after elections of the Knesset, but also often between Knesset elections when a coalition that already was formed dissolves for one reason or another. In fact, during the first eight Knesset there were 20 Cabinets.[17]

Table I shows those parties belonging to governmental coalitions (specifically, those holding Ministries) in the first Cabinets created in each of the nine elected Knesset. The table shows that the size of the Cabinet has varied over the years, from representing the Prime Minister and eleven governmental bureaucracies to representing the Prime Minister and 22 governmental bureaucracies. Some Ministries have been continuously in existence, others have appeared and disappeared, subsequently to be combined with other offices.

Our goal here is to examine the pattern of Cabinet payoffs over time, to see the role that the bureaucratic

structures play in the process of Cabinet formation.
Michael Leiserson wrote that some payoffs are dominated
by others; in other words, some Cabinet positions are
worth more than others. In his study of Japan, he
showed that coalition members perceived a qualitative
difference between different Cabinet Ministries and
agency positions. He assigned these Ministries and positions to six ranks and showed that coalition members
would demand at least a certain level of rewards for
their continued support.[18]

William Gameson predicted that Ministries would be
given away in direct proportion to the strength of members, but would not specify whether all Ministries
counted as the same value or whether some counted more
than others.[19] If two members form an alliance, one
with 40 seats and one with 20 seats, either the first
member will receive twice as many Ministries as the second (if they are all valued as being equal), or the
first member will receive twice the net value of the
Ministries as the second. The findings of Eric Browne
and Michael Franklin suggested that "even though parties
consider some Ministries more important than others,
they are unwilling to pay for the receipt of Ministries
they want by accepting less than their fair share of
the distribution taken as a whole."[20] These theories
may be applied to the Israeli case in order to help explain Cabinet Ministry distribution.

Table I illustrates the distribution of Ministries
in the Israeli Cabinets. What does this table tell us
about payoff distribution? It gives us information of
several types that may be used in evaluating some of
the theories of payoff distribution met above. First,
although we have not broken the Ministries down into
several categories as did Leiserson, even a brief examination of the table will indicate which Ministries
have been the most important to the various parties
participating in the governments. The government-
forming party, traditionally Mapai (subsequently Labour), has consistently held the positions of Prime
Minister and Deputy Prime Minister, and the Ministries
of defense, foreign relations, finance, agriculture,
and education and culture.[21] The religious parties
have traditionally held the Ministries of religious affairs and social welfare. The Ministries of commerce
and industry, justice, labour, health, immigration, interior, posts, tourism, development, housing, transportation, and communication have passed from party to

TABLE I

Distribution of Cabinet Ministries:
1949-1977

Ministry	First Cabinet of Knesset: 1	2	3	4	5	6	7	8	9
Prime Min.	MA	MA	MA	MA	MA	MA	L	L	LK
Deputy PM	-	-	-	-	-	-	-	L	DMC
Defense	*	*	*	*	*	*	L	L	LK
Foreign Affs.	MA	MA	MA	MA	MA	MA	L	L	ind
Finance	MA	MA	MA	MA	MA	MA	L	L	LK
Comm. & Indus.	*	MA	MA	MA	MA	MA	C	L	LK
Justice	PR	*	PP	PP	MA	MA	L	L	DMC
Labor	MA	MA	MA	MA	AH	AH	L	L	*
Health	URF	NRP	MP	MP	NRP	MP	-	L	LK
Immig. & Abs.	*	-	-	-	*	-	-	L	LK
Interior	*	NRP	AH	NRP	*	NRP	*	NRP	NRP
Rel. Affs.	URF	*	NRP	ind	NRP	NRP	NRP	NRP	NRP
Soc. Welfare	URF	A	*	NRP	NRP	NRP	NRP	NRP	DMC
Police	SE	MA	MA	MA	MA	MA	L	L	*
Posts	-	-	NRP	*	MA	-	G	-	*
Educ. & Culture	MA	MA	MA	MA	MA	MA	L	L	NRP
Agri.	MA	MA	MA	MA	MA	MA	L	L	LK
Tourism	-	-	-	-	-	*	IL	IL	*
Develop.	-	*	MP	MP	MA	IL	NRP	-	LK
Housing	-	-	-	*	*	NP	L	L	*
Trans.	-	-	-	AH	AH	AH	G	L	DMC
Communic.	MA	MA	AH	*	*	*	-	L	*
Energy	-	-	-	--	-	-	-	-	LK
Min. w/o Port	-	MA	MA	MA	MA	AH	L3	L3	NRP
							C2	NRP	
Total Ministries	12	13	16	16	16	17	22	24	17

Symbols and Party Abbreviations

*	Combined w/another Min.	LK	Likud (Gahal+Rafi+
-	Portfolio did not exist		State List+Free Center)
A	Agudat Israel	MA	Mapai
AH	Ahdut HaAvodah	MP	Mapam
DMC	Democratic Movement for Change	NRP	National Religious Party
G	Gahal (Herut+General Zionists+Liberals)	PR	Progressives
		SE	Sephardim
ind	Independant (no party)	URF	United Religious Front
IL	Independent Liberal		(later NRP)
L	Labour (Mapai, AH, MP)		

35

party over the years; and in fact their very existence has depended upon the political situation of the moment.

The theme that some Ministries are more important to one party than to another bears repeating. Although the Ministries of foreign affairs and defense are no doubt central to Israeli political life, they are not central to the concerns of the religious parties, for example. Although one would not want to go so far as to say that the religious parties do not care about these areas, one can assert that the religious parties see their primary function in the state as being more concerned with the role, strength, and rebirth of religion, moral development, and supporting and maintaining religious laws.

Therefore, for example, the National Religious Party will be more oriented to the Ministries of religious affairs, interior, and social welfare. From the Ministry of interior it can control through bureaucratic regulation and the broad policy-implementation process a number of important (to its members) components of daily life in Israel: dietary laws (through granting certificates of kashrut to restaurants, for example), maintaining the sabbath (through regulations governing licenses for restaurants, movie theaters, buses, and the like), and moral values (through censorship regulations affecting movies and magazines, for example). Similarly, the Ministry of religious affairs and the Ministry of social welfare give the National Religious Party a number of avenues to enforce its policy preferences. (Some would argue that these go against the wishes of majority of Israelis, but due to its importance in the government coalitions, NRP demands have always been granted.)

Another point to note is that some of the Ministries appear to serve more of a bartering function than do others. Tourism, development, housing, and transportation have been combined with each other, dissolved and recreated more than all the other Ministries combined.

It would appear to be the case, then, that to some degree Leiserson's theory is correct. We cannot specify that in order to keep, for example, the Progressive party active in the coalition in the ninth Cabinet, the Prime Minister had to offer it the Ministry of justice, but we can say with some confidence that all indications point to the fact that the National Religious Party had demanded the Ministries of religious affairs and social welfare as its "share of the pie" in return for its support. In recent Cabinets the NRP's demand has extended to the Ministry of the interior, as well. Overall, however, once we have excluded the Ministries that Labour has kept for itself, there does not appear to be a major and significant hierarcy of Ministries as Leiserson indicates exists in Japan.

Turning to Table II, we can begin to evaluate the theory of Browne and Franklin. Table II shows us the parties represented in coalitions, the number of Ministries they received, and the number of seats in the Knesset they represented as well as their "key" to the Cabinet--the ratio of the number of Ministries they received to the number of seats they controlled.

What is evident from this table is the validity of the Browne and Franklin statement that "the number of Ministries received by partners in a governing coalition is indeed explained, almost on a one to one basis, by their contribution to seats to that coalition."[22] In only a few cases was there a marked difference between "keys". Excluding the two situations (Knesset 4 and 9) in which an independent received a Ministry and consequently had a key of 1.0, we find that in only a few cases did the range among parties of the ratio of number of Ministries to number of seats controlled exceed 0.10.

The evidence seems to show quite conclusively that the number of Ministries parties receive as rewards for belonging to coalitions is a direct function of the number of seats (of support for the government) that they control. This finding is consistent with conclusions reached by Browne and Franklin and derived from the theory of Gameson. Browne and Franklin found a correlation coefficient of 0.926 between the number of seats and the number of Ministries received in European parliaments since World War II, with an overall regression equation of $Y = -.01 + 1.07X$. Our results certainly are in the same vein as those of Browne and Franklin.

It appears that in a political system such as one finds in Israel, in which a minority party must ally itself with other minority parties to attempt to form a majority coalition, the parceling out of the rewards

TABLE II

"Keys" to the Cabinet

First Cabinet of Knesset	A	AH	DMC	G	PR/IL	L	LK	MA	MP	URF NPP		Party
1. # Seats					5			46		16	A	Agudat Israel
# Mins					1			7		3	AH	Ahdut Ha-Avodah
Key					.20			.15		.19		
2. # Seats	3							45		8	DMC	Democratic Mvmt. for Change
# Mins	1							10		2		
Key	.33							.22		.25		
3. # Seats		10			5			40	9	11	G	Gahel
# Mins		2			1			9	2	2	IL	Independent Liberals
Key		.20			.20			.23	.22	.18		
4. # Seats		7			6			47	9	12	L	Labour
# Mins		1			1			9	2	2	LK	Likud
Key		.14			.17			.19	.22	.17	MA	Mapai
5. # Seats		8						42		12	MP	Mapam
# Mins		2						11		3	NRP	Nat'l Religious Party
Key		.25						.26		.25		
6. # Seats					5			45	8	12	PR	Progressives
# Mins					1			8	2	3	URF	United Religious Front
Key					.20			.18	.25	.25		
7. # Seats				26	4	56				12		
# Mins				5	1	13				3		
Key				.19	.25	.23				.25		
8. # Seats					4	51				10		
# Mins					2	17				4		
Key					.50	.33				.40		
9. # Seats			15				43			12		
# Mins			4				9			3		
Key			.27				.21			.25		

must be on an egalitarian basis. That is, the dominant party (the one forming the government) may have a right to claim certain Ministries for itself, but the ratio of Ministers to seats is one that must be maintained. In all cases where there is a large difference in party keys to the Cabinet, it is the smaller parties that receive the "bonus" Ministries, not the larger, government forming party.

One of the best arguments supporting this theory in the Israeli case is that it appears operational no matter who forms the government. That is, if all of the above were applicable to the coalition-formation periods of Mapai/Alignment/Labour, but did not apply to the Likud in 1977, we would have to conclude that our theory was insufficiently developed, that it applied only to one party. The data show, however, that when a party that had been in the opposition for almost 30 years suddenly found itself in the position of having to form a coalition with other minority parties, its behavior was virtually identical with that of Mapai earlier.

Conclusions

Although we have made several observations about structural and behavioral characteristics of the administrative system of Israel, certainly among the most prominent aspects noted was its politicization. This is important both in terms of its effects upon bureaucrats and constituents, as well as in terms of its effect upon policy. Moreover, the process of distributing the leadership positions in the respective bureaucracies--Cabinet positions or Ministries--exacerbates the politicization of the administrative machinery. Thus the administrative system of Israel continues to be a central actor in the Israeli political world, as well as serving as a major structure for policy operationalization.

Footnotes

¹Unless otherwise indicated, the information in this section is based upon David Nachmias and David H. Rosenbloom, Bureaucratic Culture: Citizens and Administrators in Israel, New York: St. Martin's, 1978.

²Leonard Fein, Politics in Israel, Boston: Little, Brown, 1967, p. 190.

³Donna Robinson, "Patrons and Saints: A Study of the Career Patterns of Higher Civil Servants in Israel" (Ph.D. Dissertation, Department of Political Science, Columbia University, 1970), p. 51.

⁴See discussion infra. Robinson, "Patrons and Saints" comes to a somewhat different conclusion from Nachmias and Rosenbloom, Bureaucratic Culture, concerning the extent of patronage in the civil service. See also Fein, op. cit., and Gerald Caiden, Israel's Administrative Culture, Berkely: Institute of Government Studies, University of California, 1970.

⁵Fein, op. cit., p. 189.

⁶Ibid.

⁷Brian Chapman, The Profession of Government, London: Unwin University Books, 1959.

⁸United Nations, Technical Assistance Programme, The Training of the Israel Civil Service, prepared by F. B. Hindmarsh, 1956, p. 3; quoted in Robinson, "Patrons and Saints," p. 248.

⁹Quoted in Robinson, op. cit., p. 225.

¹⁰Caiden, op. cit.

¹¹Jon Kimche, "Tel Aviv: Messiah in a Business Suit." Commentary 6 (December 1948), p. 531.

¹²Quoted in Robinson, op. cit., p. 234.

¹³Ibid.

¹⁴Unless otherwise noted, this discussion of Israel's administrative culture is based upon Caiden, op. cit., pp. 17-18, et passim.

40

[15]Nachmias and Rosenbloom, op. cit., p. 49.

[16]Valerie Herman and John Pope, "Minority Governments in Western Democracies," British Journal of Political Science 3 (1973), p. 192.

[17]Gregory Mahler and Richard Trilling, "Coalition Behavior and Cabinet Formation: The Case of Israel," Comparative Political Studies 8 (1975), p. 212 n. 6.

[18]Michael Leiserson, "Factions and Coalitions in One-Party Japan," American Political Science Review 62 (1968), pp. 770-787.

[19]William Gameson, "A Theory of Coalition Formation," American Sociological Review 26 (1961), pp. 373-382.

[20]Eric Browne and Michael Franklin, "Aspects of Coalition Payoffs in European Parliamentary Democracies," American Political Science Review 67 (1973), p. 458.

[21]Fein, op. cit., p. 232.

[22]Browne and Franklin, op. cit., p. 458.

CHAPTER IV

THE PUBLIC BUREAUCRACY AND NATIONAL DEVELOPMENT IN SINGAPORE

Jon S. T. Quah

Introduction

When Singapore was founded by Stamford Raffles in January 1819, there was only a small fishing community of about 120 Malays and 30 Chinese. Needless to say, there was no tradition of a separate civil service at that time, and Raffles established the nucleus of the civil service by appointing his deputy, Major Farquhar, as the Resident, his brother-in-law as the Master-Attendant, and four other officials.[1] Today, some 162 years later, Singapore is a modern city-state with a multi-racial population of 2.36 million people. Its civil service has a total of 68,569 employees and the 82 statutory boards employ about 65,000 persons, with a public official/population ratio of 57 public employees per 1,000 population.[2]

The public bureaucracy in Singapore has played a very important part in national development especially after the attainment of self-government and the assumption of political power by the newly elected People's Action Party (PAP) government in June 1959. The PAP government has been in power for 22 years and its durability can be attributed mainly to its ability to use the public bureaucracy effectively as an agent for national development. The purpose of this chapter is to describe and explain how the public bureaucracy has contributed to national development in Singapore. More specifically, the major thesis of this chapter is that, within the constraints imposed by the Singapore environment, the public bureaucracy has contributed to the attainment of national development goals by performing three tasks: (1) ensuring quality control of its personnel through the Public Service Commission (PSC); (2) preventing and controlling corrupt behavior among its employees by means of the Corrupt Practices Investigation Bureau (CPIB) and the Prevention of Corruption Act (POCA); and (3) implementing socio-economic development programs (such as public housing and family planning) which have significantly transformed the way of life of most Singaporeans.

To illustrate the above thesis, we will begin by
highlighting the various features of the Singapore
context which are crucial for understanding the public
bureaucracy's role in national development. After
providing such background information, we can proceed
to describe the structure and functions of the public
bureaucracy. The next three sections deal in turn with
the PSC, the CPIB and POCA, and the implementation of
socio-economic development programs. The concluding
section identifies the reasons for the success of the
public bureaucracy and assesses its prospects for the
future.

The Singapore Context

Four aspects of the Singapore environment imping-
ing on the public bureaucracy's role in national development deserve mention here: its geography, its
economy, its population and its political system.

In terms of geography, the most important point to
note is Singapore's smallness. The Republic of Singapore consists of the main island and 54 islets. The
main island is about 41.8 kilometers long and 22.5 kilometers broad, and has a coastline of 193.7 kilometers.
The total land area of Singapore including the islets
is 617.8 square kilometers.[3] This makes Singapore one
of the smallest nations in the world. In addition to
its small size, Singapore is also essentially a city
state as its rural sector is negligible.

The compactness of the island and its high degree
of urbanization have aided the public bureaucracy in
the performance of its various tasks. For one thing,
the diminutive size of Singapore is an advantage as
problems of communication seldom arise and there is also
relative ease of political control by the leadership.
Another advantage of smallness is that it facilitates
administrative coordination and integration and promotes
responsiveness on the part of public officials.[4] Unlike
the case of larger countries like Indonesia or Malaysia,
the smaller size of Singapore contributed to a highly
centralised public bureaucracy. It does not suffer the
same problems afflicting a federal public bureaucracy
in its interaction with the state or provincial public
bureaucracies. The absence of a sizeable rural sector
not only reinforces the centralized nature of the public
bureaucracy, but also implies that the latter is not
burdened by problems arising from rural development

programs because there is no need for such programs in the first place.[5]

Since Singapore has no natural resources except its strategic location, its level of economic development is an important factor influencing the public bureaucracy's performance because it determines the amount of resources that will be allocated by the politcal leadership for meeting the goals of national development. The Singapore economy has been transformed from a purely entrepôt economy to an entrepôt-manufacturing economy as a result of the industrialization program initiated by the PAP government in August 1961 with the creation of the Economic Development Board (EDB).[6] Ever since its founding in 1819 by Stamford Raffles, who was searching for a trading center to restrict the growing trade of the Dutch in Southeast Asia, Singapore's economy has been hinged on its position as a distributing port for the neighboring countries as well as its policy of free trade. Since Singapore does not have any natural resources, it handles the vast output of rubber, tin, timber, petroleum and other products of the neighboring areas; and serves as a processing center and money market for the region.[7]

However, when the PAP government assumed power in 1959 the economic prospects for the country were unfavorable for two reasons. First, entrepôt trade had declined because of increased direct trading by Singapore's neighbors. Second, unemployment was becoming a serious problem given the high rate of population increase of 3.3 percent. Accordingly, the PAP government had no choice but to launch an intensive industrialization program spearheaded by the EDB. The EDB was established to provide loans and technical assistance to new industries, to promote investments, and to establish self-sufficient industrial estates.[8] In 1968, the Jurong Town Corporation (JTC) and the Development Bank of Singapore (DBS) were formed to take over the functions of industrial infrastructural development and in industrial financing respectively, thus leaving the EDB with the function of investment promotion.

Singapore's success in economic development is visible to any visitor to the island. Its per capita Gross National Product (GNP) has increased from S$1,330 in 1960 to S$8,233 in 1979.[9] This means that Singapore has the highest standard of living in Asia after Japan. One obvious manifestation of affluence is the increasing number of new private cars on the roads in spite of the rising gas prices and the fiscal disincentives imposed by the government.[10] During the last two decades the manufacturing sector has emerged as the most important pillar of the economy because of the government's industrialization program. In 1960 the manufacturing sector accounted for 9.1 per cent of the Gross Domestic Product (GDP); in 1979 its contribution to the GDP increased by more than thrice to 31 per cent. The manufacturing sector has also grown in terms of the number of industrial establishments and the number of workers employed by these establishments. There were 548 industrial firms with a total of 26,697 employees in 1960. Nineteen years later, the size of the manufacturing sector has swelled to a total of 3,209 industrial establishments employing 270,284 workers.[11]

In short, Singapore has a sound and stable economy which is based on entrepôt trade and manufacturing. Its impressive economic growth during the last 22 years has enabled the PAP government to allocate more resources for socio-economic development programs such as the public housing and family planning programs. The focus on economic development by the PAP government is not accidental but a deliberate part of its approach to nation-building. The PAP leaders realized that nation-building could only succeed if the people were committed to the country and one of the most effective ways of ensuring their political allegiance to Singapore was through the promotion of economic development. Because of the immigrant nature of the population, the citizens must be given a stake in the country by providing them with a comfortable standard of living, which was after all the major reason for the migration of their ancestors to Singapore. Needless to say, without economic development and industrialization, Singapore's high standard of living would not only have been impossible but also cannot be maintained.[12]

The third aspect of the Singapore context that is relevant for our discussion is the size and nature of its population. By the end of June 1979, the population was estimated at 2,362,700 persons and its density was 3,834 persons per square kilometer.[13] The population is heterogeneous in three respects: it is multi-racial, multi-lingual and multi-religious in nature. In terms of ethnic composition, the population consists of 76.2 per cent Chinese, 15 per cent Malays, 6.8 per cent Indians (including those of Pakistani or Sri Lankan

descent) and 2 per cent of other ethnic groups.[14]   The
existence of four official languages--Malay, Mandarin,
Tamil and English--reflects the linguistic diversity of
the population.   In addition, there are also several
Chinese dialects (Hokkien, Teochew, Cantonese, Hainan-
ese, Hakka and Foochow) and Telugu, Malayalam, Punjabi,
Hindi, and Bengali are spoken by ethnic Indians.   As
far as religion is concerned, there are about 1.3
million Buddhists, 400,000 Muslims, 75,000 Roman Catholics, 75,000 Protestants, 15,000 Sikhs, 500 Jews, 200
Jains, and 100 Zoroastrians.[15]   The heterogeneous nature
of the population imposes on the public bureaucracy two
important responsibilities.   First, it means that the
public bureaucracy must also be committed to the goal
of nation-building by implementing programs that will
enhance the integration of the various races.   Second,
it must be fair and impartial in its treatment of its
clientele regardless of their race, language or religion.   In other words, there is no room for discrimination of any sort in the public bureaucracy in a plural
society.   This also implies that the processes of recruitment, selection and promotion must be based on
achievement criteria and not ascriptive criteria like
race, language, or religion.

        The final and most important facet of the Singapore
environment that must be considered is the nature of
the political system.   After 140 years of colonial rule
by the British, Singapore attained self-government in
June 1959 with the PAP forming the government.[16]   Apart
from the PAP, which captured 43 of the 51 seats in the
Legislative Assembly, there were two other political
parties and an independent member which together occupied eight seats.   In other words, there was a competitive party system with the PAP as the dominant party
in the legislature and the Singapore People's Alliance
(SPA) and the UMNO-MCA Alliance as the two opposition
parties.[17]   In the September 1963 general election,
PAP won 37 seats and the Barisan Sosialis constituted
the opposition with 13 seats.[18]   With the boycott of
parliament by the Barisan Sosialis in October 1966, the
competitive party system was transformed into a de
facto one party dominant system.   The latter acquired
de jure status when the PAP captured all the 58 parliamentary seats in the 1968 general election.[19]   Since
then, the PAP has retained its status as the only party
in parliament as it has repeated this feat of winning
all the parliamentary seats in the September 1972, December 1976 and December 1980 general elections.   In

short, the most important feature of the political
system in Singapore is the predominance of the PAP in
the political arena after 1959 and the concomitant
political stability and continuity during the past two
decades.

The PAP's predominance in Singapore politics can
be attributed mainly to its success in delivering the
goods and services to the population and the resulting
reservoir of legitimacy that it has accumulated during
the last 22 years. The lack of a credible alternative
to the PAP and the nature of the political culture in
Singapore have reinforced the PAP's predominance and
durability. On the basis of his research on the political attitudes of 209 Chinese farmers in Singapore,
David S. Gibbons has suggested the concept of the spectator political culture to describe the political attitudes of those farmers who were aware of the political
system as a whole, its output and input objects, but
did not consider themselves as active participants in
the political process. He found that one-third of the
farmers studied were political spectators i.e., they
were knowledgeable about Singapore politics but were
not politically active.[20] Although Gibbons' research
is based on a small sample of Chinese farmers, his introduction of the spectator political culture is useful
in terms of describing the political attitudes of Singaporeans. Needless to say, whether most or all Singaporeans are political spectators is an empirical question; but the reluctance of most Singaporeans to participate in politics and the difficulties encountered by
the PAP in finding new candidates for political office
suggest, perhaps, that there is some truth to the contention that Singapore has a spectator political culture.

The PAP's long term of uninterrupted rule for over
22 years has contributed to the effectiveness of the
public bureaucracy. If political continuity is lacking
in the sense that there are frequent changes of government, such changes are usually also transmitted to the
various government departments in the form of personnel
changes, departmental reorganization, changes in functions, and other forms of disruption of the previous
administrative setup. And such disruptions are not
conducive to the effective functioning of the public
bureaucracy. Conversely, the continuity of the PAP
government from its election in May 1959 to the present
day provides a partial explanation for the high level

of effectiveness of the public bureaucracy in Singapore.

Structure and Functions of the Public Bureaucracy

The public bureaucracy in Singapore has undergone five stages of development, namely: (1) the pre-colony phase (1819-1867); (2) the period of crown colony rule (1867-1942); (3) the postwar period (1945-1955); (4) the Labour Front coalition government period (1955-1959); and (5) the PAP government period (1959-present).[21] What is perhpas most important for our purposes is the structure and functions of the public bureaucracy during the post-1959 era.

The public bureaucracy consists of two major components: the SCS or Singapore Civil Service and the various statutory boards. Before the advent of the PAP government, the public bureaucracy did not play a significant role in national development as it was an instrument of the British colonial authorities and was subject to their control and policies. However, after May 1959, it has grown not only in size but also in terms of the workload and responsibilities it has to shoulder. Also, there is now a more balanced division of labour between the SCS and the statutory boards. During the pre-1959 period, the SCS did most of the work as there were only a few statutory boards in existence. Thus, the creation and subsequent proliferation of statutory boards by the PAP government served two purposes: it reduced to a great extent the SCS's workload, and entrusted to the statutory boards the task of expediting the implementation of socio-economic programs as they would not be hindered by the procedural delays and regulations faced by the SCS.[22]

In June 1959, the SCS consisted of nine Ministries employing 28,253 persons.[23] In addition to the Prime Minister's Office, the other Ministries were the Deputy Prime Minister's Office, the Ministry for National Development, the Ministry for Health, the Ministry for Finance, the Ministry for Labour and Law, the Ministry for Culture, the Ministry for Home Affairs, and the Ministry for Education. The Culture and National Development Ministries were created by the newly elected PAP government to take care of nation building and economic development respectively. In 1961, the Ministry for Social Affairs was formed to take over the Social Welfare Department from the Ministry for Labour and Law.[24] Three years later, the Ministry for Labour and Law was reorganized and a separate Ministry for Law was created in October 1964.

Several other Ministries were established after the attainment of independence on August 9, 1965 for two reasons.[25] First, such Ministries as the Ministry for Foreign Affairs and the Ministry for Interior and Defence were formed to take charge of functions which had hitherto been performed by the British and Malaysian governments. The Ministry for Home Affairs was given the additional function of defence and renamed the Ministry of Interior and Defence in 1966. This arrangement lasted for four years until August 1970 when the latter was divided into the Ministry for Defence and the Ministry for Home Affairs.

Second, four new Ministries were created to take care of new responsibilities. After the April 1968 general election, the PAP government was returned to power for the third time and it increased the size of the Cabinet with the addition of two new portfolios: the Ministry of Science and Technology and the Ministry of Communications. These two Ministries were formed because of the "growing importance of science and technology in the development of the economy" and the need to combine the vast transport and communications portfolio under one Ministry. Similarly, another new Ministry--the Ministry of the Environment--was established after the PAP government had won the September 1972 general election to implement plans for the control and prevention of pollution and the preservation of public health.[26] Finally, the Ministry of Trade and Industry was set up in March 1979 to assume responsibility for "all economic matters and duties that were previously under the purview of the Development Division, Ministry of Finance."[27] At the end of March, 1981, the Ministry of Science and Technology was dissolved and its functions were transferred to the Ministry of Trade and Industry and the Ministry of Education.

Like the SCS, the number of statutory boards increased rapidly after 1959. During the colonial period, there were only five statutory boards viz., The Board of Commissioners of the Currency, the Singapore Harbour Board, the Singapore Improvement Trust, the Singapore Telephone Board, and the Central Provident Fund. However, these statutory boards were not effective and were reorganized after 1959. The Housing and Development Board (HDB) was the first statutory board created by the newly-elected PAP government on February 1, 1960 to tackle the serious housing shortage facing the country. The HDB's formation was soon followed by a proliferation of other major statutory boards. Indeed according to the latest edition of the <u>Singapore Government Directory</u>, there are now as many as 82 statutory boards in Singapore which perform, between them, the following eight functions: economic development, development of infrastructure and essential services, public housing and urban redevelopment, education, promotion of tourism, development of Singapore as a financial center, family planning, and promotion of sports and recreational activities.[28]

In short, the public bureaucracy in Singapore today is quite different in size and workload from its counterpart 162 years ago. From a mere nucleus of six individuals in 1819, the public bureaucracy has grown to its present size of 15 Ministries and 82 statutory boards, which together employ a total of nearly 134,000 persons. The rapid growth of the public bureaucracy can be attributed not only to its increased workload, but also to its direct involvement in national development activities after 1959.

The PSC and Quality Control of the SCS

The Public Service Commission (PSC) is the most important central personnel agency for the Singapore Civil Service (SCS). According to Article 78 of the Constitution of Singapore, its duty is "to appoint, confirm, emplace on the permanent or pensionable establishment, promote, transfer, dismiss and exercise disciplinary control over public officers."[29] In addition, the PSC is also responsible for the awarding of scholarships, training awards and bursaries to deserving students and civil servants. Moreover, since April 1981, career development and training of all Division I officers (which had hitherto been the responsibility of the Establishment Unit of the Prime Minister's Office) has come under the jurisdiction of the PSC.

The PSC was originally established on January 1, 1951 as a result of the recommendation made by the Trusted Commission in 1947.[30] More specifically, there were two reasons for the creation of the PSC: to keep politics out of the SCS and to accelerate the latter's pace of localization.[31] The second reason is no longer relevant today as the localization of the SCS has already been achieved sometime ago.[32] Nevertheless, the primary aim of keeping politics out of the SCS is still important because the purpose of the PSC's program is "to meet the staffing requirements of the Government in accordance with the merit principle."[33] In other words, the PSC relies on achievement criteria rather than ascriptive criteria in the performance of its various functions.

The PSC's major function is the recruitment and selection of candidates for Divisions I and II appointments. Division III appointments or for promotions from Divisions III to II tasks are handled by selection boards appointed by it. Division IV employees are selected by the relevant Ministries and departments, but those selected must be approved by the PSC. For recruitment, the PSC is informed of the vacancies in the SCS by the different Ministries and it publicizes details of such vacancies by means of circulars within the SCS and advertisements in the local (and sometimes foreign) newspapers. The completed application forms received by the PSC for an advertised post are examined and eligible candidates are short-listed for interviews by the PSC members.[34]

The PSC relies solely on interviews for selecting qualified candidates for the SCS. To be eligible for appointment to the SCS, a candidate must satisfy these criteria: citizenship, age, education, experience, medical fitness and character (i.e., no criminal conviction).[35] Candidates for Divisions I and II appointments who meet such criteria are interviewed by the PSC members. Letters of appointment are only issued to the successful candidates if they pass their medical examination and security screening (by the Internal Security Department and the Criminal Record Office) and after their educational certificates and relevant documents have been verified. The PSC thus serves as the gatekeeper to the SCS by ensuring fair play and impartiality in recruiting and selecting candidates for appointments to Divisions I and II on the basis of merit. Indeed, the PSC controls the quality of personnel entering the SCS by "keeping the rascals out" and attracting the best qualified candidates to apply for entrance to the SCS.[36]

Similarly, civil servants are promoted by the PSC on the basis of official qualifications, experience and merit.[37] Eligible candidates for promotion are interviewed by the PSC members and selection boards. The actual procedure for the promotion of serving officers has five stages: (1) invitation to apply for promotion, (2) testing the eligibility of applicants by reviewing their applications, (3) selecting the most suitable applicants by means of the interview method, (4) approval of the promotion, and (5) informing the officer of promotion, salary and conditions of service in the new appointment.[38]

The PSC also plays an important role in training through the granting of scholarships and training awards for courses of study or training programs at foreign or local institutions. Candidates applying for bursaries and study loans at local institutions of higher learning are selected by the PSC. Competition for the above awards is quite stiff and the PSC ensures that only highly qualified candidates are selected. Thus, the PSC contributes to the quality control of the SCS by ensuring and maintaining the high caliber of its members through the provision of scholarships and training awards.

The final function of the PSC is to take disciplinary action against civil servants who are guilty of any of the 18 offences listed in the Schedule to the Public Service (Disciplinary Proceedings--Delegation of function) Rules, 1970.[39] The PSC was first entrusted with this function in 1956, but it only assumed full responsibility for disciplinary matters in 1963 when it was given executive power of disciplinary control over public officers by the Constitution. If a civil servant is found guilty of a disciplinary offence, the PSC can either dismiss, demote, impose some lesser penalty (stoppage or deferment of increment, fine or reprimand, or a combination of such penalties) or retire him, depending on the seriousness of the offence.[40] Allegations of corrupt behavior by civil servants are referred by the PSC to the Corrupt Practices Investigation Bureau for further investigation and action.

During its 30 years of existence, the workload of the PSC has increased tremendously. For example, in 1951 the three member PSC interviewed 556 candidates for appointments and promotions.[41] In 1980, the PSC interviewed 1,154 applicants for appointment and promotion to senior positions in the SCS, and considered 3,365 candidates for scholarships and training awards. The PSC was assisted by 173 selection boards which

52

interviewed 12,374 candidates for various appointments and promotions.[42] The number of disciplinary cases handled by the PSC has increased in workload, the size of the PSC has grown from three members in 1951 to its present size of nine members.[44] At the same time, the size of the PSC Secretariat has also been increased from nine persons in 1951 to 149 persons in 1980.[45]

We have seen that the PSC's role as the central personnel agency for the SCS is crucial for the latter's quality control. Its gatekeeping function ensures that only suitably qualified candidates are appointed to the SCS. Similarly, promotions and the awarding of scholar-ships and training awards are based on merit. Finally, the PSC maintains a high standard of discipline within the SCS by taking appropriate action against those civil servants found guilty of disciplinary offences.

Control of Bureaucratic Corruption

Bureaucratic corruption is perhaps one of the most serious and embarrassing obstacles to national develop-ment in the developing countries in Asia, Africa, and Latin America.[46] Whether bureaucratic corruption is a fact or way of life is important because the extent of its pervasiveness among civil servants in a country will adversely affect national development. According to Gerald E. Caiden:

> Bureaucratic corruption is a particularly
> viral form of bureaupathology. Once it en-
> ters the blood of a public organization, it
> spreads quickly to all parts. If untreated,
> it will eventually destroy public credibility
> and organizational effectiveness. Even if
> treated, there is no guarantee that it will
> be eliminated or that all infected areas will
> be reached or that as soon as vigilance is
> relaxed, it will not reappear.[47]

However, Singapore is fortunate because bureaucrat-ic corruption is not a serious problem. In a special issue of the Far Eastern Economic Review devoted to "Corruption: The Asian Lubricant," a survey of this problem in ten Asian countries has indicated that Sing-apore is "the least corrupt of all Asian states" and is reputed to be the "Mr. Clean" of Asia.[48] This view was shared by Lord Shawcross of Britain three years later, when he identified Singapore and the People's Republic of China as the only two countries in the world that are curruption-free.[49]

To further substantiate the above contention that bureaucratic corruption is incidental and not institutionalized in Singapore, we can refer to two indicators for measuring the reported extent of such behavior. First, the Index of Corruption among Policemen (ICAP) is higher during the colonial period than during the post-independent period. More specifically, the average value of the ICAP for the colonial period is 0.008 indicating that eight out of every 1,000 police officers were involved in corruption during 1845-1921. The average value of the ICAP for the 1965-77 period is much lower (0.0008) and shows that only a very small proportion (eight out of every 10,000) of the members of the Police Force was connected with corrupt behavior during that period.[50]

A second indicator of corruption is the number of offences recorded against those laws prohibiting corrupt behavior in Singapore. As corruption is a seizable offence, all offences against the Prevention of Corruption Act (POCA) Chapter 104 are recorded on an annual basis in the Statistical Report on Crime in Singapore, which is prepared by the Criminal Intelligence Unit of the Criminal Investigation Department in the Singapore Police Force. In other words, the number of offences against the POCA is an indication of the reported extent of corruption in Singapore. Using this indicator, it can be seen from Table I below that the level of corruption in Singapore is quite low as there were only 182 offences against the POCA recorded during 1968-1979.[51]

Table I. Number of Offences Against the Prevention of Corruption Act Chapter 104 in Singapore, 1968-1979

Year	No. of Offences
1968	13
1969	11
1970	28
1971	4
1972	19
1973	28

Year	No. of Offences
1974	10
1975	14
1976	10
1977	20
1978	13
1979	12
Total	182

Source: Criminal Intelligence Unit, CID, Singapore, Statistical Report on Crime in Singapore 1977 and 1979 (Singapore: CID, 1978 and 1980), p. 54, Table 11 and p. 50, Table 7.

Governments usually punish those civil servants found guilty of corruption because such behavior is considered to be detrimental to national development.[52] This assumes, of course, that the political leaders are themselves committed to the eradication of bureaucratic corruption in their country. If such leaders pay only lip service to this goal of eliminating bureaucratic corruption, it will be difficult for them to enforce the various anti-corruption measures impartially and without implicating themselves. In short, the acid test of a government's sincerity in wiping out bureaucratic corruption depends not only on the formulation of anti-corruption measures, but also on the actual implementation of such measures and their effects on the behavior of civil servants and the society at large.

Indeed, bureaucratic corruption is not a serious problem in Singapore because the incumbent PAP government, which has been in power for 22 years, is committed to the eradication of corruption both within and outside the public bureaucracy. The PAP government under the leadership of Prime Minister Lee Kuan Yew has not only accepted the desirability of formulating anti-corruption measures, but has also ensured the feasibility of such measures by creating the necessary machinery for implementing the desired changes.[53] The raison d'etre of the various anti-corruption measures is to reduce, if not extirpate, both the need to be corrupt and the opportunities for corrupt behavior among civil servants in Singapore.

Some scholars have argued that bureaucratic corruption becomes a serious problem in a society where the civil servants are generally paid very low wages and where there is an unequal distribution of wealth.[54] In other words, a civil servant or a member of the public might be forced by financial reasons to indulge in corrupt acts as he is not earning enough to support his family. In the words of Colin Leys:

> The incentive to corrupt whatever official purposes public institutions are agreed to have is expecially great in conditions of extreme inequality and considerable absolute poverty. The benefits of holding an office --any office--are relatively enormous; by comparison the penalties for attempting to obtain one by bribery are fairly modest, in relation to the low standard of living of the would-be office holder, or in relation to the pressure of relatives' claims on his existing standard of living. Generally, corruption seems likely to be inseparable from great inequality.[55]

The linkage between low salaries and bureaucratic corruption is best illustrated in Indonesia, where civil servants receive among the lowest salaries in the world.[56] It is difficult, if not impossible, for Indonesian civil servants to survive on their salaries alone because the latter amount to about one-third of the amount needed by them to sustain their families' standard of living. A survey of regional officials in Indonesia by an American scholar has indicated that these officials consider low salaries to be the most important factor responsible for corruption.[57]

Accordingly, the PAP government has reduced the need to be corrupt among civil servants in Singapore by constantly improving their salaries and working conditions. The salaries of Singaporean civil servants are quite high by Asian standards because the PAP government has to compete with the attractive private sector by offering comparable salaries and fringe benefits. For example, from March 1972 all civil servants are given a thirteen month non-pensionable allowance, which is comparable to the bonus in the private sector. A year later, the salaries of the senior officers were increased substantially to narrow the gap with the private sector.[58] The most recent salary revision was announced in Parliament by the Minister for Trade and Industry, Goh Chok Tong, in May 1979. He justified the salary increase in the following way:

> The quality of a nation depends on the quality of its people and government. Good government requires political and administrative leadership of indisputable integrity, ability and dedication.... The Singapore Administrative Service, as the premier service in the public sector, must therefore be attractive enough for it to recruit and retain a fair proportion of the cream of our graduates. The terms and conditions of the Administrative Service must match the best in the private sector.... It is the problem of gross disparity between what the outstanding graduates are earning in the private sector compared to what the highflyers are earning in the Administrative Service. This revision of the salary structure of the Administrative Service is to put right this gap in earnings of top graduates.[59]

As a result of the latest salary increase, the highest position in the SCS (Staff Grade II) commands a monthly salary of S$15,000 or S$19,508 including allowances.[60] So far, the three most senior civil servants in the SCS are in Staff Grade I and drawing a monthly salary of S$11,000 or S$14,305 including allowances.[61]

Apart from improving the salaries and working conditions in the SCS, the PAP government relies on two important measures to curb corruption by reducing the opportunities for corruption and by increasing the price to be paid for corrupt behavior if one is caught. The POCA was first enacted in December 1937 to ensure "the more effectual prevention of corruption." Fifteen years later, the Corrupt Practices Investigation Bureau (CPIB) was formed as the first autonomous anti-corruption agency outside the jurisdiction of the police because of the inability of the Anti-Corruption Branch of the Criminal Investigation Department of the police to curb the rising incidence of corruption in the country.[62] However, before 1960, both the POCA and the CPIB were not effective in controlling the problem of

57

corruption. Consequently, the PAP government amended the POCA by increasing its scope and its powers for dealing with corrupt practices. The definition of what would constitute corrupt behavior was specified and the penalty for such behavior was increased to imprisonment for five years and/or a fine of S$10,000 in order to increase the POCA's deterrent effect. Furthermore, the CPIB was given a new lease of life by the 1960 revision of the POCA as the latter identified for the first time the CPIB and its Director and the additional powers entrusted to them for performing their anti-corruption duties.[63]

In 1960, the POCA was amended to give CPIB officers the power to require the attendance of witnesses, and to examine such witnesses. The purpose of this amendment was to reduce the difficulty in getting witnesses to appear before CPIB officers for the purpose of helping them in their investigations. Three years later, two further amendments were made to strengthen the POCA. First, according to section 28, a person could be found guilty of corruption even though he did not actually accept the bribe. The intention on his part to commit the offence would provide sufficient grounds for his conviction. Second, section 35 stated that Singapore citizens would be liable for corrupt offences committed outside Singapore and would be dealt with as if such offences had been done within Singapore. In short, no Singaporean, regardless of whether he resides within or outside his country, can be immune from the "tentacles" of the POCA.[64] On October 23, 1981, the Prevention of Corruption (Amendment) Bill was introduced in Parliament by the Minister for Law, E. W. Barker. The purpose of this Bill is to increase the deterrent effect of the POCA by requiring those convicted of corruption to repay all the money received besides facing the usual court sentence. Those who are unable to make full restitution will consequently receive heavier court sentences.[65]

The CPIB is the anti-corruption agency which enforces the provisions of the POCA. When the POCA was amended in 1960 the CPIB had only eight officers. Today, the CPIB has a total staff of 76 persons and a budget of S$1.85 million.[66] In 1970, the CPIB came under the jurisdiction of the Prime Minister's Office and has remained there ever since. This ensures that the CPIB is able to obtain the necessary cooperation from all the ministries and statutory boards, and is thus able to function effectively with its small staff.[67]

We have seen that the POCA is a comprehensive piece of anti-corruption legislation which has constantly been strengthened by subsequent amendments since its enactment in 1937. The 1960 amendment of the POCA gave the CPIB the necessary ammunition for eradicating corruption in Singapore. The relationship between the POCA and the CPIB is a symbiotic one: the CPIB is powerless without the POCA, and the POCA cannot be implemented without the CPIB. The close linkage between the CPIB and the POCA is responsible, in part, for the low incidence of bureaucratic corruption in Singapore today because this effective combination has not only reduced the opportunities for corruption, but has also increased the price to be paid for indulging in corrupt behavior.[68]

Finally, in addition to the role played by the POCA and the CPIB in reducing the opportunities for corruption, the Ministry of Finance issued a circular in July 1973 to all Permanent Secretaries instructing them to review and improve the measures taken to prevent corruption among their officers by minimizing the opportunities for corrupt practices. More specifically, the Permanent Secretaries were first asked to instill in their officers "an awareness of the serious efforts of Government to eradicate all corrupt practices and all officers should be advised to report any case of offer or acceptance of, or demand for gratification." They were also requested to take appropriate measures to prevent corruption in those departments particularly exposed to corruption. Such measures included the improvement of work methods and procedures to reduce delay; increasing the effectiveness of supervision so that superior officers can check and control the work of their staff; rotating officers to ensure that no officer or group of officers remain too long at a single operational unit; carrying out surprise checks on the work of their officers; making the necessary security arrangements to prevent unauthorised persons from having access to a department's premises; and reviewing the anti-corruption measures taken once in three to five years with the aim of introducing further improvements.[69]

Implementation of Socio-Economic Programs

The task of implementing the various socio-economic programs of the PAP government is the responsibility of the major statutory boards created after 1959. The division of labor between the SCS and the statutory boards is a rational one and is based on the assumption that the SCS, which is handicapped by procedural delays and regulations, is better suited for performing regulatory and routine functions; while the statutory boards, which do not face the same constraints as the SCS, are therefore more suitable for implementing socio-economic development programs.

Two methods are available to a government to improve the performance of its public bureaucracy: increase the latter's capabilities by increasing its manpower and resources; or reduce the latter's workload by creating new organizations to take over part of the workload. The PAP government has not only reduced the SCS's workload by creating statutory boards to take care of the implementation of the socio-economic programs, but has also increased the capabilities of both the SCS and the statutory boards. In other words, the PAP government has been able to combine successfully both the methods of improving administrative performance.

The PAP government's strategy of relying on the statutory boards to implement socio-economic programs is best illustrated in the areas of public housing and family planning.

To solve the housing shortage which it inherited from the previous Labour Front coalition government, the PAP government created the Housing and Development Board (HDB) and gave it the necessary support, statutory powers and resources, which its predecessor--the Singapore Improvement Trust (SIT)--lacked. The SIT was a statutory board set up by the British colonial government in July 1927 as a town planning authority. However, in 1932 it assumed the burden of public housing because of the deterioration of the housing situation. The SIT was not a de jure public housing authority because it lacked both the legal powers and adequate resources for implementing the public housing program. To make matters worse, the economic, demographic and political aspects of the environment were not conducive for the SIT's performance, and the caliber of its personnel was not high, as manifested in the corrupt activities of its senior expatriate and local junior officers in the areas of building contracts, planning and development control, and the allocation of housing

60

units. It is therefore not surprising that the SIT failed to solve the housing problem as it was able to build a total of 23,264 housing units during its 32 years of existence.[70]

In contrast, the HDB has succeeded in providing low cost public housing for 67 per cent of the population and has completed an impressive total of 357,413 housing units during its first two decades.[71] The HDB has benefited from the SIT's experience in public housing and has avoided the mistakes made by its predecessor. Unlike the SIT, the HDB was formed as the de jure public housing authority and was thus given the things which the SIT lacked: governmental support, sufficient financial assistance, an efficient recruitment and selection system, and the necessary legal powers for implementing the public housing program. The caliber of HDB personnel is also much higher because of the efficient and careful recruitment and selection system. In short, the HDB succeeded where the SIT failed because of the commitment and support given by the PAP government to public housing and the HDB's ability to solve the various problems encountered in the implementation of its public housing program.[72]

The same phenomenon of success is repeated in the case of family planning. The small size of Singapore has not only necessitated the construction of low cost high-rise public housing, but has also dictated the need for small families. Accordingly, the Singapore Family Planning and Population Board (SFPPB) was created in January 1966 to reduce the annual population growth rate by encouraging the acceptance of family planning among the population. Apart from injecting the required dose of manpower, legislation and resources, the PAP government has also relied on a system of incentives and disincentives and national campaigns to "motivate" Singaporeans to accept family planning as a way of life. Those with large families are penalised by having to pay higher delivery charges in government hospitals, removing the income tax relief for the fourth child onwards, no paid maternity leave for delivery of the third and subsequent children, no priority in the allocation of HDB flats, and lower priority for choice of primary school for the fourth and subsequent children.[73] To spread the message of family planning, the SFPPB has also launched national campaigns to encourage Singaporeans to stop at two children (the two child family norm) and to postpone marriage and

61

child-bearing.

The success of the SFPPB in promoting family planning among Singaporeans can be demonstrated in two ways. First, it has successfully completed three five-year national programs in family planning. The birth rate has been reduced from 28.3 per thousand in 1966 to 16.6 per thousand in 1977. The rate of natural increase for the same period has dropped from 2.29 per cent to 1.14 per cent.[74] A second indicator is the level of knowledge, attitudes toward, and actual practice of family planning among the population. The First National KAP Survey conducted by the SFPPB in 1973 revealed that 97.8 per cent of the married women respondents knew at least one contraceptive method, 69.1 per cent of them approved of family planning, and 77 per cent of them had practised family planning.[75]

Thus, it is obvious that both the HDB and the SFPPB have succeeded in implementing the public housing and family planning programs respectively. The impact of both programs has been tremendous because they affect all Singaporeans. The public bureaucracy in Singapore serves as a powerful force for social change as it has succeeded in making public housing and family planning a way of life for most Singaporeans.[76]

What are the reasons for the successful implementation of the public housing and family planning programs? The most important reason is the quality of the political leadership in Singapore. The ability of the PAP leaders to plan ahead and to anticipate problems as well as their willingness to enforce necessary but unpleasant measures, have all contributed to their ability to deliver the goods and their legitimacy in the political arena. The commitment of the PAP government to the successful completion of the public housing and family planning programs is the first step to success because it ensures that the HDB and SFPPB receive the necessary manpower, legislative backing, financial resources and equipment to implement their programs. Second, both the HDB and the SFPPB are highly effective statutory boards and are staffed with qualified and competent personnel. Third, as corruption is not a serious problem in Singapore, the implementation of the public housing and family planning programs have not been hindered by this problem. This means that scarce resources have not been wasted on bribes and delays are rare because of the severe penalties for corrupt

behavior. Fourth, the PAP government relies on national campaigns to persuade the people to support its
policies on the one hand, and disincentives have been
introduced to ensure compliance with such policies on
the other hand. In other words, the population is
quite disciplined and has cooperated with and supported
the PAP government's policies on public housing and
family planning.[77] Finally, the smallness of Singapore
is an asset as the HDB and SFPPB are not plagued by
logistical and communication problems in the implementation of their programs.

It should be noted that the other statutory
boards such as the Economic Development board, the Port
of Singapore Authority, the Public Utilities Board, the
Telecommunication Authority of Singapore, the Jurong
Town Corporation and the Post Office Savings Bank, to
name only a few examples, are also quite successful in
implementing their programs. In other words, the HDB
and SFPPB are not unique in being successful statutory
boards. Space constraints necessitated our focus on
the HDB and SFPPB because these two organizations have
a greater impact on the lives of Singaporeans than the
above mentioned statutory boards.

Conclusion

From the preceding analysis, it is obvious that
the public bureaucracy plays an important and effective
role in national development in Singapore. It is the
largest employer and provides employment for nearly six
per cent of the population. It is also responsible for
implementing the various socio-economic development
programs which have transformed the way of life of
Singaporeans during the last two decades.

When the PAP government assumed power in June 1959,
it realized that it had to transform the colonial public bureaucracy it inherited in order to implement the
various development programs. Accordingly, the PAP
leaders initiated a comprehensive reform of the SCS and
created statutory boards for three reasons. First, the
time was ripe for the PAP government to introduce comprehensive administrative reforms because its assumption
of power marked the end of nearly 140 years of colonial
rule by the British and the beginning of internal self-
government for Singapore. Since administrative reform
is a deliberate attempt by political leaders to change
the structure and procedures of the public bureaucracy

as well as the attitudes of its members for the promotion of organizational effectiveness and the attainment of national development goals,[78] the PAP leaders not only reorganized the SCS and created statutory boards; they sought also to rid the civil servants of their colonial mentality and aloofness from the population. The comprehensive reform of the public bureaucracy took the form of (1) structural reorganization of the SCS (e.g., creation of new Ministries) and such statutory boards as the Singapore Improvement Trust (which became the HDB) and the Singapore Harbour Board (which became the Port of Singapore Authority) to promote efficiency; (2) reduction in the salaries of civil servants by discontinuing their variable allowances in order to promote economy; and (3) the Political Study Centre which was established to mould the attitudes of the civil servants.[79]

In addition to the right timing, the PAP leaders also had a favorable attitude towards reform and this was manifested in the critical speeches made by them in the Legislative Assembly on various aspects of the administration of the colony. The introduction and reliance on statutory boards to accelerate the implementation of socio-economic development programs was an innovation that reaped dividends for the PAP government. We have seen that the handful of statutory boards created during the colonial period did not play an active role in national development. Statutory boards have proliferated during the post-1959 period because the PAP government has found them to be useful and reliable instruments for promoting national development. The contributions of the various statutory boards to Singapore's development was acknowledged symbolically for the first time through their participation in the National Day Parade on August 9, 1976, the eleventh anniversary of the country's independence.

The third reason why the PAP leaders introduced the comprehensive reform of the public bureaucracy was that the degree of risk involved in not reforming the latter was greater than the risk accompanying the implementation of the reform. The PAP leaders felt that they had nothing to lose if the hostile and alienated civil servants were reorientated and "persuaded" to contribute towards the attainment of national development goals. On the other hand, the PAP government was uncertain of its long term survival and its ability to deliver the goods if the status quo was maintained and if the civil servants were allowed to behave as they did during the colonial period.

In short, the PAP government initiated the comprehensive reform of the public bureaucracy after its ascension to power because of the favorable timing, its commitment to reform, and the lower degree of risk in undertaking reform compared to maintaining the status quo. In retrospect, it can be said that the public bureaucracy will not be as effective as it is today if the PAP leaders had not embarked on the task of comprehensive administrative reform. If the members of the public bureaucracy had not been resocialized to adjust and adapt to the needs and aspirations of post-colonial Singapore, they would not have cooperated with the PAP leaders in the formulation and implementation of public policies. The PAP leaders realised from the outset the prime importance of the public bureaucracy in national development. Since the colonial public bureaucracy was not contributing effectively towards national development goals, the PAP government had to change the attitudes and behavior of the civil servants so that they would promote and not hinder the implementation of development programs.

Thus, the most important reason for the effectiveness of the public bureaucracy in national development is the ability of the PAP government to change the attitudes and behavior of the civil servants. Moreover, the PAP government has been in power for 22 years and its durability and stability had not only ensured continuity in public policy-making, but also led to a predictable style of government. Apart from changing the attitudes and behavior of the civil servants, the PAP government provided them with the necessary legal powers, financial resources and equipment to perform their tasks.

To buttress the positive effect of the sponsorship and support of the public bureaucracy by the political leadership, the public bureaucracy is aided in the performance of its task by the small size and high level of economic development of the country. Singapore's smallness facilitates considerably the task of policy implementation for the civil servants. Moreover, the country's relative affluence and rapid economic growth imply that it can afford to divert the required resources to socioeconomic development programs.

However, political sponsorship, the smallness of the island, and its sound economy constitute only the environmental factors responsible for the effectiveness of the public bureaucracy. The other set of factors are those organizational features of the public bureaucracy which contribute to its high level of effectiveness. The PSC guards the entry to the SCS carefully and only allows those who are suitably qualified to become members. It also selects deserving candidates for training at local or foreign institutions. It promotes civil servants on the basis of their performance, and punishes those guilty of disciplinary offences. In other words, the PSC serves to maintain the high caliber of the SCS members. This function is especially important in a multi-racial society like Singapore because the situation can become quite explosive if candidates to the SCS are selected or promoted on the basis of race, language or religion. If this happens, the minority groups will be discriminated against and such discriminatory practices will not contribute to nation building. Fortunately, the PSC has been scrupulously fair in the performance of all its functions and no complaints of discrimination have been made against it by the public.

To reinforce the quality control of the personnel in the SCS, the political leaders have repeatedly stressed the importance of an incorrupt and efficient public bureaucracy. The commitment of the PAP government to eradicate bureaucratic corruption is high and the anti-corruption measures--POCA and CPIB--are adequate and effective. If bureaucratic corruption is not checked it will spread like cancer within the public bureaucracy and debilitate it.

In short, for the public bureaucracy in Singapore to continue being an effective instrument of national development, the following conditions must be satisfied; (1) continued political stability and continuity under the PAP government; (2) absence of serious economic crisis which could reduce the amount of resources allocated for socio-economic development programs; (3) continued reliance on achievement criteria in the recruitment, selection, training, promotion and disciplinary control of civil servants; (4) constant vigilance and commitment of political leadership to eradicate bureaucratic corruption; and (5) continued use of the public bureaucracy as an agent of social change through the implementation of socio-economic developments programs by the statutory boards. For the foreseeable future, it is likely that the PAP government will remain in power because of its ability to deliver the goods and the weaknesses and lack of unity among the various opposition political parties. Barring unforeseen circumstances, the reign of the PAP government will be extended and so will the other policies continue to be used.

The political leadership has undergone "self-renewal" in the sense that second generation leaders have been groomed to take over from the old guard. In the public bureaucracy, the recent injection of young scholars into senior positions can be interpreted as an attempt by the PAP government to upgrade and renew the public bureaucracy. However, such an exercise is fraught with risks because the accelerated promotion of university graduates without the relevant experience can cause resentment among those civil servants who have experience but not the required educational qualifications. A less controversial and also more effective method of renewing the public bureaucracy so that it can effectively meet the challenges of the years ahead is to give more emphasis to training. The public bureaucracy in Singapore has not emphasized the importance of training because of the British colonial tradition of focusing only on on-the-job training. Perhaps, the time is now ripe for the public bureaucracy to transform the existing Civil Service Institute into an authentic Institute of Public Administration which will take care of the training needs of all civil servants.

Footnotes

[1]J. Kathirithamby-Wells, "Early Singapore and the Inception of a British Administrative Tradition in the Straits Settlements (1819-1832)," Journal of the Malaysian Branch of the Royal Asiatic Society 42, Part 2, (December 1969), pp. 48-49.

[2]Singapore Facts and Pictures 1980, Singapore: Information Division, Ministry of Culture, 1980, p. 37.

[3]Ibid., p. 1.

[4]Jacques Rapoport, Ernest Murteba, and Joseph J. Theratil, Small States and Territories: Status and Problems, New York: United Nations Institute for Training and Research, 1971, pp. 148-149.

[5]Jon S. T. Quah, "Administrative Reform and Development Administration in Singapore: A Comparative Study of the Singapore Improvement Trust and the Housing and Development Board," (Ph.D. dissertation, Florida State University, 1975), p. 584.

[6]See Lim Chong Yah and Ow Chwee Huay, "The Economic Development of Singapore in the Sixties and Beyond," in You Poh Seng and Lim Chong Yah (eds.), The Singapore Economy, Singapore: Eastern Universities Press, 1971, p. 5; and Lee Soo Ann, Industrialization in Singapore, Camberwell: Longman Australia, 1973.

[7]For more details, see Ronald Ma and You Poh Seng, The Economy of Malaysia and Singapore, Singapore: MPH Publications, 1966, pp. 13-14.

[8]These Functions of the EDB are discussed at length in Lee Soo Ann, op. cit., Chapters 4-5.

[9]Republic of Singapore, Economic Survey of Singapore 1979, Singapore: Ministry of Trade and Industry, 1980, p. viii. (The exchange rate for the US$ has decreased from US$1 = S$3 to US$2 = S$2.2 during the same period.)

[10]The number of private cars sold has risen by 47 percent from 10,411 cars during January-June 1979 to 15,348 cars for January-June 1980. Straits Times [Singapore], July 12, 1980, p. 6. The number of private cars registered in Singapore in 1979 was 143,402. Yearbook

of Statistics Singapore 1979/80, Singapore: Department
of Statistics, 1980, p. 160.

[11]Lim and Ow, op. cit., pp. 4 and 8; Republic of
Singapore, op. cit., p. 11; and Yearbook of Statistics:
Singapore 1979-80, op. cit., p. 80.

[12]Quah, "Singapore: Toward a National Identity,"
Southeast Asian Affairs 1977, Singapore: Institute of
Southeast Asian Studies, 1977, p. 209.

[13]Singapore '80, Singapore: Information Division,
Ministry of Culture, 1980, p. 175.

[14]Ibid., p. 175.

[15]Singapore Facts and Pictures,op. cit., pp. 171
and 173.

[16]For a concise summary of this period, see C. M.
Turnbull, "Constitutional Development, 1819-1968," in
Ooi Jin Bee and Chiang Hai Ding (eds.), Modern Singapore, Singapore: University of Singapore, 1969, pp.
181-196.

[17]For more details, see Ong Chit Chung, "The 1959
Singapore General Elections," (B.A. academic exercise,
University of Singapore, 1973).

[18]See Frances L. Starner, "The Singapore Elections
of 1963," in K. J. Ratnam and R. S. Milne (eds.), The
Malayan Parliamentary Election of 1964, Singapore:
University of Malaya Press, 1967.

[19]See Alex Josey, comp., The Crucial Years Ahead:
Republic of Singapore General Election 1968, Singapore:
Donald Moore Press, 1968, pp. 68-71.

[20]David S. Gibbons, "The Spectator Political Cul-
ture: A Refinement of the Almond and Verba Model,"
Journal of Commonwealth Political Studies 9, No. 1,
(March 1971), pp. 29-32.

[21]For a Historical Background, See Quah, "The Origins of the Public Bureaucracies in the ASEAN Countries," Indian Journal of Public Administration 24, No.
2 (April-June 1978), pp. 17-21; and Seah Chee-Meow,
"Bureaucratic Evolution and Political Change in an Emerging Nation: A Case Study of Singapore," (Ph.D.

dissertation, Victoria University of Manchester, 1971), pp. 2-110.

[22]Quah, "Statutory Boards and National Development in Singapore, 1959-1979," (Paper prepared for the Government and Politics of Singapore Project, 1980), pp. 10-13.

[23]State of Singapore, Annual Report 1959, Singapore: Government Printing Office, 1961, p. 41, and State of Singapore, PSC Annual Report 1959, Singapore: Government Printing Office, 1962, p. 4.

[24]Seah, op. cit., pp. 82-84.

[25]Lee Boon-Hiok, "The Singapore Civil Service and its Perceptions of Time," (Ph.D. dissertation, University of Hawaii, 1976), pp. 129-133.

[26]Singapore Facts and Pictures 1973, Singapore: Publicity Division, Ministry of Culture, 1973, p. 131.

[27]Singapore Facts and Pictures 1980, p. 33.

[28]Quah, "Statutory Boards and National Development in Singapore, 1959-1979," pp. 6-8.

[29]S. Jayakumar, Constitutional Law, Singapore: Malaya Law Review, Faculty of Law, University of Singapore, 1976, p. 101.

[30]Quah, "Origin of Public Service Commission in Singapore," Indian Journal of Public Administration 18, No. 4 (October-December 1972), p. 564.

[31]Quah, "The Public Service Commission in Singapore: A Comparative Study of (a) Its Evolution and (b) Its Recruitment and Selection Procedures vis-a-vis the Public Service Commissions in Ceylon, India and Malaysia," (M.Soc.Sci. dissertation, University of Singapore,1970), pp. 8-10.

[32]Seah, op. cit., pp. 111-139.

[33]Republic of Singapore, The Budget for the financial year 1980/1981, Singapore: Singapore National Printers, 1980, p. 78.

[34]Quah, "The Public Service Commission in

Singapore," op. cit., pp. 171-172, 181-182, and 185-186.

[35]Where there are no suitable citizens to fill the vacancies or where non-citizens are better qualified than citizens, the PSC has appointed Malaysians and other expatriates to Divisions I and II posts.

[36]A. P. Sinker, "What are Public Service Commissions for?" Public Administration (London) 31 (Autumn 1953), p. 206.

[37]See Jayakumar, Constitutional Law, op. cit., p. 101.

[38]Government of the Republic of Singapore, Instruction Manual No. 2 Staff (except daily-rated staff appointments), Singapore: Ministry of Finance, 1972, Section E Appointment--by promotion, paragraph 16.

[39]For a listing of these offences, see Quah, "Administrative and Legal Measures for Combatting Bureaucratic Corruption in Singapore," Singapore: Department of Political Science, University of Singapore, Occasional Paper No. 34, 1978, p. 21, fn. 18.

[40]Ibid., p. 7.

[41]Colony of Singapore, Reports of the Public Services Commission for the years 1951, 1952, and 1953, Singapore: Government Printing Office, 1954, p. 2.

[42]Republic of Singapore, Public Service Commission Annual Report 1980, Singapore: Singapore National Printers, 1981, pp. 4-5.

[43]Colony of Singapore, Report of the Public Services Commission for the year 1957, Singapore: Government Printing Office, 1959, p. 8.

[44]Recently, the Constitution was amended to increase the size of the PSC to 12 members, including the Chairman.

[45]Republic of Singapore, Public Services Commission Annual Report 1980, op. cit., p. 20.

[46]For studies on corruption in these countries, see: S. N. Dwivedy and G. S. Bhargava, Political Corruption

71

in India, New Delhi: Popular Book Services, 1967; A. K. Galied, "Bureaucratic Corruption in Developing Countries: A Comparative Analysis and Conceptual Inquiry," (D.P.A. dissertation, Syracuse University, 1972); L. M. Hager, "Bureaucratic Corruption in India," Comparative Political Studies 6, No. 2 (July 1973), pp. 197-219; Joseph G. Jabbra, "Bureaucratic Corruption in the Third World: Causes and Remedy," Indian Journal of Public Administration 22, no. 4 (October-December 1976), pp. 673-691; Victor T. Le Vine, Political Corruption: The Ghana Case, Stanford: Hoover Institution Press, 1975; Quah, "Tackling Bureaucratic Corruption: The ASEAN Experience," in Gerald E. Caiden and Heinrich Seidentopf (eds.), Administrative Reform Strategies, Lexington: D.C. Heath and Co., 1981; James C. Scott, Comparative Political Corruption, Englewood Cliffs: Prentice-Hall, 1972; and Ronald Wraith and Edgar Simpkins, Corruption in Developing Countries, New York: W. W. Norton, 1963.

[47]Gerald E. Caiden, "Public Maladministration and Bureaucratic Corruption," Hong Kong Journal of Public Administration 3, No. 1 (June 1981), p. 58.

[48]Peter Jordan, "The 'Mr. Clean' of Asia," Far Eastern Economic Review (September 6, 1974), p. 23.

[49]"No Corruption in Singapore and China," New Nation (Singapore), November 2, 1977, p. 4.

[50]Quah, "Police Corruption in Singapore: An Analysis of its Forms, Extent and Causes," Singapore Police Journal 10, No. 1 (January 1979), p. 42.

[51]Quah and Seah, "Bureaucratic Corruption in Singapore: Major Findings and Implications," (Revised version of paper presented at the Fourth Working Meeting of the Bureaucratic Behavior in Asia Project in Hong Kong, August 1978), pp. 18-19.

[52]See Edward S. Mason, "Corruption and Development," Cambridge, Mass.: Harvard Institute for International Development, Harvard University, Development Discussion Paper No. 50, 1978, and Joseph S. Nye, "Corruption and Political Development: A Cost-Benefit Analysis," American Political Science Review, Vol. 61, No. 2 (June 1967), pp. 417-427.

[53]Quah, "Administrative and Legal Measures for

Combating Bureaucratic Corruption in Singapore," op. cit., p. 20.

[54]Ralph Braibanti, "Reflections on Bureaucratic Corruption," Public Administration (London) 40 (Winter 1962), pp. 357-372.

[55]Colin Leys, "What is the Problem about Corruption?" Journal of Modern African Studies 3, No. 2 (1965), p. 225.

[56]The most junior civil servant in Indonesia receives a monthly salary of Rp. 12,000 (US$19.50) and the most senior civil servant has a monthly salary of Rp. 120,000 (US$195). (The exchange rate is US$1 = Rp. 615) See Cyrus Manurung, "The Public Personnel System in Indonesia," in Amara Raksasataya and Heinrich Siedentopf (eds.), Asian Civil Services: Developments and Trends, Kuala Lumpur: Asian and Pacific Development Administration Center, 1980, p. 162.

[57]Theodore M. Smith, "Corruption, Tradition and Change," Indonesia, 11 (April 1971), pp. 28-31.

[58]Peter Y.S. Tan, "Recruitment for the Civil Service," Kesatuan Bulletin 12 (July 1973), p. 5.

[59]Republic of Singapore, Parliamentary Debates Singapore Official Report 39, No. 5, Tuesday, 15th May, 1979, cols. 358-360.

[60]The current exchange rate is US$1 = S$2.09.

[61]Straits Times (Singapore), February 14, 1981, p. 1.

[62]For more details, see Quah, "Administrative and Legal Measures for Combatting Bureaucratic Corruption in Singapore," op. cit., pp. 14-15.

[63]For example, section 15 of the POCA gave CPIB officers powers of arrest and search of arrested persons. They did not have such powers during the CPIB's first eight years of operation. Section 17 empowered the Public Prosecutor to authorize the CPIB Director and senior special investigators to investigate "any bank account, share account or purchase account" of any person suspected of having committed an offence against the POCA. Section 18 provided for the inspection by CPIB

officers of a civil servant's banker's book and those of his wife, child or agent, if necessary. <u>Ibid</u>., pp. 11-12.

[64]<u>Ibid</u>., p. 13.

[65]<u>Straits Times</u>, October 26, 1981, p. 1.

[66]Republic of Singapore, <u>The Budget for the Financial Year 1981/1982</u>, Singapore: Singapore National Printers, 1981, pp. 363-364.

[67]Quah, "Administrative and Legal Measures for Combating Bureaucratic Corruption in Singapore," <u>op</u>. <u>cit</u>., pp. 15-18.

[68]<u>Ibid</u>., p. 17.

[69]Government of the Republic of Singapore, <u>Instruction Manual No. 2 Staff</u>, Section L Conduct and Discipline, paragraphs 120-124, Finance Circular No. 25/73 (Try S9/4-005), "Measures recommended to prevent corruption for general observation and compliance by departments," dated 24th July, 1973.

[70]For a detailed analysis of the causes of the SIT's failure in public housing, see Quah, "Administrative Reform and Development Administration in Singapore," <u>op</u>. <u>cit</u>., pp. 210-300.

[71]HDB, <u>Annual Report 1979/80</u>, Singapore: HDB, 1980 , pp. 50-51.

[72]A detailed analysis of the causes of the HDB's success in public housing can be found in Quah, "Singapore's Experience in Public Housing: Some Lessons for other New States," in Wu Teh-yao (ed.), <u>Political and Social Change in Singapore</u>, Singapore: Institute of Southeast Asian Studies, 1975, pp. 133-149.

[73]See Peter S. J. Chen, "Policies affecting the Family and Fertility Behavior," in Peter S. J. Chen and James T. Fawcett (eds.), <u>Public Policy and Population Change in Singapore</u>, New York: The Population Council 1979, pp. 187-202.

[74]Quah, "The Public Bureaucracy and Social Change in Singapore," <u>Hong Kong Journal of Public Administration</u> 2, No. 2 (December 1980), p. 31.

[75]Wan Fook-Kee and Saw Swee-Hock, Report of the First National Survey on Family Planning in Singapore, 1973, Singapore: SFPPB and National Statistical Commission, 1974, pp. 15-16.

[76]See Quah, "The Public Bureaucracy and Social Change in Singapore," op. cit., 22-34.

[77]See Mollie and Warwick Neville, Singapore: A Disciplined Society, Auckland: Heinemann Publishers, 1980.

[78]Quah, "Administrative Reform: A Conceptual Analysis," Philippine Journal of Public Administration 20, No. 1 (January 1976), p. 58.

[79]Quah, "Administrative Reform and Development Administration in Singapore," op. cit., pp. 345-346.

CHAPTER V

BUREAUCRACY BY DECREE:
PUBLIC ADMINISTRATION IN THE PHILIPPINES

Linda Richter

Public administration in the Philippines in its roots and in its current manifestation is a product of at least two colonial administrations. It is also a system that has evolved dramatically during nine years of martial law (1972-1981) and which is still being shaped according to executive dictates under President Marcos' continued rule.

The Colonial Legacy

The Philippines was colonized twice by the West, first by Spain for some 300 years, followed by the United States for half a century. The long era of Spanish control left its administrative imprint primarily on the Catholic Church and in terms of the highly centralized organization of the bureaucracy. It is, however, the U.S. administrative norms and traditions that have shaped the basic form and substance of Philippine public administration. The process was not accidental:

> U.S. colonial rule and commonwealth tutelage
> in the Philippines represent the most deter-
> mined and most extensive attempt to export
> American ideals and institutions to another
> country.[1]

This American legacy in terms of public administration has had four major elements. First, American zeal and energy toward the Philippines was in part the consequence of the Philippines being America's only colony. So thoroughly did the U.S. pursue its effort at transplanting American values and organization, that 35 years after Philippine independence, Philippine public administration continues to bear a striking though sometimes superficial resemblance to the public sector in the U.S.

Until 1972, the same could be said about the Philippines' political organization with its presidential form of government, separation of powers, non-ideological two party system, single-member district, and its sprightly if sensational press. The economic milieu was similarly familiar with the emphasis placed on the

76

private sector as "the engine of development." Martial law would affect the political and economic spheres with both intended and unintended consequences, which we will consider later.

Secondly, the successful American efforts at developing mass education meant that the resulting "availability pool" for the public bureaucracy was far larger than in any other country in the region. This had two major consequences: First, Filipinization of administration was feasible much earlier in the American colonial experience than in those of other Western powers. Secondly, the civil service was more permeable than the more elitist bureaucratic establishments characteristic of third world countries modelled on British, French, or Dutch patterns. Bureaucrats in the Philippines do not then represent a distinct social class or a cohesive occupational group.[2]

The openness of the bureaucracy encouraged many women, now found in prominent positions and in impressive numbers throughout the administrative structure.[3] Today over 15 percent of the positions in the Philippines higher civil service are held by women.[4] The Americans can scarcely take all the credit, however. Though mass access to education was a major prerequisite to public sector employment, the proportion of women at the highest levels in the civil service is higher than in the United States. Philippine culture has been more conducive to the mobility of able women than is true in most so-called "developed" societies.[5]

The government observes a secular approach to recruitment. The dominant religious group, Roman Catholics, has almost exactly its proportion of positions in the higher civil service. The Protestants with only one percent of the population have nearly four percent of the higher positions--an advantage that probably can be traced to the American Era. Muslims on the other hand are considerably under-represented. Though five percent of the population, they hold only 1.6 percent of the higher civil service jobs.[6] Several reasons for this situation are possible. First, the Muslim population is concentrated in the southern Philippines, an area neither subdued nor successfully incorporated under Spanish or American colonial rule. As a consequence, Muslims were largely unaffected by American educational efforts and today have educational backgrounds below that of Filipinos in general. Secondly,

Muslims are in an area not significantly bureaucratized. Thirdly, representation of Muslims while higher in areas of Muslim strength, typically do not include many women, who because of Muslim customs tend to be less likely to work outside the home than other Filipinos. Finally, the fact that there has been sporadic warfare, historically, between some Muslim groups and the government has dampened the enthusiasm of even non-combatant Muslims to work for the government. The government has also been incredibly insensitive to the particular legal and cultural traditions of the Muslim community, be it in terms of land reform, government negotiations, or cultural interchanges.[7]

A third element of the American legacy is the emphasis on the trained "technocrat", though the label wasn't in vogue till recently. Unlike the more common pattern in European bureaucracies of preparing "generalists" for the higher reaches of the civil service, and channeling all others into positions of circumscribed mobility, the American pattern reinforced the notion of the "specialist." The detailed job description, the expectation of particular expertise were considered central to recruitment. School and aristocratic ties were subordinate.

Fourthly, Americans would willingly waive credit for another phenomenon which accompanied but did not originate with American colonization--corruption. The era in which Philippine bureaucracy was being shaped to an American model corresponds to both the seamiest and most idealistic political period in American history, reflecting the pressures of both.

On the one hand, the "made-in-America" format reflected goals rather than realities of American public organizations. The Pendleton Act creating the "merit system" for the American Civil Service was only 15 years old when the Philippines became an American colony. Optimism about the new system encouraged its export abroad.[8]

Still, this same American era produced such colorful characters as Plunkitt of Tammany Hall who decried the civil service as "unpatriotic" because it prevented party bosses from rewarding the faithful. This point of view could be especially appreciated in a nation characterized by patron-client relationships.[9] Moreover, "conflicts of interest" or "honest graft" as

Plunkitt once called it became a political fact of life in both societies. In fact, one observer of Philippine politics, F. Sionil Jose, professed to see no "conflict" at all but more candidly characterized the phenomenon as a "convergence of interest."

Because politics and public administration offered such an entré to economic prosperity, ideology played little role. Parties jockeyed for control of factions whose vertical linkages controlled the electoral outcome. As in the U.S. at that time, this meant paying off people all along the chain of alliances--directly, by kickbacks, contracts, etc. It also meant the primacy of attention politically and administratively was directed at <u>initiation</u> of projects--preferably infrastructure--rather than <u>maintenance</u>. Implementation was sadly neglected as was true in the U.S.

Public Administration Under Martial Law

Though all but the first of these features continues to be characteristic of Philippine public administration, new objectives and patterns emerged with the imposition of martial law, Sept.21, 1972. Ostensibly martial law was imposed to "save the Republic and reform Philippine society."[10] Specifically it sought to deal with problems of sporadic violence, a Muslim secessionist movement in the Southern Philippines, Communist-inspired revolutionaries in the North and a general deterioration in law and order. None of these conditions were new or novel, however. In fact, many analysts of Philippine society contend the nation was in relatively good condition, economically stable, and politically secure at the time martial law was announced.[11]

A more persuasive scenario to some, was the fact that the lame duck President's tenure was constitutionally required to end December, 1973. Also, an increasingly nationalist Congress was challenging many of the initiatives the President was taking (initiatives intensified many times by decrees during martial law) as encouraging Philippine dependency and as neo-colonial in character. Whether subsequent American acquiescence is seen as encouraging martial law for U.S. economic and political motives or as simply an unhappy resignation concerning American inability to prevent it, depends chiefly on personal ideological inclinations. The evidence so far is mixed.[12]

79

The circumstances which triggered martial law were by no means the only political issues that concerned the government. The President, from the outset, announced his intention to create a "New Society," free from oligarchical control, the increasing gap between the rich elite and the poor majority, and the pervasive corruption and inefficiency that characterized "the Old Society."

To do so, he proposed a number of reforms intended to increase equity and self-reliance in the nation. Land reform was announced in rice and corn lands breaking up the huge estates (but leaving intact U.S. plantation businesses in export crops and the substantial holdings of many close to the ruling elite). Private armies were abolished and military pay and "perks" dramatically increased. Despite the ostensible "crisis" requiring martial law, the government proceeded within months to create as its first martial law Cabinet-level post, a Department of Tourism.[13] Tax amnesties, followed by impressive improvements in revenue collection demonstrated the renewed will of the Bureau of Internal Revenue (BIR), which had long been characterized by mediocre performance and hindered by widespread public fraud in reporting.

At the same time, the President announced that there would be important changes in the public sector. These would include not only an upgrading of the prestige of public administration but its expansion.[14] No longer was it to be assumed that the public sector would have only a supporting role with private enterprise enjoying center stage in the government's development program.

New public sector enterprises include the former Manila Electric Company, previously owned by a rival faction and Philippine Airlines, whose majority stockholder fell from grace with the President.[15] The government has also moved to establish the Philippine National Oil Corporation, though most of Philippine energy exploration and development will be in multinational hands for the foreseeable future.[16]

More important than increased size and prestige was the President's contention that the public sector would be harnessed for development goals not mere system maintenance. "Change agents" in the form of increased numbers of technocrats were to direct the various departments, now presumably less constrained by political competition.

The government has stressed administrative goals for the New Society that are consistent with Western values widely shared at least in theory by Philippine administrators. These values of planning, "change-oriented" administration, and de-centralization are also held dear by such external influences as the United States, the International Monetary Fund and the World Bank. The willingness of the U.S., western international aid organizations, technocrats, scholars and indeed the Philippine people to give "constitutional authoritarianism" a chance appears to indicate an initial ability of the government to present martial law as a temporary dose of discipline by which the lively, but untidy Philippine democracy could be put on a rational, modern course for national economic development. Under martial law, the "hard" decisions would be taken that would redistribute wealth and encourage national self-reliance. Such a view of the potential utility of authoritarianism was especially fashionable in development administration circles at that time.[17] Although a few voices demurred, most provided a reasonable rationale for such a course.[18]

Administrative Culture

The government has under martial law reiterated the intention of making the bureaucracy achievement-oriented in its recruitment procedures rather than ascriptive. But saying so has not made it fact. Philippine public administrators have consistently affirmed in questionnaires the desirability of Weberian norms of impartiality and "merit"-based recruitment and promotion. However, Philippine culture, like all others, has certain mores that operate to change actual practices from the formal values of modern administration.

"Constitutional authoritarianism," as Marcos characterized martial law, was supposed to by-pass political requisites and nepotism and usher in a new era of rationality, modernity, technical decision-making, value-free recruitment. It didn't happen. Instead de facto recruitment and promotion norms remain primarily defined in terms of reciprocity, political reliability, kinship ties, and regionalism. Prior to 1972, the check on such norms was the political competition for patronage spoils. After 1972, pluralist forces were in retreat.

Though few studies of public administration have focused on personnel policies under martial law, those that have, concur that meritocracy has made little progress.

Even among the newest departments, the Department of Agrarian Reform and Department of Tourism exhibit traditional features. The DAR, like its predecessor takes on the regional characteristics of the Secretary. A personnel evaluation conducted in 1976 after a period of enormous growth in the organization found that over 38% of the central office personnel were from Pangasinan the Secretary's home province and political base. The odds of this occuring naturally in a country with 72 provinces approach the astronomical.[19] Similarly, the Department of Tourism's Secretary, now Minister, is from La Union, one of the tiniest Philippine provinces. Nevertheless, one of the 12 tourism field offices, and by far the largest in size, is in Baung, the capital of La Union.[20]

Similarly, provisions for the hiring of "technical" and "casual" employees have been means by which administrators have been able to recruit loyalists, relatives, or those particularly sought by the regime without confronting Civil Service criteria.[21]

In the name of depoliticizing the bureaucracy, i.e. making it a so-called neutral instrument for development of the nation, the bureaucracy, like other sectors of society, has been increasingly politicized. Not all who are in Philippine public administration are enamoured of the President, even fewer of his activist wife, Imelda. But those who serve do so at the pleasure of the First Couple. Cooptation of the "best and the brightest" has lent an aura of credibility and legitimacy to the "New Society" but in fact decisions of talented technocrats are sometimes amended away from their redistributive thrust toward particularistic, often personal, political and economic objectives of the leadership.[22]

So pervasive has this politicization been, that by 1975 a restudy of government influentials found only half the number of individuals suggested as influential as were named in 1969. The 1975 nominees were also noteworthy for their general political homogeniety, reflecting the impact of the President's hold under martial law.[23]

Rationalizing the Philippine Bureaucracy:
Civil Service Reform

On October 6, 1976, President Marcos signed Presidential Decree No. 807, the New Civil Service Law. The new law was intended to help departments pursue programs consistent with national goals. Among the major changes in structure are the following:

1) New role for the Civil Service Commission--"The Civil Service has changed from a processing body to one which exercises leadership functions--such as policy formulating standards and rule-setting, and post-auditing."

2) Decentralization of personnel action.

3) The merit system--A system of personnel administration and professionalization of the service is required.

4) The new structure of the Civil Service Commission--The CSC was re-structured from a single to a three person commission.

5) The Career Executive Service--A corps of higher executives in government has been formed to act as catalysts for administrative efficiency and agents of administrative innovation.

In conjunction with the reorganization of the Civil Service, the CSC directed committees composed of scholars and bureaucrats to do personnel evaluation studies of each of the departments of the government, beginning with the central offices of each. These were done in 1976 and represented a major effort at surveying not only worker satisfaction, but the distribution of personnel by function, geographic background, by Civil Service eligibilities, and by office within each department.[24]

One of the most striking characteristics was the degree to which individuals assigned to regional or district offices managed to get informally transferred to Manila. Though the commission reports stressed the need to get these people back to their "home bases" for efficiency and fair distribution of workloads, this writer found department personnel both in central and regional offices unwilling to sacrifice popularity by taking steps to return personnel to the "boondocks." While the performance evaluations represented an important effort at getting a picture of de facto conditions in the civil service, it will be the willingness of the CSC to pursue follow-up studies and extend the performance

evaluations to other levels that will determine whether
achievement norms really do receive more than rhetorical encouragement.

Planning

During the spirited days of political democracy
prior to 1972, a finely-tuned system of Congressional
log-rolling frequently meant regular raids on the Treasury. The Philippines was a faithful mirror of American
politics in this regard, but unfortunately such "pork
barrel" products did not serve development needs very
well. Hence, earlier planning institutions often saw
their elaborate plans crumble before the political compromises of various Congressional groups.

Under martial law, planning assumed a special primacy. Just three days after martial law, September 23,
1972, the President "decreed" into existence the Integrated Reorganization Plan, part VI of which provided
for the establishment of a National Economic Development Authority (NEDA) charged with the responsibility
for national planning. NEDA was subsequently established by Presidential Decree No. 107 on January 24,
1973.[25] While the NEDA is today a generally respected
Philippine institution, it has not succeeded in preser-
ving its immunity from political blandishments. What
it has done is create a framework for informed policy-
making which the President can either utilize or ignore.

Regionalization and Decentralization

Regionalization has been another New Society goal
aimed at moving fundamental decision-making to intermediate levels.

The Integrated Reorganization Plan (IRP) was
the first decree issued after martial law.
Since then several decrees have been issued
amending the original purpose and logic of the
plan....The deviations and changes were
brought about now not by Congressional, but
by bureaucratic "politics". Administrators
and others who would be affected either favorably or adversely by the proposals sought,
not from Congressmen and Senators, because
they were no longer around, but from people
close to the decision-making centers in the
government. What was an integrated plan as

adopted "disintegrated" as a result of "bureaucratic politics."[26]

The country was divided into 12 major political regions
with most Ministries organized accordingly. A capital
was chosen for each region which, in contrast to pre-
martial law days, was the common center for Ministries
in that region. Region-wide planning was introduced.
The habits of centralization begun under the Spanish
and never effectively challenged since have been hard
to remove. The primacy of Manila as the political,
economic and cultural center has also worked against
continuity of talented regional directors of the various
Ministries. Success is usually defined in terms of
movement to Manila. There has also been a corresponding
unwillingness to meaningfully devolve authority to lower levels.

At least part of the reluctance to pursue with concerted vigor de-centralization or regionalization stems
from the historic tendency to consider all politics a
zero sum game. Thus, if the center is giving up power,
it is perceived as weaker. Add the other historic pattern of using government power for private economic advantage and the incentive structure for devolution of
power is even less persuasive. Also, local government
in the Philippines has been noteworthy chiefly for its
weakness and venality.

The government's announced intent to make regionalization and decentralization a reality has had, however strong intellectual support, especially from the
prestigious University of the Philippines College of
Public Administration. The school's influence rests
not only on its reputation as a center of public administration but also in its special consulting role vis-
a-vis the administration.

Local and regional personnel view devolution of
authority with some ambivalence. They may welcome and
horde what little spheres of discretion exist, but they
realize that any effort on their part to encourage a
greater lattitude for decision-making at their level
will be viewed with suspicion even as they'd regard
such pressures from still lower levels.[27] After eight
years of martial law, the reality of decentralization--
and regionalization still seems more symbolic than substantive.

Where there is more regional autonomy as in the Southern Philippines, war-time conditions still leave administrators with few options and many constraints.

Corporatism

Another structural effort of the New Society is President Marcos' decision to draw interest groups of a certain type together in industry-wide umbrella organizations. Such bodies are designed to rationalize communication channels for administration policy and theoretically serve as a conduit of opinion to the government. How benignly one views this policy of incorporation depends on both one's ideological perspective and practical objectives. Filipino political scientist Remigio Agpalo sees such a policy as characteristic of Filipino politics since 1872. It is consistent with the "organic hierarchical paradigm" in which the leader sees himself as the head of the nation with government departments and interest groups operating as his arms.[28] American social scientist, Robert Stauffer is less sanguine about incorporation, viewing it primarily as a ploy to control and disarm rival centers of influence.[29]

Some sectors have moved toward incorporation with fewer qualms than others. Tourism, already highly centralized, incorporated with only private grumbling. Agricultural groups have resisted strongly the broad hints that they should mold into a common body.[30]

Other efforts at rationalizing bureaucracy have been directed less at structure than at raising administrative standards and improving worker morale and productivity. As with most systems the actual practices remain at considerable variance from the ideals.

Perhaps most unusual is the fact that an ostensibly reformist regime has often taken the lead in aborting genuine efforts at administrative reform. For example, the Department of Tourism developed a thoughtful plan aimed at developing tourism gradually and with due attention to diffusing its impact and profits. The plan was scuttled for a disastrous policy of building luxury hotels in Manila at a breakneck speed to accommodate the prestigious IMF-World Bank conference for one week. Moreover, those close to the regime ignored the guidelines of the Philippine Tourism Authority by borrowing beyond PTA limits at low interest without prior approval of projects.[31]

Other sectors invested, against IMF-World Bank loan guidelines, in capital rather than labor-intensive projects. Again, regime supporters profited from investment in such priority projects at low interest and from cuts at each stage of the negotiation, contract and building process.[32] There is nothing novel about such behavior in Philippine administration except its current levels of magnitude and the narrowing of those who enjoy the spoils. When asked about the impressive economic success of those close to the President, the First lady replied: "Some are smarter than others."[33]

Part of the contrast between performance and pretense has been attributed to what one Filipino scholar termed a "split level system of values."[34] It is seen in the behavior of individuals throughout the political system. Even in the President one sees evidence of the twin desires to succeed along both contemporary and traditional lines, to be remembered as the architect of the modern Philippines and the head of the richest family in Asia.[35]

The best description of this process is "prismatic" bureaucracy, a term Fred Riggs coined to describe administrative behavior in the Philippines and Thailand but which is common in many developing nations.

> ...A rule is formally announced but is not effectively enforced. The formalistic appearance of the rule contrasts with its actual administration....Apparent rules mask without guiding actual choices.[36]

The implications of the split-level value system show up in public administration in the simultaneous enthusiasm for the latest in administrative techniques and organizational theory and the equal ease with which such values are discarded if they prove inconvenient or a source of controversy. Some examples will illuminate the problem.

Training is associated with advancement not necessarily job performance. Hence, training in some controversial sectors, like land reform is a means of promoting oneself away from controversial issues not a way of learning to resolve such problems.

There is also an emphasis on education in western public administration. Though the Philippines has

quality facilities in both public administration and
other types of education, there is more prestige attached to a foreign diploma, a tendency sometimes exacerbated by American aid efforts.

The degree--foreign or otherwise--does not however,
leave the recipient immune against the cultural barriers
to efficiently utilizing new ideas. Often the person
who attempts to make suggested reforms is teased or
made to feel like a show off. Such a pattern has been
referred to as "a sociostat," because it effectively
regulated social behavior even as a thermostat regulates
heat.[37] Individualism, if it includes an unwillingness
to agree with the prevailing opinion, is also criticized. Such a person is called a "pilosopo." The term
implies not only disagreement with the individual's
viewpoint, but the much harsher assessment that the opinion itself is being advanced only to attract attention. In such a milieu, only those at the very top have
the political and social clout to bring about reform,
so it's of special importance to look at the issues they
choose to emphasize and the way they support them.[38]

The government has embraced a variety of techniques
designed theoretically to improve public administration,
but which often-times seem more directed at impressing
foreign observers, bureaucrats, and raising morale.
For example, at the top echelons many of the brightest
bureaucrats are channeled into Junior Executive Training (JET). At other levels programs with such acronyms
as "STREAM" and "MORE" demonstrate a superficial commitment to administrative modernization. While this
writer was in the Philippines, Management By Objectives
(MBO) was instituted by Presidential decree. Vast numbers of worker hours were devoted to "unfreezing" or
other fashionable endeavors.[39] In a department like
land reform which supposedly works only with speed and
executive commitment, the sums spent on such dubious
luxuries as MBO seem misplaced, the time required an
unnecessary diversion. Older, more tradition-bound
departments, which might have benefited from the MBO
were, in fact, the least likely to pay more than lip
service to the President's decree.

Budgeting, too, has mimicked the fads and foibles
of American budgeting, though with a difference. Lacking a federal structure, Philippine budgetary experimentation starts at the top.[40] Despite the fact that
the Minister of Finance has found that efforts to

modernize Filipino budgeting have been generally futile, the government has switched from one budget format to another and another in an effort to project a facade of "development."

Though 3/4 of government offices have ignored attempts at performance or even program budgeting, preferring to continue with line-item presentations, the government fearlessly decreed PPBS (Planning, Programming Budget Systems), [41] an approach already abandoned in the U.S. as dysfunctional in terms of time, information and expense required. Then, in an almost echo effect of President Carter, President Marcos decreed Zero-Base Budgeting. [42] What scarce resources will be diverted to new veneers of budgeting, one cannot predict, but perhaps more tragic than the monies involved is the psychological dependency that encourages such inappropriate copying.

The Bureaucratic Role in the Developmental Process

Under martial law, the bureaucracy's role in development has been both enlarged and constricted. It is enlarged in the sense that it no longer competes for influence with a lively and combative Congress, a determinedly independent judiciary or a no-holds-barred collage of interest groups. But these political forces, though they exacted a toll in bureaucratic autonomy, also kept the bureaucracy from being the exclusive tool of the executive as it is today.

Freed of political pressures from the mass groups or their representatives the bureaucracy now can presumably focus on "the big picture": national development. Policy studies, however, illustrate that such Olympian perspectives only occur when they coincide with the priorities of the First Couple. [43] Even then, the actual implementation of policy may lose its developmental thrust if it interferes with private political or economic objectives of the ruling elite.

The problems of scarcity, skilled expertise, public apathy or a lack of informed executive ability which are so frequently the cause of development plans going awry are not, in fact, the major obstacles in the Philippines --particularly under martial law. Scarcity exists; but inequity is a more serious problem. Talent abounds and yet it is often coopted to lend credibility for schemes at considerable variance with thoughtful planning. The public is "progressive" in most sentiments, literate, and willing to give martial law a chance to deliver, but it is disenchanted by exchanging competitive oligarchic control for a monopoly by the Marcos family and its close supporters. President Marcos is himself given by supporters and critics alike, high marks for intelligence, political skill and understanding of the development process that few national leaders can match. Unfortunately, he and his associates have other more persistent traditional qualities which keep developmental criteria trailing private economic and political objectives.

Control Mechanisms

Since 1972 the control mechanisms on the political system have changed dramatically. The Congress, independent judiciary, party system, press, and people through the election or interest group process have been rendered impotent. The new controls come in the form of the expanded and greatly enriched military, the officers and new recruits of which are overwhelmingly drawn from the President's regional and linguistic (Ilocano) political base; a new group of technical and political experts who have "burned their bridges" to conventional politics by their lucrative association with the "New Society"; and an international group of donor organizations to whom the Philippines owes some 12 billion dollars, giving the country the highest per capita debt level in Asia.[44]

These groups, like the IMF and World Bank, have enormous potential to affect Philippine development. To date, however, the President has been persuaded more by their arguments against protectionist tariffs or barriers to external investment, than by their encouragement of projects with lower profiles and more labor-intensive possibilities. Another new constraint is the growing criticism of the powerful Catholic Church, a force he sought to defuse with a papal visit. The pope did urge the church to avoid political issues, but he also took the President to task for human rights violations.

Two earlier constraints on Presidential control, the Muslim secessionist efforts in the Southern Philippines and the New People's Army in the North have grown even stronger since 1972 and have been joined by establishment political elements both in the Philippines and in exile.

As a consequence martial law did not streamline or rationalize administrative decision-making but merely changed the nature of the political environment in which those decisions are reached.

The formal lifting of martial law on January 7, 1981, did not change actual control any more than the June 1981 "election" challenged the dominance of the Marcos government. Serious candidates were either declared ineligible or boycotted the election. The lackluster opposition that did contest the election was reputedly "hired" to make the election look credible.

Footnotes

¹David Rosenberg, ed. Marcos and Martial Law in the Philippines, New York: Cornell University Press, 1979, p. 15.

²Carl Lande, "The Philippine," a reprint from the volume Education and Political Development, East Asian Series Reprint No. 8, Lawrence: International Studies Center for East Asian Studies at the University of Kansas, n.d., p. 342.

³These observations are based on my field research focusing on the Department of Agrarian Reform and the Department of Tourism during 1976-1977 under the auspices of a Fulbright scholarship.

⁴Edward M. Masa, "The Higher Civil Service of the Philippines," a paper presented at the Philippine Political Science Meeting, Quezon City, July 1977.

⁵See Justin Green, "Female Elite Goals and National Development: Some Data from the Philippines," in Sylvia A. Chipp and Justin J. Green, eds., Asian Women in Transition, University Park: Pennsylvania State University Press, 1980.

⁶Also grossly under-represented are non-Tagalog or non-Ilocano speakers who have less than 30% of all higher civil service positions. Masa, "The Higher Civil Service in the Philippines," op. cit., p. 2.

⁷Lela Noble, "Keeping an Ethnic Movement Mobilized: The Moro National Liberation Front 1972-1980," a paper presented at the Association for Asian Studies meeting, Toronto, March 13-15, 1981.

⁸O.D. Corpuz, The Bureaucracy in the Philippines, Manila: Institute of Public Administration, 1957, p. 243.

⁹Carl Lande, "Networks and Groups in Southeast Asia: Some Observations on the Group Theory of Politics," in Schmidt, Scott, Lande, and Guasti, eds., Friends, Followers and Factions: A Reader in Political Clientelism, Berkeley: University of California Press, 1977, p. 86.

¹⁰Raul P. DeGuzman, and Associates, Citizen

Participation and Decision-Making Under Martial Law: A Search for a Viable Political System, Manila: University of the Philippines College of Public Administration, 1976.

[11]Rosenberg, "Marcos and Martial Law in the Philippines," op. cit. The author refers to a Rand Study describing the Philippines in 1972.

[12]See Robert Stauffer, "The Political Economy of Development: A Philippine note," Philippine Journal of Public Administration, (April 16, 1972) pp. 129-146; Carl Lande, "Philippine Prospects After Martial Law," a paper circulated for private discussion.

[13]Linda Richter, Land Reform and Tourism Development: Policy Making in Martial Law Philippines, Massachusetts: Schenkman, 1982. It should be noted that government departments became Ministries, and secretaries, Ministers following the irregular national election of an advisory legislature in April, 1978. The terminology is virtually the only indication of the government's determination to create a parliamentary system after martial law--a goal apparently abandoned in early 1981 for the stronger executive possible under a French-style government.

[14]Russell Cheetham and Edward Hawkins, The Philippines: Priorities and Prospects for Development, Washington, D.C.: World Bank, 1976, pp. 30-31.

[15]Richter, "The Political Uses of Tourism: A Philippine case Study," Journal of Developing Areas 14, (January, 1980), pp. 237-257.

[16]Richter, "Priorities in Philippine Policy-Making: The Energy Crisis," a paper presented at the Association for Asian Studies meeting, Toronto, March 13-15, 1981.

[17]See Samuel Huntington, Political Order in Changing Societies, New Haven: Yale University Press, 1968.

[18]Abdo Baaklini, "Comparative Public Administration: The Persistence of an Ideology," Journal of Comparative Administration 5, (May, 1973), pp. 109-121; Mark Kesselman, "Order or Movement? The Literature of Political Development as Ideology, World Politics 26, (October, 1973) p. 144.

[19]"Report of the Performance Evaluation Committee on the Department of Agrarian Reform, 1976." The Secretary announced both his surprise at the proportion of employees from Pangasinan and his intention to correct such geographic imbalance. Whether there has been such a correction, is not known.

[20]Interview with the Department of Tourism Personnel Director, 1977. La Union is also the only province with a sub-field office, in this case located in Agoo, the home town of the secretary. Agoo has become more important recently with a major highway connecting it and the chief resort town of the Philippines, Baguio.

[21]Some of the innumerable ways in which the Civil Service requirements are circumvented are included in Richter, Land Reform and Tourism Development, op. cit.

[22]Ibid.

[23]Perla Makil, Mobility By Decree, Vol. II, Quezon City: Ateneo de Manila University, 1975.

[24]Interviews with faculty of the U.P. College of Public Administration, November, 1976.

[25]The National Economic Development Authority, a pamphlet published by the Philippine government, no date.

[26]de Guzman, op. cit., p. 29.

[27]These comments are based on my interviews with officials in eight of the twelve agrarian reform regional offices and in ten of the twelve tourism field offices from November 1976 through July 1977.

[28]Remigio Agpalo, The Organic-Hierarchical Paradigm and Politics in the Philippines, Manila: University of the Philippines Press, no date (but after 1974).

[29]Robert Stauffer, "Philippine Corporatism: A Note on the New Society," Asian Survey 17, No. 4 (April 1977), pp. 393-407.

[30]Interviews with representatives of the various tourism associations and farmers groups, 1976-1977.

[31]Richter, "The Political Uses of Tourism," op. cit.

[32]Richter, "Priorities in Philippine Policy-Making," op. cit.

[33]Rueben R. Caroy, The Counterfeit Revolution, Manila, Philippine Editions Publishing, 1980.

[34]The term has been attributed to noted Philippine scholar, Frank Lynch.

[35]Carl Lande, a paper for discussion at the Association of Asian Studies meeting, Toronto, March 13-15, 1981.

[36]Fred Riggs, Administration in Developing Countries: The Theory of Prismatic Society, Boston: Houghton Mifflin, 1964, p. 201.

[37]Frank Lynch as quoted by Mary Hollnsteiner, "Social Control and Filipino Personality," in J.B.M. Kassargian and Robert Stringer, Jr., eds., The Management of Men, Cases and Readings on Human Behavior in Philippine Business Organizations, Manila: Solidaridad Publishing, 1971, p. 429.

[38]Ibid., p. 431.

[39]Despite the generally accepted action of the importance of speed in pursuing a controversial land reform, MBO training was seized upon almost as a welcome respite from the problems of task accomplishment.

[40]Cesar Virata, "Government Budgeting--The Philippine Experience," Fookien Times Yearbook, 1975, pp. 74-80.

[41]Ibid., p. 78.

[42]Bulletin Today (Manila Daily), August 27, 1977. See also Presidential Decree No. 1177.

[43]Richter, Land Reform and Tourism Development, op. cit.

[44]Senator Benigno Aquino in a speech before the Association for Asian Studies, Toronto, March 13, 1981.

CHAPTER VI

HIGHER CIVIL SERVICE IN INDIA

Krishna K. Tummala[*]

Independent India was spared the trauma that is characteristic of many an emergent nation in that it not only retained the administrative system developed by the British but also utilized the services of some of the expatriates initially.[1] Some foreign observers even credited it to be among the dozen or so advanced governments, following its independence in 1947.[2] Yet, the metamorphosis of the state from that of a purely regulatory to one which is service-oriented and developmental showed the inadequacies of the system. The colonial service was operating within the context of a "limited government", maintaining law and order and collecting revenues. In the absence of representative political institutions to enforce responsibility, the guardian bureaucrat tended to be despotic, benevolent though.[3] But, independent India is another story, and the following pages are devoted to provide a panorama of the changed circumstances that led to the several administrative reforms and to explain and analyze the administrative system, with an assessment of the current situation. The focal point here would be the Indian Administrative Service, the highest public service position that India could offer, and one most every young college graduate must have fancied, fantacized or pretended to be an aspirant for. All top administrative positions are filled by the Indian Administrative Service officer, and all other Services look towards these either as role models or with envy.

After independence, India declared itself to be a sovereign democratic republic with a parliamentary system of government. While a republic ruled out allegiance to a hereditary monarch, democracy demanded representativeness, participatory politics and also responsiveness. The parliamentary system not only buttressed these but also was intended to assure control over the executive part of the government by providing

[*]I wish to acknowledge my appreciation to the Indian Council of Social Science Research, New Delhi, who twice in the past gave me Fellowships to do field research in India. Part of the material here is from that effort.

an organic link between the legislature and the executive. It also adopted a federal form of government, albeit with some peculiarities.

The word "Union" is deliberately used in preference to "federal" to emphasize the need to check the centrifugal tendencies which are the natural products of immense diversity--linguistic, regional, religious and otherwise. The same Consitution governs the Union as well as the state governments. Although the Seventh Schedule of the Constitution provides three separate Lists of powers-- Union, State and Concurrent (the last could be exercised either by the Union or the states, but precedence is given to the Union), the Union has the superior position. Article 248 confers residuary powers on the Union. Any matters in the State List could be dealt with by the Union Parliament in the name of national interest, if the Council of States (Raj Sabha, the upper House of Parliament) by a two-thirds majority so decides. Two or more states' legislatures may also make such a request (Art. 252). During an Emergency, any matter in the State List could be dealt with by the Union for the whole of India (Art. 250). And in case of any inconsistency between laws passed by the states and the Union, the latter will have precedence (Art. 251). In fact, by the use of the Emergency provisions (Arts. 352-360), the country could be transformed into an unitary one by the President of the Union with the states governments dismissed, and the Union taking over altogether.[4] State Governors are appointed by the President of India and hold office at his pleasure. It is also required that the executive power of the states be exercised to ensure compliance with Union laws, and should in no way impede or prejudice the executive power of the Union (Arts. 256-257). The Union government is empowered to issue directions in this regard from time to time.

In tune with the federal principle, the states governments are allowed to have their own administrative services. The state legislatures are empowered to regulate the recruitment, selection and service conditions of their own civil servants, just as the Union government controls its own. And at each level, independent and impartial Public Service Commissions are constitutionally created to take care of recruitment and selection. Yet, there is something unique in what is known as the All-India Services.

Article 312 of the Constitution provides for the creation of All-India Services, recognizing two of them initially: the Indian Administrative Service (IAS) and the Indian Police Service (IPS). (More could be created and were, by a special resolution by the Council of States). These are common in the sense that the services of the officers could be made use of either by the Union or the states to whose cadres they belong. (At the time of selection, these are asked to denote their preferences regarding the state cadre to which they would like to be attached.) These cannot be dismissed, removed or reduced in rank, except for cause and after an inquiry, and serve at the pleasure of the President of the Union even while they are in the pay and service of the state government. In addition to the IAS, the Union government also draws upon the Class I Services,[5] besides the non-gazetted services (which constitute the lower echelons).

The district as an administrative unit, with the District Collector (Collector from now on) as its chief executive officer, not only was the mainstay of Imperial Rule in India but also continues to occupy a very important position in the administrative structure--unique and even incomparable since independence.[6] Immediately below the state, and as its integral part, the district is the highest local government unit. Selected, trained and controlled (service-wise) by the Union government, the Collector serves the state government (to which posting has been made) as the head of the district administration in charge of revenue, law and order and developmental functions. (In some states, he continues to exercise magesterial funtions too.) And it is the IAS officer that gets to be the Collector. Having served a stint as the Collector, most are drawn back to the Secretariats--the policymaking and administrative hubs of the Union as well as the states, though mostly to the former. Thus, he serves as a linch-pin among the levels of government, ironic and untenable though it may seem in terms of traditional principles of hierarchy, command and control and decentralization. The Secretariat denotes the Ministerial type of organization with the elected politician--from the party in government, as the Minister with the Secretary- the permanent civil servant, immediately below him. The Secretary thus not only serves as the chief aid and advisor to the Minister but also as the administrative head of the Ministry/Department.

A word of explanation is in order regarding the decentralization scheme, otherwise famously known as Panchayati Raj. The Balwantray Mehta Committee in 1959 advocated the establishment of a new setup (replacing the old District Boards) which should be "statutory, elective, comprehensive...controlled and directed by popular representatives of the local area," and entrusted with all the planning and developmental functions.[8] Accordingly, a three-tier system of local self-government was established: at the lowest level the village, the Block at the intermediate level and the district at the top. The stutory bodies were named respectively as the Gram Panchayat, Panchayat Samithi and Zilla Parishad. An organic link among these levels was also established in that the elected representatives at the village level in their turn elect the next higher level representatives. The Samithis were conceived as executive bodies with the Parishads as performing coordinating and supervisory functions with the Collector as the Captain of the team of all developmental officers. The Government of India accepted the recommendations, but left the actual implementation to state governments, as local government is a state subject. The result is a wide variety of patterns too numerous to mention here.[9] However, contrary to the Mehta Committee recommendation, the distrcit continues to be a critical link in the administrative chain, with the Collector at its administrative helm, though his role varies slightly from state to state. The role of the district in the developmental activity, besides its unquestionable regulatory functions, was further confirmed by the Administrative Reforms Commission which realized that the district is the principal point of contact between the citizen and the state.[10]

Independent India meant more than a simple transfer of power to the natives; it foresaw a transformation of the purpose and functions of the state. And Democratic Socialism provided the blue-print. In an effort to rebuild a new India politically, economically and socially out of an ancient, traditional and substantially unequal society according to liberal democratic principles, Democratic Socialism was used both as a guide and support.[11] While the Preamble of the Constitution set the tone, Fundamental Rights (Part III) and the Directive Principles of State Policy (Part IV) provided substance (at times even bitter conflict) in this context. By the establishment of the Planning Commission in 1950, India became the first non-Communist country in the world to have comprehensive planned economic development through the Five Year Plans. In 1952, the National Extension Service and Community Development Programmes were started. And as mentioned above, by 1959, the Panchayati Raj scheme came into vogue. Congress Party (currently, Congress (I), I-to denote Indira, the first name of the Prime Minister, Mrs. Indira Gandhi), which is the dominant party, except for a brief spell in 1977-79, had been preoccupied with socialist thoughts ever since the Karachi Resolution of 1931. And in 1964, it set up Democratic Socialism as a goal for the nation, with certain militancy added to its thought as well as public policies since 1969, when Mrs. Gandhi became the Prime Minister.[*]

Ambiguous though it continues to be, Democratic Socialism in India has certain distinctive features. Insisting on flexibility, the leaders, especially in the past, refused to be doctrinaire about it. It is not based on class war. There is an emphasis on tolerance and peaceful change. There is an interesting mix of individualism and socialism. In contrast with the Marxian conception of the legal-political order being after all a superstructure reinforcing the economic system, Democratic Socialism contends that state power, through the planning process, is to be an instrument of social engineering. The emphasis has been on socialism within the context of a democratic system. Thus the transformation of the state from a regulatory agency to a service-oriented one, with innumerable planning and developmental functions, placed a large premium on the administrative services which in the past were used only to the maintenance and regulatory functions. The result was a series of unending reforms, which at times leave the impression of being ritualistic.[12]

The voluminous reform reports in India since independence may be classified under three headings:[13] reforms suggested by the higher civil servants, initiated by the legislature and in a few instances advised by foreign experts. An examination of these several

_____

[*]The 1977-79 interlude with the Janata rule after the defeat of Mrs. Gandhi, did see some backtracking, even to the point of a "soft state". Even after the return of Mrs. Gandhi in 1979, the socialist rhetoric appears to have been toned down to an extent.

reports and a survey of their evaluative literature reveal some important points. (a) There had been an united approach to the problem of reform in that the initiative came from a combination of several sources such as the Parliament and the executive, and also all types of elite--political, administrative and academic. (b) They are all intellectually well-conceived in the sense they had been products of serious thinking of able scholars and experienced administrators and politicians. (It should however be noted as a caveat that this is an impression one gathers from reading the recommendations and not the actual implementation. Certainly some of the recommendations were criticised for the lack of any empirical evidence, thus leaving the impression that they are after all products of arm-chair speculation.) (c) There appears to be a gap between profession and performance, the important consideration being the avaialable political support and the prevailing social climate. (d) The original administrative structure had not been radically changed and whatever reforms were undertaken were all within that framework. (e) As reform attempts mostly dealt with only the structural aspects of administration, it was felt that sufficient emphasis was not placed on the process of administration. (f) Though the changes in the character of the civil service had not kept pace with the social and political developments in the country, it should be noted that the service did change from time to time to fit in with the objectives of the state. (g) At times, .contradictory and conflicting goals may have been pursued. For example, while emphasizing the concepts of efficiency and economy all the time in public service, undue premium was also placed on the state as an employer of the last resort, which in turn led to the criticism of overstaffing and wasteful expenditures.

The 1960's and 70's continued the reform trend, and in 1964 the Department of Administrative Reforms was created in the Ministry of Home Affairs. Among other things, it was supposed to have prepared the ground for a comprehensive investigation of the administrative system in the country. Since then two major reform attempts were made. One was the work of the Administrative Reforms Commission (ARC) appointed in 1966, and the other the Committee on Recruitment Policy and Selection Methods (Kothari Commission, after the Chairman) reporting in 1976. While this is not the place for a critical assessment of their work, a few general remarks and comments are not out of place.[14]

Despite protestations and unlike in the past, the influence of foreign thought and experience is marked.[15] The ARC was charged with the task of a rather comprehensive reform, and drawing upon a variety of talent and expertise, it resulted in the most voluminous reform effort.[16] The Kothari Commission on the other hand, is more modest in both its assignment and output, as may be seen below.

The ARC made some important recommendations besides repeating several that were made over the years.[17] Some of them are: (a) Introduce specialists into the administrative hierarchy; (b) Devise a functional grouping of positions; (c) Fill senior management positions in these functional areas by its own members; (d) Provide for lateral entry into the prevailing closed system; (e) Create more career opportunities for lower level officers by increasing the quota of promotions to Class I to 40%; (f) Change the annual confidential report to a performance report; (g) Rationalize pay by establishing 9 pay scales with junior, middle and senior levels. The Third Pay Commission in 1973 however, neutralised or dampened several of these when it leaned back towards a generalist service. It also concluded that pay scales ought not to be a vehicle for administrative reforms or further changes in staffing policy. Arguing against parity of pay scales, it tried however to narrow the disparities.

II
A change in public service could be brought about by manipulating the area of recruitment, altering the selection criteria and improvising and improving the training process. The same may also be attempted by a general restructuring of the society as is the case with revolutions, coup d'etat and the like. But a democratic country that it is, coercion has little place, if any, in India, which also brings us to the rights of the civil servants vis-a-vis the citizenry.

The Union Public Service Commission--an independent and impartial body, handles the recruitment and selection processes for the All-India Services and other Class I Services for the Union government.[18] The combined civil services examinations given annually seek to obtain a diverse group of civil servants while assuring merit and equal opportunity. As each year's examination determines the eligibility and ranking of the candidates for that year, the age limits and the number of attempts at the examination are important determinants of the area of recruitment. The Kothari Commission recommended a minimum of 21 and a maximum of 26 years of age with two attempts during that life span of a candidate. But as of now, the upper age limit is set at 28 years with three attempts.[19]

Art. 15 of the Constitution, while prohibiting discrimination on the basis of race, religion, caste, sex or place of birth, does not prevent any special provisions for women, children and socially and educationally backward classes, and Scheduled Castes (SC) and Scheduled Tribes (ST). In fact, Art 16, section 4, permits reservation of appointments and posts in favor of any backward class that is not adequately represented (in the opinion of the state) in the Services under the state. Further, Art. 335 enjoins that special claims of SCs and STs be considered "consistently with the maintenance of administrative efficiency in the making of appointments..." (This provision was originally to last only for 20 years since the commencement of the Constitution, but was extend in 1969.) Accordingly, 15 per cent of appointments each year are reserved for SCs and 7½ per cent for the STs. Experience so far however showed difficulty in finding eligible ST candidates, and the quotas often remained unfilled or transferred to the SCs. For example, in 1975, out of the total 64 positions reserved for STs only 31 were filled, and 5 transferred to the SCs. There are no reservations for women, but they constitute 11 to 13 per cent. In fact, in 1974, 16 per cent of the candidates chosen for the IAS alone were women, 8 of whom were among the top 20. [20] Similarly, there are no quotas based on either ethnicity or religion, which might suggest some sort of inequality. For example, moslems constitute 12 per cent of the Indian population, but have only 2 per cent of the positions in the government services, police and the army. To ensure mobility and to provide for diversity, 1/3 of the promotions to the IAS are required to be from state Services.

Although whether the Services are representative or not is a debatable point, there surely is an increase in the number of candidates taking the examinations, which prompted the Kothari Commission to suggest some reform in the selection process. They showed that whereas 3,647 people applied for the various positions, in 1975 nearly 8 times more--28,538, applied. While in

1950, of those taking the examinations 8.58% were recommended for appointment, in 1974 the number fell to 4.35 per cent. It was also seen that 70-80% of the candidates scored less than 40% of the points in the examination on an aggregate. Hence the recommendation in favour of a winnowing process, involving a three-step selection method.[21]

Since 1978, the first step is the Preliminary Examination given to all those eligible, in the nature of two objective tests: General Studies and any one of choice out of the given list of 20 optional subjects. This is a simple screening test in that it determines who could take the second step--the Main Examination. In doing this, a ten to one ratio between candidates admitted to the Main Examination and the vacancies to be filled will be maintanied. The Main Examination itself is in two parts: written and interview. The written, essay type examination comprises of eight papers. Paper I is in one of the 15 Indian languages mentioned in the Eigth Schedule of the Constitution. Paper II is in English, with III & IV in General Studies The other four are in two of the several optional subjects (two papers in each). Papers I & II are of qualifying nature, with the minimum standards set by the Commission. Each paper is of a three-hour duration, carrying 300 points. Based on the cumulative score on the last six papers, candidates are called for an interview to test the personal suitability of the candidate for public service. It carries 250 points with no minimum requirement. The number called for the interview will be twice the vacancies to be filled. Final selection and ranking are made on the basis of the cumulative score obtained in the written and interview tests. (Neither scores on the Preliminary Examination, nor of those in Papers I & II are counted here.)

Noteworthy here is an effort at nativising the process. English has long been in use as the medium of examination, and as a foreign language this was felt to be restrictive of opportunity. Consequently in 1969, a Parliamentary Resolution permitted candidates to answer the first two papers (general knowledge and general essay under the old scheme) in any of the 15 languages listed in the Eighth Schedule of the Constitution. The Kothari Commission observed:

> A young person who lacks proficiency in one
> of our languages suffers from a major lacuna

and is ill-fitted for public service. Indeed for the development of a well-rounded personality, it is necessary that our young people should have some interest in the language and the related literature of our country.[22]

This was accomplished by having not only Paper I (which tests proficiency in one of the Indian languages, but also by the inclusion of the various languages/literatures in the optional subjects category.[23] The examinations (other than languages) are also set in Hindi and English, and the candidates can answer in any language noted in the Eighth Schedule (except for the language papers, which need be answered in the given language).

A case can be made without much difficulty, despite occasional pleas to the contrary, that the higher civil service exhibits some homogeneity.[24] Several empirical studies showed that the service is predominantly of middle class origin, though of late, on a slight downward scale. One study showed that wereas in 1947-56, the middle class per centage of IAS probationers was 93.75, it was 81.20 in 1957-63.[25] In a more recent, but a smaller sample, 76% of the newer entrants and 97% of the older officers identified themselves as middle class. Nineteen per cent among the new entrants, as opposed to 3% of the older group identified as of lower class.[26]

The Universities of Delhi, Punjab, Allahabad, Calcutta and Madras (in that order) constantly provided the majority of the selectees, with a particular prediliction towards certain subjects such as British, European and Indian histories, Physics and Political Science.[27] Insitutions of higher learning, being located in urban centers, and most professionals of urban domicile, it is but natural that most of the candidates are of urban origin and orientation. Also, nearly half of the probationers are the progeny of civil servants, which may suggest some perpetual in-breeding. Indeed, there is a slight increase in candidates of rural background--from 21% during 1948-60 to 26% during 1972-1974.[28] But further socialization process and self-interest of the new candidate would transform that in no time, as may be seen below. So is the case with promotees. Although the middle class dominance of the Service is not unique in India, what is important is that nearly 70% of the Service is drawn from 10% of the

Indian population--the middle class, urban professional group. This becomes critical when such a Service is charged with the responsibility of being a "change agent". Similar concern was expressed by the ARC when it recommended against drawing the civil servants, either imlicitly or explicitly, from a small stratum of society, while insisting that the best available talent be netted from all over the country.

In the absence of professional examinations (they are still, more or less scholarly) and rank inhering in the person and not in the position (there is no classification of position scheme; candidates are selected on the basis of knowledge and potential), the type of training imparted for the higher civil servant becomes crucial. It in fact acquires added significance in that the selectees come from a variety of educational background. Particularly so is the case of those graduates in sciences who may not have had any humanities/social sciences background, not to speak of knowledge of the Constitution, law or public administration.

This need was recognized and institutionalized by providing pre-entry training to each of the Services through specialized schools/staff colleges. In the recent past, it was also provided that every officer shall have at least two in-service training opportunities: one, between 6-10 years of service,and the other, between 11-15 years. A total of 24 months of training leave with pay is also permitted for these. The training program in the Lal Bahadur Shastri National Academy of Administration (Academy) located in Mussoorie is of prime importance as it provides pre-entry training to all probationers from the All-India Services and the Class I (non-technical) Services in a Foundation Course. It also doubles up as a staff college for the IAS, besides providing some mid-career training opportunities.

The training for the IAS probationers is divided into three phases. Phase I consists of the Foundation Course lasting for four months. The aims and objectives here are to provide basic understanding of the constitutional, political, economic, legal and social framework within which the civil servant operates; to promote a common outlook and understanding and purpose of public service among all ranks; and to help build appropriate attitudes, values and qualities of leadership and organizational skills. Herein is a study of "core" subjects such as public administration, law, political theory, Constitution of India, planning and economic policy and Indian history and culture. Each probationer is examined in these subjects and interestingly enough, the performance here does not affect in any way the overall performance of an officer.

Each probationer is required to take a qualifying examination early on in the regional language (of the state to whose cadre one has opted), elementary Hindi (which is the official language in India) and physical fitness. One is given 2-3 chances. It is quite unlikely that a person who passed a rigorous initial selection examination would fail these. But there have been rare cases when one did; but no case has been cited when one is thrown out of service altogether.

After the completion of the Foundation Course, an additional five month professional training is given to all the IAS probationers before the second phase starts with a field posting. During the one year in field, the probationer is posted to several lower level line positions to observe and learn particularly revenue, law and order and judicial administration, local government in action (Panchayati Raj), and agriculture and other developmental functions. On completion, he returns to the Academy to continue the third phase for 3 more months when the field experience comes up for scrutiny, along with some supplemental training. According to the director of the course, this phase "has been designed to bring together their earlier theoretical understanding and appreciation and their field observations together." Just as the previous year's training shows a decided rural bias, the last three months are sort of summing up.[29] And the time now is spent in syndicate studies, seminars on law and order, district planning, management techniques, development programs, and with case studies and guest lectures.

Characterizing this training as an attempt at "the induction of a new generation into the language of administrators," Theo Mars concluded: "The major difficulty in coming to terms with the programs is the inadequacy of received ideas of training, derived from other situations and efforts, to capture the essence of what it does, as opposed to its more ephemeral incidentals."[30] One cannot deny the necessity of socializing the young university graduate into the prevailing administrative culture, and this the Academy does. As a matter of fact,

the Academy has a distinct departmental flavor, although
the faculty is equally drawn from academicians and administrators. Academicians are selected by the Union Public Servcie Commission, and the administrators are sent
on deputation by the Department of Personnel, Ministry
of Home Affairs, Government of India. Yet, all directing staff are deputationsists, and one cannot fail to
notice the secondary position to which the academician
is relegated to. Similarly, the treatment accorded to
the probationer is rather very protective, and they
respond with more than deference--even obedience. It
is often clained that the official influence is less
than what it appears to be as many guest lectures are
arranged from time to time. But the following table
tells a different story. The 38 guest lectures organized
for the last phase of the course held during April 10
and July 4, 1978, may be broken down thus, for example:

Government Servants	18	(of whom 5 were listed as retired I.C.S. officers)
Planning Commission	2	
Public Enterprises	1	
Members of Parliament	3	
Newspapermen	2	
Governors of State	1	
Academician & Researcher	5	
Private Sector Manager	1	
(Five of the lecturers could not be identified and categorized as the listing did not provide the background information)		

Thus, it appears that there is a decided bias in
favor of administrators as trainers (as the first three
categories shown above constitute more than 55% of the
total lecturers in addition to the administrators as
faculty), and one is compelled to conclude that there
is an effort at passing on the tradition of the bureau-

crat. But one of the officers of the Department of Personnel defended the arrangement thus: "That these are people from the field with first-hand experience of what the administrative situation is and what the problems are, gives an added measure of credibility, and the probationers to that extent feel secure. As opposed to these, the academicians are people to an extent like the arm-chair philosophers. The theoretical knowledge that they impart is necessarily to be tempered by practical experience."[31]

Turning to administrative ethos, the policy-administration dichotomy finds its place. The First Five Year Plan read: "Its (political executive) sphere is, in the main, one of policy and the principles that lie behind policy....The public service stands outside the arena of political life....Even though their (administrators) views generally influence decisions, their main role is to implement and to administer policies..."[32] Accordingly, the service conditions and practices reflect the effort at protecting neutrality. Though free exercise of franchise is in no way hampered, the civil servants are not to give any indication of the way they voted. And active political participation is forbidden, just as their right to strike is denied.[33]

One would also observe a rather strict adherence to rules and regulations, and a deference to superior officers.[34] A rule of procedure is given for the benefit of both the civil servant and the public. For the civil servant, it is a guide to action. For the public, it affords guarantee against discriminatory and arbitrary action. From the systemic point of view, it enhances objectivity while assuring consistency. It is democratic in that it provides for equality by preventing the possibility of undue favors. Yet, an indiscriminate adherence to the letter of the rule would deny the flexibility needed in a developing situation and prevent timely decisions. While it is realized that rules after all are man-made and can be changed, no such effort comes forth. Even those who prefer that they should use their judgement to meet the demands of a particular circumstance succumb to the line of least resistance and follow the established rules. This is so because to change a rule, the civil servant has to make a case and take it to the policymaker and persevere, which means a lot of time and effort and perhaps bother.

More importantly, prevailing rules also serve as

a defensive mechanism. In the name of good constituency relationships, it is normal for a politician to approach the civil servant for favors. The Panchayati Raj scheme by further narrowing the distance between the civil servant and the public and the politician only accelerates this process. In this context, a rule provides a ready-made shield to ward off political pressures. Also, the same Panchayati Raj scheme led to the loss of anonymity of the civil servant as he became highly visible and accessible. In the absence of voluntary assumption of responsibility for all political and administrative decisions by the politician--a prerequisite for anonymity of the civil servant and his neutrality, the civil servant is often dragged into acrimonious political debate. This in its turn encourages defensive behavior, and established rules and regulations provide a convenient cloak. Similarly, deference to the superior administrative officials is seen to be a cherished value.[35] But in the process of referring to the higher-ups, responsibility is passed on, security is obtained, distrust institutionalized and innovation smothered.

Admitting the large area of interaction and overlap between administrative and political functions, particularly at the local level, and the political nature of many an dministrative decision, the attitude of the civil servants towards public policy becomes crucial.[36] And their rule-oriented, hierarchical behavior led the Prime Minister, Mrs. Gandhi to criticise that they had become the "stumbling blocks" in the developmental path. As a corrective measure, the concept of "committed bureaucracy" was advocated in 1969.

Although no precise definition of commitment to what or whom was ever provided, the general feeling was expressed thus:

> That the present bureaucracy under the
> orthodox and conservative leadership of
> the ICS[*] with its upper class prejudices
> can hardly be expected to meet the require-
> ments of social and economic changes along
> socialist lines. The creation of an adminis-
> trative cadre committed to national objectives

---

[*]The Indian Civil Service (ICS) during the British Raj even while recruited in India from the elite, was trained in England. And the current IAS is a progenitor of the ICS, since indpendence.

110

and responsive to our social need is an
urgent necessity.[37]

Mrs. Gandhi, denying any implication of partisanship,
suggested that "the bureaucracy should be committed
to the nation, and also the welfare of the people."[38]
But the ensuing political rhetoric clouded the issue as
it suggested a failure to distinguish between the policies of the government and the party mandates, and 'commitment' was understood by some, particularly the opposition, as an exhortation to tow the party line--an
attempt to make the bureaucrat "compliant". The party
in power was criticized as attempting to use this as a
ploy to perpetuate its ideology and consequently its
rule. For those wedded to the concept of neutrality,
any such suggestion seemed to be unprofessional, and
threatened the objectivity of civil servants.

Amidst all this controversy, one may discern that
"commitment" implied an effort at injecting some passion
and enthusiasm as opposed to the Weberian view when "a
spirit of formalistic impersonality" dominates, and the
bureaucrat works "without hatred or passion and hence
without affection and enthusiasm."[39] There are three
options open to achieve this. One, the composition and
structure of bureaucracy may be manipulated hoping for
consequent behavioral changes. Two, rigorous training
may be imparted to alter attitudes and behavior. Three,
coercion may be used to obtain compliance.[40]

As seen above, even with the latest round of reforms, the composition and structure remained more or
less intact. And in terms of training, the one year
posting to the field is the only innovation which indeed does some good in terms of providing some first-hand
local experience. Although overt coercion is not particularly obvious, subtle pressures over the upper echelons of the civil service have come into vogue in the
last few years. The two succeeding governments that
criticized Mrs. Gandhi for having used transfers of senior civil servants as a weapon to have compliant higher
administrators, or at least to get rid of those who
were perceived to be not sympathetic to her government
policies,[41] themselves indulged in the same to the point
where they were criticized of being vindictive (see
below). The net result is that the civil servant not
only remains entrenched but also threatened; hence very
cautious.

All the recommendations of the reforms committees made no dent in the administrative structure which remained stable. Not only that, some problems persist.

That the IAS stands at the top of the heap is understandable. This continues to be a sore point and causes resentment among the technical and specialist classes of the civil services. As far back as in 1973, some engineers refused to accept an IAS officer as their chief, and doctors demanded equal status. That year, the All-India Confederation of Central Government Officers' Association demanded a "common discipline" among all officers, including the IAS, and parity of scales.[42] Neither was acceded. So long as there is no parity of pay scales, the higher paid continue to have an inherent privileged position.

With the given recruitment and selction process, it is easily seen that the emphasis so far has been on a generalist administrator. A generalist administrator is understood to be one who, after demonstrating general intellectual capabilities through the examination process, was selected for the potential to discharge administrative functions in any area or situation, as opposed to the specialist whose training has been in a particular area and was selected to man that particular position. This 'jack of all trades' attitude served adequately within the context of a 'limited government'. But within the developmental nature of the current task, the ARC felt that "...a new approach is necessary which should integrate selected specialists into the administrative hierarchy and enable them to participate more directly in the process of policy formulation..."[43] After more than a decade, such an assimilation is yet to come by, and the class consciousness persists.

In an effort to impart a common outlook, the four month long Foundation Course common to all Services was developed. But to hope that this would serve an integrative function is rather doubtful. For one thing, it is too short a period to lead to any comraderie among the multitude. For another, and more importantly, the probationers come to the Foundation Course, having been chosen to the various Services, which means that the differential seed has already been sown. The French system provides an interesting contrast in this context, as the entrance examination there only guarantees admi-

ssion to the training school. All selectees receive
the same training in administration for 2 years and 5
months after which time only they join the administrative cadre. Selection of a career is made at the end
of the academic term, and on the basis of performance.
While it cannot be denied that differences do indeed
exist among French Services, this system could be expected to provide some commonalty.[44] But the Indian system as it obtains, cannot fulfill this promise. It only
captured part of the structure from the French and missed the spirit altogether.

The trend that the majority of the civil servants
are drawn from a rather small segment of the country's
population continues. Several writers drew critical
attention to this. And the Kothari Commission, while
acknowledging an improvement in the number of entrants
with rural background and lower class origin, declined
to draw any inferences.[45] Whether such a Service could
be considered "representative", is a matter for further
debate.[46] Noteworthy here is a dissent from a member
of the ARC:

> The present system of recruitment...is such
> that even a very brilliant boy who has passed
> out of a small college hardly stands any chance
> of success against even a mediocre student who
> has had the benefit of a public school educa-
> tion or who has had the advantage of moving in
> higher society. This leads to boys belonging
> to higher income groups and urban centers mono-
> polizing the all-India competitive examinations.
> My colleagues in the Commission appear to have
> closed their eyes to this dangerous trend where
> western-oriented young men are in a position
> to annex most positions in all-India and Central
> Services. [47]

Most assuredly, the number of candidates competing
for civil service positions has gone up, and the Kothari
Commission recommendation and the subsequent implementation of the Preliminary Examination work as screening devices. While one can argue that this large number
provides a wider recruitment pool from which the best
can be chosen, there appears to be some debate as to the
quality of candidates. With the private sector providing job opportunities with better pay and less stress,
the number of first class graduates competing for civil
service positions has been on the decline.[48] If the

attractiveness of the Service were to be measured by the type of candidates competing, the trend thus seems to indicate that public service is slipping in its appeal.

Since the 1969 Parliamentary Resolution, native languages are permitted as the medium of examination, and as seen above, the Kothari Commission pushed this nativization further. All this was done in the light of evidence that shows that regional languages are not only not popular but also pose some administrative problems. In 1980, it was reported by the Chairman of the Union Public Service Commisison that 86% of the candidates opted English as the medium; only 12% preferred Hindi--the official language.[50] This was said to be due to several reasons. Not all these languages are used as the medium of instruciton at the college/university levels. In fact some of the universities that switched to the regional languages are going back to the English medium. There is paucity of textbooks in the languages. And at times, it was even found to be difficult to obtain qualified examiners. There was also the problem of secrecy in translating the tests into 15 languages. In addition, there is the problem of uniform grading of the examinations in different languages.[50]

In the absence of a national language--Hindi is designated as the official language due to the opposition from the southern states--the advocacy of regional languages as media of examination may result in consequences that may not necessarily be pleasant. Does this encourage more fissiparous tendencies, and what type of communication problems might arise between the Union and states and the administrator and the client, and what would happen to national integration in general are some of the imponderables in this context. (This is not necessarily a plea for the retention of English as the medium, but an argument for the developemnt of a national medium.)

As mentioned initially, the Constitution-makers were concerned about the centrifugal tendencies and created the Union, and the All-India Services have a special role to play in this context. As a report of the Estimates Committee of the House of the People (Lok Sabha, the lower House of Parliament) reads:

In a vast country like India, with different religions, languages and customs, All-India Services play a vital role. They provide administrative stability, national solidarity, and continuity in administration. They also act as invisible catalytic agents in strengthening national integration. With their broader outlook, these services also provide a bulwark against the forces of disruption, parochialism and regionalism. It is important that the All-India Services should be strengthened and expanded, wherever possible.[51]

As seen above, though only two such Services were initially recognized by the Constitution, attempts were made to create more. The States Reorganization Commission in 1955 recommended the creation of technical All-India Services, which was unanimously accepted by the Chief Ministers Conference in 1961. And three such-- Forestry, Medical/Health and Engineering were created in principle, with Education and Agriculture added in 1965. But developments since then had not augured well, and if any, the question of national integration surfaces once again here. In 1966, the Indian Forest Service was indeed created, but as of January 1979, only 1329 of the sanctioned 1737 positions were filled. Some of the states governments, in the hands of the opposition parties, had shown reluctance not only to the expansion of the All-India Services but also for the present ones. For example, the Government of West Bengal argued in favour of the total abolition of the All-India Services. The states of Jammu & Kashmir, Tamilnadu and Maharashtra voted against Medical/Health Service, and the states of Jammu & Kashmir and Tamilnadu against Engineers. Although some specious reasons were given, the major factor is that the All-India Service as constituted, is controlled by the Union government as mentioned earlier, and non-Congress governments tend to view them as agents of the Congress Party which is in power at the Union level. Thus, a new phenomenon--the question of states autonomy and rights, came up, and if successful, would have serious consequences for not only the All-India Services but also for states' cooperation and national development.[52]

Speaking of the developmental process, indeed one would have to concede that India is secure politically and economically; more so when compared with her sister states--Pakistan and Bangladesh. While most of the credit shall go to political stability at least thus far, part of it shall be given to the civil service that not only adapted itself but also had proven its mettle vis-a-vis the developmental functions. However, the oft asked question is whether the administrative services are adequate. Using Anthony Downs' typology one would indeed find a few "advocates" among the civil servants who show zest and zeal for their work and the various programs, with an effort to break new ground. But there are powerful disincentives against 'breaking the tradition', so to speak. At the other end of the spectrum, there are also a few totally submissive, compliant civil servants who would be glad to trade their expertise and independent judgement for the security that is offered and/or obtained by tacking on to a powerful politician. Mercifully, these are in a microscopic minority. The majority, on the other hand, are of the "conserver" category, and exhibit what Victor Thompson called, "bureau pathology".[53] Whether such a bureaucracy is in general conducive to development is answered doubtfully.[54] All this, however does not mean that the Indian administrator cannot perform. On the contrary, several times in the past, the civil service demonstrated its ability to successfully undertake gigantic tasks, if only the leadership was available. Sardar Patel with the integration of the states soon after independence, Rafi Ahmad Kidwai doing away with controls on food commodities, the resettlement of several millions of refugees consequent to partition, and also in the 1970s from Bangladesh are but only a few examples of massive success stories, not to mention the great strides that were taken in the growth of agriculture, health and the like, since independence.

For that matter, one cannot make a sweeping argument against the over-cautious, rule-oriented, and non-risk-taking civil servant, which is also deferential to the administrative superiors. As a matter of fact, they may constitute a bulwark of stability, in an otherwise unstable political climate as was the case following the ouster of Mrs. Gandhi from power in 1977-1979. At the local level, they may even do the balancing act in terms of providing a check against the over-zealous, parochial politician and consequent petty politics, and thus maintain the status quo.

Yet, of late, the morale of the civil service seems to be at a low ebb with a pervading sense of insecurity. When the Janata Party came to power after Mrs. Gandhi's defeat in 1977, it was reported that as many as 500 senior IAS and IPS officers were transferred.[55] Quite understandably, with the return of Mrs. Gandhi in 1980,

attempts to restore these back to their former prominence have been made under the plea that they were after
all victimised. And those who favoured by and or identified with the two previous governments automatically
find themselves shunted around. Thus, the proximity of
the higher civil servant to the elected politician (Minister) under these conditions put the concept of neutrality to its severst test. Insecurity in its wake,
leads to execessive caution to the point of abrogating
reponsibility, if not overtly. Certainly, one would not
do anything beyond what is absolutely mandated; in
other words live by 'the book'. The point is not lost
and Mrs. Gandhi in a recent confidential memo said:

> A major cause of deterioration (in administra-
> tion) is the tendency of higher officers to
> shirk responsibility. The feeling has grown
> that taking decisions is risky and invites
> criticism. The file-pusher feels safe because
> he commits no mistakes. This tendency must be
> combatted. Officers should be judged on the
> basis of the results they show and the contri-
> bution they make to the fulfilment of the obje-
> ctives of the organization they serve. They
> should be assured that the Government will
> draw a distinction between genuine errors
> of judgement and those based on fraudulent
> motives. It is essential that full protect-
> ion is given to officers in all cases where
> their action is bona fide even though they may
> have committed mistakes.[56]

The problem seems to be compounded by the rather
fluid political situation and not so strong a leadership as it exists today. In spite of her continued
popularity, Mrs. Gandhi seems to have lost some of her
verve. Her ouster from office in 1977, after the 1975
Emergency should have made her more cautious. Sanjay
Gandhi, her son and confidant, was being groomed for
future leadership. But his sudden and tragic death soon
after acquiring some political legitimacy, having been
elected to the Parliament, was a sure blow, though not
admitted by her. Since then, the Congress (I) as well
as the government seem to be listless despite the
resurrection of old charters such as the Twenty Point
program.

On the other hand, politics of personality came to
prominence mainly going in concentric circles around

Mrs. Gandhi. Political squabbles within the government and the Congress (I) party, conflict between the executive and judiciary, ineffective opposition, deteriorating law and order, growing social and communal tensions, expanding population, continuing economic problems-- all are taking their toll. On top of all this, corruption in public office, particularly elected offices, has grown to a new height. R. K. Nehru summarized thus:

It is unfortunately undeniable that corruption has spread to every part of the governmental apparatus: the record in office of no political party is better than of any other. We are powerless prisoners of the system within which we must operate. An uncomfortably large number of politicians and ministers are corrupt; corruption is universal in the lower ranks of public services; it has affected the middle ranks as well and is now infecting the apex of our administrative structure--the all-India services--who used at one time to be, like Ceasar's wife, wholly above suspicion.[57]

Whether all this is evidence to prove that rot has already set in deep into the body politic or this is only a temporary lull-- a passing phenomenon, waiting for a corrective course to be provided by a strong and dynamic leadership is yet to be seen. In the meanwhile, the civil service continues to play it safe.

Footnotes

[1]For example, nations such as Burma, Congo and Indonesia, on becoming independent, expelled foreign civil servants en masse, thus creating an administrative vacuum. See Merle Fainsod, "The Structure of Development Administration," in Irving Swerdlow, ed., Development Administration: Concepts and Problems, Syracuse: Syracuse University Press, 1963, pp. 4-5.

[2]See Paul H. Appleby, Public Administration in India: Report of a Survey, New Delhi: Cabinet Secretariat, Government of India, 1957, p. 8. However, in fairness to Appleby, it should be noted that he was highly critical of some of the bureaucratic practices in India.

[3]For a good account of colonial service, see Philip Woodruff, The Men Who Ruled India: The Guardians, New York: Schoken Books, 1964; Sir Edward Blunt, The I.C.S., London: Faber & Faber, 1937; L.S.S. O'Malley, The Indian Civil Service, 1601-1930, London: Frank Cass, 1965. For an account of the British Raj as "limited government", see B.B. Misra, The Administrative History of India, 1834-1947, London: Oxford University Press, 1970.

[4]These provisions in fact led some to dub it a "quasi-federal" system. See, K.C. Wheare, Federal Government, London: Oxford University Press, 1953, p. 28.

[5]There are twenty-two of these meant exclusively for the Union government service such as the Indian Audit and Accounts Service, Indian Defense Accounts Service, Central Secretariat Service, etc.

[6]The department and prefect in France come close to the District and District Collector in India, respectively. But unlike the Collector, the prefect supervised the popularly elected councils of the departments. See the classic by Brian Chapman, Introduction to French Local Government, London: Allen & Unwin, 1953. Calling that "we must rid of what remains of Napoleon's ancien regime," the Prime Minister of France, Pirre Mauroy, in tune with President Francois Mitterand's decentralization platform, proposed the abolition of the position of prefect. New York Times, July 17, 1981.

119

[7]C.P. Bhambri, Administration in a Changing Society, Delhi: National, 1972, p. 38. There is an abundance of literature on the Collector, too numerous to be listed here. For a summary of the history of the position of the Collector and relevant issues and cocnerns, see the special issue, Indian Journal of Public Administration (IJPA) XI, No. 3 (July-September 1965).

[8]Government of India, Committee on Plan Projects, Report of the Team for the Study of Community Projects and National Extension Service, New Delhi: 1959, p. 7.

[9]As one administrator quipped, Panchayati Raj scheme generated the most literature, after Marxism. The one best source is the Administrative Reforms Commission Study Team, Report on District Administration, Vol. II, New Delhi: Government of India Press, September 1967. A brief assessment of the working of the scheme may be seen in S.V.S. Juneja, "Panchayati Raj- A Survey," IJPA XIX, No. 1 (January-March 1973), pp. 54-81.

[10]Administrative Reforms Commission, A Compendium, New Delhi: Government of India, July 1970, pp. 146-147.

[11]For the development of socialist thought in India see for example, Sankar Ghose, Socialism, Democracy and Nationalism in India, Bombay: Allied Publishers, 1973.

[12]For a thesis that administrative reforms in India are ideological, as is the case with other developing nations, see Krishna K. Tummala, The Ambiguity of Ideology and Administrative Reform, New Delhi: Allied Publishers Private Limited, 1979, and also the monograph, Dynamics of the Politics of Confrontation: The Case of India, Institute of Policy Research Paper # 226, Laramie, Wyoming: The University of Wyoming, 1977.

[13]For an elaboration of the several points made in this section see, Tummala, The Ambiguity of Ideology and Administrative Reform, op. cit., Chapter VI.

[14]For contrasting views on the working of the ARC, see, Shriram Maheswari, The Administrative Reforms Commission, Agra: Lakshmi Narain Agarwal, 1972, and Tummala, The Ambiguity of Ideology and Administrative Reform, op. cit.

[15]One cannot but notice the striking similarities in thinking and some of the recommendations of the Fulton Committee Report in England which was dated June 19, 1968, and the ARC Report on Personnel Administration, April 18, 1969. Similarly, the Kothari Commission Report, Civil Services Examination: Report of the Committee on Recruitment Policy and Selection Methods, New Delhi: Union Public Service Commission, 1976, reflects heavily the French influence. In fact, Appendix IV contains a note dealing with the French system and was prepared by Dr. Pierre Racine, former Director, L 'Ecole Nationale d'Administration, Paris. And Appendix III is a note on the British system.

[16]The ARC   produced as many as 19 reports, relying upon the work of 20 Study Teams, 13 Working Groups and one Task Force, plus 4 Expert Groups to assist one of the Study Teams. While this was expected to provide a balanced and thorough picture, some felt it to be overcautious and halting, unable to be radical enough to transplant a new system, due to the necessary accommodations among the diverse groups. See Bata K. Dey, "Administrative Reform--A Perspective Analysis," IJPA XVII, No. 3 (July-September 1971), pp. 558-576.

[17]V. Shankar, Member-Secretary of the ARC had this to say: "Now, if you follow, many of the recommendations that we made on the question of administrative machinery are not novel; there is nothing new in them. They have been repeated ad nauseum." Interview, New Delhi, July 2, 12, 20, 1973.

[18]Part XIV, Chapter II of the Constitution of India provides that the Chairman and the members of the UPSC be appointed by the President of India. He also determines from time to time the number of members on the Commission keeping in view that one half of them must be with at least 10 years of government service. All hold office for six years or 65 years of age, whichever comes first, and are not eligible for reappointment or for any other service with the government. They may be removed from office only by the President for misbehavior, after an inquiry by the Supreme Court of India, and for being insolvent, or for holding any other paid government position,or in the opinion of the President unfit to hold office by reason of infirmity of mind or body. Similar provisions govern the State PSCs.

[19]Kothari Commission, op. cit., pp. 44-45, and Rules published by the Ministry of Home Affairs (Department of Personnel and Administrative Reforms), Gazette of India Extraordinary, December 18, 1980.

[20]UPSC, Twenty-Sixth Report, April 1, 1975 to March 31, 1976, pp. 91-92, passim.

[21]Kothari Commission, op. cit., pp. 35-36, 5-22, and passim. In 1979, the number of candidates applying for examination stood at 100,742. UPSC Twenty-Ninth Report, April 1, 1978 to March 31, 1979, p. 7.

[22]Kothari Commission, op. cit., pp. 52-53.

[23]However, only one of the several languages may be opted. In other words, of the 4 optional papers, only two could be in the language. Noteworthy is the addition of German, French, Russian, English, Arabic, Persian, Chinese, Pali languages besides those other Indian languages listed in the Eighth Schedule.

[24]For example, N.N. Chatterjee argued against the concept of "the culture of a privileged, exclusive club of men," in his "The Developing Role of the Indian Administrative Service," Public Service Commissions in India, 1926-76, New Delhi: UPSC, November 1976, pp. 87-97.

[25]V. Subramaniam, Social Background of India's Administrators, New Delhi: Government of India Publications Division, 1971, p. 145. Also, Bhambri, op. cit., p. 27. For a wider discussion and bibliography, see Tummala, The Ambiguity of Ideology and Administrative Reform, op. cit., Chapter VII. Many of these used the father's occupation/profession as an indicator of class. Using income levels, the Kothari Commission came up with different figures that do not violate the argument. Kothari Commission, op. cit., p. 39

[26]Tummala, Higher Civil Service in India: 'Establishment' or 'Commitment'," Politics, Administration and Change VI, No. 2 (July-December 1981), pp. 17-40. Here the respondents were asked to identify themselves in terms of the class, as they see it. This section on training heavily draws from the above cited article.

[27]Kothari Commission, op. cit., pp. 40-41.

[28]Ibid, p. 40.

[29]S.S. Sharma, Course Director, Interview, Mussoorie, July 5, 1978.

[30]Theo Mars, "The National Academy of Administration: Normative Vocabularies and Organizational Realities," in Bernard Scheffer, ed., Administrative Training and Development: A Comparative Study of East Africa, Zambia, Pakistan and India, New York: Praeger Publishers, 1974, pp. 315-382.

[31]Interview, Department of Personnel, New Delhi, June 28, 1978. (This high-ranking officer wished to remain anonymous.)

[32]Government of India, Planning Commission, First Five Year Plan, New Delhi: Planning Commission, 1952, p. 112. That Indian civil servants are steeped in the concept of neutrality was argued by many. See for example P.R.Dubashi, "Committed Bureaucracy," IJPA XVII, No. 1 (January-March 1971), pp. 33-39. This is not necessarily so in practice as argued by S.P. Aiyar, "Political Context of Indian Administration," IJPA XVII, No. 3 (July-August 1971), pp. 337-354. Also, see Tummala, The Ambiguity of Ideology and Administrative Reform, op. cit., Chapter VII.

[33]Challenges to the July 1981, Essential Services Maintenance Ordinance, which prohibited strikes, were dismissed by the Supreme Court. The Hindu (International Edition), August 15, 1981.

[34]For example, in one sample, 58.5% thought that rules shall be followed strictly; only 22.6% disagreed. See Shanti Kothari and Ramashray Roy, Relations Between Politicians and Administrators at the District Level, New Delhi: Indian Institute of Public Administration, 1969, p. 43. In another, civil servants scored high on points of hierarchy, division of labor and system of rules. See Pai Panandikar and S.S. Kshirasagar, "Bureaucracy in India: An Empirical Study," IJPA XVII, No. 2 (April-June 1971), pp. 187-208.

[35]Kothari and Roy, op. cit., p. 45, and Tummala, "Higher Civil Service in India: 'Establishment' or 'Commitment'," op. cit.

[36]For a discussion of bureaucracy's vast coversion role and its political functioning, see for example, Nimrod Raphaeli, "Civil Servants as Gatekeeprs," Public Personnel Review XXXI (October 1970), pp. 261-264, and Bhambri, Bureaucracy and Politics in India, Bombay: Vikas Publications, 1971.

[37]Chandra Sekhar and Mohan Dharia, "Committed Bureaucracy," Hindusthan Times (New Delhi), December 1, 1969.

[38]Mrs. Indira Gandhi, Interview, New Delhi, July 11, 1978. See also Vishnu Sahay, "What Does it Mean?," Seminar 168 (August 1973), pp. 19-23. (The entire issue of Seminar deals with the concept of "Committed Civil Service," and has an extensive bibliography.)

[39]Max Weber, The Theory of Social and Economic Organization, trans. A.M. Henderson and Talcott Parsons, The Free Press of Glencoe Publication, (Oxford University Press copyright), 1947, p. 340.

[40]See the discussion in Tummala, "Higher Civil Service in India: 'Establishment' or 'Commitment'," op. cit.

[41]Indeed the Shah Commission, while declaring the 1975-77 Emergency unconstitutional, showed that several mala fide arrests and illegal detentions were made, and false criminal charges were lodged and proceedings launched under the Maintenance of Internal Security Act (MISA) in pursuit of a "grand conspiracy", but later court action has exonerated Mrs. Gandhi.

[42]Editorial, Times of India (New Delhi), July 2, 1973, and Indian Express (New Delhi), July 19, 1973.

[43]ARC Report on Personnel Administration, op. cit., p. 11. The generalist/specialist issue is a controversial one exercizing several minds. See for example, Roy Lewis and Angus Maude, Professional People, London:

Phoenix House, 1952; F. F. Ridley, ed., Specialists and Generalists,London: Allen & Unwin, 1968; Subramaniam, "Specialists in British and Australian Governments," Public Administration (London) 42 (Winter 1963), pp. 357-374, and "The relative Status of Specialists and Generalists:An Attempt at a Comparative Historical Examination," Public Administration (London) 46 (Autumn 1968), pp. 331-340; Thomas Balogh, "The Apotheosis of the Dilettante: The Establishment of the Mandarin," in Hugh Thomas, ed., Crisis in the Civil Service, London: Anthony Blond, 1968; B. Shivaraman, "Generalist and the Specialist in Administration," IJPA XVII, No. 3 (July-September 1971), pp. 383-396.

[44]Differences in the French system do exist in that some services are considered to be top: Three of them are, Conseil d'Etat (State Council), La cour des Comptes (Audit Office), and Inspecteur Generale des Finances (Inspector General of Finance). See Racine's note, in Kothari Commission, op. cit., Appendix IV.

[45]Kothari Commission, op. cit., p. 40. For critical comments on the class composition, see Appleby, op. cit.; A.K. Chanda, Indian Administration, London: George Allen & Unwin Ltd., 1967; ARC Study Team Report on Personnel Administration, August 1968.

[46]The question of "representativeness" continues to be a controversial one ever since the term was first used by Donald J. Kingsley, Representative Bureaucracy: An Interpretation of the British Civil Service, Yellow-springs, Ohio: The Antioch Press, 1944. For a more recent discussion of the issue within the American context see, Samuel Krislov, Representative Bureaucracy, Englewood Cliffs, NJ: Prentice Hall, 1974.

[47]T. N. Singh, "Note of Dissent," ARC, Report on Personnel Administration, op. cit., pp. 163-164.

[48]ARC Study Team Report on Center-State Relations, September 1967, p. 246. Also, The Third Pay Commission Report, Vol. I, 1973, p. 67.

[49]The Hindu, (International Edition), January, 1980.

[50]See A.K. Dhan, "Indian Languages as Media in the Civil Service Examinations," in Public Service Commissions in India (Golden Jubilee Souvenir, 1926-76), New Delhi: UPSC, 1976, pp. 119-125.

[51]Quoted by K. K. Katyal, "Catalytic Agents for National Integration," The Hindu (International Edition), August 23, 1980.

[52]Ibid.

[53]To Anthony Downs, conservers consider convenience and security as nearly all-important. They avoid risk-taking. "...Many conservers eschew even the slightest deviation from written procedures unless they obtain approval from higher authority." Further developing the thought, Downs came up with the Law of Increasing Conserverism: "In every bureau, there is an inherent pressure upon the vast majority of officials to become conservers in the long run." See his Inside Bureaucracy, Boston: Little, Brown & Company, 1967, pp. 88, 96-101. Also, Victor Thompson, Modern Organizations, New York: A.P. Knopf, 1961, Chapter 8.

[54]Several writers in the past had argued this point. For example, Appleby, op. cit.; Bert F. Hoselitt, "Tradition and Economic Growth," in Ralph Braibanti and Jospeh Spengler, eds., Tradition, Values and Socio-Eonomic Development, Durham, NC: Duke University Press, 1961; Jospeh LaPalombara, "An Overview," in his edited Bureaucracy and Political Development, Princeton, NJ: Princeton Univeristy Press, 1963, pp. 3-33; A.H. Hanson, The Process of Planning: A Study of India's Five Year Plans, 1950-64, London: Oxford University Press, 1966, p. 261.

[55]See India Today, January 15, 1982, p. 84

[56]The Hindu (International Edition), Week ending March 27, 1982, p. 9.

[57]As quoted in India Today, op. cit., p. 82.

CHAPTER VII

ADMINISTRATIVE REFORM AND THE EVOLUTION
OF THE ADMINISTRATIVE SYSTEM OF PAKISTAN

Robert LaPorte, Jr.

In 1979, the Civil Services Commission of the Government of Pakistan prefaced its recommendations for reform with the following passage:

> Public services in Pakistan have been the object of persistent and mounting criticism by the public. There are complaints of inefficiency, dishonesty, discourtesy, arrogance and unhelpfulness, so much so that many a time bureaucracy is derisively referred to as afsar-shahi, daftar-shahi or naukar-shahi, or a relic of the colonial past. All these terms are meant to denote public resentment against the apathy, the insensitivity, the lack of responsiveness and accountability of the public services to the needs and requirements of the public. Sometimes, even the abolition of the bureaucracy, as an institution, is suggested as a possible way out of the impasse. However, that evidently is a counsel of despair. What is needed is to make the bureaucracy perform effectively and efficiently within the bounds and norms set by, and in the manner reflective of, the popular will.[1]

Let us juxtapose this observation with one made fifty years ago by the Simon Commission:

> Of no country can it be said more

---

*The author wishes to thank the Institute of Public Administration and the College of the Liberal Arts of the Pennsylvania State University for granting sabbatical leave and the American Institute of Pakistan Studies for providing a Senior Research Grant to undertake field research for this work. The Institute of Public Administration also provided the time and secretarial support required to complete this work.

than of India that 'government is administration', and the success of the
constitutional changes which we have
proposed will depend, in no small degree,
upon the maintenance of the high standards which the services have established. . .
    No one of either race ought to be
so foolish as to deny the greatness of
the contribution which Britain has made
to Indian progress. It is not racial
prejudice, nor imperialistic ambition,
nor commercial interests, which makes us
say so plainly. It is a tremendous
achievement to have brought the concep-
tions of impartial justice, of the rule
of law, of respect for equal civic rights
without reference to class or creed, and
of a disinterested and incorruptible
civil service. These are the essential
elements in any state which is advancing
towards well-ordered self-government.[2]

To the uninitiated, either one perception was wrong or
that during the intervening 50 years, something or
things went askew. Perceptions or observations of the
same phenomena are based on facts filtered through value
systems. This is especially true when the phenomena
are human behaviors in human organizations. To the de-
parting British, the bureaucratic/administrative inheritance they were bestowing on Indians and Pakistanis in
1947 was a near perfect one. To the new leaders and
their populations in both countries, the imperfections
of the administrative system were more glaring than were
the benefits.[3] The question of facts and values, therefore, are part of the process of understanding administrative system evolution and reform.

    The purpose of this chapter is to examine the evo-
lution of the administrative system of Pakistan in the
context of established facts and the values of Pakistani
leadership--values which have contributed to the design
or redesign of the system over the past thirty years.
Of necessity, a historical perspective is employed to
illustrate what has changed and what has remained essentially unchanged during the independence period. The
issue of administrative reform (or attempts at reform)
will be a critical one in this examination. Although
the past is essential to understanding the present and

the future, the latter two will not be neglected--rather, an examination of the present will be made so that some forecast of further administrative system evolution can be made.

The Colonial Period

Although one might reach back as far as pre-Moghul times in attempting to provide background on administrative system evolution, the critical starting point in examining modern administration in Pakistan is the British period. It was the British who established the foundations of public administration in the Subcontinent. The fact that they built their governmental rule upon the Moghul foundation (with the Moghuls layering their administrative system on those which preceded them) does not diminish the importance of this period to the development of administration in India, Pakistan, and Bangladesh. Therefore, the British Colonial Period is a logical place to start.

The area of modern-day Pakistan (the provinces of Punjab--which were divided between India and Pakistan in 1947--Sind, the Northwest Frontier, and Buluchistan) was the last part of the Subcontinent to come under the control of the British Empire in India. The British conquest of this area occurred during the middle of the 19th Century by which time they had already exercised power in the rest of the Subcontinent for close to one hundred years. By then, the structure of British administration in India had been developed and tested in other parts of the Indian Empire so that certain concepts of area administration (the district concept) were well-established, although the British did adapt some practices to the newly acquired territories.

The fact that this area (which included both settled and tribal enclaves) was the last to be included in the Empire reveals an important factor which has influenced political and administrative development in Pakistan over the last thirty years. The factor is this--as a "fringe" area (or "outpost" of the Empire as it was popularly portrayed a la "Kipling's Empire"), parts of it (especially the Northwest Frontier, Baluchistan, and northern Punjab) were viewed by the British as essential to the security of the rest of the Indian Empire. Consequently, the British concentrated large detachments of troops (the areas of the Punjab and Northwest Frontier were also prime recruiting grounds

129

for the British Indian Army) in what is now modern-day Pakistan. In fact, Rawalpindi was initially developed as a cantonment area for the Northern Command of the Indian Army. As in other parts of the Indian Empire, the British employed both direct and indirect rule. Parts of the Punjab, Northwest Frontier, Sind and Baluchistan were incorporated into British India (ruled directly by British civil servants) while others were part of "Princely India" (British advisers--members of the Indian Political Service--advised native princes on "how to rule" especially on the conduct of their external relations). Although the Indian princes were "phased out" during the 1950's and 1960's, areas north of Rawalpindi, parts of the Northwest Frontier Province, and Baluchistan, are still administered as "tribal areas"--the Government of Pakistan controls the roads but the tribal <u>jurga</u> (council) administers tribal law. But unlike other areas of the Indian Empire, these provinces were politically passive (in a national sense) and their indigenous leaders, with few exceptions, did not become involved in the independence movements of the 20th Century.

This factor, coupled with the economic isolation of the area, stamped it as a "backward" area and one which had to be administered carefully. More than other areas of India under the British, law and order, the administration of justice, and the collection of revenue were the principal tasks of British civil officers. The presence of the military which could reinforce civilian authority impressed upon the population the concept of authoritarian rule.

In terms of administration, the district was the focus of power. The Deputy Commissioner (D.C., a position held by an Indian Civil Service officer) had great powers over life and death. He was law-maker, enforcer, and adjudicator. He commanded both the civil police as well as the military units within his domain. Because of the lack of communications and transportation, the Deputy Commissioner had to rely upon his own knowledge of his district and his judgement. If ever an administrator was cast in the role of a despot, it was the D.C. in pre-independence Pakistan.

This area was overwhelmingly rural in composition. In 1947, only Lahore (in the Punjab) was a densely populated city. Karachi (the port city in the Sind) had only a few hundred thousand citizens. Rawalpindi was

130

still a small cantonment and Lyallpur (now Faisalbad) was a small town. Politics were regional in nature and political leaders were not concerned with national issues.

For the British, this situation had positive overtones. These provinces were easy to control and administer, especially as Indian nationalism began to make strident demands for independence. There were relatively few demands for participation in government stemming from leaders in this area. Mahatma Gandhi, the Indian nationalist leader, had only a few followers in the Northwest Frontier, and thus his influence was rather limited. Further, the landed aristocracy in the Punjab and Sind remained true for the Muslim population, although before Partition, the Punjab and Sind had sizeable populations of Hindus and Sikhs.

The basic concepts of British civil administration in India evolved over a period of approximately 200 years. Although Britian's first foothold in the Subcontinent was established during the reign of Elizabeth I,[4] the idea of a permanent Empire was not established until the signing of the Treaty of Paris (1763) which ended French ambitions in India and the granting of diwan (the right to collect revenue) by the Moghul Emperor for Bengal, Bihar and Orissa in 1765) to the East India Company. During the early period of Company rule, Company employees were "covenanted" (the process of signing covenants or contracts covering conditions of service, etc.), but towards the end of the 18th Century, corruption and adverse affects of patronage appointments interfered with the smooth collection of revenues. Consequently, the first reform of the civil service led to the establishment of an elite corps of administrators, the Indian Civil Service.[5]

With this change from a mercantile orientation, the functions of revenue collection, law enforcement, and administration of justice at the District level became the principal responsibilities of the civil officers. The administrative system was designed, therefore, around the district concept with the performance of these functions assumed by a generalist-educated administrator.

Subsequent refinements of the system during the 19th and 20th centuries maintained the elite generalist approach. Through a series of Royal Commissions,[6] the

131

British sought to adjust the system to changes in policies established in the India Office and in Parliament as well as to changes resulting from the application of new technology.[7]

Initial Attempts At Reform: the 1940's and 1950's

The evolution of the administrative system after Independence was influenced by several factors, including the political leadership's values, its political and economic priorities, the internal political and economic environment, and the political and economic relationships Pakistan established and maintained with other nations in the world, particularly with the United States. During the 34 years since Independence, 34 government-sponsored inquiries have been made on all or parts of the public administrative system in Pakistan. Of these 34 inquiries, nine[8] attempted to examine the broad issues of structure and functioning of the administrative system. However, before discussing these inquiries and their impact (or lack of) on the evolution of public administration in Pakistan, some commentary must be offered to place administrative evolution in the context of the political, economic and social dynamics of the Independence period.

The Partition of India and the establishment of Pakistan as a "Muslim homeland" in 1947 did not just come about. Although there was little mass agitation for a separate nation until the 1940's, the intellectual, economic and social basis for it began to emerge in the 19th Century. However, it was not until the late 1930's that the Muslim League under the leadership of Mohammad Ali Jinnah--who drew his support not from the indigenous peoples of present-day Pakistan but from among the millions who would come to Pakistan after 1947 as muhajirs (refugees)--began to publicly articulate the demand for a separate state. These muhajirs[9] became the power base for the League in its agitation and negotiations with both the British and the Indian Congress leadership.

Jinnah himself was not a native of pre-partition Pakistan. As a western-educated lawyer, he preferred speaking in English and dressing in western-styled clothes. His fondness for things western and British also spilled over into his desire to maintain the administrative inheritance (the so-called "vice regal" system) for at least the first ten years of independence.[10] The agenda facing the new state of Pakistan (tensions and war with its neighbors, India and Afghanistan, the establishment of a total governmental apparatus almost from scratch) was too massive to make major changes as well in the British designed administrative system. Although Jinnah lived for only one year after independence, he did confer upon the inherited administrative system his personal stamp of approval. His use of the elite civil service (a mixture of British and Pakistani ICS officers and later the officers of the newly created Civil Service of Pakistan--CSP) as the control mechanism for governing the country was continued by his successors. The bias in the late 1940's was against any radical tampering with the administrative system. Only the gradual replacement of British officers by Pakistanis was accepted.

This acceptance by Jinnah and others following him of the inherited system was not shared by all political leaders, or members of the civil service. The elite group (ICS-CSP) was purposively kept small and since it was a career-type service, it controlled key administrative and policymaking positions through its control of personnel assignments through the Establishment Division. It "policed" its own ranks, controlling entry into the the CSP and the other Central Superior Services through an extrance examination procedure which was biased towards those individuals who had received an elitist, liberal arts university education through the medium of English.[11] Those recruited through the Provincial Civil Service Commissions (and became part of the PCS-Provincial Civil Service) could not aspire to the top federal, provincial, or district level positions on a permanent basis.[12] Unlike India which expanded its central superior services after independence to include PCS officers, Pakistani leadership excluded them, thus creating animosity and resentement among Pakistani PCS officers. In addition, those with technical and professional training (engineers, doctors, and scientists) could not aspire to the top administrative posts in their own Ministries since these were reserved for CSP officers. These individuals within the system coupled with political leaders[13] who harbored resentment towards the CSP "clique" formed the basis for agitation against the inherited system and articulated the demand for administrative reform.

In the early 1950's, this demand for reforming the system began to emerge. Pressure from within the system

began to be coupled with pressure from without in the
form of inquiries conducted by administrative experts
from abroad. In 1953, the Government of Pakistan invited Rowland Egger (from the United States) to examine
public sector organization and management and to make
recommendations for possible change.[14] Egger's report
criticized the civil service for "living in the past"
and characterized the administrative system as a "system designed for a day that has gone by."[15] He then
recommended a series of radical changes in the organization, structure and functioning of the system. The
intent of the recommendations was to eliminate the
elite nature of All-Pakistan services (especially the
CSP) and to open-up the system to other types of talent
and training. The Government's response to these recommendations was negative--Egger's recommendations were
not acceptable. In 1955, still another U.S. expert
(Bernard Gladieux) was contacted to undertake an analysis of government organization for national development.
Although his focus was slightly different, in terms of
general administrative structure and functioning, he
agreed with Egger's findings and recommended virtually
the same regarding the services structure (and the need
for opening up the system). With the exceptions of his
recommendations regarding the establishment of planning
boards at the Federal and provincial levels and the establishment of national administrative training institutions (recommendations that were not adopted until General Mohammed Ayub Khan took power in 1958), his other
recommendations were rejected by the Government.

In analyzing the period of the 1950's from an administrative systems perspective, the question that often occurs is why were these recommendations rejected?
The usual response has been that they were rejected because of the strong counter-pressure exerted by the
ICS/CSP lobby within the government.[16] Other analyses
suggest that political factors and the inability of the
experts to effectively recognize the political and social implications of their attempt to "Americanize" the
administrative system of Pakistan[18] tended to result in
non-acceptance of these inquiry recommendations. It
might be suggested that all three analyses are correct--
that each contributed to the eventual postponement of
action on these recommendations. One must remember that
the period of the 1950's was one of political instability and non-consensus. After the assassination of Liaquat Ali Khan (Jinnah's trusted associate who succeeded
him in 1948) in 1951, an intense struggle occured over

134

the relative powers of the Governor-General vis-a-vis the Prime Minister. This conflict lasted until 1958. In addition, non-consensus over the constitutional basis of the country also marked this era. Unlike India, which adopted its Constitution in 1950, Pakistan did not have a Constitution until 1956 (and it was abrogated in 1958). Federal Cabinets and Prime Ministers averaged less than one year in office from 1951 to 1958. No general, country-wide elections were held. In short, although external aid donors might have desired changes in the administrative system and there existed internal support for administrative reform, those in policy and decision-making positions felt they could not afford to experiment with the administrative system since it was this system which provided continuity during the political turmoil which followed Liaquat Ali's death.

In summary, the first ten years of Independence saw only small changes in the public administrative system. Pakistanis replaced British in key administrative policy and decision-making positions. Centralized economic development planning was begun (although it was Ayub Khan who gave it its greatest boost) and economic development became a national, provincial and district level responsibility. However, the "nerves of government" were still in the firm control of a small cadre of generalist-educated and trained individuals. District administration was virtually left untouched by ten years of political independence. By the end of the first decade, the "steel frame" that the British left behind was still in place.

Reform Attempts During the Ayub and Yahya Periods

The political instability of the 1950's was brought to a close with the declaration of Martial Law by President Iskandar Mirza who appointed General (later Field-Marshall Mohammed Ayub Khan (Army Commander-in-Chief) as Chief Martial Law Administrator. This coup has been described as the October 1958 "revolution"[19] In less than one month, Ayub toppled Mirza and gained undisputed control of the country. The reasons for Pakistan's first military coup are complex and not directly related to our analysis. Suffice it to say, Ayub felt that he had a mandate to intervene and govern. During the early part of his rule, Ayub established over two dozen "reform commissions" in almost all areas of activity in Pakistan, including government administration. In 1959, Ayub appointed the Chief Justice of the Supreme Court of Pakistan, A. R. Cornelius, to head the Pay and Services Commission. Its mandate was to examine, comprehensively, the organization, structure and functioning of the administrative system and to make recommendations to Ayub. It took the Commission until 1962 to submit its report. In essence, its recommendations paralleled those of the Egger and Gladieux reports, with a strong advocacy for revamping district level administration. As with the reports of the two outsiders, the Cornelius Commission advocated an opening up of the civil services to all qualified Pakistanis, regardless of their professional, educational backgrounds. The domination of the CSP was to be eliminated.

Ayub's reaction was unfavorable. In one statement, he characterized the Commission's recommendations as "radical changes involving a complete redesigning of the existing scheme and organization of public services but nothing should be done at this time which might disrupt the administrative fabric."[20] The report was not made public until 1969.

What Ayub did instead was to open-up the CSP to military officers. After purging a little more than a dozen members of the Central Superior Services (including a few CSP officers), he sought to develop a coalition between the civil and military services that he would control. Hence, the "militarization" of civil administration through the entry of military officers was begun in the early 1960's.

To a great extent, the basic organization, structure and functioning of the administrative system continued as it had existed prior to October 1958 throughout the Ayub period. He did increase the role of the public sector in all areas of national economic endeavor, particularly in economic development. The National Planning Commission was elevated from its previous minor status as a planning board and the Field Marshall assumed the position of Chairman. The Planning Commission was made responsible for economic policymaking and directing Ayub's grand plan for the economic development of Pakistan through massive government incentives to private industry and through direct government involvement in the economy by the establishment of hundreds of public enterprises. In both endeavors, the elite CSP played major roles.[21] The results of development efforts in the 1960's, using the vice regal system as modified by Ayub, have been rated positive when compared to the earlier period (the 1950's) and the later period (the 1970's).22

At the sub-national level (provincial, district and village), Ayub sought to modify the traditional "administrative state" nature of government administration by the introduction of his own local government scheme. The scheme (known as 'Basic Democracies") was a multi-tiered system of elected representatives of the people who would have input into the formation and implementation of economic development programs below the national level. Although not as "democratic" or "radical" as the advocates of this scheme portrayed it, nevertheless, the Basic Democracies Scheme did introduce Pakistanis, for the first time, to participation in governmental affairs and administration. Again, the instrument to implement this scheme was the vice regal administrative system.

In summary, although Ayub was not the "revolutionary" he styled himself to be, he did introduce changes into the administration of the country. Through the success achieved in attaining his economic development objectives (although these objectives have been criticized), he demonstrated that the vice regal system, under his tutelage, could function in a modern context. The system may have relied heavily on the principles of elitism and exclusivity at its apex; nevertheless, it could administer the country for purposes other than those for which it was designed. Ayub did not alter, radically, the administrative system. He modified it to serve his purposes by expanding its role in economic development and the management of economic and social change. In a sense, he attempted to modernize the vice regal system through the introduction of new public institutions (public enterprises, economic development planning units, the Basic Democracies) and by expanding the role of the public sector. A "pillar" of his rule was the vice regal system with its reliance upon the small, tightly knit group of generalist administrators. However, with the exception of the public enterprises he established, his other institutions, including the strong Presidential form of government he imposed, did not endure beyond his tenure as chief of state. In 1969, under extreme pressure, he resigned as President and appointed General Mohammed Yahya Khan (Army Commander-in-Chief) as his successor.

The Yahya interlude (1969-71) was absorbed with

the political problems of transferring power from the military to a civilian successor and the regional issues dividing Pakistan between the Western provinces (principally Punjab) and East Pakistan (now Bangladesh). Yahya further changed the composition of civil administration by purging more than 1,300 civil officers (including members of the CSP and the other Central Superior Services) and by replacing them with military officers. Thus, further militarization of civil bureaucracy occurred during 1969-71. Other than this personnel replacement, Yahya did not alter the organization, structure and functioning of the administrative system.

Before considering the Bhutto period, there is one issue in administration that should be discussed--the issue of morale. The civil bureaucracy had undergone a series of "jolts" which had shaken its philosophical foundations. The first occurred with Ayub's downfall. The mass agitation against Ayub was also mass agitation against the vice regal system as the prime administrative instrument of government. Civil officers who had served Ayub had begun earlier (than Ayub's resignation) to question the meaning of the economic "miracle" they had orchestrated in the 1960's. Events which followed Ayub's resignation caused great concern within the bureaucracy. First, the 1970 elections and the emergence of Bhutto in the West and Mujib in the East--leaders known for their distrust and dislike of the apex of the vice regal system (the CSP)--raised serious questions as to the continuation of the system itself. Second, the inability to resolve the regionally-inspired issues separating Bhutto and Mujib which prevented a political settlement and led to civil war further eroded the confidence of the civil services to function in this type of political turbulence. Finally, the civil war itself reduced the ranks of the CSP and the other Central Superior Services. The unity that characterized the service before Ayub's departure and the political uncertainties of the post-1970 era must have had a negative impact on civil service morale. The formal organization, structure and functioning may not have been changed but the qualitative character of the administrative system was not the same after 1969.[23] As we shall see, the decade of the 1970's not only continued this trend but reinforced it through the adoption and partial implementation of the 1973 reforms.

The Bhutto Period and the "Great Reform"

At the end of civil war in December 1971, General Yahya transferred power to Zulfikar Ali Bhutto, the Chairman of the Pakistan People's Party (PPP) who had captured a clear majority of national assembly seats in the Western provinces in the 1970 election. Bhutto, who first emerged nationally as a member of Ayub's Cabinet in the 1960's, was a charismatic leader who espoused a political philosophy known as "Islamic Socialism", a mixture of populism with social democratic and Islamic overtones.[24] The 1970 election has been described as a significant watershed in Pakistani politics for a number of reasons, including the mobilization of the "common man" in opposition to elite control in the rural areas.[25]

Upon assumption of power, Bhutto sought to achieve complete control over the instruments of power and government in Pakistan. This meant achieving control over (1) the military, (2) the civil bureaucracy, and (3) the industrial elite.[26] How he accomplished this vis-a-vis the military and the industrial elite is only indirectly related to this analysis. His strategy of achieving control over the administrative system is of great importance to understanding administrative evolution during this critical period.

Before his assumption of power, Bhutto was known to harbor great antipathy towards the CSP, which controlled, from the apex, the administrative system. His dislike, as Burki relates,[27] was derived from two sources--his experience during the Ayub period when, as a abinet inister, he saw his ideas sabotaged by CSP's who were technically subordinate to him but who could and did secure Ayub's reversal of Bhutto's plans; and his desire for a highly centralized, non-institutionalized policy and decisionmaking process which began and ended with him.

He initiated his control and restructuring strategy by purging the civil service of real and potential opponents so that by the end of his rule (July 1977), thousands of civil servants had been forced out.[28] At the same time he began the process of fashioning a new Constitution for Pakistan (to replace Ayub's 1960 constution which had been abrogated by Yahya)--a Constitution which, when ratified in 1973, would abolish the Constitutional guarantees afforded to the civil service which had been part of the earlier Constitutions (1956 and 1962). To replace the Constitutional guarantees, he had enacted a Civil Service Law which provided him with greater flexibility in the selection, assignment, and retainment (or dismissal) of all civil officers.

His vehicle for administrative reform was the report of the Meer Commission,[29] a Commission established in 1972 and given a mandate similar to that Ayub gave to Cornelius in 1959. However, unlike Ayub, Bhutto accepted the Meer Commission recommendations.[30]

In essence, the Meer Commission, using the rationale provided by the Cornelius, Gladieux and Egger inquiries, recommended: (1) the disestablishment of the Central Superior Services and the merger of all services into the All-Pakistan Unified Grades scheme (APUG); (2) the discontinuation of the use of the old service labels (CSP, PFS, etc); (3) the opening-up of the civil bureaucracy (at the highest level) to non-career civil servants through a lateral entry mechanism; and (4) the need to make all appointments to the civil bureaucracy on the basis of merit. The result of this reform was to further politicize appointments to the civil services. Members of the PPP could now be legally appointed to positions formerly reserved for career civil officers (and, in particular, CSP officers). The "steel-frame" of the administrative system, already shaken by Ayub and Yahya, was formally dismantled by Bhutto. Or, so it seemed. Actually, those CSP's who worked well under Bhutto's tutelage continued to occupy positions of importance. The "acid test" was loyalty to the Prime Minister, not to the service.

Although service labels were abolished and the services merged into the APUG, clearly a remnant of the old service groupings remained. The APUG was divided into about a dozen groups whose labels were now "Office Management Group," "District Management Group", "Foreign Affairs Group," "Accounts Group," etc. Identity and service in a particular group for example the District Management Group (DMG), was still preferred over other groups by incoming recruits.[31]

Bhutto's reforms also "indigenized" the upper echelon of the services. The sons of the middle class could now secure appointments to the upper grades of the APUG. The almost exclusive recruitment of the sons of the upper class (the landed, propertied families who

140

sent their offspring to the exclusive English medium
universities--Government College, Lahore, for example--
with post-graduate work at Oxford or Cambridge) was altered. The "class nature" of the services was changed
under Bhutto. Finally, Bhutto deinstitutionalized policy and decision-making in a number of critical areas,
centralized these processes and incorporated them into
the Prime Minister's office, and expanded further the
role of the public sector in the economy. A few examples will illustrate these changes. In the critical
area of economic management and development, Bhutto
nationalized a number of private sector operations (the
banking sector--except foreign banks, shipping, the
production and distribution of certain consumer goods--
cooking oil and rice, for example, among others) and
established public enterprises in place of private corporations and companies. These actions generated great
uncertainty in the private sector causing the drop-off
of private investment and the actual "flight" of capital from the country. The public enterprises added
additional burdens on the already over-taxed managerial
capabilities of the public sector. In the area of economic development, Bhutto retained Ayub's National Planning Commission but usurped its power, reduced its role,
and assigned its powers and role to his office. Plans
continued to be formulated but economic development
memoranda issued by the Prime Minister's office replaced
directives issued by the Planning Commission. Unlike
Ayub, Bhutto's personal style inhibited decision making
,based on criteria other than those established by him
(which were often more influenced by political variables
as opposed to economic ones). As some officials who
worked under both men have revealed,32 Ayub could be
persuaded to change the direction of economic development resource allocation if he could be persuaded that
economic and social factors dictated the change.
Bhutto, however, did not tolerate such arguments since
his view of decision-making was highly personal and
political. Consequently, although Ayub had his share
of obsequious "yes" men, he was amenable to rational,
professionally sound analysis and input. Bhutto, towards the end of his rule, became a victim of his own
creation and, consequently, when his opposition challenged him in March 1977, he misjudged it. Bhutto failed
to cultivate (or tolerate) the capacity to generate and
utilize information from the political, economic and
social environment regarding the effect of his policies
and decisions. The capacity to generate and utilize
such information is often found in the administrative

system. The vice regal system as designed by the British, utilized by Jinnah, and modified by Ayub had this capacity. The irony was Bhutto's disregard for the system he inherited coupled with his inability or unwillingness to create a viable substitute.

The last analysis has not been made regarding the evolution of the administrative system during the critical years of 1971 to 1977. It does appear clear, however, that Bhutto formally and actually changed the organization, structure and functioning of the system through both formal reform and through his leadership style. His political rhetoric and charismatic relationship with the masses aroused their passions and expectations. However, neither appear to have been satisfied, even partially. He was not an effective administrator (a characteristic he shared with his rival, Sheikh Mujib) and the way he refashioned the administrative system he inherited is testimony to this conclusion. By the time General Zia-ul-Haq seized power on July 5, 1977, the public sector was in disarray.

The Present Situation

On July 5, 1977, the military, led by Army Chief of Staff, General Mohammad Zia-ul-Haq, seized power in a bloodless coup. This action followed months of rioting and bloodshed resulting from the March 1977 elections. Upon seizing power, General Zia placed Bhutto, leaders of his party, and leaders of the opposition under detention. Zia's announced intentions were to restore order, mediate between the feuding civilian factions, hold new general elections, and return to soldiering. Elections were scheduled to take place in October 1977. On October 1, 1977, General Zia announced the postponement of the October elections until a "process of accountability" could be completed regarding crimes allegedly committed by Bhutto. This announcement followed some observations made by Zia in September:

> I wish I had known one-hundredth of this (actions by Bhutto) before I took over on July 5 . . . He (Bhutto) was running this country on more or less Gestapo lines, misusing funds, blackmailing people, detaining them illegally and even, perhaps, ordering people killed.

142

Subsequently, Bhutto was charged with conspiracy to murder a political opponent and placed on trial.[33] During his incarceration and trial, the Government began the "process of accountability" and produced several White Papers recording the misuse by Bhutto of his office and power. These documents (a total of six), in combination with radio and television broadcasts, were the Government's case against Bhutto.

Part of Zia's intention to restore order and stability to the country involved dealing with the changes made in the organization, structure and functioning of the administrative system. In February 1978, General Zia appointed a Civil Services Commission to be chaired by the Chief Justice of the Pakistan Supreme Court, S. Anwarul Haq. This Commission's charge was to "recommend measures for making the public services an effective instrument for national development and for the promotion of the good and the welfare of the people."[34] The Egger and Gladieux reports of the 1950's, the Cornelius and Power reports of the 1960's, and the Administrative Reforms of 1973, were "virtually the take-off point for this Commission."[35] Before dealing with this Commission's recommendations and their fate, some additional actions taken by General Zia should be mentioned.

During the first two years in power (1977-79), Zia restored hundreds of civil servants who had been dismissed during the Bhutto period to their services. Not only were those who had been dismissed from the service reinstated, but also many who had been reassigned from positions of importance were reassigned (under Zia) to their former positions or their equivalents. Those civil servants who prospered during the Bhutto era were now vulnerable to the repercussions of change in government leadership. In many instances, Bhutto's "political" civil servants have been replaced by military officers.[36]

In addition to the formal study of the administrative system by the Civil Services Commission, an examination of the public enterprise sector (which had increased significantly as a result of Bhutto's nationalization efforts) was undertaken. As a result, the present Government has begun the process of reversing the tight restrictions imposed on the private sector in the mid-1970's and has denationalized most of the agricultural processing units as well as some of the industrial units. The 1973 Constitution was amended to provide safeguards to private investors against additional arbitrary nationalization. Finally, the Board of Industrial Management (a Bhutto creation) was abolished by Zia and sector holding corporations were reduced to eight (from 11 under Bhutto). Whether or not these steps will enhance the performance of individual public enterprises or the management and organization of the public enterprise sector as a whole remains to be seen.

The Civil Services Commission submitted its report to General Zia in November 1979. Although this report has not been made public, a number of its recommendations have been released through the mass media. The Commission leveled criticism at the 1973 reforms indicating that many were not fully implemented. Its recommendations called for the implementation of the 1973 recommendations in the areas of position classification (that is, the development of a systematic classification of all positions in government), position description (description of all positions in terms of duties, responsibilities and qualifications for positions), performance evaluation (the establishment of standardized, valid, reliable, objective performance evaluation procedures), training, and recruitment. Also criticized was the non-implementation of equal opportunity procedures for all government employees. Its greatest criticism of the Bhutto reforms, however, was leveled at the elimination of constitutionally-based service security. It recommended immediate restoration into the existing Constitution of the Constitutional safe-guards to civil servants found in Articles 181 and 182 of the 1956 Constitution. Further, it recommended the establishment of a "Pakistan Public Service" (PPS) which would encompass all posts in the Federal Government. This would lead to a "truly unified services structure with different branches representing a distinct occupation to be called 'occupational branches.'"37

In the areas of ministerial/divisional organization and district administration, the Commission had essentially two recommendations. Divisions "engaged in allied and related activities could be combined together" citing the example of the Industries Division with the Production Division. Regarding district administration, the Commission recommended that the "Deputy Commissioner should retain the regulatory functions relating to law and order, police, treasury, jail, and certain matters pertaining to general administration. Local government institutions should be established and delegated power "in respect to development."38

On the surface, the Commission's recommendations did not advocate a return to the pre-Bhutto era vis-a-vis government administrative organization, structure and functioning. However, the advocacy of constitutional guarantees of service security indicated a desire to return to a basic characteristic of the vice regal system. Further, the powers to be retained at the district level by the Deputy Commissioner clearly reflect the report's bias towards the continuation of a paternalistic, authoritarian approach regarding the administration of the traditional regulatory functions of government at this level. Finally, advocating the delegation of economic development authority to local bodies of elected officials has traces of the Ayubian Basic Democracies Scheme.

As was mentioned earlier, this Report was submitted to General Zia in November 1979. So far as can be determined, the Government has yet to act upon the recommendations. General Zia did enact a Local Bodies Ordinance (August 1979) and elections were held in the fall of 1979. However, it is unclear as to the precise allocation of power and resources these institutions will have and what their relationship will be to the administrative structure at the district and provincial levels. On the whole the fate of the Civil Services Commission's Report appears to be similar to the fates of the other inquiries (the exception being the Meer Report of 1973).

Before concluding our examination of the present situation, two additional factors must be considered: (1) the attempts to "Islamisize" Pakistani government and economy through state intervention (an avowed purpose of the Zia regime); and (2) the increased domination of the military (and its institutions) over the civilian administration.

Although the rationale for a separate State of Pakistan was to provide a homeland for Indian Muslims,39 the founders of this new state, including Mohammed Ali Jinnah, were not sympathetic to Islamic orthodoxy. Jinnah often spoke of the secular nature of Pakistan-- a state which would welcome individuals of all religious creeds. All political regimes which followed Jinnah's, until the present, appealed to both Islamic as well as the secular traditions of the state. The present regime, however, has repeatedly proclaimed the Islamic nature of Pakistan and has actively promoted the "Institutionalization" of the state, its economy and society as the most important priority.

What does Islamization mean? How does it affect the governance of the country? Unlike Iran, Islamization in Pakistan has not meant rule by Islamic clergy. In fact, the orthodox Islamic political parties and their leaders have been at odds with General Zia, from time to time, over matters of state. So far, Islamization has meant the imposition of Islamic criminal penalties (flogging and the amputation of limbs--the latter having been imposed in some cases but not executed), prohibition of the sale to and consumption of alcoholic beverages by Muslims (foreigners are permitted to consume them under official restrictions), the establishment of shariat (the whole of Muslim law) courts, the imposition zakat (a tax to raise revenue for distribution to the poor) and the abolition of riba (a fixed rate of interest on loans or investments). The economic measures (zakat and riba, in particular) have caused alarm among the population. Zakat has been opposed by the Shi'a[40] Muslims, while the abolition of riba without a viable substitute has been opposed by the professional[41] and business communities. The impact of Islamization on public administration is difficult to assess, given the relatively brief period since the enactment of these measures.

Militarization of the civil bureaucracy, on the other hand, has created changes in the administration of the country. Although it is impossible to calculate the magnitude of military officer appointments to civil positions, an impressionistic assessment is that it has been considerable. Many high ranking federal and provincial civil positions are now occupied by military officers. Further, judgements rendered by military tribunals cannot be appealed through the civilian court system.[42] Hence, policymaking, administration, and adjudication are firmly in control of the military. These ominous developments do not provide optimism for an early return to civilian rule.

CONCLUSIONS: Lessons of the Past and Implications For the Future

In analyzing the public administrative system of

Pakistan over the three decades of its existence, several themes have emerged: (1) the desire of each successive political leader and/or regime to control[43] the apex of the system so as to effectuate the public policies and programs these leaders believed were necessary during their period of tenure; (2) the non-acceptance of formal administrative reform proposals (the exception being the reforms during the Bhutto period); (3) the adaptability of the administrative system to whomever gained central executive power; (4) the continuity of district level administration throughout periods of political uncertainty and turmoil; (5) the gradual erosion of civilian control over both civil and military administration and, as a corollary, the growing influence of the military over both civilian political leadership and the public administrative system; and (6) the change in the class basis of the apex of the administrative system (the emergence of the middle class[44]) and the further "indigenizition" of the administrative system. What is the significance of these themes or tendencies for the future? How will the administrative system evolve further? Will "reform ritualism"[45] continue to be a characteristic of administrative reform attempts in Pakistan?

First is the issue of controlling the bureaucracy. Every chief executive since independence has attempted to establish control over at least the apex of the system. Some have been more successful (Ayub and Bhutto) than others. It would be unrealistic to think that future chief executives will not attempt to do so. But controlling the apex is not controlling the system. Forcefully retiring or dismissing higher civil servants will not affect the system as a whole. As long as government procedures and information systems remain unchanged (in these areas little has changed since independence), control of the administrative system will be confined to Islamabad or the provincial capitols.

Second is the issue of "reform ritualism." Given the frequency of administrative reform inquiries (one per year for the past 34 years, on average), this type of activity will continue to be pursued. Only if there is a confluence of reform proposals with political, economic and social receptivity (that is, the political leader accepts the proposals because they fit into his design for the maintenance and use of power), will formal administrative reform occur. Even in these rare cases (the Bhutto period is the example), the effect of formal reform on the system is or will be limited. I have argued elsewhere[46] that adjusting organizational forms and structural characteristics of administrative systems without considering the output and impact end of the system is an exercise in futility.

Third, the adaptability of the administrative system (in particular, its apex) to work for the person in power will continue. There is enough historical evidence to support this assertion. It is the nature of the higher bureaucracy to reach some accommodation with whoever is in power. The higher bureaucracy may not be representative of the people it governs, but high level civil officers in all societies understand power and its use.[47] The history of Pakistan supports this conclusion.

Fourth is the continuity of district level administration. Until there is a viable system of elected local government, nothing short of a mass revolution will alter the scope and nature of district administration or the powers possessed and exercised by Deputy Commissioners. Ayub's Basic Democrats and Bhutto's party members came close to altering administration at this level but only temporarily. The reluctance of political leadership at the center to delegate power and resources to provincial and local levels has been a characteristic of government in Pakistan since 1947. The Islamic Republic of Pakistan is a federal republic only in a formal sense. It has been a highly centralized, unitary-type government in practice. Only if and when political leadership at the center delegates power and resources to elected local leaders will changes occur in local administration.

Fifth is the gradual erosion of civilian control and the increasing influence/domination of the military over civilian leadership and administration. The erosion began in the early 1950's when Ayub, as Army Commander-in-Chief, through his "special relationship" with the U.S. (the U.S. was the source of military assistance to Pakistan), began to assert himself in civilian affairs, and military intervention was legitimized in State Versus Dosso.[49] Although Ayub became a civilian leader, and the military after the first few months of the coup ceased to be a direct participant in his government, he did introduce military officers into civilian administrative roles as was mentioned earlier. His successor, General Yahya, used military officers

extensively in civilian administrative positions from
1969-1971. With the exception of the first five years
of independence, the only other extensive period when
military influence was in remission was during the
Bhutto period (1971-77). Civilian control over both
civil and military administration was exerted. However,
military influence and domination re-emerged more viru-
lent than ever after July 5, 1977. Today, military
control extends down to the district level (all provincial Governors are military officers--initially after
the July coup, Zia appointed High Court justices as
Governors) and many Federal and provincial Secretaries,
Joint Secretaries and Deputy Secretaries (or their equivalents) are or have been military officers. The independence of the judiciary has been abridged by the
substitution of military court for civil court decision.
The influence of the military in civilian administration
(if not its domination) has become a part of Pakistani
government and politics. Its curtailment in the near
future is a very remote possibility. Its continuation
is more assured. It took a civil war to cast doubts
upon the military as an institution. Only something
comparable to the events of 1971 will dislodge the military from its present position.

Finally, the changed class nature of the administrative system is important. The change in the class
basis of the higher bureaucracy is related to the process of indigenization and even Islamization. The
"Macaulay" generation[50] of political leaders and high-
level civil administrative and military leaders has
been replaced by individuals from the middle class and
only on occasion will the former reassert themselves
in government. The push by the present government for
greater use of Urdu as the medium of instruction in
primary, secondary, and, most important, university education has and will have significant impact on future
generations of administrators and the administrative
system. Where English was once understood in the major
cities, towns and even at the village level, it has been
replaced either by Urdu, or by the regional languages
(Punjabi, Sindhi, Pushtu, Baluch, etc.). Bhutto's nationalization of private schools (except foreign ones)
accelerated the movements towards non-English medium
instruction. Now, the major universities are required
to allow their students to complete written assignments
as well as to verbally respond in the classroom in Urdu
instead of English. In effect, the indigenization of
Pakistani society, which may seem to be a conflict in

149

terms, has created uncertainties regarding public values and the use of public power and resources in pursuit of these values. Generational differences in terms of popular expectations and demands is further complicated by differences in values--the pursuit of western-inspired values versus those which characterize a more indigenous, non-western experience. Within this situation is the issue of Islam. Is Pakistani society becoming more "Islamic" or is the current emphasis on Islamization only a passing aberration? Regardless of what the eventual outcome will be, the interim uncertainties have created strains on the administrative system.[51]

In conclusion, although the evolution of the public administrative system in Pakistan has pursued its own unique pattern, this experience is not totally different from those of other developing countries. Viewed from the perspective of its history and within its political, economic and social environment, bureaucracy in Pakistan has changed over time. Although vestiges of the inherited system remain, it would be inaccurate to conclude that it is still the same system left by the British. Its future role in society will be determined largely by decisions and actions yet to be taken. Efforts to "reform" administration in Pakistan, if successful, must take into account what has happened in the past and the extent to which the future can be anticipated with some measure of certainty.

Footnotes

[1]*Report of the Civil Service Commission*, Islamabad: Government of Pakistan, November 1979, p. i.

[2]*Indian Statutory Commission Report* (referred to as the Simon Commission after its Chairman), 1930, pp. 286 and 316.

[3]This last statement was more accurate in the case of India, as has been noted by such scholars as Krishna K. Tummala, *The Ambiguity of Ideology and Administrative Reform*, New Delhi: Allied Publishers Pvt. Ltd., 1979, than of Pakistan. For a recent treatment of this thesis, see M. M. Khan, *Bureaucratic Self-Preservation: Failure of Major Administrative Reform Efforts in the Civil Service of Pakistan*, Dacca: University of Dacca, 1980.

[4]The British East India Company, chartered in 1600, secured a concession from the Moghul Emperor to establish a trading post (factory) outside modern-day Bombay in 1609.

[5]See Philip Woodruff, *The Men Who Ruled India*, two volumes, London: Jonathan Cape, 1954 .

[6]For a discussion of the Commission reports and their impact, see Khan, *op. cit.*

[7]The advent of railway transportation and its development in India as well as telegraphic communications had its impact on administration. However, the basic unit of administration, the district, and the role of the district officer remained relatively unchanged-- new responsibilities were added to existing responsibilities in the case of the Deputy Commissioner.

[8]These included: (1) "Improvement of Public Administration Report" (the Egger inquiry) 1953; (2) "Reorganization of Pakistan Government" (the Gladieux inquiry) 1955; (3) "Administrative Reorganization" (the G. Ahmed inquiry) 1958; (4) "Pay and Services Commission" (the 1st Cornelious inquiry) 1959; (5) "Reorganization of Service Structure" (the Power Committee) 1969; (6) "Services Reorganization" (2nd Cornelius inquiry) 1969; (7) "Administrative Reforms" (Meer Commission) 1973; (8) "National Pay Commission" (2nd Anwarul Haq inquiry) 1978. The year given for the inquiry is the year of

appointment of the committee/commission/investigation. Most of the 34 inquiries had committees or commissions of more than one individual with the exception of the Egger and the Gladieux inquiries. Source: "History of Administrative Reforms," O & M Wing, Government of Pakistan, 1978, mimeographed report.

[9]Interestingly enough, this term is still applied to those who migrated to Pakistan during partition and to their descendants, even though they have resided in Pakistan for over thirty years and hold Pakistani citizenship. For the most part, these refugees settled in Pakistani Punjab and Karachi.

[10]See the last chapter in Hector Bolitho, Jinnah: Creator of Pakistan, London: J. Murray, 1954.

[11]For a discussion of this process, see Ralph Braibanti's chapter on Pakistan in Braibanti (ed.) Asian Administrative Systems Emergent from British Imperial Tradition, Durham: Duke University Press, 1966.

[12]PCS officers could occupy, temporarily, positions normally assigned to ICS/CSP officers but only until an ICS/CSP officer could be found to be assigned to them.

[13]A noteable example was Zulfikar Ali Bhutto although his role in political affairs was not to emerge until the middle 1960's.

[14]The Ford Foundation assisted in the selection of Professor Egger. This period roughly corresponds to the beginning of U.S. interest in and military/economic assistance to Pakistan. See: Robert LaPorte, Jr., Power and Privilege, Berkeley: University of California Press, 1975.

[15]See Khan, op. cit., p. 91.

[16]Ibid, pp. 96-98.

[17]See Shahid Javed Burki, "Twenty Years of the Civil Service of Pakistan: A Re-evaluation," Asian Survey IX (April 1969), pp. 239-254.

[18]See Albert Gorvine, "Administrative Reform" in G. Burkhead, Administrative Problems in Pakistan, Syracuse: Syracuse University Press, 1966, pp. 185-211. See also Khan, op. cit., p. 98, for his comments on

these analyses.

[19]The term "revolution" was used by Ayub to indicate the radical change he planned to make in the political, economic and social direction of the country. This term was also used to describe the initial years of the Ayub period. See Herbert Feldman, Revolution in Pakistan, Karachi: Oxford University Press, p. 196. Feldman later changed his mind. More recent analyses indicate that although Ayub did change directions, his "revolution" was of a more conservative nature than is usually associated with the term. See Shahid Javed Burki, Pakistan Under Bhutto, 1971-77, London: Macmillan, 1980; and Khalid B. Sayeed, Politics in Pakistan: The Nature and Direction of Change, N.Y.: Praeger Publishers, 1980.

[20]Government of Pakistan, Speeches and Statements, Field Marshall Mohammed Ayub Khan, Karachi: 1964, as quoted in Khan, op. cit., p. 106.

[21]See Burki, "Twenty Years of Civil Service of Pakistan: A Re-evaluation," op. cit., who maintains that, CSP officers assumed leadership positions in the public enterprise sector.

[22]See Burki, "Pakistan's Development: An Overview," in S. J. Burki and R. LaPorte, (eds.) Pakistan's Development: Choices for the Future, forthcoming.

[23]The Public Services Commission (1978) refers to this as a problem of "low morale."

[24]A number of works have been written on the subject of Bhutto and the PPP. Perhaps the best analyses to date include: Burki, Pakistan Under Bhutto, 1971-77, op. cit.; and Philip E. Jones "The Pakistan People's Party: Social Group Response and Party Development in an Era of Mass Participation," (unpublished Ph.D. dissertation, the Fletcher School of Law and Diplomacy, 1979).

[25]See Burki and C. Baxter, "Socio-Economic Indicators of the People's Party Vote in the Punjab: A Study at the Tehsil Level," Journal of Asian Studies XXXIV, No. 4 (August 1975), pp. 913-930.

[26]For an analysis of his strategy, see LaPorte, Power and Privilege: A Study of Decision Making in

Pakistan, op. cit.

^{27}Burki, Pakistan Under Bhutto, op. cit.

^{28}For an account of the "mass purges" of 1972 and 1976, see the White Paper on The Performance of the Bhutto Regime, Vol. II, Government of Pakistan 1978 .

^{29}The formal title was the "Administrative Reform Commission."

^{30}For an analysis of these recommendations, see LaPorte "Civil Bureaucracy: Twenty-Five Years of Power and Influence," Asian Survey XIV, No. 12 (December 1974) pp. 1094-1103; and L. Ziring, "Administrative Reforms," Asian Survey XIV No. 12 (December 1974), pp. 1086-1093.

^{31}Bhutto also engaged in symbolic degrading of the old elite civil service. He retitled the Civil Service Academy, the Academy for Administrative Training, and moved it from its spacious surrounding on the Mall in Lahore to more modest quarters in Walden, a remote suburb of Lahore. It remains in Walden at present.

^{32}Personal interviews with the author, 1971 and 1979.

^{33}He was convicted and after the Supreme Court denied his appeal, he was executed on April 4, 1979.

^{34}Report of the Civil Services Commission," op. cit., p. ii.

^{35}Ibid.

^{36}Recently (December 1980 - January 1981) several hundred civil servants were retired from the service. These individuals had completed the 25 years of service required for retirement but had not reached retirement age. The upper levels of the APUG (grades 18-22) were affected and many Joint Secretaries and Deputy Secretaries were retired "in the public interest" under clause ii, Section 13, of the Civil Servants Act, 1973 (LXXI of 1973). See: Gazette of Pakistan for December 3 and 17, 1980.

^{37}"Proposals to Reform Services," Viewpoint, November 25, 1979.

[38]Viewpoint, op. cit.

[39]Not all Indian Muslims opted for Pakistan. At present, more Muslims in the Subcontinent live outside Pakistan than within its borders.

[40]Shi'a Muslims compose roughly 20 per cent of the total Muslim population in Pakistan. In Iran, Shi'a Muslims are in the majority. In Pakistan, Sunni Muslims are in the majority.

[41]See, "An Agenda for Islamic Economic Reform," A Report of the Committee on Islamization, May 1980. This committee was appointed by Ghulam Ishaq Khan, Federal Minister for Finance, Planning, Commerce, Economic Affairs and Co-ordination in April 1980. Professor Syed Nawab Haider Naqvi, Director, Pakistan Institute of Development Economics, served as the Committee Chairman.

[42]The Chief Justice of the Supreme Court, Anwarul Haq (who chaired the Civil Services Commission referred to above) refused to take the new oath of office and resigned from the court.

[43]Chief executive control of the administrative/ managerial class of public administrative systems is a universal desire. In the U.S. case, every modern President has attempted some type of reform, reorganization or action to enhance political control of the bureau-cracy. Roosevelt established the Executive Office of the President as a staff agency to help supervise the bureaucracy. Eisenhower's Administration saw the establishment of Schedule C--close to 2,000 positions of a "confidential or policy determining" nature reserved for Loyal Republicans after 20 years of Democratic Administrations. Carter's 1978 Civil Service Reform Act established the Senior Executive Service (an idea that goes back to at least the Roosevelt era) as a means to separate the highest General Schedule grades (the old GS 16 through Executive Level IV) from other "competitive service" personnel.

[44]One observes this not only in the class basis of the higher civil service but also in the industrial/ commercial sector, the agricultural sector, and the military. General Zia is the most obvious example in the military.

[45]This is Tummala's term. See Tummala, op. cit.

[46]See LaPorte in S. J. Burki and R. LaPorte (eds.), op. cit.

[47]This understanding is a prerequisite for occupying civil positions at this level. If certain civil officers "forget", they often lose their positions. If they contest the use of power by chief executives, they are often dismissed or forced to resign.

[48]See his Friends Not Masters, N.Y.: Oxford University Press, 1967; and Paul Y. Hammond, Military Aid and Influence in Pakistan: 1954-1963, Santa Monica, California: The RAND Corporation, 1969. Hammond contends that Ayub's position vis-a-vis his civilian colleagues was greatly enhanced since he "brought home the bacon" (i.e. military and economic assistance).

[49]PLD 1958 Sc (Pak). The Supreme Court, in its decision, gave legal sanction to the military coup. Later, the principle laid down in the Dosso case was overruled by the Supreme Court in Asma Jilani versus The Government of the Punjab, etc. For further discussion, see Hamid Yusuf, Pakistan in Search of Democracy, 1947-77, Lahore: Afrasia Publications, 1980, p. 53.

[50]For lack of a better term, I have used it in reference to Lord Macaulay because of his impact on education in India and the products of the educational system established by the British. Lord Macaulay's Minute on Education (1835) is perhaps, most remembered for the stricture "We (the British) must at present do our best to form a class who may be interpreters between us and the millions whom we govern; a class of persons, Indian in blood and color, but English in taste, in opinions, in morals, and in intellect." Quoted from Thomas Babington Macaulay, Speeches by Lord Macaulay, London: Oxford University Press, 1935 (reprinted in 1979), p. 359, as cited in Shuja Nawaz, "The Mass Media and Development in Pakistan," Burki and LaPorte (eds.), op. cit. See this chapter for an interesting analysis of the indigenization of communications and education in Pakistan.

[51]Public institutions such as the Pakistan Institute of Development Economics and the administrative training units (National Institutes of Public Administration, Lahore and Karachi, the Administrative Staff College, the Academy for Administrative Training, and the Academy for Rural Development) have been assigned

the difficult task of developing "Islamic economics" and "Islamic administration" with virtually no guidelines from the Government. Administrators and members of the judiciary have to deal with Islamic Law and its implementation/adjudication.

CHAPTER VIII

PUBLIC BUREAUCRACY IN BANGLADESH

Mohammad Mohabbat Khan
&
Habib Mohammad Zafarullah

During the British rule, the Indian subcontinent witnessed the predominant role of the bureaucrats in the administration of the colony under the direct control and supervision of the Secretary of State in London. The East India Company and successive colonial governments gave only lip service if any, in developing representative systems and relied solely on centrally recruited British officers and, later, British trained Indian elite to rule the sub-continent. Under this viceregal system, the Governor General (the chief executive) was responsible to the Crown of England. And as the centrally recruited officers, most notably the members of the well-known Indian Civil Service (ICS), were hierarchically linked with the Governor General, they became extremely powerful and disdainful of the native politicians and mainly concerned themselves with the protection of the paramountcy of the British empire. The bureaucrats managed as well as moulded all spheres of life be it social, political or economic. Everything emanated from them and ended with them. There was very little popular participation in the affairs of the state. It was a 'bureaucratic state' all the way.[1]

The character of bureaucratic preeminence in every facet of the daily lives of the citizens did not change even after 1947 when two independent states--India and Pakistan, came into being after years of struggle against alien rule and patterns of administration. The bureaucracy in independent Pakistan manifested all the institutional trappings of the ICS and presented the most remarkable instance of influences of the British imperial heritage. Its prevalence in all aspects of national life continued till 1971 when a civil war disintegrated the political system and its Eastern wing seceded to form an independent nation--Bangladesh.[2]

Background

The bureaucrats in Pakistan (1947-71) enjoyed tremendous power and exercised substantial influence in the adoption of key policies and their implementation.

The members of the elite corps, the Civil Service of
Pakistan (CSP), were well-disciplined. Innoculated
with strong esprit de corps they maintained high morale.
Bureaucratic dominance of the state apparatus was complete in 1951 after the assassination of Liaquat Ali
Khan, the first Prime Minister of Pakistan. Liaquat,
like Mohammad Ali Jinnah, the omnipotent first Governor
General of Pakistan and 'father of the nation', depended
more on senior bureaucrats rather than experienced political leaders to run the state. The bureaucrats were
in effective charge of the government and took key decisions on their own.[3] Immediately after independence
in 1947, senior bureaucrats belonging to the ICS were
posted by Jinnah as Governors in three of the four provinces of the country with wide-ranging powers. Two
of them presided over Cabinet meetings. All of them
maintained close watch on the activities of the political leaders in their respective provinces and, following
the past colonial practice, sent fortnightly reports to
Jinnah detailing not only the administrative and economic situations, but also the intrigues in the Cabinets
or parties.[4] Bureaucrats and senior military officers
after the coup of 1958 monopolized most of the key positions in the government such as the Presidency and
Governorships of the provinces and captured vital
policy-making institutions such as the National Economic
Council, the Central Secretariat, the Planning Commission and the important public corporations. In effect
they became the ruling elites instead of public servants.[5] Consequently, the role of the politicians in
statecraft became rather limited and inconsequential.
It has been claimed that as early as 1951 politicians
had been relegated to a subordinate position by the
civil-military bureaucracy which by then had assumed
full powers for running the state of Pakistan.[6]

Bureaucratic dominance over the state machinery
was made possible through the continuation and strengthening of an administrative system which was paternalistic, repressive, non-responsive, and hostile to the
idea of playing a subordinate role to the political
leadership. Jinnah's, and to some extent Liaquat's,
patronizing attitude towards the bureaucrats at the
expense of political norms and values made them boastful
and arrogant. With the support of the military assured,
the bureaucrats, especially the Civil Service of Pakistan (CSP) and the Police Service of Pakistan (PSP)
started playing 'God' and were sharply resentful of any
attempt to change their status quo. Efforts at

reforming the administration met with stiff and organized resistance especially from the CSPs resulting in the nonimplementation of major reforms.[7] By 1970 Pakistan epitomized all the features of a bureaucratic state. And large-scale corruption, abuse of official powers and gross misconduct on the part of the bureaucrats became common.

The tradition of bureaucratic dominance in the affairs of the state was broken to a large degree with the emergence of Bangladesh as a sovereign nation in 1971 after two decades of struggle against exploitation and domination of the people of the then East Pakistan (Bangladesh) by the West Pakistani military-bureaucratic -entrepreneurial oligarchs. The Awami League, the party with the largest following in East Pakistan, spearheaded the movement against this 'internal colonialism'.[8] The bureaucracy was considered to be one of the main instruments through the use of which the West Pakistani ruling coterie perpetrated their dominance over the region that now comprises Bangladesh. As anticipated, the Awami League believing in the political control of bureaucracy, initiated under the direct guidance of its leader Sheikh Mujibur Rahman, the Prime Minister of Bangladesh (1972-75), several measures to keep the bureaucracy under check. The 1972 Constitution included provisions which made the position of the bureaucrats, to a great extent, insecure and weak. They could be dismissed or removed or reduced in rank at the pleasure of the President.[9] Negation of the use of cadre affiliations by the elite bureaucrats,[10] reduction in their pay, and placement of non-generalist bureaucrats in top administrative positions which were previously reserved for the elite generalist bureaucrats in erstwhile Pakistan were some of the means of downgrading the one time supremacy of the bureaucrats. The pivotal power of the elite bureaucrats was further weakened by intra-bureaucratic conflicts and tensions that featured during the initial years of independence and gradual strengthening of the political infra-structure at the administrative level.[11] Consequently, the nation was left with a denounced, demoralized and demotivated bureaucracy.

This isolation of the bureaucrats from the political power base however could not be continued for long. Economic recession and famine conditions, increasing corruption, deteriorating law and order situation, social degeneration and deepening political morass led

the regime to change its 'anti-bureaucratic' stand to
one of gradual dependence. The political-bureaucratic
hiatus began to narrow down and concrete moves were
made to politicize the bureaucracy to the extent of in-
ducting some of its senior members into political positions.[12] This revival of bureaucratic eminence has been
further consolidated and strengthened at the wishes of
the present regime* that came to power through a military coup d'etat in November 1975 but later legitimized
by democratic elections.[13]

Organizing the Civil Services: The Built-in Constraints

The civil services in Pakistan were classified
both vertically and horizontally. The main criterion
of vertical classification was the type of work performed and on the basis of this there were three main categories: a) generalist-administrative services; b) functional services; and c) specialist services. Horizontally, the services were classified into four classes
I, II, III, and IV on the basis of levels of responsibility, educational requirements and admissable pay
range. Top policy-making and managerial positions were
the preserve of the members of the elite cadre, the
Civil Service of Pakistan (CSP).[14]

After independence, the civil service system in
Bangladesh was in complete disarray with the inheritance
of three main categories of regularly constituted services from former Pakistan. These were: a) the former
All-Pakistan services; b) the former Central services;
and c) the former Provincial services. The Awami League
regime did not officially affirm the exact status of all
the above services which resulted in anamolies, confusion and contradictions. Instead of amalgamating and
unifying all the civil services on a rational basis,
members of the elite service were not only allowed to
use their former cadre titles[15] (like CSP, PSP, PA&AS,
etc.) after their names with only the prefix 'ex-' for
the purpose of identification, but also given extraordinary preferences in terms of postings and promotions.
This created dissatisfaction and dissension among members of other services.

---

* Since this piece was written, there has been another
coup (in March 1982) by Lieutenant General Hosain Mohammed Ershad, army chief of staff, who ousted President
Abdus Sattar (who himself was elected in November 1981).

Conflicts with the civil services[16] were further aggravated on the issue of 'collaboration' versus 'patriotism'. During the nine months of the war of liberation some civil servants crossed over to India, the majority remained in the country, and many were stranded in Pakistan. The first group claimed themselves 'patriots' and maligned the other two as having collaborated with the Pakistan military regime in its attempt at crushing the liberation struggle of the people of Bangladesh. After the end of the war, returnees from India were 'rewarded' with undue, irrational and accelerated promotions. Other seniors became juniors overnight and many lost their jobs on charges of collaboration. Simultaneously, the built-in conflict between the erstwhile central and provincial civil services gave birth to open friction and strong factionalism developed among the members of these services.[17]

The CSPs advocated that members of their cadre should form the nucleus of administrative services in Bangladesh and be a 'meritocratic model' for other services.[18] On the other hand, the members of the former East Pakistan Civil Service (EPCS) demanded that the erstwhile provincial services be transformed into the premier civil service in the country. They also pleaded for reappraising the status of the CSP's in the new administrative system.

The specialist-generalist controversy which existed during the days of united Pakistan sharpened and engulfed the entire administrative set-up after the emergence of Bangladesh. The specialists claimed that the generalists were usually indecisive in their administrative pursuits and there was nothing professional in general administration and felt that the continuance of a generalist cadre was not necessary. They demanded higher status and appropriate pay and a greater degree of participation in the policy-making process.[19]

Administrative Reforms/Reorganization

Reforming an elitist institutional bureaucracy is an Herculean task; more so in a post-colonial country, where roots of bureaucratization are deeply ingrained. It is believed that political leadership of a country which gains independence through armed struggle is ideologically committed to bring about drastic changes in the demands of the society. In Bangladesh the party that took over the reins of power at the end of the traumatic events of 1971 declared its intent to recast the administrative system in keeping with its commitment to democracy and socialism.

In March 1972 the Administrative and Services Reorganization Committee (ASRC) was appointed by the government with Professor Muzaffar Ahmed Choudhuri, Vice Chancellor of the University of Dacca and an eminent political scientist, as its Chairman. An economist, a parlimentarian and a member of the erstwhile elitist CSP were also in the Committee. The terms of reference of the ASRC were:

a) To consider the structure of various services, both technical and non-technical, and determine the future structure keeping in view the functional needs and requirements of the government;

b) To consider the question of amalgamation of all the civil service (i.e., services other than defence) into one unified service;

c) To determine the principles of integration of the personnel of the various services in the new structure, and to determine the inter se seniority of personnel of the different services having a similar academic background and job experiences in the process of merger or amalgamation, in case structural changes are envisaged;

d) To determine the future recruitment policy in Government services at various levels keeping in view the educational and other job requirements; and

e) To prepare and recommend a comprehensive scheme for administrative reorganization.[20]

The committee submitted its volumnious Report in April 1973. One hundred and eighty three services associations submitted their representations with their opinions for the consideration of the Committee. Additionally, thirteen Ministers and fifty five top-ranking officials were interviewed. To comprehend the working of a socialist administrative system, the members of the Committee visited the Soviet Union. Furthermore, the views of a cross-section of the people and local level

163

officials were also ascertained.

The recommendation of the ASRC, largely influenced by the recommendations of the Fulton Committee in Britain, called for the shedding off of traditional class status consciousness by the bureaucrats and creating a close rapport between the former all-Pakistan services, central superior services and the former provincial services and the higher and lower classes and, in its stead, recommend the organization of a single classless unified grading structure with an appropriate number of different pay scales matching different levels of qualifications, skills and responsibilities. Each post should be graded on the basis of job analysis and same scales of pay be given to posts belonging to the same grade.[21] Accordingly, ten grades covering all jobs of the entire civil service (that included generalists, specialists, technicals and non-technicals of all classes) from the highest to the lowest tiers were recommended for introduction.[22] Grades I, II and III were grouped into Senior Policy and Management Posts and were to be filled up with officers having relevant areas of specialization. They would ultimately be concerned with policy planning and management. The selection system for entry into these posts, however, would be highly competitive.

The Committee recommended several measures for developing an integrated public personnel management system encompassing a rational selection process based on merit, long-term career planning, formulation of a general training policy and coordination of institutionalized training and an employee promotion procedure based on merit-cum-seniority.

Although the Committee made some far-reaching recommendations to drastically transform the colonial institutional bureaucracy into an instrumental and service-oriented one, the political leadership shelved the Report and barred it from public circulation. By the time it was submitted to the government in October 1973, politics in the country took a new turn with the gradual alienation of the regime from the masses and the inclination of the leadership to run the country through dictatorial means. All these resulted in undue dependence on bureaucrats who convinced the leaders in power that in order to maintain the 'effectivity' (sic) of the administration their (bureaucrats) status should not be disturbed for the time being. The opposition to the implementation of the recommendations of the Report was successfully orchestrated by the senior members of the elite cadre, the CSP. Thus, the first major effort in administrative reform failed due to bureaucratic resistance, intrigues and manoeuvers similar to the days of united Pakistan.[23]

Shortly after the appointment of the ASRC, the National Pay Commission (NPC) was constituted in July 1972 "to comprehensively review the existing pay structure relating to all employees in the public sector (including defence services, employees of autonomous and semi-autonomous bodies, statutory corporations and nationalized enterprises, but excluding 'workers')... and recommend a national pay structure embracing the entire public sector". In making its recommendations, the Commission was specifically asked to consider a number of factors: the cost of living, the resources of the government, the need to attract and retain in the public sector highly talented and technically and professionally qualified persons; requirements of efficiency, equity and incentives for work; and demand and supply in respect of different professions and occupations. The terms of reference also stipulated the Commission to suggest means to rationalize and standardize the pay scales of all civil servants--both central and provincial in former Pakistan.[24]

The NPC, composed of both full-time and part-time members, was headed by A. Rab, a former retired high-ranking civil servant belonging to the provincial government of erstwhile East Pakistan. One of the members was Colonel (later retired Lieutenant General) Ziaur Rahman, the then Deputy Chief of Staff of the Bangladesh Army, who later became the President of the country. The full-time and part-time members included a professional economist, a banker, a high-ranking retired police officer, and engineer-cum-academician, a chartered accountant and an incumbent civil servant. The NPC was instructed to work in close cooperation with the ASRC.

The Commission observed that the existing pay structure in Bangladesh was characterized by sharp cleavages maintaining disproportionately high dispersals. With the total absence of functional specificity for pay administration, wide proliferation and overlapping were flagrant. The Commission thus faced the perplexing task of suggesting a rational pay structure

evolving out of the anarchical disorder of nearly 2200
pay scales with several hundred for each class of employees.[25] The NPC recommended national scales of pay
and fringe benefits for ten grades adhering to the
grouping of existing posts in national grades as proposed by the ASRC. The Commission opined that the pay
structure had to be based on a floor pay scale with
complementary fringe benefits as would constitute a
living wage in socio-economic milieu obtaining in the
country. It maintained:

> The pay plan should be simple and within the
> comprehension of most of the people. It should
> have logical pay policy, involving sharing of
> hardship in an equitable manner. The pay
> structure should be in harmony with its al-
> most unclassified society, and it should
> be easy to administer...it should have a pay
> administration which is responsible, efficient
> and fair...embracing institutional arrange-
> ments for eradicating evils like administra-
> tive corruption, conspicuous consumption and
> unplanned family life.[26]

Accordingly, the highest pay (national grade I) was
fixed at Taka 2,000[27] and the lowest (national grade X)
at Taka 130-240 thereby reducing the disparity between
the highest (former CSP secretary's) pay and the lowest
(peon's) pay including fringe benefits down from 1:28·1
to 1:11·5.[28] In keeping with the rising prices of essential comodities and services, the NPA urged upon the
government to grant appropriate dearness allowances for
different grades of employees. It also envisaged the
creation of a separate Ministry of Personnel and Pay
Administration. Besides managing the personnel and pay
matters of all employees in the public sector, it would
undertake an indepth study of existing organizations
for bringing about organizational rationalization and
improvement for achieving efficiency and economy.

The ASRC, as indicated earlier, devised a ten grade
service structure for the public services. The NPC,
working in close cooperation with it, also designed a
ten grade pay structure to bring harmony into the entire
scheme of reform. Interestingly, while the ASRC Report
was rejected, the NPC's recommendations were accepted.
However, the latter's proposals could not be implemented fully. Only the pay scales for grades X upwards
to V (messengerial, clerical and entry level junior

officers) were put into effect and that also without proper job evaluation. The non-effectuation of pay scales for the higher grades was due to the manipulation of the senior bureaucrats (especially erstwhile CPSs and EPCSs) who demanded enhancement in their salaries and associated fringe benefits and were enraged with the Commission for recommending less pay for them. This only shows the tremendous hold of senior bureaucrats in the implementation of major personnel policies in the country. Moreover, the compressing of over 2200 existing scales into only ten pay grades created contradictions and anamolies. It has been observed:

> supervisory posts were downgraded in terms of pay and equalized with the grade of the supervised, creating deleterious effect on efficiency, morale and performance.29

Furthermore, the recommended pay scales were totally out of place with the galloping price hikes of essential commodities thereby creating dissension and dissatisfaction among public servants of all grades leading a large number of them to resort to legal process and in most cases getting the verdict in their favor.

Within a few months (in February 1976) of its coming to power, the military regime of Ziaur Rahman set up a twelve member Pay and Services Commission (PSC) to formulate recommendations for streamlining the service and pay structure of the employees in the public sector.30 A. Rashid, a retired secretary in the former central government in Pakistan, was the Chairman of the Commission. Of the other five full-time members, two were retired senior civil servants, one was a high-ranking police officer, one was a retired judge and the remaining one was a serving generalist civil servant. A corps of six part-time members represented various professions, i.e., engineering, accounting, business, medical science, journalism and generalist civil service.

Questionaire administration and interviews, eliciting of opinions of 154 service associations/groups/ unions, scanning of reference materials, attitude surveys of university students and their parents towards the civil services, and study tours both within and outside the country formed the bases of the PSC's findings and recommendations. Three drafting committees were constituted--the first and the second were on

167

services and pay respectively while the third was created for moderating the reports of the first and the
second committees.

The policy guidelines and terms of reference empowered the Commission to examine the existing pay and
service structure of the public sector employees and
recommend:

a) A suitable service structure for the civil
services along with their methods of recruitment, training and deployment;

b) Rational and simple principles for the amalgamation of the employees of the erstwhile
central and provincial governments performing
similar duties and functions;

c) A suitable pay structure including fringe
benefits for (i) civil services, i.e., the
traditional government sector, and (ii) the
employees of the autonomous and semi-autonomous
bodies, statutory corporations, the universities
(excluding teaching posts) and nationalised
enterprises;

d) Suitable minimum and maximum pay limits
within which the University Grants Commission
should formulate the pay scales of the various
teaching posts of the universities for the
approval of the government;

e) Suitable death-cum-retirement benefits for
all categories; and

f) Suitable scales of leave and compensatory
benefits.[31]

It can be said that the PSC was given wide-ranging
responsibilities encompassing the entire spectrum of
the public service. It was asked to keep in mind the
recommendations of the ASRC and NPC and the actions taken in the implementation of some of the recommendations
of the latter body. The creation of the CSP in the ICS
model and its sustenance in former Pakistan was an inappropriate move in the view of the PSC. Growing consciousness of the people and democratization of their
outlook and the elevated importance of the functions of
the specialists/technocrats have all resulted in

considerable erosion of the hitherto unchallenged power base and authority of the CSPs.

The major recommendations of the Commission included the amalgamation of all erstwhile services and the creation of an all-purpose civil service to include all functionaries in the traditional government sector, emphasis on the merit principle as the determining factor for recruitment and promotion, removal of barriers existent between the erstwhile CSP and other services through the introduction of equal initial scales of pay and provisions for equitable scope of advancement towards the top of the administrative hierarchy, constitution of a new apex cadre with 'talented, efficient and experienced' officers drawn from all functional cadres through approximately designed tests for providing administrative leadership and high-level coordination, adoption of the cadre concept of the civil service structure for major functional areas in the government as opposed to position concept and the organization of cadre services at the top tier to constitute the nucleus of the civil structure.

The Commission further recommended that the proposed Civil Service of Bangladesh should consist of four broad tiers of services in hierarchical order: 1. The Administrative/Top Management/Specialized Group; 2. The Executive/Middle Management Group; 3. The Inspectorial/Ministerial/Technical/Support Group; and 4. The Messengerial/Custodial Group. The bases of this division, according to the Commission were: nature of work and the level of responsibility assigned to various posts in the civil service hierarchy and corresponding educational, mental and physical standards of the incumbents. All four tiers of the services would have provisions for direct recruitment with scope for advancement from one tier to the next higher one. The Commission also proposed that twenty-nine organized services be constituted.[32] Each of these services would have two levels of entry at points 'A' and 'B'. Recruitment to 'A' level posts would be made through higher standard examinations and to 'B' level posts through average standard examinations. 'A' level recruits would be placed directly in the 'A' level service junior scale posts while 'B' level entrants would be placed in the 'B' level service with provisions for promotion to level 'A' service.

The Pay and Services Commission recommended to

broadband the marginally different scales in respect of posts in which practically the same type of work is done by persons with similar qualifications and abilities. This was done to reduce multiplicity of pay scales. Alternative sets of scales for particular categories which can be adopted without disturbing the overall pay structure were proposed. Taking into consideration the problems encountered in the implementation of the NPC Report, the Commission proposed fifty two scales of pay ranging from Taka 230 to Taka 4000. The PSC was of the opinion that persons undergoing highly specialized professional training should be adequately remunerated. Also, it recommended the proper valuation and upgrading of jobs demanding creativity and innovation.

Some of the major recommendations of the Pay and Services Commission were accepted in principle but implemented in modified forms. Five Cabinet committees were formed to work out the details of implementation. The Council Committee looked into disputes arising out of conversions of lower posts (particularly the non-gazetted ones).[33] The Committee on Supersession and Superior Appointments examined matters regarding gazetted posts. The Pay Committee dealt with conversions of posts in the autonomous bodies, corporations, banks and other financial institutions. The High Level Committee was given the responsibility of considering the recommendations of Pay Committee and for presenting them in their final form to the Council of Ministers. The Appellate Committee heard the appeals against anamolies arising out of new adjustments.

Incorporating the Commission's modified recommendations, the government through the Services (Grades, Pay and Allowances) Order 1977 introduced New National Grades and Scales of Pay (NNGSP) providing for twenty one grades. The lowest salary ranged between Taka 225 and Taka 317 while the highest was fixed at Taka 3,000.[34]

The declaration of the NNGSP created dissension, discontent and dissatisfaction among various sections of public employees. Frequent strikes and absentions from work, meetings and demonstrations nearly paralyzed the administration. Deputations and representations from different employee bodies met the authorities to point out the gross discrimination in fixing pay scales for all categories of public employees. Protests came not only from lower level employees but also the high-ranking personnel who took recourse to strikes.[35] The Professionals in particular, felt ignored and accused the generalist civil servants of relegating their positions to that of underprivileged ones.[36]

The Commission, as indicated earlier, had recommended twenty nine organized services in major functional areas but the Council Committee on Services Structure proposed certain alterations. Consequently, twenty eight services were created under fourteen main cadres aiming at the reorganization of the civil services into a 'classless' bureaucracy named as the Bangladesh Civil Service. All the services would be equal with the elimination of the concept of 'rank and status'. All designations would be functional and pay scales would be the sole criterion of determining the position and privileges of a civil servant. The unified career service includes all functionaries in the traditional government sector consistent of both administrative and specialised professional groups.[37] The report of the Council Committee further provided for the creation of the Senior Services Pool in the model of the Superior Policy Pool as recommended by the Pay and Services Commission.[38]

Included in the Senior Services Pool (SSP) of 523 automatically were 520 generalist officers with a maximum fifteen years of service of the ranks of Secretary, Additional Secretary, Joint Secretary and Deputy Secretary. But only three professionals with an average of twenty years of active experience could find places in it. While the SSP Order of 1979 specifically mentions that encadrement of Pool officers shall be made by the government on the basis of selection tests conducted by the Public Services Commission, the automatic induction of such a large number of generalist officers mostly belonging to the erstwhile CSP has effectively nullified the purpose of creating this 'open' structure. In effect, a 'super elite' cadre of generalist 'policy makers' has emerged. Consequently, the way the SSP has been constituted has angered all categories of specialists (i.e., medical doctors, engineers, educationists, agricultural experts and others) as well as members of erstwhile provincial and central superior services. The specialists justifiably feel that the SSP is a built-in device to protect and promote the interests of the members of the CSP.

Bureaucracy and Politics

Politicization of the bureaucracy in Bangladesh began during the war of liberation in 1971. The Awami League political leadership and bureaucrats--both high-ranking and mid-level--who crossed over to India came in close contact with each other while forming and running the Bangladesh government-in-exile. The political leadership with little or no experience in policy making and management of government depended on the bureaucrats who in turn influenced the former's decisions considerably. After the surrender of the Pakistani army in December 1971 and the return of the leaders from India (where the government-in-exile was stationed), these bureaucrats, irrespective of seniority and service affiliations came to occupy key positions in the administrative hierarchy. This group even included bureaucrats with proven corruption charges against them during Pakistani days and the liberation period.[39]

As stated earlier, the dependence of the Mujib government on bureaucrats increased considerably by the end of 1974. The transformation of the multi-party parliamentary system into a one-party presidential type in January 1975 in effect banned representative politics. All political parties were disbanded and a 'national' party was created which was in reality the Awami League plus some of its allies like the Communist Party of Bangladesh and the National Awami Party (Muzaffer Ahmed faction), both pro-Russian. An unprecedented decision of far-reaching implications was to include senior bureaucrats--civil and military in the central committee of the only legitimate party--the Bangladesh Krishak Sramik Awami League (Bangladesh Peasants Workers People's League or BAKSAL). The government's intent to involve high-ranking bureaucrats of its choice in active political posts was further evidenced by their appointments as district Governors. These Governors were to be under the direct command of the President of the country and Chairman of the 'national' party of BAKSAL and were to work hand-in-hand with the party district secretaries. However, the fall of the Mujib regime in August 1975 inhibited the scheme from being put into practice.

Civil bureaucrats in Bangladesh have not only been concerned with routine policy (political) decisions but have also been involved in the change of regimes. It has been alleged that high-ranking bureaucrats in the

police service were aware of the plans of the August
'75 coup leaders but did not purposely bring those to
the notice of the President as they were a party to the
coup.[40]

During the military regime of Ziaur Rahman nearly
all members of the President's Advisory Council were
either retired or incumbent civil servants. Even after
the withdrawl of the martial law in the spring of 1979,
Zia's Council of Ministers has included a large number
of civil and military bureaucrats with all of them holding crucial Cabinet posts. Such moves have emboldened
the bureaucrats to become politically ambitious and de-
fiant of Ministers with 'pure' political backgrounds.

The creation of the posts of district development
coordinators somewhat similar to the district Governors
scheme of Mujib, and selection of members for the envoys
pool (a diplomatic corps) with only members of Zia's
Bangladesh Nationalist Party (BNP) are attempts at in-
filtrating political elements into the bureaucratic
hierarchy. The bureaucrats in the foreign and administrative services feel indignant at these moves and are
apprehensive of continuous political meddling in administrative affairs. The district development coordinators chosen from among the members of the Parliament
belonging to the ruling BNP with the rank and status of
Deputy Ministers and responsibilities of overseeing all
the developmental activities within the district will
certainly come into conflict with the district officer
(the Deputy Commissioner), an officer of mid-level seniority. As a coordinator belonging to the district for
which he has been appointed for it would be very difficult for him not to be motivated by local political
considerations as opposed to the Deputy Commissioner
who is a career bureaucrat under the supervision of the
Secretariat (the machinery of the national administration) in the capital.

Attempts at Making the Bureaucracy "Representative"

From independence in 1947 to disintegration in
1971, the higher bureaucracy in Pakistan was manned
mostly by individuals with upper and upper-middle class
backgrounds. Of the total number, the majority came
from rich landowning families who were either natives
of the Punjab or settlers from Northern India. These
officers maintained close ties with the military and
were, in most cases, related to one another by

blood or marriage.[41] The ratio of East and West Pakistani representation in the CSP was highly disproportionate. Till 1968, of the 450 CSP officers, only 190 were Bengalis.[42] These Bengali officers, unlike their West Pakistani colleagues, largely came from families with middle and lower middle class economic status. Interestingly, East Pakistan enjoyed a higher literacy rate than the West[43] but disparity between the two provinces as far as development of educational facilities was concerned obstructed the Bengalis from preparing themselves academically for entering the CSP or other elite cadres. To achieve 'parity' in the ratio of representation between East and West Pakistan, the government of Pakistan introduced the 'quota system'. The system provided for the filling up of 20% of the total number of vacancies on the basis of merit regardless of geographical factors and the remaining 80% to be equally divided between the two wings. Inspite of this, the much craved 'parity' was never achieved and the bureaucracy in united Pakistan continued to be dominated by the West Pakistanis.

After independence, steps were taken by the Awami League government in Bangladesh "to achieve a more equitable representation of the people of all the districts of Bangladesh in various services and posts under the government (including the defence services), autonomous and semi-autonomous organizations and nationalized enterprises".[44] The quota varies between the upper two classes (I and II) and lower two classes (III and IV): 40% of posts in the upper two classes are staffed on the basis of merit. The remaining 60% are reserved for women (20%), freedom fighters (30%) and others (10%) include people from minority communities and backward areas). The emphasis on merit is negligible (10%) for the lower two classes. District-wise quota is calculated on the basis of population and pervades all the criteria for selection as indicated earlier.

The introduction of the system of reservation of posts for persons belonging to different regions, sex, group and religious communities defeats the very purpose of building up and sustaining an efficient administrative machinery instrumental in the attainment of nation-building goals and socio-economic progress. The 'quota' system is discouraging young people with sound academic background and coming from regions which are already well-represented in the public services from taking examinations with the fear of their being relegated to less attractive services inspite of the possibilities of their performing better in these examinations. Placements in the different services made on the basis of performance of candidates in the first two Superior Posts Examinations conducted by the Bangladesh Public Service Commission (BPSC) have confirmed the apprehension of these young people.

Both the ASRC and the PSC justifiably recommended the introduction of merit principle as the basis of recruitment in the higher civil services. The PSC, in particular, rightly observed that the system of reservation of posts would severely restrict the range of selection to mediocres in preference to brighter ones. This policy would have serious repercussions on the quality of the services particularly in positions which are meant to have country-wide functions.[45] But the advocates of this system claim that it would assist people from 'backward' regions to enter the public services thereby reducing regional disparity.[46]

Training and Development

Public administration training (PAT) in Bangladesh still suffers from a lack of clear, bold and innovative national policy.[47] This is a legacy from the past. During the British rule of the subcontinent institutionalized training for public servants was non-existent. Pakistani rulers were more interested to indoctrinate carefully the members of the elite civil services but had little inclination to spread training facilities to non-cadres who were actually responsible for most of the routine and day-to-day functions of administration. In effect, the benefits of training were denied to the majority of the public servants in Pakistan.

Bangladesh's experiences in PAT have not been satisfactory. Very little attention was given to it during the first six years (1972-78) of independence. But the need for training was forcefully advocated by the ASRC and the First Five Year Plan, 1973-78. The Plan formulated an ambitious program to train a large number of public servants but a bulk of it did not materialize. The military regime of Ziaur Rahman, after consolidating its power, also started taking particular interest in reorienting and revitalizing existing programs and institutions for attaining developmental goals.

At present public officials are being trained in

three major institutions. The Bangladesh Administrative Staff College (BASC), established in 1977, offers a regular three-month long course on administration and management and a number of short courses for senior officials. Middle level officials are sent to the National Institute of Public Administration (NIPA) which was established in 1961. The Advanced Course in Administration and Development of three and a half months duration is the main course that NIPA offers twice a year. From time to time the Institute also offers an innovative and action-oriented training program called Own Village Development (OVD). Trainees are sent to their own villages to gather information and to make in-depth study of the various aspects of rural administration and development. The Civil Officers Training Academy (COTA) is solely responsible for imparting a twenty-two week long comprehensive preparatory training to those young university graduates who successfully qualify in a country-wide open competitive civil service examination. Considerable emphasis in the entire training program is placed on field training or 'village assignment' which is designed to train the officers in the basic process of decision-making in the rural areas by inculcating in them the competence in problem identification, analysis and solution.

PAT in Bangladesh has reached a state when its reassessment is in order. It must be admitted that some piecemeal efforts were initiated in the recent past to introduce 'development' elements in the training programs but these were ill-conceived, unplanned and haphazard. Concerns of substantive nature like the formulation of a national training policy is still awaited though the country's Second Five Year Plan, 1980-85 has specifically recommended the   setting up of a National Training Council under the aegis of the Establishment Division of the government to formulate, develop and review the training and career development/ planning policy of the bureaucrats. In the absence of a comprehensive and long-range national policy the present morass vis-a-vis public sector training cannot be overcome.

The existing institutions for training the higher civil servants have limited physical facilities and suffer from the shortage of well-trained and professional corps of trainers. In almost all instances, training courses are conducted by public servants who had little, if any, exposure at all, to the modern methods and techniques of training. Institutes have, in effect, become dumping grounds for civil servants who could not be placed, for one reason or another, in other positions. This has seriously undermined the usefulness of training. Moreover, all the three prime institutes (BASC, NIPA and COTA) are headed by senior members of the erstwhile elite services--the Civil and Police Services of Pakistan. This apparent policy of reserving top-most directorial positions of the training institutes for members of the public services has incited qualified, competent and experienced trainers to leave the institutes to join educational institutions as faculty members while at the same time dissuading young professionals from seeking a career as trainers.

It has been observed that trainees, especially the higher bureaucrats, do not take training programs seriously because of three reasons: first, most of the civil servants-cum-trainers are anything but good trainers; second, trainees do not like archaic training techniques which are dished out to them in a disjointed and incoherent manner; lastly, most of the trainees have nothing but contempt for institutionalized training, as they confidently profess they are better off without any training.

In effect, public administration training now available in Bangladesh has very little impact on the bureaucrats. Attitudinal changes hardly take place. This is because human relations training is hardly emphasized in the existing program content. Evaluation of training programs are kept restricted to academic exercises. Attention is more on the building of huge training complexes than on the substantive content of programs. As a result, training has little relevance to the realities obtaining in the country. There is hardly any difference in terms of performance, interaction with the public, etc. between a public servant who has been trained and one who hasn't.

Motivating the Bureaucrats

In most of the developing countries, especially the newly independent ones, one of the tasks of formidable dimension is the motivation of the bureaucrats. The task is even more difficult in post-colonial society where the bureaucrats had been accorded high social status and matching economic rewards. A state of disequilibrium exists between expectations of the

177

bureaucrats and the ideological orientations of the political leadership. While the former craves far more power and prestige, the latter attempts to establish political control over the public officials and shun bureaucratic elitism.

We have seen how the Awami League in Bangladesh during the initial years of its rule tried to keep the bureaucracy subdued. We have also seen why the recommendations of the ASRC and NPC as far as achieving egalitarianism in the civil services is concerned were not accepted fully and could not be appropriately implemented. We have also discussed some of the mechanisms, i.e., withdrawl of constitutional guarantees and promulgation of P.O. 9, etc., and their impact in demotivating the bureaucrats.

The PSC, as we have indicated, adopted a more moderate stand vis-a-vis the status and pay of the bureaucrats. This conciliatory measure has to some extent pacified them. It has been pointed out by a senior official belonging to the erstwhile CSP as to what motivates the bureaucrats in achieving what he calls "the general quality, tone and efficiency, integrity and morale" in administration. He argues rather passionately:

> The members of the erstwhile Civil Service of Pakistan constitute the corps de elite in the civil service of Bangladesh. Their predecessors had set up an excellent tradition and a very high reputation for integrity, initiative, objectivity and efficiency. The sense of belonging to such a corps has motivated them to a great extent to maintain their professional standards and has acted as incentives to put in their best for the country. Monetary benefits (which could be available to them better in other fields, e.g., trade, commerce or industry) was not the sole criterion to attract them to join the civil service; status and rank which assured them social prestige, placement in key positions allowing them to participate in the decision making process at the highest level, and the sense of belongingness to the elite corps to the highest traditions, more compensated for the monetary benefits that could be available to them elsewhere.[48]

It appears from the above that bureaucrats in Bangladesh advocate elitism and demand access to political (high level policy making) power as the two major criteria for motivation. A recent empirical study[49] confirms that 88% of the bureaucrats interviewed are motivated by such concerns as glamour of the service, rapid promotions, security of service, pay, power and prestige. Only 12% expressed that their main motivating factor was a sense of public good. Moreover, 80% of the bureaucrats strongly favor guardianship orientation and "a kind of limited popular participation within the framework of a paternal rule." [50]

Control Mechanisms

The bureaucracy in Bangladesh is plagued with corruption ramifying the entire administrative machinery. Corruption is institutionalized and an accepted order of the day. It takes several forms--graft, depravity and kickback. Besides, the administration is ulcerated with inefficiency, insubordination, misconduct and misuse of official positions. All these have increased the miseries of the common populace and created a class of bureaucrats who unabashedly enjoy a life style far beyond their actual means.

Since the British-India colonial days several mechanisms have been used to control the bureaucrats and to combat corruption. But past experience proves their futility. Since independence, successive governments in Bangladesh have been introducing devices to mitigate administrative inefficiency and indiscipline. Some of these are President's Order No. 9 of 1972, Government Servants (Discipline and Appeal) Rules 1976, Public Servants (Special Provisions) Ordinance 1979 and Civil Services (Prevention of Corruption) Rules. The 1979 Ordinance makes special provisions for maintaining discipline among the public officials through certain penalties which include dismissals from service, discharge from service and reduction in rank and pay. A penalized official can however appeal against the order to an authority immediately superior to the appointing authority.[51] The Government Servants' Conduct Rules of 1979 prevent public servants from accepting gifts or foreign awards, raising of funds, lending and borrowing or buying or selling of valuable property, taking part in politics and elections, etc.[52] Observers feel that the 1979 Ordinance may not serve the purpose for which it has been issued; rather it might prove counterproductive.[53]

Bureaucrats and the Development Process

The traditional administration (dealing only with law and order and revenue collection) in the British colonial days gave an opportunity to the bureaucrats to participate in the development activities of the government. Between 1947 and 1971 the bureaucrats in Pakistan played a predominant role in formulating and implementing development policies and programs. In Bangladesh today bureaucrats are increasingly being involved in developmental activities especially at the field level.

From the very beginning, attempts were made to assert the preponderance of the political leadership in nation-building and socio-economic activities. Mujib's ill-fated district Governors scheme was one of the steps in this direction. The active participation of the bureaucrats at the micro-level began in early 1976 during the martial law regime. Ziaur Rahman repeatedly stressed the need to narrow down the gap between the people and the bureaucrats to bring about meaningful development, particularly in the rural areas. He encouraged innovativeness among the bureaucrats to design and implement developmental projects to inculcate a spirit of self-reliance among the masses. Several self-help schemes, conceived and developed by public officials, were directly patronized by the national leadership. These were experimental in nature and aimed at "the enrichment of the quality of life of all social classes through emphasizing both the fulfillment of their finer values as well as economic aspirations". Entailing a decentralized bottom-up planning process with people's particupation, the bureaucrats acted as the 'change agents' with the task of motivating preparing and activating the rural poor.[54]

One of the recently established institutions for development at the grass roots level is intended to embolden the rural masses to take care of their problems using their own inventiveness and local resources. In this micro-governmental system, known as the Swanirvar Gram Sarker (Self-Reliant Village Government) the people of a particular village are to elect through consensus a number of representatives from among different occupational groups to form the nucleus of this 'government'. Each representative is allocated a particular developmental sector (i.e., food production, health and population, education, etc.). But this 'democratization' process in the rural areas is being controlled and manipulated by the bureaucrats posted at the <u>thana</u> and subdivisional levels[55] sometimes at the authoritative command of the ruling party. This shows unwarranted bureaucratic intervention in the affairs of the local people in their efforts towards attaining self-reliance.

Paradoxically, at the regional levels governmental bodies for the development of different areas of the country, the bureaucrats manning important positions in them are being replaced by Ministers and members of the Parliament belonging to the ruling party. Another recent move by the government aims at providing considerable opportunities for ruling party members in Parliament to guide and coordinate development activities in the district. These moves will obviously reduce the influence of the bureaucrats in the development process at different levels.

Conclusions

Public bureaucrats in Bangladesh have shown a remarkable capacity to stick together to frustrate any effort to weaken their power, positions and status. Major administrative reform proposals intended to break away with the past have floundered at the altar of stiff bureaucratic resistance and the unwillingness of the political leadership to chart a new course for the much-maligned administrative system. The bureaucratic machinery is top heavy, elitist, decadent, inefficient and expensive. It can no longer justify its existence in its present form except on the selfish ground of self-preservation. The system which badly needs total and radical overhaul has survived mainly due to a combination of a number of factors such as mass iliteracy, wide-scale poverty, politics and apathy of the educated citizenry towards the affairs of the state. It is difficult to perceive any end to this bureaucratic rot and the consequent citizens' nightmare unless there are radical reforms in the socio-political and economic spheres in the country.

Footnotes

[1]See Sir Edward Blunt, The ICS, London: Faber
and Faber, 1937; L.S.S. O'Malley, The Indian Civil
Service, London: John Murray, 1931; Philip Woodruf,
The Men who Ruled India, New York: Schocken, 1954.

[2]See Robert LaPorte Jr., "Pakistan in 1971: The
Disintegration of a Nation," Asian Survey 12, No. 2,
(February 1972), pp. 97-108; W.H. Morris-Jones, "Pakis-
tan Post Mortem and the Roots of Bangladesh," Political
Quarterly 18, No. 2, (April-June 1972), pp. 187-200;
and K.B. Sayeed, "The Breakdown of Pakistan's Political
System," International Journal 27, No. 3 (Summer 1972),
pp. 381-404.

[3]Some cogently argued that the bureaucrats in
Pakistan had been in effective command of the state
power right from the beginning of 1947, though they
functioned behind a parliamentary facade in the '50s.
With the military coup in 1958 they openly 'seized'
power. See, for example, Hamza Alavi, "The State in
Post-Colonial Societies: Pakistan and Bangladesh,"
in K. Gough and H.P. Sharma (eds.), Imperialism and
Revolution in South Asia, New York: Monthly Review
Press, 1973, p. 152; and Angus Maddison, Class Structure and Economic Growth: India and Pakistan since
the Moghuls, London: George Allen and Unwin, 1971,
p. 136.

[4]See K.B. Sayeed, Pakistan: The Formative Phase,
Karachi: Pakistan Publishing House, 1960, pp. 262-
285.

[5]See Emajuddin Ahamed, Bureaucratic Elites in
Segmented Economic Growth: Bangladesh and Pakistan,
Dacca: University Press Limited, 1980, p. 29.

[6]Lawrence Ziring, "Militarism in Pakistan: The
Yahya Interregnum,"in W.H. Wriggins (ed.), Pakistan
in Transition, Islamabad: University of Islamabad
Press, 1975, p. 200.

[7]See Mohammad Mohabbat Khan, Bureaucratic Self-
Preservation: Failure of Major Administrative Reform
Efforts in the Civil Service of Pakistan, Dacca: Un-
iversity of Dacca, 1980, pp. 90-133; and "Ruling Elites
and Major Administrative Reforms: The Case of the
Civil Service of Pakistan", unpublished paper, 1980.

[8]The new left writers like Herbert Marcuse, Angela Davis and others use the term 'internal colonialism' to signify the process of domination and exploitation of one ethnic group by another within the same country.

[9]See Articles 134, 135 (3) of the 1972 Constitution of the People's Republic of Bangladesh. Presidential Order No. 9 of 1972 also provided for the dismissal of any officer without any right of appeal. Between July and November, 1972 over 300 government officials were dismissed under this Order. See Talukder Maniruzzaman, "Bangladesh in 1974: Economic Crisis and Political Polarization," Asian Survey 15, No. 2, (February 1975), pp. 117-128.

[10]The Civil Service of Pakistan was considered the elite corps.

[11]Emajuddin Ahamed, "Dominant Bureaucratic Elites in Bangladesh," Indian Political Science Review 13, No. 1, (January 1979), p. 36.

[12]Twenty one senior bureaucrats were nominated to the central committee of the only legitimate 'national' party of Mujib. Fourteen senior bureaucrats were also selected as district Governors.

[13]A nation-wide referendum to assess President Ziaur Rahman's popularity was held in May 1977; he received a mammoth support. A presidential election was held in June 1978 with Zia winning it. In February 1979 in the second general elections Zia's party BNP won comfortably.

[14]See Government of Pakistan, The Civil Services (Classification, Control and Appeal) Rules, 1951 (First Edition).

[15]For example members belonging to the former Civil Service of Pakistan were identified as ex-CSP or those belonging to the Police Service of Pakistan as ex-PSP.

[16]See Manirruzzaman, "Administrative Reforms and Politics within the Bureaucracy in Bangladesh," Journal of Commonwealth and Comparative Politics 17, No. 1, (March 1979), pp. 47-59.

[17]Ibid, pp. 48-49.

[18]The CSP Association, The Service Structure of Bangladesh: A Proposal, memorandum submitted to the Pay and Services Commission, Part I, p. 14.

[19]See, for example, the memorandum of the Engineers' Association submitted to the Pay and Services Commission.

[20]Government of Bangladesh, Cabinet Division, Report of the Administrative and Services Reorganization Committee, 1973, Part I, The Services, p. 1.

[21]The Committee used the term 'grade' to include all classes of posts that although different in kind or subject matter of work are sufficiently equivalent in difficulty, responsibility and the level of qualification required. This they did to justify their inclusion within one range of rates of basic pay.

[22]The ten grades were: I. Senior Administrative/ Top Specialist Grade; II. Administrative/Chief Executive Grade.; III. Junior Administrative/Higher Executive/Higher Professional Grade; IV. Senior Executive/ Senior Professional Grade; V. Junior Executive/ Junior Professional Grade; VI. Lower Executive/Lower Professional Grade; VII. Lower Supervisory/Higher Ministerial/ Higher Technical Grade; VIII. Lower Ministerial/ Lower Technical Grade; IX. Semi-skilled Grade; and X. Unskilled Grade. See Government of the People's Republic of Bangladesh, Report of the Administrative and Services Reorganization Committee, Part I, 1973, pp. 30-31.

[23]See Khan, Bureaucratic Self-Preservation, op. cit.

[24]Government of Bangladesh, The National Pay Commission Report, Vol. I, Main Text, 1973, pp. 1-2.

[25]Ibid, pp. 5, 14, 15.

[26]Ibid, pp. 17-18.

[27]One US Dollar is approximately Taka 15.78.

[28]The National Pay Commission Report, p. 87.

[29]Government of Bangladesh, Cabinet Division, Report of the Pay and Services Commission, Part II, Vol I, 1977, p. 8.

[30]Included were the civil service, autonomous, semi-autonomous bodies, statutory corporations and nationalized enterprises (excluding the workers).

[31]Report of the Pay and Services Commission, Part I, Vol I, p. 7.

[32]These were: 1. Bangladesh Administrative Service; 2. Bangladesh Agricultural Service; 3. Bangladesh Ansar Service; 4. Bangladesh Audit and Accounts Service; 5. Bangladesh Customs and Excise Service; 6. Bangladesh Defense Civil Service; 7. Bangladesh Defense Intelligence Service; 8. Bangladesh Economic Service; 9. Bangladesh Education Service (General); 10. Bangladesh Education Service (Technical); 11. Bangladesh Engineering Service (Public Health); 12. Bangladesh Engineering Service (Roads and Highways); 13. Bangladesh Fisheries Service; 14. Bangladesh Foreign Service; 15. Bangladesh Forest Service; 16. Bangladesh Food Service; 17. Bangladesh Health Service; 18. Bangladesh Livestock Service; 19. Bangladesh Military Lands and Cantonment Service; 20. Bangladesh Police Service; 21. Bangladesh Information Service; 22. Bangladesh Judicial Service; 23. Bangladesh Postal Service; 24. Bangladesh Railway Service; 26. Bangladesh Secretariat Service; 27. Bangladesh Statistical Service; 28. Bangladesh Taxation Service; 29. Bangladesh Trade Service.

[33]In Bangladesh, as is the case with the Sub-Continent, there are two types of employees: gazetted and non-gazetted. Usually the higher officials belonging to classes I and II are termed gazetted and information regarding their appointment, promotion, transfer, etc. appears in the official Gazette. Lower level employees belonging to classes III and IV are known as non-gazetted.

[34]Government of Bangladesh, Ministry of Finance, Indtroduction of New National Grades and Scales of Pay, Grades I to XI, Government Sector, 1977, p. 2.

[35]Maniruzzaman, "Administrative Reforms and Politics within the Bureaucracy in Bangladesh," op. cit., pp.54-56

[36]See New Nation, October 15, 22 and 29, 1978; and Holiday, January 29 and March 12, 1978.

[37]The fourteen cadre services are: 1. Bangladesh

185

Civil Service (B.C.S.) (Administrative) having two sub-cadres: administrative and food; 2. B.C.S. (Agriculture) having four sub-cadres: agriculture, forest, fisheries and livestock; 3. B.C.S. (Education) with two sub-cadres: general education and technical education; 4. B.C.S. (Economic and Trade) with three sub-cadres: economic, trade and statistical; 5. B.C.S. (Engineering) with four sub-cadres: public works, public health, roads and highways, and telecommunications; 6. B.C.S. (Finance) with three sub-cadres: audit and accounts, customs and excise, and taxation; 7. B.C.S. (Foreign Affairs); 8. B.C.S. Health and Family Planning); 9. B.C.S.(Information); 10. B.C.S. (Judicial); 11. B.C.S. (Postal); 12. B.C.S. (Enforcement) with two sub-cadres: Police and Ansar; 13. B.C.S. (Railways) with two sub-cadres: transportation and commercial and engineering; and 14. B.C.S. (Secretariat).

38The Bangladesh Times, November 12, 1979.

39One such bureaucrat who was earlier removed from service by the Martial Law regime of General Yahya Khan in 1969 was appointed Secretary General of the administration for his 'contribution' during the liberation war.

40See Lawrence Lifschultz, Bangladesh: The Unfinished Revolution, London: Zed Press, 1979, pp. 98-149.

41K.B. Sayeed, The Political System of Pakistan, Massachusetts: Houghton Mifflin, 1968, p. 151.

42See Khan, "Ruling Elites and Major Administrative Reforms," op. cit.

43According to the 1961 population census, the literacy rate was 21.5% for East Pakistan and 16.3% for the West.

44Office Memorandum of the Establishment Division, Government of Bangladesh, as quoted in the Report of the Administrative and Services Reorganization Committee, Part I, p. 50.

45Report of the Pay and Services Commission, Part I, p. 212.

46Of the 138 candidates who appeared before the

interview board in the first Superior Posts Examination, 46.43% had their secondary education in urban areas, and 53.57% in rural areas. See Bangladesh Public Service Commission, Annual Report, 1979, p. 4.

[47]For a wide-ranging discussion of PAT in Bangladesh see, Khan and Zafarullah, "Public Administration Training in Bangladesh: An Overview," International Review of Administrative Sciences 46, No. 4. (December 1980).

[48]K.M. Asaduzzaman, "The Civil Service System in Bangladesh," Indian Journal of Public Administration 26, No. 1, (January-March 1980), p. 19.

[49]Emajuddin Ahamed, "Bureaucratic Elites in Bangladesh and their Development Orientation," The Dacca University Studies 28, Part A, (June 1978), pp. 52-67.

[50]Ibid, pp. 66-67.

[51]Habib Mohammad Zafarullah (ed.), Administrative Affairs in Bangladesh: 1979, Dacca: Center for Administrative Studies, 1980, pp. 75-76.

[52]Ibid, p. 76.

[53]See The New Nation, March 4, 1979.

[54]B.K. Jahangir, "Local Action for Self-Reliant Development in Bangladesh," IFDA Dossier, No. 15, (January-February, 1980), pp. 1(31)-15(45).

[55]Thanas and subdivisions are two tiers of the administrative hierarchy. The country is first divided into divisions; each division is divided into districts; a district is further divided into sub-divisions; a sub-division is further broken up into thanas; a thana is subdivided into unions composed of villages.

CHAPTER IX

THE EVOLUTION OF PUBLIC BUREAUCRACY IN NIGERIA

PETER H. KOEHN

Introduction

Over the past 25 years, a relatively small colonial service in Nigeria has been transformed into 20 indigenous civil services that jointly employ more than 700,00 persons. While expansion and extension constitute the most striking and consistent forms of bureaucratic development in Nigeria, the organization and conduct of public administration also have been shaped in important ways by regime change, indigenous political culture and pressures, external influences and approaches, intergovernmental relations, and reform efforts. This chapter describes the principal developments in Nigerian public bureaucracy, from its colonial origin through the establishment of a second civilian republic in 1979, with particular reference to political changes affecting the environment in which public administration operates.

Historical Overview

The Nigerian governmental apparatus has been divided into several independent civil services since 1954. Prior to independence, the regional governments succeeded in attracting many of the most highly qualified senior Nigerian staff into their services.[1] And the independent competitive position of regional/state civil services had been preserved over time by various personnel policies and practices.[2] Yet, in spite of their separate and exclusive constitution, the formal organizational arrangements of the Nigerian civil services have evolved in remarkably similar fashion. In broad outline, this structural evolution has incorporated colonial secretariat organization, British administrative patterns, indigenous adaptations and practices, and (recently) the adoption of selected ideas based on the conduct of administrative affairs in the United States.

The Colonial Secretariat Structure

Under the colonial administrative system, all communications to and from the Governor were channeled through the Chief Secretary in Lagos, who also played the dominant decision-making role and, supported by a number of assistant secretaries and clerks, served as the effective head of the civil service. Almost all higher civil servants were British colonial officers.[3] Residents and district officers served as local chief executives with general responsibility, similar to that exercised by the Chief Secretary, for all government activities in their provinces or districts. These officers possessed considerable autonomy and discretion in the field.[4] Functional departments, formally directed on technical matters from London, organized their field administration according to provincial and/or district boundaries.

The Ministerial System

The Macpherson Constitution of 1951 introduced a Council of Ministers allowing their collective participation in the policy-making process. While each Ministry assumed work within its assigned sphere of activity previously handled by the secretariat, the British professional officers who headed the departments continued to operate independently of ministerial supervision until 1954. "The final act in the process of developing a Nigerian Ministerial organization patterned on the Whitehall model," however, occurred in 1959 with the decision to amalgamate federal departments and ministries.[5]

Under the ministerial system as adopted in Nigeria (see Chart I), each ministry is divided into a number of functional divisions, including an Administration and General Division, with the latter handling housekeeping chores such as supplies, accounts and personnel matters. Divisions are further subdivided hierarchically into branches, sections, and subsections. Differences, however, exist between administrative and technical Ministries, primarily concerning the role and status of the permanent secretary. In the administrative Ministry, the permanent secretary serves as the chief administrator and advisor to the Minister. As the chief advisor, the permanent secretary is expected to elaborate policies and plans and assist in determining the best means of implementing them. As administrative head, he is responsible for interpreting

189

CHART I

ORGANIZATIONAL STRUCTURE OF A "TYPICAL" ADMINISTRATIVE
AND TECHNICAL MINISTRY (1966)

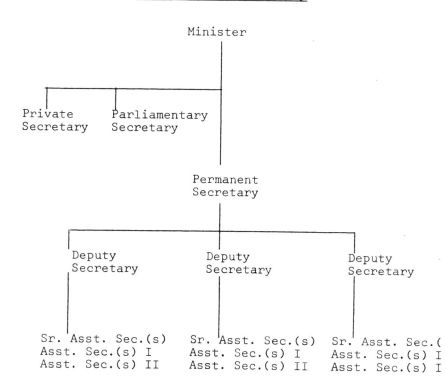

Continued next page

CHART I

ORGANIZATIONAL STRUCTURE OF A "TYPICAL ADMINISTRATIVE
AND TECHNICAL MINISTRY (1966)

<u>Technical Ministry</u>

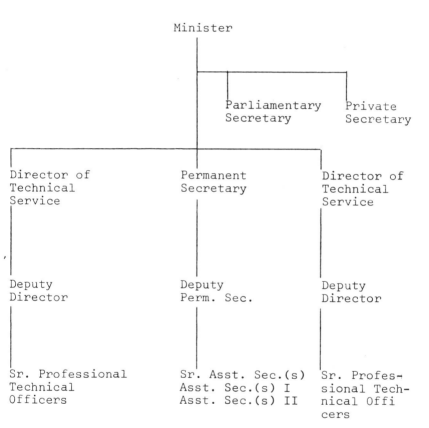

Minister

Parliamentary   Private
Secretary   Secretary

Director of   Permanent   Director of
Technical   Secretary   Technical
Service   Service

Deputy   Deputy   Deputy
Director   Perm. Sec.   Director

Sr. Professional   Sr. Asst. Sec.(s)   Sr. Profes-
Technical   Asst. Sec.(s) I   sional Tech-
Officers   Asst. Sec.(s) II   nical Offi
                                          cers

Source: Lapido Adamolekun, "High Level Ministerial
         Organization in Nigeria and Ivory Coast," in
         D. J. Murray, ed., <u>Studies in Nigerian Admini-</u>
         <u>stration</u>, 2nd ed., London: Hutchison & Co.,
         Ltd., 1978, p. 15-16.

191

policies, coordinating Ministry activities, supervising functional execution and monitoring results, defending Ministry budget proposals and serving as chief accounting officer, deciding on the selection, placement, promotion, and discipline of lower-level officers (i.e., GL 01-06) and passing recommendations on such matters with respect to higher officers (GL 07 and above) to the Civil Service Commission, and upholding the Ministry's interests in inter-ministerial meetings and in relations with other agencies and external groups.[6]

In the technical Ministry, the technical service directors share executive responsibilities with the permanent secretary. Each director supervises the performance of a cluster of technical services. However, the permanent secretary (along with his deputy and assistants) retains exclusive authority for personnel and financial matters and remains responsible for overall coordination of ministry functions. Moreover, the permanent secretary is expected to serve as chief advisor even in the technical Ministries, with the added responsibility of informing the Minister of the professionals' point of view on policy matters. Technical directors may consult directly with the Minister, but must inform the permanent secretary of all such high-level discussions.[7]

Generalists vs. Specialists

Two important observations can be made from the above description. First, the permanent secretary occupies a powerful policy-formulating and executing position in technical as well as administrative ministries. In addition, the specialist class of civil servants have encountered deeply felt frustrations over policy and administrative matters under both types of Ministries. Professional officers have criticized their administrative counterparts for lack of technical competence and understanding, relative youthfulness and inexperience, and short tenure dealing with the specialized affairs of their particular Ministry. Although professional officers are not formally barred from assuming the post of permanent secretary, the prevailing practice has been to appoint administrative officers even in technical Ministries.[8] This practice has not only led to conflicts between specialists and generalists in technical Ministries, but also had aggravated the frustrations of technical officers in securing promotions to influential and prestigious positions.[9] The conviction that technical expertise and perspectives should prevail in policymaking and functional supervision contributed to the demand by professional officers that the permanent secretary of all technical Ministries be appointed from their ranks.

Administrative-Executive Class Dichotomy

The British colonial legacy of dividing general service positions into two clearly defined classes the senior service and the junior service, has resulted in additional intra-bureaucratic conflicts. Racial barriers (until 1946), strictly enforced entry qualifications based upon formal educational attainments, and the lack of any connection between performance in the lower class and promotion to the higher one served to reinforce the rigid distinction drawn between the two compartments.[10]

In 1956, the four governments began to implement recommendations contained in the Gorsuch Report for the establishment of an executive class (with a corresponding "higher technical" class) that would bridge the gap between junior and senior officers. The Report aimed principally at eliminating routine tasks performed by high-level administrative and professional officers and at providing performance incentives for middle bureaucratic personnel by allowing promotion into the administrative class based on a candidate's record in the executive ranks, rather than on competitive examination. The duties to be assigned to executive class officers involved "routine but responsible work of a general administration, personnel, or accounting nature."

Although neither of the two principal objectives of the Gorsuch Report was realized by 1970, a new caste had arisen in the civil services. This intermediate class of executive officers[12] has failed to take over more responsible tasks from the administrative class and to carve out unique functional roles. At the same time, most administrative grade officers have continued to utilize executive officers as chief clerks. As a result of their reluctance to delegate responsibility, higher officers still devote a considerable amount of time to routine work. In most respects, then, the executive grades have continued to be regarded and treated as a junior service rather than as a middle-management cadre. The junior status of the executive class has been further reflected in and perpetuated by the vastly superior salaries and emoluments given to

administrative officers.[13]   The failure to satisfy
raised expectations generated considerable resentment
within the executive ranks and exacerbated inter-class
conflicts.[14]   Furthermore, by 1970 few executive officers had been appointed to the administrative class
as a reward for superior job performance, and most
continued to believe that a university degree provided
the only certain avenue of entry into the administrative ranks. In short, the Nigerian civil services had
failed to fashion the connections envisioned by the
Gorsuch Report between middle management performance,
training programs, and promotion policies.[15]

Bureaucratic Expansion

In the decades following independence in 1960,
the Nigerian civil service have experienced rapid expansion at all levels. From a colonial service base
of 1,100 at the time of the unification of north and
south in 1914 and 39,100 established posts in 1952, the
total number of federal and regional government personnel had grown to 71,693 by 1960.[16]   By 1974, the
total size of the Nigerian public service (excluding
local government, judiciary, and military personnel)
was estimated to be as follows:

Public Sector Categories	Number of Employees
Federal Civil Service (including Police)	102,000
State Civil Services	140,000
Education Services	160,000
Parastatals	230,000
TOTAL	632,000

Source: Public Service Review Commission, Report on
Grading and Pay, Vol. I, Lagos, 1974, p. 13,
as cited in Paul Beckett and James O'Connel,
Education and Power in Nigeria, New York:
Africana Publishing Co., 1977, p. 8.

Much of the enoromous expansion can be attributed
to growth in state government and parastatal employment
due to political pressures and to increased governmental
activity at all levels. Between 1960 and 1966 for instance, the number of Ministries in the Western Region
rose from 12 to 19. The creation of 12 states out of
the four former regions in 1967 and the addition of
seven new states in 1976 provided another major impetus

behind bureaucratic expansion.[17] Similarly, between
1966 and 1977, the number of public enterprises (utilities, banks, commerical and industrial operations) increased from about 30 to nearly 300.

Nigerianization

The accelerated replacement of colonial and expatriate officers with Nigerian personnel constituted a
major objective for the public services in the immediate
pre- and post-independence periods. Prior to the abolition of racial barriers in 1946, all administrative,
professional, managerial, and technical positions in
the senior colonial service had been filled by British-
ers. By 1954, Nigerians had been promoted or appointed
to 19 percent of the senior service posts.[18] Rapid
Nigerianization characterized the period 1957-1966,
when all Public Service Commissions were directed to
appoint qualified Nigerians to vacant public service
posts.[19] By 1960, Nigerians held 62 per cent of all
senior officer posts, and by 1962 they held all permanent secretary posts in the Western Region, two-
thirds at the federal level, more than half in the
Eastern Region, and four in the Northern Region.[20]
However, the extent to which Nigerianization policy
had been implemented varied considerably among the
respective services as shown below:

Percentage of Senior Officer Posts Occupied
by Nigerian in 1960 by Service

Service	Per Cent
Eastern Region	80%
Western Region	82%
Northern Region	28%
Federal Government	57%

Source: Omorogbe Nwanwene, "The Nigerian Public
Service Commissions," in D. J. Murray,
ed., Studies in Nigerian Administration,
2nd ed., London: Hutchinson, 1978, p. 201.

Protecting Regional/State Interests

In spite of the importance placed upon accelerated
Nigerianization of the public services following independence, substantial numbers of expatriates continued
to be employed at high levels on a contract basis in
the early 1960's, particularly in the northern and

federal services. The continued preference in the
northern region/states for expatriate officers employed
on temporary contracts must however be understood in
the context of the comparatively small number of indigenes of that region possessing the minimum entry educational qualifications. As early as 1957, the Public
Service Commission of the Northern Region adopted an
explicit policy of "Northernization" of the public
service: "If a qualified Northerner is available,
an expatriate may be recruited or a non-Northerner on
contract terms."[21] By the time of independence, application of the Northernization policy had already indicated that "few Southerners would be allowed to remain long in any conspicuous positions in the service
of the Northern Regional Government".[22]

With the creation of the Mid-West Region in 1963,
moreover, Chief Akintola's government dismissed all
Mid-Westerners (more than 3,400 employees) from the
Western Region's public service.[23] The Eastern and
Midwestern regional governments also pursued extreme
regionalization of their civil services. The personnel
redeployment exercises which followed the creation of
states occurred primarily on the basis of employee
state of origin. And the goal of staffing higher
service ranks exclusively or preponderantly with indigenes of one's area continues to be pursued by each of
the present 19 states.[24]

The practice of giving priority to individuals
from one's own region may be justified in terms of
providing employment and experience opportunities that
might not otherwise be available, facilitating bureau-
cracy-public relations,[25] and promoting closer relations between local politicians and civil servants.
On the other hand, discrimination against non-indigenes
virtually eliminates opportunities for inter-state
labor mobility, perpetuates bureaucratic exclusiveness
and divisiveness[26] and involves the risk of inferior
job performance.[26] The emphasis on self-sufficiency in
all classes of personnel has, in a number of states,
perpetuated reliance upon expatriate staff (particularly in certain professional ranks, such as engineers,
planners, doctors),[27] led to frequent turnover among
temporary employees, and resulted in a higher proportion of vacant posts and "acting" appointments.[28]

At the federal level, regional political pressures
have resulted in sustained attention and sensitivity
to the goal of establishing a representative public

service.[29] Historically, indigenes of the northern
states have been grossly underrepresented in the federal
civil service. In 1960, official figures showed that
"only 29 out of 4,398 'officers in C Scale and above'
listed the Northern Region as their 'region of origin'."[30]
Ten years, two coup d'etats, and a civil war later, the
situation had changed to the extent that one participant at a national conference on administrative development in Nigeria could, without challenge, categorize
the total federal civil service as "now fairly representative of all groups."[31]

Thus, following independence, the Nigerian civil
services maintained certain distinctive structural features of British administrative tradition. Yet, in the
face of rapid bureaucratic expansion, Nigerianization
and politicization of the civil services, and increasing
government involvement in development-oriented activities
controversy and criticism grew over the performance,
status and role of the public bureaucracy.[32] This reaction provided a further stimulus to modify British
colonial administrative principles and practices in accordance with Nigeria's unique political circumstances
and culture.

Post-Coup Developments

The political context within which the Nigerian
public services must operate has fluctuated dramatically
over the past 15 years, beginning with the violent
January 1966 military coup d'etat that overthrew the
First Republic and placed General Ironsi at the Head
of the imposed Federal Military Government. Ironsi's
rule was short lived, largely due to opposition among
all northern groups to his hasty moves to institute a
unitary system of government and unify the separate
regionally based civil services under a single Public
Service Commission.[33] In July 1966, a second coup resulted in the death of General Ironsi and the emergence
of Lt. Colonel Yakubu Gowon as the new Head of State.
Gowon (who retained power until deposed in 1975 by
ranking officers) was committed to return Nigeria to
Civilian rule within four years. After the assassination of Gowon's successor, General Murtala Mohammed,
in an abortive coup the following year, the new Head
of the Federal Military Government, General Olusegun
Obasanjo, oversaw the implementation of plans and policies that culminated in return to elected civilian rule
on 1 October 1979.[34]

As a result of these events, political-administrative developments in post-coup Nigeria must be analyzed according to three broad but distinctive time frames: the Gowon regime (1966-1975), the Murtala/Obasanjo regime (1975-1979), and the second Republic (1979 to the present). While issues of particular salience for public administration in Nigeria have found recurring place on the political agenda over the past 15 years, there have been marked differences in the style and substance of each regime. These persistent and pressing issues are treated below under the broad categories of inter-governmental relations, administrative innovations and adaptations, and the role of higher civil servants in public policymaking and national developments.

Inter-governmental Relations

In spite of the negative reaction to Ironsi's abortive attempt to impose a unitary system on Nigeria, the nature of inter-governmental relations changed considerably under subsequent military regimes in the direction of increased federal power and authority. The success of federal forces in the civil war fought to preserve national unity against the Biafran secessionist movement underscored the de facto and symbolic supremacy of the federal government. The numerous measures designed to centralize political power during this period reflected both the military leaders' preference for familiar hierarchical command structures and commitment to national unity as well as federal civil servants' interest in and attachment to the concept of a strong and effective central government.[35] Under the Murtala/Obasanjo regime, for instance, state military administrators no longer sat on the Supreme Military Council. They served as military officers to the Supreme Headquarters' Chief of Staff, who in their turn exercised authority to transfer or remove them.

By the late 1970's thus, successive military regimes had decisively revamped the Nigerian political system in a manner which ensured federal dominance and rendered the states incapable of acting as co-equal units of government.[36] These tendencies have been entrenched in the Second Republic Constitution which took effect on October 1, 1979.[37] The 1979 Constitution grants the national legislature "exclusive" authority over a list of 64 functions,[38] concurrent authority with state Houses of Assembly over another lengthy list of functions, supremacy in the area of tax collection, and sole authority to provide for the allocation of public revenues among federal, state, and local governments.[39] In addition, the Constitution provides for a directly elected President, and seeks to ensure that federal and state government agencies, as well as political parties, reflect "the federal character of Nigeria."[40]

The role and status of local governments in the Nigerian political system also have undergone important changes in the post-coup period. In particular, the 1976 local government reform introduced by the Murtala/ Obasanjo administration reversed the trend toward regional/state domination over governmental activity at the local level. The reform established 303 independent, single-tier local government units, each assigned a nearly uniform set of exclusive and concurrent (with state government) functions. Voters selected three-fourths of their local council members through direct or indirect elections held without political party involvement in 1976 and the state Governor appointed the chief administrative officer (secretary to the local government), usually on secondment from the state civil service. State governments continued to supervise local government activities closely, but the new units had managed to develop a variable degree of autonomy by 1979. Article 7 of the 1979 Constitution, moreover, guarantees the existence of democratically elected local government councils and its Fourth Schedule grants them certain specific principal and shared responsibilities, as well as "such other functions as may be conferred on a local government council by the House of Assembly of the State." Many local officials are currently pressing for greater de facto structural autonomy and the delegation of additional functional responsibilities and financial capacity.[41]

Structural and Administrative Innovations and Adaptations

The upper levels of the Nigerian political-administrative system have been thoroughly reorganized and revamped in the post-coup period, first by the ruling military leadership and most recently under the Second Republic Constitution. The military rulers vested supreme legal, policy-making, and executive authority in two new organs which replaced First Republic political institutions (parliament, cabinet, and parties): the Supreme Military Council (SMC) and the Federal Executive Council (FEC). The SMC, composed of 24

199

ranking military officers (including the Head of State and Commander-in-Chief of the Armed Forces, and the Supreme Headquarters Chief of Staff) functioned as the paramount official decision-making structure during military rule.[42] The military and civilian commissioners who served as heads of Ministries made up the FEC, a body charged with overseeing policy execution and the coordination and administration of government programs. A third organ, the National Council of States (NCS), consisted of the Head of State, all armed forces Chiefs of Staff, the Inspector-General of Police, and all state military Governors. From 1975 through 1979, the NCS functioned as a consultative forum for the articulation of state interests and harmonization of federal and state government activities.[43]

With the abolition of all elected political offices, the Nigerian civil services became directly accountable to the military leadership. Under the Gowon regime, in particular, many career civil servants seized the opportunity provided by the replacement of politicians with military men, who shared common administrative values and depended upon their support and expertise, to assume a more central and powerful role in fashioning public policies. General Gowon encouraged this development by personally inviting permanent secretaries and other civil servants to participate fully in FEC deliberations. However, Gowon's policy of more directly involving civil servants in running the affairs of state eventually led to dissension within the ranks of the army based on perceptions that the military bore the onus of responsibility for policies primarily shaped by civil servants.[44] Role expansion concomitantly drew top civil servants into an increasing number of conflicts with army brass and tightly linked their position and the reputation of the civil service to the fate of the ruling military faction with whom they had forged an alliance.[45]

On the heels of the July 1975 coup, General Murtala Mohammed removed all 12 military Governors and most federal and state commissioners.[46] Within a year, more than 10,000 federal and state civil servants, including the high-level administrative officers who had been closely linked to the Gowon regime, had been dismissed. Widespread recognition that civil servants had become deeply involved in the policy-making arena had only heightened their vulnerability to dismissal or involuntary retirement.[47]

The sweeping 1975 purge and other civil service reform measures introduced by the Murtala/Obasanjo administration appear to have had negligible positive long-
term impact on bureaucratic performance. As an immediate response to the mass dismissal exercise, "the personal performance of public officials improved enoromously, people arrived on time, worked harder and spent
less time on private business."[48] There is no evidence,
however, that the purge, the establishment of new in-
vestigatory bodies, and the promulgation of formal
codes of conduct have served as major deterrents to
corruption, abuse of authority, lack of accountability,
or laxity in the discharge of responsibility by public
servants. Indeed, Adamolekun concludes that "the balance
sheet of all these new measures suggests that no qualitative change has occurred in . . . the behavior and
performance of the public servants."[49]

In conducting the 1975 exercise, the military
ignored existing Civil Service Rules and resorted to
what the SMG at the time has characterized as "revolutionary legality".[50] The leadership eventually conceded
that its purge had brought about 'panic and uncertainty
in the ranks of serving officers' and terminated the
program in November 1975 because of its 'unsettling
effect on the services'.[51] Subsequent to the 1979
elections, however, a fresh series of allegations sur-
faced in the press concerning the dismissal, forced
retirement, and unjust reassignment of public officers
by some of the new state executives as part of an effort to consolidate the position of their political
party within the civil service.[52] These attacks on
security of tenure are alleged to have resulted in
civil services plagued by low morale, reluctance to
assume responsibility and render advice, an impunged
public image, and increased difficulty in attracting
and retaining qualified manpower.[53]

Under military rule and the Second Republic, the
principal structural features of the Ministerial system
of administration remained essentially unchanged at the
national and state levels. However, the position of
parliamentary secretary had been abolished at the outset of military rule. The 1979 Constitution (Articles
139, 177) provides for the appointment of special advisors to the President and each Governor. Special
advisors hold temporary political rather than civil
service appointments and serve "at the pleasure of"
the President/Governor. The authority and influence
of many special advisors rival or exceed those exercized

by federal Ministers/state Commissioners.[54]

The military also created the single post of secretary to the military government and head of the civil service (commonly abbreviated as SMG) at the apex of the federal and state bureaucratic hierarchies. Appointees quickly built the office of SMG into the most powerful and prestigious administrative position in the military government. Self-designated as "super perm secs," SMG's possessed unrivaled access to the Head of State and the Military Governors. They served as secretary to the Federal and State Executive Councils. The secretary to the federal military government even sat in on most SMG meetings.[55] In addition to functioning as chief advisor to the military leadership, the SMG exercised important supervisory powers over the top ranks of the civil service. In an effort to centralize control over state government operations further, military Governors appointed a number of permanent secretaries to newly created posts within their own office. This practice, which has been continued by many elected chief executives under the Second Republic, had the effect of reinstituting a powerful secretariat office and reducing the authority and range of functional responsibilities possessed by ministries and departments.[56]

The Second Republic Constitution split the office of SMG (at both federal and state levels) into the two separate posts of secretary to the government and head of the civil service. The person appointed to fill the latter office must be a member of the respective federal or state civil service (Articles 157 and 188). Beyond this, the Constitution is silent regarding the two newly created positions. The absence of any precise legal definition and division of responsibilities for the two offices allows ample opportunities for conflict and variability in role performance. Based upon expectations that the secretary to the government will assume the more powerful political and policy advisory aspects of the former SMG's role (i.e., act as "chief" advisor) and will participate in Executive Council deliberations, informed commentators have predicted that the head of the civil service will be a secondary and perhaps even isolated figure under the new system.[57]

More fundamentally, the 1979 Constitution altered the status of the top echelon of the public bureaucracy by allowing elected chief executives to appoint individuals from outside the career civil service as permanent secretaries, heads of extra-ministerial departments, and

secretary to the government.[58] With the return to civilian rule, the newly elected chief executives made
sweeping personnel changes in these ranks. A number of
individuals from outside the civil service (most notably from the universities) have been appointed permanent
secretary or secretary to the government, particularly
by certain state governors, although a majority of the
initial appointees have been civil servants.[59] This
result does not alter the fact that, under the Second
Republic, the primary criteria for appointment at the
level of permanent secretary have become increasingly
and explicitly political. According to one state commissioner, Dr. Ray Ofoegbu, the critical bases for
appointment now are "competence, loyalty and total
commitment."[60] These changes constitute a decided
shift away from British conventions of bureaucratic
neutrality and anonymity toward the deeper politicization of top administrative ranks that characterizes the
U.S. and French presidential systems of government.[61]
As a condition of holding appointment in the Second
Republic, permanent secretaries, heads of extra-Ministerial departments, and secretaries to the government
"will be expected to pursue with absolute commitment
the manifestoes, programmes, and policies of the Chief
Executive."[62]

The politicization of the top echelons of the administrative machinery under Nigeria's multi-party
political system militates against greater cooperation
among, no less unification of, the federal and state
civil services and increases the likelihood that, upon
assuming office in the future, newly elected Presidents
and Governors will replace incumbent permanent secretaries and heads of departments (as well as the secretary to the government) with fresh appointees of their
own choosing. In short, under Nigeria's present system
of government, "permanent secretaries are no longer
permanent."[63] Nevertheless, the office of the federal
head of service announced in 1980 that government officials who take up political appointments are not
automatically deemed to have resigned or retired from
the civil service and may elect to remain a member of
the service when their political assignment is terminated.[64]

No discussion of administrative reform efforts in
Nigeria would be complete without reference to the
impact of the Public Service Review Commission's study
and recommendations. After two years of inquiry conducted under sweeping terms of reference, the Commission

appointed by the Gowon regime and chaired by Chief
Jerome Udoji submitted its report in September 1974.
The major recommendations of the Udoji Commission can
be divided into two categories: (1) structural reforms designed to "increase the efficiency and effectiveness of the Public Services in meeting the challenge of a development-oriented society" and (2) the
regrading of civil service posts, changes in salary
scales, and the establishment of a unified, "harmonized"
remuneration scheme for the public and private sectors.

To realize developmental objectives, the Commission advocated integrated project management in preference to the existing organizational practice of dividing government work into separate functional ministries.
It called for the creation of ad hoc task forces or
teams composed of relevant specialists drawn from
throughout the service that would design and manage
the execution of specific development projects. Upon
completion of an assigned project, task force members
would revert to their former position in the bureaucracy until called upon to participate in another undertaking. However, the Gowon government chose to ignore
these recommendations for organizational and management
reforms.[65]

Under considerable pressure from public servants
at all levels, the Gowon administration reacted more
favorably to the Public Service Review Commission's
grading and salary proposals. The Udoji Commission had
recommended that the multitude of differentially graded
and remunerated posts existing in the various civil
services be systematically reclassified under a single,
unified position and salary scheme composed of 17
grade levels. The Commission based its specific position classification proposals on the results of systematic job analyses conducted within each civil service
that revealed which posts possessed essentially equivalent duties, responsibilities, and required qualifications. The FMG not only adopted the unified grading
scheme proposed by the Udoji Commission for the civil
services, but extended it to encompass the entire public sector.

By 1970, public servants in Nigeria, particularly
senior management personnel, generally received considerably lower salaries and less attractive benefits
than their counterparts working for large private
enterprises. The lucrative material rewards offered
by multinational firms led public administrators to

demand equivalent benefits for themselves. In response to these demands and growing competition over highly qualified personnel, the Adebo and Udoji Commissions carried similar charges to explore areas in which the harmonization of public and private sector wages, salaries, and other conditions of employment would be desirable and feasible.

In January 1975, the FMG acted favorably on the Udoji Report's recommendations that the wages and salaries of certain classes of civil servants be increased dramatically in order to bring about comparability with private sector pay scales. The government doubled many salaries, including the rates paid to daily laborers at the bottom of the scale and to top-level administrators. The Gowon administration also decided to backdate the increases to April 1, 1974 and to exempt half of the arrears from taxation. Moreover, the FMG implemented an even more generous civil service pension scheme than the Udoji Commission had proposed and substantially raised the rate at which it paid supplementary allowances.

The combined effect of the regrading exercise and the government's differential "catch-up" salary awards triggered a spate of protests on the part of workers who perceived that they would suffer an erosion in their status and/or income relative to the categories of civil service personnel most favored by the new policies. Public service employees in technical and professional positions complained that the government's regrading of posts worked to their disadvantage, and joined intermediate scale civil servants in protesting the smaller salary increases they had received relative to the administrative cadre. Workers in public cooperations and the private sector, who had been excluded from the initial "Udoji" awards, agitated for comparable salary increases. Confronted by a series of private and public sector strikes and other labor actions, the Gowon regime eventually capitulated, allowing employees to negotiate wage settlements comparable to the Udoji awards (with full arrears) and granting specialist public servants a greater measure of parity with administrators.

The long-term impact of the Udoji Commission has been considerable, although the results have differed in important respects from those envisioned in its report and recommendations. In the federal service, operation of the unified grading scheme, ministerial reorganizations, and expansion of the number of directorships at the head of newly created specialized departments have enhanced promotion prospects for professional and technical personnel. In a crucial departure from past practice that enables more professional officers to take advantage of improved career opportunities, including appointment as permanent secretary, the federal government adopted a new approach to training in the post-Udoji period. The Cabinet Office now "endeavors to ensure that the professional and non-professional alike attend general management courses designed to prepare them for the highest appointments in the Service."[66]

Nevertheless, neither the imposition of a unified grade structure nor the attempt to harmonize salaries have produced the intended effect of attracting qualified private sector personnel into the public services. Indeed, inter-sectoral mobility has continued to flow overwhelmingly in the opposite direction during the post-Udoji years, with high ranking professionals and administrators exhibiting the greatest propensity to leave government work.[67] The government's failure, in spite of its generous Udoji awards, to alter this situation must be viewed in the context of a political economy characterized by rapid expansion of multinational operations in the midst of an oil boom, indigenization measures that have dramatically improved the position of Nigerian businessmen, and perceived skilled manpower shortages.[68] As long as such conditions persist, the realization of comparable public and private conditions of employment will continue to be an elusive policy objective. Thus, privately employed professionals and managers still manage to pay lower taxes, receive more lucrative fringe benefits, and secure higher incomes than their public service counterparts.

The Udoji awards rapidly exerted their own substantial impact on the Nigerian economy. The payment policies adopted and sanctioned by the government in the first quarter of 1975, which ignored the Udoji Commission's warning about the inflationary effects of large and retroactive public service salary increases and the Central Bank's opposition both to the size of the awards and to the payments of arrears, generated a dramatic monetary expansion. The spending spree unleashed by the sudden growth in aggregate demand, coupled with shortages of available commodities and constraints on domestic production, fueled rampant,

uncontrolled inflation. Spiraling inflation rates, in
turn, prompted a new wave of worker protest demonstrations. Subsistence farmers and the unemployed, moreover, possessed virtually no protection to mitigate the
inflationary consequences of the Udoji exercise. When
the dust had settled, Nigeria's experience with "harmonization" had produced few beneficiaries and a multitude of losers.

Between 1975 and 1979, the Murtala/Obasanjo regime
essentially froze the unified salary scheme that was
established following the Udoji review. The new civilian regime enacted a minimum wage of 100 naira per
month and increased the salary structure accordingly
in 1980, but only in the lower grades (GL 01-06).
Table 2 presents the basic monetary dimensions of
Nigeria's unified salary scheme for the public services
following these revisions. Throughout 1980, the
civilian government resisted labor pressures to increase the minimum wage to 300 naira per month. Demands for special treatment on the part of university
employees, and other pressures for a general upward
revision of the unified salary structure met with
the same fate.

The Role of the Bureaucracy in Public Policy Making

Nigerian public servants have consistently played
a major role in the public policy initiation process,
although the extent of their involvement has ebbed and
flowed with historical, legal, and political changes
in the environment of public administration at the
federal, state and local government levels. They have
operated under a nearly universally shared norm which
not only permits, but expects that ranking public
servants will both take the initiative in developing
public policy alternatives and implementation strategies and in advising their Ministers "on the full
implications of policy options open to the Government."[69]
Such behavior can be seen as a legacy of a colonial
system of government that had been predominantly administrative in character.[70] This tradition has been
readily sustained under a Ministerial government structure in which career officials are appointed to posts
much higher in the hierarchy than in the U.S., and
therefore serve in positions of greater influence and
political responsibility in the decision-making process.

207

TABLE 2

UNIFIED SALARY SCHEME FOR THE PUBLIC SERVICES (1980)

Grade Level	First Step (₦p.a.)	Last Step (₦p.a.)	Annual Step Increment (₦p.a.)
01	1,200	1,350	24/30
02	1,236	1,416	30
03	1,284	1,524	36/42
04	1,500	1,752	42
05	1,740	2,172	72
06	2,196	2,772	96
07	2,832	3,552	120
08	3,564	4,464	150
09	4,668	5,640	162
10	5,760	6,732	162
11	6,744	7,284	180
12	7,404	8,052	216
13	8,064	9,024	320
14	9,168	10,128	320
15	10,296	11,328	516
16	11,568	12,720	526
17	12,996	14,268	636

One naira (₦) = approximately US $1.80.

*There are 7 steps for GLs 01-10, 4 steps for GLs 11-14, and 3 for GLs 15-17.

208

In practice, higher civil servants (particularly permanent secretaries) have played more than an advisory role in the public policy formulation process. Policy papers initiated and prepared by permanent secretaries have frequently formed the basis for Executive Council deliberation and sanction.[71] And the drafting of annual budget proposals has been given over almost exclusively to civil servants. Political instability, lack of experience and educational qualifications on the part of ministers, the delegation of broad discretionary authority over policy and program implementation, and the better informed, more expert and realistic perspectives reputedly brought to bear on development issues by members of the administrative and professional classes have figured prominently in explaining and justifying bureaucractic encroachment in the policymaking domain. In sum, higher civil servants have been central, and often dominant participants in the policymaking process throughout Nigeria's history.[72]

The onset of military rule drew higher public servants even deeper into policy-formulating role. According to Robin Luckham, "the Ironsi regime relied heavily on its permanent secretaries, and virtually all important decisions were taken by a narrow group of half a dozen military leaders, together with a handful of civil servant advisors." Although General Ironsi did not appoint Commissioners, he vested ministerial powers in the Federal Executive Council rather than in permanent secretaries. However, the FEC delegated broad authority to promulgate subsidiary statutes as well as extensive rule-making powers to the permanent secretaries.[73]

By all accounts, the direct involvement of public servants in the policy-making arena reached its zenith under General Gowon. Lack of experience on the part of most military officers with government processes and public decisionmaking coupled with an unwillingness to appoint former politicians to authoritative or advisory posts in the new regime and the absence of any organized constituency, left the Head of the FMG and the supreme military Governors dependent upon the policy advice and alternatives proferred by civil servants. Through personal access, "super perm secs" and other ranking civil servants secured the backing of the Head of State (and the military Governors) for their proposals in advance of SMC and Executive Council meetings. Joint authorship with the chief executive practically guaranteed that the policy memoranda advanced by public servants would not be substantially changed by the SMC. In addition, whenever necessary, permanent secretaries utilized standing invitations to participate fully in SMC and FEC deliberations to counter any objections raised by council members to memoranda they had drafted, or to present a strong case advocating adoption of policy proposals as submitted -- even though their own ministers may have already articulated a contrary position on the issue. As Major-General Joseph N. Garba confirmed on the eve of the return to civilian rule, "during the nine years of the Gowon Regime, senior civil servants literally held sway over decision-making, and some of them could in fact over-rule their commissioners and get away with it."[74]

Following the overthrow of General Gowon, the Murtala/Obasanjo regime moved to check bureaucratic "excesses" and to narrow the scope of civil servants' authority in the policy-making realm. In addition to retiring the super permanent secretaries and other powerful senior public servants, General Murtala banned permanent secretaries from FEC meetings unless specifically invited to attend and participate. Nevertheless, policy formulation continued to occupy the attention of permanent secretaries under the new regime. General Obasanjo's 1977 affirmation that the "role of the civil servant is to initiate policies and to offer professional and technical advice to the government . . ." indicates that no fundamental changes had occurred in prevailing norms and expectations and suggests that the new military government merely sought a return to pre-1966 administrative practices.[75]

With the return to civilian rule in 1979, renewed efforts have been made to establish political control over the bureaucracy. The Second Republic Constitution, for instance, substantially undermines the formal standing of higher civil servants in both policy formulation and policy execution. Constitutional provisions that call for the appointment of special advisors to the President (and the Governors) and a secretary to the government (who is expected to serve as the overall political advisor to the chief executive) have added powerful non-career competitors with whom permanent secretaries and the head of service must vie when attempting to influence public policy making. Furthermore, permanent secretaries no longer serve as the administrative heads of their Ministries. Federal

Ministers and state Commissioners are to be delegated
this responsibility as the representatives of the chief
executive under articles 136 and 174 of the 1979 Constitution.

In light of these constitutional innovations,
along with those that make the post an explicitly political appointment, Bach envisions the permanent secretary acting in the role of Deputy Minister/Commissioner
under Nigeria's new political system.[76] The norm that
civil servants initiate policy alternatives and provide
programmatic and political advice is consonant with
the conception of permanent secretaries acting as
deputy ministers/commissioners, while the expectation
that civil servants dominate policy formulation clearly
is not. We have seen that both behavioral norms have
played an important part in Nigeria's experience with
public policy making. While present prescriptions
overwhelmingly favor adherence to norms that are consistent with a subordinate (but important) role for
permanent secretaries and other higher civil servants,
the weight of past behavioral conditioning leads one
to conclude that these career officials will not
readily disengage from their dominant place in the
policy-making arena. By 1980, numerous conflicts and
considerable confusion had already arisen over the
policy-formulating role of permanent secretaries at
the federal and state levels. On October 31, 1980,
President Shehu Shagari felt compelled to invite
federal permanent secretaries to the State House for
the second time, mainly to reemphasize the limitations
placed on the authority of civil servants under the
presidential system of government.[77]

It is in the area of policy execution, however,
that newly elected chief executives have expressed
greatest frustration with the bureaucratic apparata
they inherited. Many permanent secretaries have not
been willing to accept a subordinate position when it
comes to the administrative affairs of their ministry
and have resented and resisted ministerial interference
in the policy-implementation process. In his 1980
meeting with the permanent secretaries, President
Shagari directed his strongest criticism at federal
civil servants who "obstruct the smooth and speedy
implementation of the programmes of this administration. . . ." These officials, he warned, would be
"removed" from the service.[78] Such confrontations
and frustrations are likely to persist as Nigerian
chief executives struggle within the context of a

multi-party political system to establish political control over a large, powerful bureaucracy that has been accustomed to self-initiative and advocacy, and views itself as the guardian of professional and public interests.

The Nigerian Public Bureaucracy: Participant in National Development or Underdevelopment?

Although burned by their intimate association and identification with official levers of political power under the Gowon regime, shaken by the mass purge of 1975, and threatened by the loss of formal authority under provisions of the 1979 Constitution, civil servants have managed to preserve a prominent position in Nigerian society. Higher public servants, in particular, remain a politically powerful and economically privileged elite.[79] The most important and controversial issue concerns the bureaucracy's role commitments. Will civil servants utilize their elite social status and powerful policy-shaping position in the political system primarily to pursue the further aggrandizement of bureaucratic self-interests, or to promote the design and execution of effective public projects that enhance indigenous, sustained economic development and bring about substantial improvements in the living conditions encountered by the vast majority of the country's rural and urban populations?

Relative to many other countries, Nigeria is fortunate in that its recently discovered and exploited petroleum resources have provided at least a temporary opportunity to attain national development objectives and address the basic needs of its citizens. However, the performance record compiled to date by Nigerian bureaucrats offers little ground for future optimism. Most civil servants have principally devoted their ample social prestige and political power to reaping personal or corporate group benefits. Developmental leadership through example, sacrifice, and commitment to the primacy of long-term, mass interests has been the exception rather than the rule among the administrative and professional elite.[80]

The harshest critics contend that the Nigerian public bureaucracy acts as a "parasitic class," exploiting the wealth of the nation and the labor of its dispossessed masses in alliance with foreign capitalist interests. There is considerable evidence that supports these charges. To begin with, civil servants receive salaries far in excess of national per capita income. In 1980, the salary of the lowest level civil servant (GL 01) amounted to ₦ 1,200 per year, roughly 4 times higher than the nation's estimated per capita GDP.[81] Moreover, federal, state, and local governments have incurred escalating budgetary commitments for staff salaries and emoluments as a result of the enormous growth in the size of all public service ranks described earlier in this chapter. A major proportion of the new capital investment expenditures authorized in recent years at all levels of government has been devoted to the construction of staff housing and office buildings, and to the purchase of imported, labor-saving machinery and equipment used exclusively for administrative convenience.[82] The creation of additional states and units of local government has required massive outlays of public funds for the employment of locally based staff, the construction of new headquarters and staff residences, and the provision of basic infrastructural facilities and elite services.

While peasants, contract workers, and petty traders have been left to cope with the inflationary consequences of such oil-fueled public expenditures, high-level bureaucrats who have realized the largest salary gains also have been granted real income protection by the government through a host of generous, untaxed subsidization schemes. Government subsidies range from home leave allowances and free use of agency vehicles through transportation allowances, low-interest car loans, overseas educational leaves at full pay plus transportation, tuition expenses, and generous maintenance and shipping allowances, free health care and medical supplies, and the provision of low-rent, furnished government housing. Taken together, Ladun Anise estimates that government subsidies result in "real shadow wages" for the average high-level public servant that are "twice as high as the direct, taxable nominal wages quoted on the official payrolls."[83]

Nevertheless, the salaries and fringe benefits of public servants pale in significance by comparison with the more indirect opportunities for individual enrichment that government service provides given the nature of the Nigerian political economy. For many, the principal attraction attached to holding a strategic position in the public bureaucracy is "the opportunity which it may provide for income, experience, and contacts, which can be used contemporaneously and subse-

quently in independent economic activity."[84]   Private
firms, in turn, are heavily dependent upon government
contracts in an economy dominated by public sector
capital investments. Acting on the basis of mutual
self-interest, officials have forged relationships that
link the top levels of public organizations with private,
domestic and foreign enterprises. In exchange for the
award of a lucrative contract or some other form of
economic advantage dispensed by the state, public decision-makers at all levels of government have been rewarded handsomely by representatives of local and/or
foreign firms.

　　Furthermore, public servants have effectively
employed the power of the state to establish a strong
position for themselves in the private sector and
thereby consolidate their central strategic location
within the domestic "organizational burgeoisie." One
of the most expedient avenues for accomplishing this
has been through the promulgation and implementation
of government decrees promoting the indigenization of
enterprises operating in Nigeria. The Nigerian Enterprises Promotion ('Indigenisation') Decree (NEPD) of
1972 mandated that "by March 1974, a range of economic
activities, then dominated to varying degrees by non-
nationals, should be partly or wholly owned by indigenes."
NEPD essentially excluded aliens from the ownership of
small-scale domestic business operations and required
40 per cent Nigerian participation in the 36 types of
large-scale manufacturing, service, processing, and
commercial industries listed in its second schedule.
In furtherance of NEPD objectives, the federal government acquired a 40 percent share in the foreign-owned
commercial banks and mandated that at least 40 percent
of their total loans be allotted to indigenous borrowers.
Civil servants ranked among the main beneficiaries of
subsequent increases in the volume of bank lending to
Nigerians. Recipients used their newly acquired capital to purchase shares in Schedule II firms at highly
favorable prices. Through privileged access to information as well as credit, public officials secured a
place at the "core of the Nigerian emergent share-
owning class."[85]

　　Civil servants have also manipulated state land
allocation policies and procedures in ways that have
further entrenched their elite economic standing and
expanded their profit-making opportunities. Access to
credit and fellow decision-makers has enabled many
public servants to acquire valuable real estate holdings,

particularly highly desirable residential[86] and commercial/industrial plots in major urban centers. They have effectively utilized inside information and the ability to satisfy requirements that allocated land be "developed" (i.e., built upon) within a short period of time to accumulate urban land use[87] rights for residential, rental, and business purposes. Following the July 1975 coup, for instance, the press published lists revealing the extensive acquisition of land in the Lagos area by top civil servants and other politically influential individuals. In spite of such revelations and promulgation of a new Land Use Decree in 1978, public servants remained one of the main beneficiaries of state government land allocation policies and practices during the Murtala/Obasanjo regime.

Conclusion

Political developments in Nigeria have sustained relentless growth in the size of the public bureaucracy, extended the scope of its authority in the public policy making arena, and expanded the privileged economic opportunities available to its members. Increases in bureaucratic power and rewards have not been accompanied, however, by noticeable improvements in the performance of public servants or gains in public sector productivity. Moreover, preoccupation with accumulating personal wealth and status has led many civil servants to engage in behavior that at best neglects, and at worst promotes exploitation of the vast majority of Nigeria's rural and urban populace.

In light of the entrenchment of the public bureaucracy and the inclination of members to enhance and protect their vested interests, civil servants will not easily be transformed from an essentially "parasitic class" into a committed, effective force for social change and sustained, mass-based economic development. In the long term, deeper politicization and tighter control of the bureaucracy by popularly elected civilian leaders offers a more viable and promising prospect for effecting such transformation of the Nigerian public services than re-education or other measures that hinge on bureaucratic initiative and voluntary compliance.[88]

Footnotes

[1]See Simeon Adebo, "Personal Profile," Quarterly Journal of Administration," (April-July 1979), p. 197; also Jerome Udoji, "Personal Profile," p. 201, and Adamu Liman Ciroma, "Personal Profile, " p. 209, in the same issue; Humphrey N. Nwosu, Political Authority and the Nigerian Civil Service, Enugu: Fourth Dimension Publishers, 1977, pp. 51, 58-59.

[2]Philip Asiodu contrasts the separate civil service of Nigeria with the unified Indian model. See his, "The Future of the Federal and State Civil Services in the Context of the Twelve States Structure," in Mahamud Tukur, ed., Administratvie and Political Development: Prospects for Nigeria, Zaria: Insitute of Administration, Ahamdu Bello University, 1970, pp. 130-133, 145.

[3]Lapido Adamolekun, "High Level Minsiterial Organization in Nigeria and the Ivory Coast," in D.J. Murray, ed., Studies in Nigerian Administration, 2nd ed., London: Hutchinson & Co., Ltd., 1978, p. 12.

[4]J. Donald Kingsley, "Bureaucracy and Political Development, with Particular Reference to Nigeria," in Jospeh LaPalambora, ed., Bureaucracy and Political Development, Princeton, NJ: Princeton University Press, 1963, p. 312; Murray, "Nigerian Field Administration: A Comparative Analysis," in Murray, op. cit., p. 105.

[5]Adamolekun, op. cit., pp. 12-14. Nevertheless, former departments (renamed as divisions) continued to act in a relatively autonomous fashion within certain Ministries. See Taylor Cole, "Bureaucracy in Transition: Independent Nigeria," Public Administration XXXVIII (Winter 1960), p. 330. The entrenchment of the Ministerial System following independence at the federal and regional levels also had the general effect (with important regional variations) of promoting administrative centralization and enhancing the status and authority of headquarters' position vis-a-vis field personnel. See Murray, op. cit., pp. 104-139.

[6]Under new regulations issued by President Shehu Shagari in 1980, the Federal Civil Service Commission has delegated full appointment power up to GL 07 to

permanent secretaries and heads of extra-Ministerial departments. New federal policies also authorize officials at GL 08 and 09 and to employ certain specialist professional staff up to GL 11. See _New Nigerian_ , October 28, 1980, p. 1.

[7]Adamolekun, _op_. _cit_., pp. 17-20.

[8]In the first decade following independence, only six professional officers served as federal permanent secretaries in three Ministries. Adamolekun, _op_. _cit_., p. 19; Nwosu, _op_. _cit_., p. 79.

[9]Adamolekun, _op_. _cit_., pp. 19-21; Allison A. Ayida, "The Federal Civil Service and Nation Building," _Quarterly Journal of Administration_ (April-July 1979), p. 223; T. M. Aluko, "Administration in our Public Services: A Profesional Officer Speaks up on Bureaucracy," in Adebayo Adedeji, ed., _Nigerian Administration and Its political Setting_, London: Hutchinson Educational, 1968, pp. 70, 77.

[10]Frederick J. Fletcher, "The Executive Class in Nigeria: Introduction, Problems, Prospects," in Murray, ed., _op_. _cit_., pp. 143-145; Asiodu, _op_. _cit_., p. 135

[11]Fletcher, _op.cit_., pp. 146-154.

[12]Ranks within the Executive Class are arranged in the following descending order: Principal Executive Officer (PEO), Senior Executive Officer (SEO), Higher Executive Officer (HEO), Executive Officer (EO), and Assistant Executive Officer (AEO).

[13]In 1970, a 17 to 1 disparity existed between the highest and the lowest salary levels. See Asiodu, _op_. _cit_., p. 144. Executive Officers generally have not qualified for major benefits such as car allowance and loans and the subsidized housing enjoyed by the administrative elite since the colonial period. Fletcher, _op_. _cit_., p. 171. In 1980, however, the new government reversed this exclusive policy by providing all workers with a monthly transportation allowance, regardless of whether they commute by car, bike or foot, and by entitling all civil servants to a housing allowance. _New Nigerian_, November 27, 1980, p. 1.

[14]Added to this are "the tensions between age groupings based on the realtively rapid promotion achieved
by the most senior administrative class officials during
the period when the service was being built up and
administration expanded, and in contrast to this, the
poor promotion prospects, at least in relation to expepe-
ctations of most junior administrative class officials."
Murray, "The Impact of Politics on Administration," in
Adedeji, op. cit., pp. 21-22. On the relatively young
age and hasty preparation of newly appointed administrative officers in 1961, see Kingsley, op. cit., pp. 311-
315.

[15]By the late 1970's, this situation had changed
somewhat with the introduction of national training
courses specifically designed to facilitate the movement of executive grade officers into the ranks of the
administrative class.

[16]Cole places the total employment figure (including local government staff and all daily laborers) at
the higher figure of 302,000; op. cit., p. 323.

[17]The creation of additional units of local government at the time of the 1976 local government reform
had the same effect on the third tier of Nigeria's political system. See A.Y. Aliyu and Koehn, Local Autonomy
and Intergovernmental Relations in Nigeria: The Case
of the Northern States in the Immediate Post Local Government Reform Period, Zaria: Institute of Administration,
Ahamadu Bello University, forthcoming.

[18]Fletcher, op. cit., pp. 143-144.

[19]According to Kingsley, district officer position
usually was the first to Nigerianize. During this period, the Public Service Commission allowed a number of
candidates without university degrees entry into the
administrative cadre. See Omorogbe Nwanwene, "The Nigerian Public Service Commissions," in Murray, ed., op.
cit., p. 201.

[20]Kingsley, op. cit., pp. 310-311; Nwanwene, op.
cit., pp. 200-201.

[21]Cited in Cole, op. cit., p. 334. Also see, J.

Isawa Elaigwu, "Federal-State Relations in Nigeria's New Federalism: A Review of the Draft Constitution," in S. Kumo and A.Y. Aliyu, eds., Issues in the Nigerian Draft Constitution, Zaria: Institute of Administration, Ahmadu Bello University, 1977, p. 147.

[22]Cole, op. cit., p. 334.

[23]Nwanwene, op. cit., pp. 200-201, and Nwosu, op. cit., p. 52.

[24]However, the compulsory National Youth Service Corps (NYSC) scheme, which deploys the vast majority of graduates from the universities and other institutions of higher learning to states other than their own, has fostered a somewhat greater willingness on the part of state governments to employ non-indegene graduates, and of the latter to accept such offers since 1973. See Folayan Ojo, "Youth Employment and the Impact of National Youth Servcie Corps on Labor Mobility in Nigeria," African Studies Review XXIII (Setpmber 1980), pp. 51-62.

[25]Robert M. Price, Society and Bureaucracy in Modern Ghana, Berkeley: University of California Press, 1975, p. 216.

[26]Kingsley, op. cit., p. 316; Ojo, op. cit., pp. 55, 61; Nwosu, op. cit., pp. 55, 79, 121; Asiodu, op. cit., pp. 129, 132-133.

[27]See Patrick Keinecke, "A Dependent Civil Service in an 'Independent' Country," paper presented at the Faculty of Administration Seminar, Ahamdu Bello University, November 13, 1979, pp. 9-10.

[28]A 1977 government study of Nigeria's manpower requirements placed the level of staff vacancies for most higher level scientific and technical posts at 40 and 55 per cent, and reported a 15-30% vacancy rate in administrative and other non-technical posts. Cited in West Africa, March 16, 1978, p. 543.

[29]Adamolekun, op. cit., p. 40. Also Bayo Kehinde, "The Politics and Administration of Public Corporations in Nigeria," in Adedeji, ed., op. cit., pp. 95-99.

[30]Cited in Cole, op. cit., p. 335.

[31]Asiodu, op. cit., p. 136. Nevertheless, in 1965 the universities and certain federal Ministries and public corporations were perceived "to be the preserve of one or another of the regional groups represented in the federal government." See Richard L. Harris, "The Role of Higher Public Servants in Nigeria: As Perceived by the Western-educated Elite," in Murray, ed., op. cit., p. 302. Moreover, "..it is not uncommon to find in a typical Ministry or department many low skilled staff such as messengers, drivers, cleaners, clerical assistants belonging to the same ethnic groups with the top superior officers of the organization." See Nwosu, op. cit., p. 79

[32]Adedeji, "The Evolution, Organization, and Structure of the Nigerian Civil Services," in Adedeji, ed., op. cit., pp. 9-10; Jospeh N. Garba, "The Military Regime and the Nigerian Society," New Nigerian, September 28, 1979, p. 1.

[33]John Ostheimer, Nigerian Politics, New York: Harper & Row, 1973, pp. 60-63; Edward Feit, "Military Coups and Political Development: Some Lessons From Ghana and Nigeria," World Politics XX (January 1968), pp. 190-191.

[34]See Koehn, "Prelude to Civilian Rule: The Nigerian Elections of 1979," Africa Today XXVIII (June 1981), pp. 18-23; Gavin Williams and Terisa Turner, "Nigeria," in John Dunn, ed., West African States: Failure and Promise, Cambridge, Mass.: Cambridge University Press, 1978, pp. 144-145.

[35]Federal civil servants, particularly key permanent secretaries, also have been credited with intervening to preserve and extend the authority of the federal government vis-a-vis the regions/states. See Robin Luckham, The Nigerian Military: A Sociological Analysis of Authority & Revolt, 1960-67, Cambridge, Mass.: Cambridge University Press, 1971, p. 132. Mahmud Tukur, "Implications of the Development Administration Model for the Practitioner," Nigerian Journal of Public Affairs 1 (October 1970), p. 21. Williams, "Nigeria: A Political Economy," in Williams, ed., Nigeria: Economy and Society, London: Rex Collings, 1976, p. 44; Aliyu, "The Executive Presidential System: A Political Imperative for Future Nigeria," in Kumo and Aliyu, eds., op. cit., pp. 266-267.

[36]According to Williams and Turner, "a unitary state had been set up in federal disguise. But it leaves local institutions, patronage and appointments in state hands, and ensures protection at the federal level for the interests of the far north." See Williams and Turner, op. cit., p. 168

[37]Elaigwu, "Federal-State Relations in Nigeria's New Federalism: A Review of the Draft Constitution," op. cit., pp.152-155; C. Achimu, "The Draft Constitution: The Division of Legislative Powers," p.170; P.C.A. Daudu, "Nigerian Draft Constitution: Anaysis of Powers in Relation to the Financial Provisions," pp. 136-141--all in Kumo and Aliyu, eds. op. cit.

[38]Including "any matter incidental or supplemental to any matter mentioned" on the list. Item 66, Second Schedule.

[39]Second Schedule, Parts I and II.

[40]Article 14 (sections 3 and 4); also, Articles 135 (3), 157 (5), 173 (2) and 188 (4).

[41]See Aliyu, Koehn and R.A. Hay, "The Involvement of Local Government in Social, Political, and Economic Development in the Northern States: 1976-79." Paper presented at the National Seminar on the Role of Local Government in Social, Political and Economic Development held at the Institute of Administration, Ahmadu Bello University, April 28-30, 1980, pp. 7-33.

[42]Under General Gowon, state military Governors (most of whom were relatively junior officers) formed a majority of the SMCs membership. They were relegated to representation on the advisory NCS after General Murtala Mohammad assumed power. M.J. Dent, "Corrective Government: Military Rule in Perspective," in Keith Panter-Brick, ed., Soldiers and Oil: The Political Transformation of Nigeria, London: Frank Cass, 1978, pp. 112-115.

[43]Adamolekun, "Postscript: Notes on Developments in Nigerian Administration since 1970," in Murray, ed., op. cit., p. 312.

[44]On the other hand, "military regimes put heavy burdens on civilian administrators. The military devolves on civil servants many tasks and decisions that it itself does not want to take." See, Henry Bienen and Martin Fitton, "Soldiers, Politicians, and Civil Servants," in Panter-Brick, ed., op. cit., p. 29

[45]Ian Campbell, "Army Reorganization and Military Withdrawl," in Panter-Brick, ed., op. cit., pp. 69-76; Paul Collins, Terisa Turner and Gavin Williams, "Capitalism and the Coup," in Williams, ed., Nigeria: Economy and Society, op. cit., pp. 185-186; T.A.Akinyele, "On Being a Higher Civil Servant," Quarterly Journal of Administration (April-July 1979), p. 237.

[46]Ten of these Governors were subsequently "found guilty of corrupt or improper conduct and dismissed from the forces..." Campbell, op. cit., pp. 69-70.

[47]For example, Dent, op. cit., pp. 115-116, 119-124.

[48]Ibid, p. 123, and Campbell, op. cit., p. 81.

[49]Adamolekun, "Postscript: Notes on Developments in Nigerian Administration Since 1970," op. cit., pp. 325-326. This outcome is consistent with Price's analysis regarding the institutionalization of the status but not the role aspects associated with organizational position in Ghana and other African countries. The Nigerian military neither introduced a disciplinary scheme systematically related to personnel behavior and performance nor replaces dismissed civil servants with a new insitutional core of development administrators who are cut off from traditional forms of social organization and thereby released from socio-cultural (corporate) constraints on bureaucratic role performance. See Fidelis Okoli, "The Dilemma of Premature Bureaucratization in the New States of Africa: The Case of Nigeria," African Studies Review XXIII (September 1980), p. 12.

[50]Allison A. Ayida, "The Federal Civil Service and Nation Building," Quarterly Journal of Administration (April-July 1979), p. 224.

[51]Cited in Campbell, op. cit., pp. 81-82; also Dent, op. cit., p. 120.

[52]Editorial, New Nigerian, February 4, 1980, p. 1.

[53]Adedeji, "Restoring Civil Service Morale," West Africa 3324 (April 13, 1981), p. 805; A.L. Ciroma, "The Civil Service Today," New Nigerian, May 9, 10, 12, 1980; Adamolekun, "Introduction: A Tentative Profile of the Higher Civil Servants," Quarterly Journal of Administration (April-July 1979), p. 194.

[54]The role of special advisors, the nature of the presidential system of government and constitutional prohibitions (Articles 135, 173) against currently holding the office of Minister/Commissioner and member of legislative bodies, all constitute further moves away from the British inspired doctrine of collective Ministerial responsibility, which had never been strictly adhered to in Nigeria. See Adamolekun, "Postscript...," op. cit., p. 327.

[55]Fidelis Okoli, "Relationships Between the Secretary to the Government and the Head of the Civil Service Under the 1979 Nigerian Constitution," Nigerian Journal of Public Affairs VIII (1978-79), pp. 10-12.

[56]Augustus Adebayo notes that "some State Government-ments, during 1966-75 had as many as seven permanent secretaries concentrated in the office of the Military Governor,...responsible to the Governor for almost the entire range of governmental activities--economic, administrative, political, commerical and industrial." See his, "Policymaking in Nigerian Public Administration, 1960-1975," Journal of Administration Overseas XVIII (January 1979), p. 10.

[57]For example, Daniel C. Bach, "The Role of Permanent Secretary in Nigeria's New Executive Presidential System." Paper presented at the Imo State top management seminar held at Oguta, January 21-24, 1980.

[58]These appointments do not require legislative consent. The only constitutional restraint placed on the exercise of the president's power of appointment with respect to those offices is the requirement to "have regard to the federal character of Nigeria and the need to promote national unity." Governors must "have regard to the diversity of the people within the

State and the need to promote national unity." Articles 157, 188.

[59]Bach, op. cit., pp. 2-3; Ciroma, op. cit., p. 5.

[60]Ray Ofoegbu, "The Chief Executive in a Presidential System." Paper presented at the Imo State seminar, op. cit.

[61]In practice of course, the Nigerian public services (and public service commissions) have never been totally apolitical and neutral. See Nwanwene, op. cit., p. 207. All public servants are however, barred by Articles 62 (f), 101 (f) and 4 of the Constitution from running for elective office at the federal, state and local levels. See Adesola Adeogun, "Contractors in Local Government Elections," Nigerian Public Affaris IX (May 1980), p. 124. In addition, the Civil Service Rules still prohibit supporting or opposing a party or its programs and campaigning for candidates for elecetive offices.

[62]Akinyele, op. cit., p. 239.

[63]Permanent secretaries have not been permanently assigned to a particular federal or state ministry since independence. The relatively rapid turnover of generalist permanent secretaries has been a distinctive feature of the Nigerian ministerial system, although the common practice had been for a small group of individuals to rotate from Ministry to Ministry or in and out of cabinet offices. Adamolekun, in Murray, ed., op. cit., p. 21. One result has been the frequent appointment of high-level generalist administrators who possess no expertise in and may not even be conversant with the primary subject matter jurisdiction of their Ministries. See Udoji, op. cit., pp. 207-208.

[64]New Nigerian, February 25, 1980, p. 24. This practice is common in France.

[65]Integrated project management along the lines advocated by the Udoji Commission has not become a characteristic feature of Nigerian public administration, although agricultural development projects sponsored by the World Bank have adopted similar principles.

Major problems have been encountered on these projects which can be attributed to the integrated management approach. These include insulation from popular local participation in planning and implementation, lack of coordination with established Ministries, and failure to improve the institutional capacity of existing, permanent administrative structure. See Tina Wallace, "'Agricultural Bonanza?' Some Crucial Issues Raised by the World Bank Agricultural Development Projects in Nigeria," Nigerian Journal of Public Affairs IX (May 1980), p. 67.

[66]Ayida, op. cit., p. 223.

[67]Ibid, pp. 222, 226-227; also Adamolekun, "Postscript..." in Murray, ed., op. cit., p. 234.

[68]See Collins, Turner, Williams, op. cit., pp. 186-187, 191-192; Paul Collins, "Pubilc Policy and the Development of Indigenous Capitalism: The Nigerian Experience," Journal of Commonwealth & Comparative Politics (July 1977), pp. 134-146.

[69]Ayida, "Federal Civil Service and Nation Building," op. cit., p. 219; S.O. Asabia, "The Role of the Administrator in the Nigerian Public Services," in Adedeji, ed., Nigerian Administration and Its Political Setting, London: Hutchinson Educational, 1968, pp. 114-115.

[70]Michael F. Lochie, "Representative Government, Bureaucracy and Political Development: The African Case," Journal of Developing Areas II (October 1967), p. 48.

[71]Aliyu, "The Role of the Chief Executive, Bureaucracy, and Assembly in Public Policy Formulation and Execution Under the New Nigerian Constitution." Paper presented at the Seminar for Commissioners and Top Civil Servants in Niger State held in Minna, November 19-23, 1979, p. 8.

[72]Adebayo, op. cit., pp. 5-9.

[73]Luckham, op. cit., pp. 203-24 and 255.

[74]Jospeh N. Garba, "The Military Regime and the Nigerian Society," New Nigerian, September 28, 1979, p.I; See also Yusuf Gobir, "Discussant's Comments," in Tukur, ed., op. cit., p. 161. As an indication of the extent of their power, the military Governors reportedly would travel to the Lagos residences of federal permanent secretaries in order to lobby for their support on matters "that might in due course come before the Supreme Military Council, the Federal Executive Council or even directly before the Head of State." Adebayo, op. cit., p. 14.

[75]See Adamolekun, "Postscript...," in Murray, ed., op. cit., p. 314.
Further evidence that adminstrators continued to determine public policies throughout the military rule has been produced by investigation of council-staff relations at the local level. In spite of the legal prescriptions to the contrary embodied in 1976 local government reform edicts, many secretaries continued to view their roles in familiar terms of Resident or Divisional Officer and therefore, endeavoured to dominate the policymaking process. At the same time, many councillors remained satisfied to ratify measures initiated by the secretary and/or department heads. See Aliyu and Koehn, "Local Autonomy," op. cit.; Elaigwu, "The Politics of Participation and Control: State-Local Government Relations Under Local Government Reforms in Nigeria." Paper presented at the National Conference on Local Government Reforms held at the Institute of Administration, Ahmadu Bello University, 1974.

[76]Bach, op. cit., p. 3.

[77]New Nigerian, November 1, 1980, p. 1.

[78]Ibid.

[79]Ayida, "Federal Civil Service and Nation Building," op. cit., p. 221.

[80]See for example, Segun Osoba, "The Deepening Crisis of the Nigerian National Bourgeoisie," Review

of African Political Economy 13 (May-August 1979), p. 67.

[81]Political power rather than collective bargaining had provided the major vehicle for the attainment of monetary rewards by public servants. "...Periodic wage increases have been the result of government awards, usually following commission enquiry...set up ...in response to general and specific strikes, or to the threat of these, and to...electoral calculations ..." Williams and Turner, op. cit., pp. 148, 161-162.

[82]Bill Freund, "Oil Boom and Crisis in Contemporary Nigeria,"Review of African Political Economy 13 (May-August 1979), pp. 93-94; Aliyu, "The Involvement of Local Government in the Administration of Social Services," Nigerian Journal of Public Affairs IX (May 1980), pp. 87-89; Koehn, "The Involvement of Local Government in Nigeria's National Development Planning for the 1980's: A Comparative Analysis of Bauchi and Kaduna Capitol Project Proposals." Paper presented at the Department of Research, Management, and Consultance seminar, Institute of Administration, Ahmadu Bello University, Zaria, June 5, 1980, pp. 24-38, 51-57.

[83]Ladun Anise, "Desubsidization: An Alternative Approach to Governmental Cost Containment and Income Redistribution Policy in Nigeria," African Studies Review XXIII (September 1980), pp. 29-33; also Williams and Turner, op. cit., p. 164.

[84]Williams, op. cit., p. 37; also, Heinecke, op. cit., pp. 2-3.

[85]Decree No. 3 of 1977 extended the scope of Schedule II and increased the idigenous equity participation requirements to 60% effective December 31, 1978. See Collins, op. cit., pp. 128-133, 145, in passim.

[86]The expropriation and acquisition of large tracts of rural land for commercial agriculture and staff housing certainly has not been ignored by state officials. See Tina Wallace, "Agricultural Projects and Land." A paper presented at the seminar on Change in Rural Hausland held at Bagauda Lake, February 29, 1980; also,

<u>New Nigerian</u>, June 12, 1980, p. 9.

[87]See A. T. Ojo, "Financing Urban Housing in Nigeria," in <u>Urbanization and Nigerian Economic Development</u>, Ibadan: Department of Economics, University of Ibadan, 1977, pp. 269, 271-274; also, Alan I. Frishman, "The Spatial Growth and Residential Location Pattern of Kano, Nigeria," (unpublished Ph. D. dissertation, Northwestern University, 1977), pp. 295-398.

[88]See Osoba, <u>op</u>. <u>cit</u>., pp. 71-72. In contrast, Abdulkadir and M.T.A. Liman advocate "extensive training and retraining...for all categories of public servants to help in development of new philohophy for the civil service..." See their, "The Judiciary, Civil Service, Police and Armed Forces," in Kumo and Aliyu, eds., <u>Issues in the Nigerian Draft Constitution</u>, Zaria, Ahmadu Bello University, 1977, pp. 231-232.

CHAPTER X

CONTROLLING BUREAUCRACY IN COMMUNIST CHINA

(1949-1980)

Anne Freedman
&
Maria Chan Morgan

Probably no leader of recent times has been more aware of the pit-falls of bureaucracy than Mao Zedong. By the mid-1960's Mao had become convinced that the bureaucrats of New China, like those of the Old, were sabotaging the government's policies. In a speech on the "Twenty Manifestations of Bureaucracy" he complained that the bureaucrats "are divorced from reality, from the masses, and from the leadership of the party; they always issue orders and the orders are usually wrong; they certainly mislead the country and the people; at the least they could obstruct the consistent adherence to the party line and policies."[1]

Mao believed that the bureaucrats had lost their "revolutionary will" and were promoting "erroneous tendencies and a spirit of reaction". Instead of serving the people and putting the public interest first, they worried only about themselves and their families and friends. As he saw it, "the greater an official becomes, the worse his temperament gets; his demands for supporting himself become higher and higher; his home and its furnishings become more and more luxurious; and his access to things becomes better and better. The upper strata gets the larger share while the lower gets high prices; there is extravagance and waste . . .they employ personal friends; they engage in factionalism; they maintain feudal relationships; they form cliques to further their own private interests; they protect each other. . . ."[2]

The Chairman was also greatly disturbed by the increasing bureaucratization he saw in China. "Government offices," he wrote, "grow bigger and bigger; things are more confused; there are more people than there are jobs; they go around in circles; they quarrel and bicker; people are disinclined to do extra things; they do not fulfill their specific duties. . . . Documents are numerous; there is red-tape; instructions proliferate; there are numerous unread reports that are not used; meetings are numerous and nothing is passed on. . . ."[3]

While Mao's hostility towards the bureaucracy came to a head in the early 1960's, he had always been profoundly suspicious of bureaucrats and bureaucratic organizations. The Chinese had had more than two thousand years of experience with bureaucracy and Mao was well aware of the many ways in which fearful, passive, "do-nothing" officials had undermined the efforts of the central governments of the past. He was also familiar with the nepotism, corruption and factionalism that had plagued the bureaucracy and of the arrogance of the elitist scholar-bureaucrats in their relations with the people.[4]

As a revolutionary, Mao had long been committed to destroying the traditional social and political hierarchy and replacing it with an egalitarian socialist system. Mao wanted to erase elitism and he no doubt would have been the happiest if he could have governed without any officials. There were periods during the Cultural Revolution when he appeared to veer toward anarchism and the elimination of all bureaucracy, and favored a Paris Commune type of organization in which officials were popularly elected and could be recalled at any time, and were paid wages similar to those of ordinary workers. But like Lenin before him, who also lauded the Paris Commune but created an elitist bureaucracy in practice in order to cope with the administration of a revolution, Mao was basically a realist. He recognized that some bureaucracy was necessary even though evil. Mao's task too was to create an organizational structure which would serve the cause of his Revolution. To him, this meant a bureaucracy which would obey the commands of the center and carry out the main lines of its policy, but would do so with creativity and imagination, adapting to local conditions as needed. This bureaucracy would give its primary loyalty to the Party and to the principles of Maoist collectivism rather than to kin, locality, or faction. The bureaucrats would have to identify with the masses of peasants and workers, avoiding arrogance and "commandism". The bureaucrats were to be satisfied with relatively small material rewards; their life style was to be that of the masses and they were not to look down on those who had to labor with their hands. Whenever possible, the bureaucrats were to mingle with the masses and to do physical labor. Above all they were to

230

encourage the active participation of the masses.

Although Mao recognized that bureaucrats might need some expertise, he did not want to create a corps of experts who would think they were superior to the masses. If anyone was to be considered superior in Maoist China, it was to be the workers and peasants with their practical everyday understanding of real problems.

In Mao's view an official or cadre could only be acceptable if he were both Red and Expert. As a good Red (or Communist), he must look "upon the interests of the revolution as his very life" and subordinate his personal interests to those of the Revolution. He must "be more concerned about the Party and the masses than about himself."[5]

Mao's conception of the ideal cadre grew out of his long years of experience as the military commander of guerilla forces. Cadres were to lead by personal example and by arousing the masses and personally directing them in the way that a combat leader directs his troops in battle. Unfortunately Mao did not adequately consider that this style of leadership was not as well suited to governing a large area through an organizational structure. There is a basic contradiction between a personal guerilla style mobilizing leadership and the exercise of leadership through an organizational office.[6]

This contradiction between organizational dictates and Mao's preferred Red leadership style became evident long before the final Communist victory in 1949. From the late 1920's on, the Communists had control of large territories and had to devise ways of governing them. It quickly became apparent that it was going to be very difficult to create a truly Red bureaucracy. Mao and his colleagues did a good deal of experimenting and by the time the People's Republic of China was established, a range of mechanisms had been developed to maintain control of the bureaucracy. They included: positioning party units parallel to the larger government establishment to watch over, direct and control the government administrators; a series of "hearts and minds" programs to create and maintain good Red attitudes in cadres and in the masses; the encouragement of mass participation (under Party control) to act as a check on officials; and a variety of techniques similar to those used in traditional China and other nations such as rotation of bureaucrats in offices, assigning officials to posts far from their native places, internal investigation, annual reviews of performance, and the use of rewards for good work. The Party also employed periodic purges of the leadership ranks in which some cadres might be demoted, dismissed or shifted around (but not physically liquidated) and administrative reorganization to reduce the number of employees and to simplify and decentralize the organizational structure.

Party Control of the Bureaucracy

The Communist Party of China is an elite organization. In theory the Party's members should be the most trustworthy and dedicated of Reds. Mao's first line of defense against bureaucracy was therefore to establish a system of dual rule in which the Party bureaucracy is used to control the state-government bureaucracy. Two parallel hierarchies - of state units and party units - were created, with the smaller, more selective party units being assigned the task of watching over the government units. Party members also serve within the government units to further tighten party control over the state organization (which contains cadres who do not belong to the party as well as those who do).

Since the Party in a Communist state supposedly speaks for the People, it constitutes the ultimate authority and is the sole policy-maker. The state bureaucracy is only supposed to carry out policy. In China to insure that the state performs its role properly, orders flow from the top where party and state elites merge, down through the ranks of administrators. Technically, basic policy is made in the Standing Committee of the party Politburo and transmitted horizontally from the Politburo to the State Council at the apex of the state structure. The State Council then communicates the policy directives of the party to the state's functional Ministries in charge of such areas as education, agriculture, and industry. However, at the top of the two hierarchies of state and party there is a complete overlap of personnel. All of the members of the State Council are also high level party members; at the top levels the leaders are responsible both for making policy and carrying it out. Only at the lower levels are there two somewhat separated hierarchies.

The larger state unit carries out policy while the party members within the Ministries are supposed to watch over their operations and personnel. For example, the party always monopolizes the posts in the government's watchdog units such as those responsible for internal investigation and for supervising personnel. Party members also occupy all of the most important leadership posts in each government agency and they are expected to give priority to party instructions. Moreover, within each government agency the party members are organized into party units. A party fraction composed of the top party members within the agency generally acts as the ultimate decision-making body for the agency.[8]

This complex structure was initially necessary in 1949 because there were not enough party members to staff the government. Although there are more party members today, the elite character of the Leninist party means that their number is still relatively small. Moreover, it is still necessary to employ the services of experts of various kinds whose complete devotion to Red principles may be suspect.

Unquestionably, these measures have resulted in party dominance of the government bureaucracy at all levels of the hierarchy.[9] However, this did not solve the problem of bureaucracy for Mao. The party itself had become a bureaucratic organization which had to be harnessed to Maoist principles. For this Mao relied primarily on the operation of the "mass line" and on programs for ideological control.

Controlling Hearts and Minds

Party members were entrusted with the job of watching over the state bureaucracy because party members were assumed to be more Red, more committed to the Revolution and the People. Supposedly only those who had proven themselves to be devoted to the cause by years of activism were admitted to the party ranks. Still, Mao never took for granted anyone's Redness. An outstanding feature of the Chinese Communist movement from its earliest days was an emphasis on study or indoctrination. Even in the midst of war, the Red Army had a program of political lectures and study. Later, this was formalized in the small study groups which were organized for nearly all the citizens of the People's Republic. In a government Ministry, for example, every bureaucrat would be assigned to a study group of ten to twenty persons. Normally, the group would meet for a half-day or evening once a week to read and discuss theoretical Marxist-Leninist writings (with special emphasis of course on Mao Zedong Thought) and special study materials and newspaper articles dealing with current party policy.

The groups are not simply an academic exercise. Each member is required to engage in criticism and self-criticism in which the individual is supposed to throughly review his own behavior and thoughts and to publicly criticize those who do not live up to the standards of Redness. This confession is also criticized and analyzed by the other members of the group with the session usually ending in the individual vowing to improve. In this fashion the study groups function to communicate the party line and inculcate party principles and to control the members' behavior by exposing it to constant public scrutiny.

While study group criticism sessions can be quite intense, over time they tend to become routinized. Many members would simply become bored with reviewing the same texts over and over. They would also try to reduce the stressful aspects of the meeting by performing criticism and self-criticism in a perfunctory fashion.10

Because study appeared to lose some of its effectiveness, Mao experimented with a number of additional techniques of indoctrination and control. Periodically, campaigns would be launched. A Chinese campaign resembles a military operation. All resources are mobilized in a single cause. Study sessions are increased in number and intensity; the mass media and other communication channels such as the loudspeaker network keep up a constant stream of exhortation and propaganda. Walls are festooned with political posters. Everyone takes time off from his normal duties to draw cartoons and write essays. In a health campaign individuals might also be given quotas - so many people to be vaccinated, for example.

There are all kinds of campaigns in China. To the bureaucrat, undoubtedly the most threatening are the rectification campaigns aimed at examining and purifying thoughts of subversive feudal or bourgeois influences. In the Thought Reform campaign of 1951-52, which was aimed at all educated people, many bureaucrats had to leave their posts completely to spend six months or more in a "revolutionary college". There they were subjected to a constant diet of study and criticism culminating in the writing of a complete autobiographical confession. This is the process that has been labelled "brainwashing" in the West.[11]

During an ordinary rectification campaign normal work would virtually come to a halt in a government bureaucracy as

> special campaign indoctrination meetings slowly increased in duration until they occupied perhaps half the working day, and later the whole of it, for perhaps a month or two. As a campaign progressed, emphasis shifted from fairly generalized propaganda and indoctrination to increasingly emotional meetings in which everyone had to engage in criticism and self-criticism. Finally a climax was reached when a number of specific cadres were singled out and made the targets of mass public denunciations within the ministry in huge "struggle meetings." In major political campaigns there had to be specific human targets to "struggle" against; errors and evils, as well as virtues, had to be personified.[12]

Short of imprisonment and execution, being struggled is probably the worst thing that can happen to a Chinese. On the basis of his interviews with ex-cadres in Hong Kong, A. Doak Barnett notes that a struggle meeting is psychologically unnerving for the observers as well as the victims. Such meetings

> are carefully planned and directed by Party personnel, and the hapless victims are pilloried with torrents of abuse in a succession of public meetings that may last several days. The victims must stand with bowed heads while accusations are shouted at them and. . . they cannot speak in self defense except when specifically instructed to do so by the Party leaders directing the meetings. The charges made in these accusation meetings generally include ones to which large numbers of cadres in the audiences may feel vulnerable - e.g. charges of having a politically-tainted past or of holding wrong general attitudes - and consequently it is fairly easy for many

cadres to identify themselves secretly with
the victims. Those who do so identify often
feel themselves under the greatest compulsion
to join publicly in the denunciations, fearing
that failure to do so might suggest that they
secretly sympathize with the person under
attack.[13]

Even when the pressure is relaxed and the campaign ended, cadres find it impossible to erase their memories
of the experience. They are strongly motivated to behave so as to avoid being a future struggle victim.
The campaign thus does have the effect of increasing
the cadres' responsiveness to the party. Out of fear,
bureaucrats avoid questioning the party or giving any
outward signs of dissent. However, out of the same
fear, they tend to avoid independent action and come
to strongly resemble the "do-nothing" dynastic officials.

Mao was never satisfied with the results of the
campaigns and tried other tactics. In the late 1950's
the xia-fang system of "sending down" intellectuals
and bureaucrats was begun.[14] Some bureaucrats were
permanently transferred to lower level posts and to the
rural areas; many were sent temporarily to the countryside to do physical labor. Mao hoped that contact with
the masses and the experience of performing manual labor would give the cadres a greater understanding of
the people and would lead to identification with the
masses. Later, during the Cultural Revolution of the
late 1960's, a network of May 7 Cadre Schools were created in the countryside. Usually, cadres attend the
schools on a rotating basis for six months to several
years. The schools are not prisons and the cadres get
their regular pay while in attendance. They do all of
the physical work of maintaining the schools from
cooking the meals to cleaning the latrines and they
also work in the fields. In all they spend 60% of
their time in physical labor and 40% in political study
and criticism and self-criticism. Although they visit
nearby communes, they do not actually live with the
peasants.

Even those cadres who are not sent to the May 7
schools or to the countryside as part of xia fang are
expected to spend part of their time in physical labor
or in the menial activities of the organization they
administer. For example, the head of a factory is

required to spend part of the week working on the assembly line while commune officials are supposed to do some field work. Even the very top leaders like Mao and Zhou Enlai engaged in symbolic stints of physical labor.

Although these programs have several purposes, they are all designed to educate the cadres and to prevent them from becoming arrogant and growing distant from the people as were the imperial bureaucrats. However, officials are still better-paid than most workers and earn much more than peasants do. They are also permitted other perquisites such as the use of official cars. Even though the privileges of officials were severely curtailed during the Cultural Revolution, they were never completely eliminated.

Although there is no reliable data which allow us to accurately assess the effect of manual labor on the bureaucracy, there are many hints that the experience did not thoroughly purge the cadres of bourgeois thoughts and traits nor make them true Communists. For example, some ex-cadres told Barnett that officials did gain some understanding of local conditions from xia fang, but that they also "resented the necessity of undergoing the hardships of life in the countryside." The experience did not seem to close the gap between urban-based bureaucrats and the rural masses, but it did often have the effect of chastening some of the bureaucrats, who tended to complain less after having worked in the fields. "Problems that had seemed important before, seemed relatively minor after exposure to the difficulties of village life."[15]

The Mass Line

A counterpart to the programs which sent officials out to mingle with the masses were those which brought the masses into the political process. The mass line policy was designed to mobilize mass energies and to use the masses to control the bureaucrats. It was meant also to be a guideline on leadership style for the bureaucrats, with its emphasis on consultation and communication. Cadres were instructed to make policy with an eye to its impact on the masses. They were to get feedback from the people and were encouraged to get out of their offices and personally investigate conditions in the field. However, the final decisions, as always, were to be made by the party leadership.

As Mao explained, the mass line would prevent a breakdown in communication between the leaders and the led. He wrote:

> All correct leadership is necessarily "from the masses; to the masses." This means: take the ideas of the masses (scattered and unsystematic ideas) and concentrate them (through study turn them into concentrated and systematic ideas), then go to the masses and propagate and explain these ideas until the masses embrace them as their own, hold fast to them and translate them into action, and test the correctness of these ideas in such action. Then once again concentrate ideas from the masses and then once again go to the masses so that the ideas are persevered in and carried through.[17]

During the Cultural Revolution, the masses were supposedly brought indirectly into the government as members of the Revolutionary Committees which were established as the ruling bodies in cities, communes, factories, schools and other institutions. The masses were also allowed to elect their leaders in basic level units such as the commune production teams. However, the available evidence indicates that the mass representatives never actually controlled the Revolutionary Committees and that the choice of leaders was strictly limited to those acceptable to the party.[18]

The masses have been encouraged to air their complaints against officials by speaking up in meetings, by putting up "big character" wall posters, by writing to the newspapers, or by using the other available channels such as the opinion boxes placed in various institutions. Cadres may also be criticized by the masses in struggle meetings or in open-door rectification sessions.[19] However, it appears that much of the participation which does occur is largely empty and ritualistic because most people fear the consequences of genuine participation. One recent study concludes that about 80% to 90% of the people fall in the "lukewarm middle," participating only as much as they have to and taking their cues from the cadres, rather than trying to control the cadres.[20] Emigré respondents told Victor Falkenheim that they would hesitate to criticize a cadre, even if asked to do so, because of the risk of retaliation. Although retaliation was not legitimate, it was apparently quite common.[21]

Falkenheim also found that his respondents had a "clear sense" of the limits of participation. It was understood that an individual could express purely personal grievances and even raise questions about local problems in applying policy, but that it was forbidden to question basic state policies. Significantly, the most effective form of influence was "quasi-legal" and quite traditional in character. Citizens "were able to work quietly for certain goals through personal networks of connections, appeals to family ties or benifit-exchange relationships" (including bribes), as well as through threats of violence.[22]

Other Techniques of Control

Presumably the programs of attitude change and thought reform should have produced the proper Communist orientation in the cadres. But to insure that the bureaucrats did not slide back into selfish bourgeois thinking and behavior, their lives were substantially collectivized and highly politicized. Most of the bureaucrat's time was taken up with work or political meetings so there was almost no free time left for purely personal concerns. Frequent transfers served to prevent the development of personal attachments to other workers or to specific organizational units and to create a sense of insecurity which made the individual more vulnerable to party influence. The extreme secrecy and security-consciousness within the bureaucracy also inhibited cadres from discussing their work with each other and thereby helped prevent the formation of individual and group ties which might compete with ties to the party and the state.[23]

Most cadres, especially those working for national units, lived with their fellow workers in state-run apartment buildings and ate in their ministry's mess halls. When he had to travel on government business, the bureaucrat would stay in official guest houses together with other cadres of similar rank. The guest houses, mess halls, and apartment buildings insured that the cadres would be isolated from those outside the bureaucracy and that their lives were public within the bureaucracies. Cadres live in an "atmosphere of mutual surveillance" in which "everyone was presumed to be observing and judging everyone else's attitudes as well as behavior."[24]

The cadres feared that these judgments would make their way into the dossiers which are kept for each employee. These files contain the individual's references as well as a lengthy personal summary written by the employee upon entrance into the organization. The summary included a detailed account of the cadre's life since childhood, his class background, his friendships and personal relationships, his ideological development and his educational and professional experience. Each year and after every campaign an assessment is made of the individual and added to his dossier. The cadre also has to write a personal summary of his work, activities and thoughts for the previous year. This summary is submitted to his study group for discussion and the comments made by each study group member are entered in the file. These dossiers are reviewed before campaigns in order to choose targets for investigation and struggle and they form the basis for promotions and demotions. While expertise and technical performance were given some consideration in making promotions, political consciousness and activity were rewarded and those whose Redness was in doubt were precluded from advancing.[25]

The anxiety created by this system is all the greater in China because of the absence of alternate careers. There are no private employers in the People's Republic. A bad file will permanently ruin the individual's chances in life. Unless he can emigrate, the individual has no other source of income, status or power.

The lack of alternatives in part explains why individuals endure the negative aspects of Chinese bureaucratic life. However, fear alone does not account for bureaucratic behavior. While there have been times when it was so dangerous to hold official positions that people avoided them, most of the time the rewards are great enough to make bureaucratic work desirable. It must be remembered that everyone in China has to put up with a severly curtailed private life and with heavy political demands. While the bureaucrat's freedom is even more restricted than that of the worker or peasant, the rewards given him are also much greater. Officials have always had a significantly higher standard of living-better food, housing, medical care, cultural opportunities, educational opportunities for their children and so on-than have the masses. Even during the Cultural Revolution these privileges were not completely eliminated, nor were the wage differentials between cadres and ordinary people nor between cadres of different ranks within the bureaucracy.

It appears that the regime has to give more rewards to its cadres in order to motivate them. Where the rewards are minimal, as they are for leaders of the commune production teams, it has proven difficult to recruit qualified people. However, the giving of rewards has some very undesirable effects from the Maoist point of view. It is all too easy for the rewards to grow and for the bureaucracy to become a new elite.

The Cultural Revolution

According to orthodox Marxist theory, classes are supposed to disappear in the socialist society. There is also no longer supposed to be any differentiation between the interests of the people and those of the government nor of the people and the party because state and party are simply the instruments of the people. Yet, as the years passed, Mao came to believe that the division between the leaders and the led had not disappeared at all in socialist China and that the leaders - the bureaucracy of the state and the party - were becoming a new and privileged class. The bourgeoisie had reappeared in the form of the bureaucracy.

Specifically, Mao was disturbed by the transformation of the corps of revolutionary cadres into bureaucrats and experts lacking in revolutionary fervor. He felt that the policy of combining the qualities of Red and Expert had failed and that increasingly the party was becoming professionalized. He was also disturbed by the related growth in the size and complexity of the administrative apparatus of the state and party; by careerism among the cadres; by the development within the bureaucracy of more and more separate rankigs and the consequent growth of a highly elite strata; and by the growth in the power of the middle and upper levels of the bureaucracy at the expense of the lower level units which were closer to the people. Overall, it appeared to Mao that the masses were losing power to the state and the party.

Bureaucrats, under conflicting pressures from above and below, were adapting to the strain of their positions in ways that Mao could only deplore. Cadres were increasingly prone to try to "minimize responsibility avoid making decisions, flatter their superiors, file false reports and engage in corruption." At the middle levels there was a tendency to create "independent kingdoms - interorganizational cliques whose members were more committed to their bailiwicks, their colleagues and themselves than to the center. These independent kingdoms produced serious disruption of Party communications and distortion of Party staffing policy. Downward communication was disrupted by distorting or pigenholing unpopular central directives, by quoting them out of context and even by forging them. Upward communication was disrupted by filing false reports, overly optimistic reports or no reports at all . . . ." In addition, cadres would make appointments on a personal basis, putting their friends in key jobs and dismissing or attacking their rivals. There was also widespread "squandering of state resources, speculation in state funds and state property, as well as extortion and bribery."26 Small wonder that in 1965 Mao thundered: "The bureaucratic class is a class sharply opposed to the working class and the poor and lower-middle peasants. These people have become or are in the process of becoming burgeois elements sucking the blood of the workers."27

Convinced that drastic action was needed, Mao launched the Cultural Revolution. Mao tried to keep alive the revolutionary spirit by recreating the actual conditions of revolution through intensifying the class struggle. The people were urged to "Learn Revolution by Making Revolution" and to wage class struggle by attacking the new class in the bureaucracy. For the first time Mao turned the masses on the party hierarchy itself, right up to Liu Shaoqi, the second most powerful man in the nation. As the agents of the masses, high school and college students organized as Red Guards, were urged to "liberate themselves" and to overthrow those within the Party who are in authority and taking the capitalist road."28 The Red Guards took Mao at his word, attacking - at times with guns and other weapons - the very party and government which Mao headed. For a time, in many areas the government was completely disrupted and many high-level officials were removed from office. The resulting anarchy and near civil war eventually led to the use of the People's Liberation Army to restore authority and order.

The entire story of the Cultural Revolution is too complicated to tell here. For our purposes, it is enough to know that when the dust finally settled, the bureaucracy and state structure were altered, but the fundamental nature of political power and organization remained unchanged. Society was still dominated by the state and its bureaucrats. Mao had wanted to strengthen the mass line, increase the power of the masses and eliminate the forces which kept the masses and the center (Mao) from communicating directly. He did not succeed in producing a new, populist, democratic political order and "in the end he settled for the reestablishment of a presumably ideologically rectified party and a presumably reformed state bureaucracy.[29]

Most of the reforms resulting from the Cultural Revolution were not new. The May 7 Cadre schools, for example, were an extension of the xia fang program. Other reforms such as simplification of the organizational structure and the reduction of cadre privileges had also been tried before the Cultural Revolution. Only the Revolutionary Committees were a real innovation and these were soon gutted and transformed into bureaucratic organs dominated by the army or the party.[30]

By the early 1970's the cadre school experience had been regularized into a kind of sabbatical for bureaucrats; some young activists had attained positions of power but 95% of the party officials had been reinstated although not always in the same job; dual rule and new party bureaucratic organs were reappearing even though the Cultural Revolution policy was to unify party and state administration; bourgeois life styles were less in evidence but material incentives and significant wage differentials remained; some power had been transferred to the local level but the center remained in control.[31]

Bureaucratic Problems in Post-Mao China

As long as Mao lived, his personal authority and prestige and the egalitarian revolutionary heritage which he embodied may have acted as a partial brake on the routinization and institutionalization of bureaucratic power in the People's Republic. After the death of Mao in September 1976 and the arrest of the so-called Gang of Four a month later, the new leaders lost no time to conduct a rectification campaign against bureaucrats within the Chinese Communist Party. The purpose of the campaign was two-fold: to restore party authority which was badly shaken by the divisive

politics within the central committee since the controversial purge of Lin Biao in 1971, and to cleanse
out party members who were supporters of the Gang of
Four. During 1977 and 1978, numerous references were
made in the Chinese press to rampant factionalism which
was deemed damaging to party unity. It was implied
that the followers of the Gang of Four formed their
own cliques--"organizing mountain tops", as the Chinese
put it,--and defied central supervision.[33] Besides
factionalism and other political variants of defiance
of central authority, officials admitted the existence
of other serious problems such as the avoidance of
responsibility, corruption, bribery, waste, poor work
style and failure to practise democratic centralism.[34]
Such vices were not news to the Chinese, as the earlier
part of this chapter indicated. The difference between
this latest campaign and the previous ones is that the
failures of the party bureaucrats this time were blamed
on their susceptibility to the Gang of Four's propaganda
against authority and discipline. When they initiated
this rectification campaign within the party, the new
leaders appeared to have hoped that by discrediting
the Gang of Four and the values they embraced, they
could restore discipline within the party. The priority for the new leaders in 1977 was to consolidate political power and support. By laying much of the bureaucratic problem at the feet of the Gang, the Peking
leaders tried to provide an easy way out for those
cadres who had been sympathetic to the Gang for a variety of reasons but who can now be coopted by the new
administration with a minimum of recrimination.

The problem of factionalism within the party
however, went much deeper than adherents to the Gang of
Four. In fact, the ease with which Ch'iao Kuan-hua,
the former vice-foreign minister, and Mao Yuan-hsin,
the former political commissar of the Shenyang Military
Region, and numerous others were removed from office
indicated that resistance by the Gang faction was minimal. Yet criticism against factionalism persisted in
the press in 1979, suggesting that party disunity and
bureaucratic in-fighting came from other sources. The
Chinese press admitted as much when they mercilessly
caricatured two other factions. These culprits were
called the "wind" faction, or the opportunists, and
the "ambivalent" faction. The opportunists referred
to those bureaucrats who survived the Cultural Revolution by singing to the tune of the radicals in their
condemnation of "capitalist roaders within the party."

These very people then protested that they were the victims of radical propaganda after the arrest of the Gang of Four.[35] The ambivalents referred to those bureaucrats who became so weary with the changes in political fortunes that they would not commit themselves to new policy changes nor would they act against the so-called deviants.[36] These two groups were dragging their feet in the anti-bureaucratic campaign against the remnants of the Gang of Four, and they too came under increasing attack in 1978.

But these factions were symptomatic of a deeper problem which has to do with the decentralization of the bureaucracy which took place before the death of Mao, the sociology of the bureaucracy since the Cultural Revolution, and the still fragile political coalition which formed to oppose the Gang of Four in 1976 but which is still divided on many other issues. Thus, when Renmin Ribao (People's Daily) complained in August, 1978 that party interests were being replaced by factional interests, it was referring to a phenomenon of factionalism which had many sources.[37] Some were based on personal loyalty, some on survival instinct, some on indifference to leadership changes in Peking, and some on opposition to new policies; but they all led to excessive independence in different levels or segments of the party organization and threatened the leadership's attempt at national consolidation.

Not surprisingly, the rectification campaign went rather badly in 1978, and produced unexpected violence as some veteran cadres who were disgraced during the Cultural Revolution tried to settle old scores with vengeance. Ye Jianying, chairman of the National People's Congress Standing Committee, was reported to have told a delegation in April, 1978 that the central committee was surprised by the violence which accompanied the campaign in which about 1.1 million people were arrested and over seven thousand PLA soldiers were killed or wounded.[38] He admitted that the campaign had the adverse effects of weakening party leadership as it raised many uncomfortable questions about the role of some present leaders during the Cultural Revolution.[39]

The Chinese press in the spring of 1978 corroborated the above report that the central leadership was frustrated by the ineffectiveness of the anti-bureaucratic campaign. Many party bureaucrats appeared too preoccupied with reversing the verdict of the

Cultural Revolution and thus created instability within the party. As a result, lower-level officials in the government were afraid to carry out the new policies advocated by Deng lest he should lose his influence. It became clear to the new leaders that factionalism should be eliminated not only in the party, but in the government bureaucracy. Renmin Ribao thus suggested in March 1978 that the rectification campaign be extended to all government units throughout the country, and that nine types of deviants should be removed from the leadership positions in the party and government bureaucracies.[40] Apart from the followers of the Gang of Four, they were: (1) those who made mistakes or had poor attitude; (2) those who practised fascist methods of oppression; (3) those who deceived or robbed the people; (4) those who engaged in factional activities; (5) those who had no production experience; (6) those who had lost their revolutionary commitment; (7) those who held political ideas similar to the Gang of Four; and (8) those who engaged in empty talk but did very little.[41] As might be expected, such ambiguous and overlapping criteria for the elimination of bureaucratic careers only added confusion to the rectification campaign. Not surprisingly, many officials conducted the campaign with neither passion nor enthusiasm.

By the end of 1978, the campaign against bureaucratism had clearly changed from one which attacked political factionalism to one which attacked administrative incompetence. The change was signalled by a Renmin Ribao editorial which suggested that problem-solving skills and the ability to take initiatives to ask questions were the criteria for a good cadre.[42] A number of factors accounted for this shift of emphasis. As the new leaders felt increasingly confident of the domestic support for their modernization program, they recognized that the implementation of such policies should be priority. But they were confronted with an administrative apparatus which was characterized by incompetence, by personnel redundancy, and by an aging leadership which might be rich in revolutionary experience but lacking in professional skills. At the same time, the modernization of the economy, the military and science and technology became even more urgent as relations with the Soviet Union deteriorated further because of Vietnamese incursions into Chinese territories. As the Chinese prepared for their so-called punitive war against Vietnam, who is allied with the Soviet Union, the mobilization for the war effort

brought home to them the inadequacy of their administrative organization.

In the exchange of hostilities between Vietnam
and China during February 1979, some Western analysts
detected, and some Chinese officials admitted later,
that the initial phase of the Chinese invasion into
Vietnam was poorly coordinated and organized.[43] The
heavy casualties suffered by the Chinese caused considerable consternation at home, and produced a serious
crisis within the Chinese leadership.[44] The debate
among the leaders concerned not so much the justifica-
tion of the Chinese invasion, but the priorities and
strategies of four modernizations. The war had obviously produced a serious strain on the meager resources of the country, but the burden on the economy came
from other sources as well. The government had decided
in early 1979 to raise the prices paid to peasants for
food in order to bring up the standard of living in
the countryside.[45] The treasury was drained further by
compensation payments to workers and former disgraced
officials for their loss of wages during the Cultural
Revolution. Large investments were also made in Capital construction in heavy industries. The war with
Vietnam was in fact the last straw that forced the
Peking leaders to re-examine their economic program.
The wholesale importation of foreign technology and
equipment was challenged by some, and the reliance on
material incentives to increase productivity was also
questioned.[46] The lack of money forced the Chinese
to suspend about U.S. $2.5 billion in contracts with
Japanese manufacturers of plant equipment in early
March, 1979.[47] In April, a work conference was held
in Peking to reassess the economic program, and a month
later, the leaders decided on a major slowdown in the
modernization plans, especially in the heavy industries.[48] At the same time, readjustment of the bureaucracies was given serious consideration.

By the summer of 1979, reforming the bureaucracy
was acknowledged as the prerequisite to four modernizations. More holdovers from the Maoist era were ousted
from the Politburo so that there was greater unity of
leadership at the very top to symbolize the solidarity
of support for new policy changes.[49] At the same time,
the leaders discouraged the removal of too many officials lower down the party and government hierarchies
who had supported the Cultural Revolution, for fear
that continuous struggle against these officials would

only distract the organizations from the task of reviving the economy.[50] Renmin Ribao warned in March, 1979 against going too far in replacing leaders at a time when the country was trying to stabilize and forge ahead economically.[51] In short, factionalism was to be healed rather than to be exposed. It was no longer viewed as the key obstacle to controlling the bureaucracy. Nor was the failure to practise democratic centralism. Although Hua Quofeng told the Second Session of the Fifth National People's Congress in June 1979 that strengthening democratic centralism among cadres was essential to the four modernizations, he went on to suggest that an overhaul of the recruitment and examination systems was even more important to make bureaucrats better public servants of the society.[52] He ridiculed the "iron rice bowl" system which gave such job security to cadres that they were promoted but never demoted, recruited but never dismissed. Hua concluded his speech by warning that there were two forms of bureaucratism that need to be overcome: the passive bureaucrats who evaded responsibility, who held conferences but never made decisions, or who never implemented decisions if they were made at conferences; and the authoritarian bureaucrats who issued commands to lower-level cadres without paying attention to objective considerations.[53] Of the two, one may infer from the customary ranking that the former is considered a greater offender.

The dependence of four modernizations on a rational administrative system was even more explicitly spelt out by Deng Xiaoping in his January 16, 1980 speech to a congregation of cadres in Peking.[54] Deng believed that modernizations required a rational party and government organization whose membership should be recruited on the basis of expertise, first and foremost. This is what he said:

> Let me say something about the relationship between red and expert. Expert does not mean red, but red required expert. If you are not an expert, and don't know much, but blindly take command. . .you will only delay production and construction. Unless we resolve this question we cannot realize four modernizations. . . . From now on, in the selection of cadres we should pay special attention to expert knowledge. . . . Unless we do so, we cannot proceed with modernizations.[55]

The professionalization of the bureaucracy in short,
is the present leaders' answer to the problem of administrative incompetence.

Since then, more rational reforms have been proposed to improve the bureaucracies. In the June, 1980
issue of the party journal Honggi, it was pointed out
that some of the 18 million party bureaucrats in the
country are "mindless, irresponsible, ignorant but
blindly taking command."[56] The writer lamented the
lack of specialists and the prevalence of aging bureaucrats in the higher echelons of the party and government organizations, and proposed to remedy the situation by abolishing life-time tenure for the bureaucrats.
He defended the suggested reform by arguing:

> There are at least these advantages (in abol-
> ishing life-time tenure); first, it helps to
> recruit young talents. . .and guarantees to
> give the various organizations a breath of
> fresh air; second, it helps to overcome bureau-
> cratism; and third, it helps to change some
> people's attitude that a bureaucratic job is
> an "iron rice bowl". . . .[57]

In another Honggi issue a month later, Song Renqiong,
head of the party Organization Department, also singled
out the age of bureaucratic leaders as the greatest
problem with Chinese organizations. He too recommended
the introduction of mandatory retirement for officials.[58] Before the openning of another session of the
National People's Congress in September, 1980, the need
for rejuvenation of organizational leadership became
the dominant theme in official pronouncements. Deng
told Oriana Fallaci in an interview:

> Enough with old men who continue to be in po-
> wer until the day of their death, enough with
> lifelong tenure of the leaders. It has not
> been put on any paper that the old men must
> rule, that the leaders must lead all their
> lives, and yet this mistaken habit continues
> to dominate our system and to be one of our
> shortcomings.[59]

Thus, in the four years after Mao's death, the
anti-bureaucratic campaign was motivated first by a desire for political stability, but later by a desire for
improved administrative capabilities. As political

opposition within the bureaucracies was neutralized, the leaders recognized that unless the modernization goals are soon realized, there will be disaffection with both the leaders and the policies they advocate. To streamline the bureaucracy for the purpose of administering effectively the modernizations program thus became the paramount concern of the Peking government. Let us examine next the means by which the Chinese leaders proposed to resolve the problems they identified.

The Means of Bureaucratic Control in Post-Mao China

Just as the rectification campaign in 1977-78 focused mainly on political issues, but shifted to administrative issues at the end of 1978, the devices used by the Chinese to control such problems can be separated into ideological and political means on the one hand, and technical, managerial means on the other. After Mao's death, the new leaders at first relied heavily on political means that were most familiar to them. The very rectification campaign itself, conducted mostly through the intensive media progaganda, and in struggle sessions against the supporters of the Gang of Four, was a political means through which the new leaders had hoped to achieve party unity and political stability. Another political device was the reiteration of the notion of democratic centralism. Hua Guofeng, for example, told the students at the Central Party School that:

We should work hard to revive and carry forward our Party's democratic style of work and uphold democratic centralism, and resolutely oppose the bad tendencies of tolerating no contrary opinions, of "what I say goes", of retaliating against comrades who make criticisms, of disregarding discipline and organization and seeking "independence" from the Party.60

This concept was echoed in official speeches and in the press throughout 1977 and 1978, culminating in the first official publication of Mao's 1962 speech on Democratic Centralism.61 The purpose was to teach the young and new members of the party about the fine traditions in this regard.

A third political device contemplated by the

present leaders for controlling the bureaucracy was to subject officials to mass supervision through the ballot. In November, 1978, Renmin Ribao suggested that the overly centralized personnel system encouraged cadre indifference to local demands because their promotion and demotion were made at the top elsewhere.[62] It proposed the direct election of basic-level cadres, but at the same time, allowed higher-level echelons to appoint officials in unspecified special circumstances. Nevertheless, it insisted that such appointees should be subject to dismissal by the people during the period of probation.[63] The election of cadres was endorsed by Hua in his speech to the Second Session of the Fifth National People's Congress in June, 1979. He suggested that not only should the leading cadres in the rural communes be elected by the people, but that mining and commercial enterprises too should have their basic-level leading cadres selected through popular election. He also advocated the gradual extension of this method to higher levels. Furthermore, in government units which are not conducive to popular election--presumably referring to the military--the performance of the bureaucrats should be evaluated at the end of each year through a public opinion poll.[64] The Chinese leaders seem convinced that the public can help to identify and promote to leadership positions those who are selfless and efficient, and who possess organizational skills and technical expertise. The validity of such assumption is of course questionable, as those objective criteria have seldom played an influential role in determining voters' choices even in an open, democratic contest. Where a candidate's political acceptability has to be predetermined, as in the case of China, it is even more questionable whether popular election will ever achieve its objective.

As the campaign against bureaucratism shifted focus from political issues to administrative issues at the end of 1978, rational managerial means were proposed to improve bureaucratic performance. Increased attention was paid to bureaucrats' old age and lack of professional skills. In the Beijing Review, for instance, it was admitted that

> According to figures available in 1978, cadres competent in specialized work accounted for less than one-third of the nation's total, and among qualified scientists and technicians, the average age of those having reached the

level of associate researchers was fifty-eight.[65]

The targets for managerial rationalization are technical specialization, recruitment on the basis of merit, and the lowering of the average age of leading cadres.

Officials now make it clear that possession of expertise is the primary requirement for leadership positions in party and government organizations.[66] This is a significant departure from the emphasis placed on seniority, as measured by one's revolutionary experience, during the Maoist period. Renmim Ribao in June, 1980 condemned the practice of giving top priority to seniority in the selection and promotion of cadres as "a manifestation of the poisonous vestige of feudalism."[67] The professionalization of the bureaucracy is fostered by educational reforms which place a premium on academic achievement.[68] An increasingly large number of Chinese students are sent abroad to acquire skills not only in science and technology, but in capitalist style management. Many government departments and enterprises try to organize various types of training classes and evening schools to help upgrade cadres' technical skills.[69] While the young are in the process of acquiring greater expertise, the older cadres who were professionally trained in the fifties are being promoted. Deng made no secret of this in his January 1980 speech:

> We need more and more people with special
> skills. But does this mean that we don't have
> any skilled people right now? No, but our
> party committees at various levels have not
> made special effort to identify, cultivate
> and help such people. . . . From now on,
> special attention should be paid to promote
> those in their forties. Why in their forties?
> Those are the people who entered into univer-
> sities in the 1950's. . . . They were about
> twenty-five years old then.[70]

Since politics had not yet replaced factual knowledge or scientific inquiry in university curricula in the fifties, and admissions to universities were based largely on academic merit, the graduates then were more professionally qualified than their counterparts a decade later. Such experts are sought not only by the government agencies which require their skills, they

252

are also courted by the communist party to become members. For the party wants the vanguards of the state organizations to be truly red and expert.

In the area of personnel recruitment, no system of bureaucratic examination similar to the U.S. Civil Service Examination exists at the time of this writing. But officials acknowledge that "set-ups for examining cadres, supervising them, giving out awards and punishments, and for seeing to their removal, rotation and retirement, all remain to be established or improved."[71] Song Renqiong announced that more and more leadership positions will be reserved for graduates of universities and secondary technical schools only, and that stress from hereon will be the selection of cadres from among outstanding young and middle-aged people with high cultural, scientific, and technological level.[72] Meanwhile, the State Council laid down temporary regulations in May 1980 with regard to the evaluation and promotion of engineering and agricultural technicians, and recommended that all those who were promoted after January, 1967 should come under closer scrutiny, and need to meet technical standards before they can retain their positions in the organization.[73] The Peking leaders dramatized their determination to make their bureaucracy a meritorious organization by publicly giving one of their vice-premiers a demerit on his record for his negligence in an oil-rig accident, and dismissing the Minister of Petroleum for his failure to take responsibility in the same tragedy.[74]

Yet another aspect of the bureaucracy the Chinese attempt to rationalize is the replacement of aging leaders. The need for organizational renewal has been a Maoist theme during the Cultural Revolution, it continues to occupy the minds of his successors even though they have repudiated his method of cultivating revolutionary successors. The National People's Congress in September 1980 underlined the leaders' determination to transfer power to a younger generation as eight of the top, aging leaders resigned their government positions as premier and vice-premiers to make room for new blood.[75] No mandatory retirement age has been set for bureaucrats, but seniority is rejected as the basis for promotion. Song Renqiong recommended that job reassignment should be made for the old and the frail, and that the incompetent cadres should be investigated and rectified, and if necessary, transferred.[76] Honggi advised old cadres to retreat to the second and third lines to make room for the young, and consoled them by suggesting that they could serve as the mentors of the young by passing their experience and legacy to the new generation.[77]

Conclusion

We have described what the present Peking leaders perceived as problems with their bureaucracies and their proposed solutions to the problems. We may now contrast in some general terms the methods of controlling the bureaucracy in the Maoist and post-Mao eras, and predict the likely consequences of the latest attempts to deal with bureaucratism.

During the Maoist period, because the chief objective in controlling the bureaucracy was to realize an egalitarian society where no one group of people would enjoy special privileges and lord over the others, the bureaucrats <u>behavior</u> was the main target of the controlling devices. In the post-Mao period, the objectives have changed from one of achieving political stability to one of realizing the ambitions of four modernizations, thus the bureaucrats' loyalty, and then their performance on the job become the main targets of reform. In both eras, the leaders used a combination of rational and radical approaches, but with important differences. During the Maoist period, the rational approach concentrated mainly on structuring supervisory procedures and organizations, and the radical approach relied chiefly on political mobilization and ideological indoctrination.[78] During the post-Mao period, the rational approach follows closely the Weberian concept of ideal-type bureaucracy, with emphasis on professionalization, division of labor, functional specialization, and well-defined rules and procedures. The radical approach, used mainly in the first stage of the anti-bureaucratic campaign, retained but a trace of communist polemics, and adhered chiefly to the socialist tenet of democratic centralism.

Anthony Downs' theory of organizational behavior has been invoked by many scholars in the past to explain the failure of Mao to control the bureaucracy.[79] In trying to predict the prospects of the present leaders to change the Chinese bureaucracy, we may be better served by taking into account the existing social and economic structures, and political constraints in the organizational environment. We would argue that the present leaders are unlikely to eliminate some of the features of bureaucratism as long as the existing social, political and economic factors remain constant.

During the Maoist era, the social and economic structures retained much of the legacies of traditional China--lack of social mobility, high level of unemployment, low level of technical skill and capital investment. As a result, the bureaucracy offered rare security and prestige for those who got recruited into it, and they were not likely to give up their privileges without resistance. In spite of impressive growth in the industrial sector since the communist takeover, the Chinese economy could not generate enough jobs to absorb the ever-increasing number of middle-school and high-school graduates. Employment and social mobility thus remained unresolved issues up to this date. But the present social and economic structures carry also the legacy of the Cultural Revolution, during which time, many lower-level bureaucratic positions in both party and government were opened to the young people from rural and poor urban background. Many leaders then and now, be they radicals or moderates, support this policy for a variety of reasons. For one thing, few leaders would repudiate the need to open opportunities for the socially disadvantaged and the poor, because they are not unaware of the price of social discontent. For another, it is always easier to place the unskilled in the lowest level of a government organization than in a factory, expecially if that government department happens to deal with such general tasks as social relief, welfare and cooperatives. The productivity of a government bureaucrat is also easier to be disguised than that of a factory worker, making it a more attractive post to place the relatively uneducated young.

After the arrest of the Gang of Four, even though people from rural and poor urban background are no longer given priority in employment, there is no massive expulsion of such people from the government or party organizations. This suggests that the present leaders are mindful of the fact that to turn the Cultural Revolution generation of bureaucrats loose is likely to create more political and social difficulties than would compensate for the rationalization of the bureaucracy. Thus the present leaders may lament publicly about overstaffing in their bureaucracies, yet they are constrained by social and political considerations to retain the less qualified bureaucrats hired during

the Cultural Revolution, and to rehire and rehabilitate
many older cadres who were dismissed during the Cultural
Revolution. Ye Jianying revealed in 1978 that there
were 2.3 million cases of cadres and technicians vic-
timized by the Gang who needed to be "liberated."[80]
The retirement of old cadres may not be fast or large
enough to prevent the Chinese bureaucracy from becoming
more bloated than ever before.

The situation with the party organization is not
encouraging either. Deng said earlier in 1980 that
there were about 38 million party members in China. In
1962, Mao spoke of a party membership of 17 million.[81]
The size of the Chinese Communist Party has therefore
more than doubled in the course of eighteen years. It
seems that the Gang of Four and their supporters were
responsible for the recruitment of a large number of
their adherents into the party in order to boost their
strength. It has led Deng to question the qualification of two types of members in the party: (1) those
who entered the party under what Deng called "extreme
leftism" policy, and (2) those old members who "adhered
to factions and thus could not be an example for the
people."[82] But Deng did not suggest their immediate
expulsion from the party either. Instead, he wanted
more professionally qualified people to lead the party,
and prevent the future entrance of extreme leftists
into the party.

Many of the means employed by the present leaders
to control bureaucratic problems seem to work at cross
purposes with one another and may eventually generate
even greater tension within the Chinese bureaucracy
and society as a whole. For example, the emphasis on
technical expertise as a necessary qualification for
bureaucrats appears to conflict with their socialist
impulse for democratic populism. For the former necessarily puts the experts above the masses, whereas
the latter calls for popular control of the bureaucrats
through election; the former espouses elitism whereas
the latter egalitarianism; the former restricts opportunities whereas the latter opens them. The leaders
try to reconcile these contradictory tendencies by arguing that given the freedom of choice, the masses will
want a technical expert over a political ideologue.
But the political experience elsewhere in the world
should put that assumption to rest quickly. The American experience with Jacksonian democracy had not helped
this country to find competent officials and had to be

replaced by the Civil Service Act which introduced a merit system to our recruitment process.

Secondly, the Chinese are pushing for decentralization while condemning factionalism. But decentralization creates two separate problems. It is a mistaken notion that decentralization is always welcomed by bureaucratic leaders. For some people who have not been accustomed to the exercise of authority and the making of independent decisions, decentralization is feared because it places the burden of responsibility directly on them. In such cases, decentralization is counterproductive to rationalization, because organizations under such leadership tend to be less efficient rather than more. On the other hand, decentralization tends to encourage factionalism because it allows bureaucratic leaders a lot of power in economic planning and administrative hiring. Under decentralization, local units have to rely on their own resources to meet many administrative expenses, but at the same time, they have greater freedom to allocate their resources to their best interests. It is difficult for the center to obtain compliance from the lower-level functionaries if central policy should conflict with local interests. Factionalism, or excessive local independence in this case, is the result of decentralized bureaucracy. Trimming personnel in a decentralized bureaucracy is also difficult. Bureaucratic leaders after all, loath to undercut their own positions by the elimination of subordinates, especially if they have the potential to cause political troubles later on. Not surprisingly therefore, some of the leaders did not cooperate freely during the anti-bureaucratic campaign when they were told to remove cadres suspected of having connections with the Gang of Four. For the same reason, one can predict the lack of enthusiasm these leaders would have for the proposal to recruit basic-level cadres through popular election, even though the rationale for such proposal is the further strengthening of decentralization.

Thirdly, the increasing emphasis placed on youth and professionalism can only generate tension within the bureaucracy and society. Within the bureaucracies, the old cadres who are urged to retire to make room for the younger professionals may feel betrayed by the leaders whom they have helped to come to power, and whom they have supported in more difficult times. The Cultural Revolution generation of bureaucrats whose prospects for promotion are dim, and whose status becomes increasingly lowly as greater prestige is accorded to expertise, will no doubt resent the younger but better trained cadres who are promoted over their heads in spite of their seniority. They are likely to be the scapegoats in future shakeups if the goals of four modernizations are not soon realized. Within the society, the achievement-oriented policies have already produced a scramble for educational opportunities among the young, and will no doubt widen the gap between the urban professional class and the rural poor.

Thus, the present leaders may find that in spite of their commitment to improve administrative capabilities in their bureaucracies, they are unable to institutionalize a legal-rational type of bureaucratic organization because of political and social constraints. On the other hand, their drive to professionalize the bureaucracies may push them further away from the socialist goals of egalitarianism, which may be politically unacceptable to the majority of peasants and the disadvantaged. In that case, the leaders may have to engage in a new search for a workable balance between politics and administration.

Footnotes

[1]Mao Zedong, "Chairman Mao Discusses Twenty Manifestations of Bureaucracy," in David Milton, Nancy Milton, and Franz Schurmann, eds., People's China, New York: Vintage Books, 1974, p. 248.

[2]Ibid., pp. 248-251.

[3]Ibid., p. 250.

[4]For an introduction to the traditional bureaucracy see: Etienne Balazs, Chinese Civilization and Bureaucracy, New Haven: Yale University Press, 1964; the essays by C.K. Yang, Charles O. Hucker and James T.C. Liu in David S. Nivison and Arthur F. Wright, eds., Confucianism in Action, Stanford: Stanford University Press, 1959, and Thomas Metzger, The Internal Organization of Ching Bureaucracy, Cambridge: Harvard University Press, 1973.

[5]Mao Tsetung, Selected Readings from the Works of Mao Tsetung, Peking: Foreign Languages Press, 1971, pp. 136-137.

[6]Franz Schurmann, Ideology and Organization in Communist China, 2nd ed., Berkeley: University of California Press, 1971, p. 166.

[7]James R. Townsend, Politics in China, 2nd ed., Boston: Little, Brown, 1980, p. 88.

[8]A. Doak Barnett and Ezra Vogel, Cadres, Bureaucracy, and Political Power in Communist China, New York: Columbia University Press, 1967, p. 19.

[9]Ibid., p. 35.

[10]See Martin King Whyte, Small Groups and Political Rituals, Berkeley: University of California Press, 1974.

[11]See Robert Jay Lifton, Thought Reform and the Psychology of Totalism, New York: Norton, 1969.

[12]A. Doak Barnett, "Social Stratification and Aspects of Personnel Management in the Chinese Bureaucracy," The China Quarterly (October-December, 1966), p. 32.

[13]Ibid.

[14]See Tensselaer W. Lee III, "The Hsia Fang System: Marxism and Modernization," The China Quarterly (October-December, 1966).

[15]Barnett, op. cit., p. 29.

[16]Richard H. Solomon, "Communication patterns and the Chinese Revolution," The China Quarterly, (October-December 1967), p. 105.

[17]Mao Tsetung, Selected Works of Mao Tsetung, v. III, Peking: Foreign Languages Press, 1961-65, p. 120.

[18]See John P. Burns, "The Election of Production Team Cadres in Rural China: 1958-74," The China Quarterly, (June 1978).

[19]See Richard M. Pfeffer, "Serving the People and Continuing the Revolution," The China Quarterly (October-December 1972).

[20]Victor C. Falkenheim, "Political Participation in China," Problems of Communism (May-June 1978).

[21]Ibid., p. 26.

[22]Ibid., p. 25.

[23]Barnett and Vogel, op. cit., pp. 58-60, 65-69.

[24]Ibid., p. 102.

[25]Ibid., pp. 48-52.

[26]Harry Harding, Jr., "Maoist Theories of Policy Making and Organization," in Thomas W. Robinson, ed., The Cultural Revolution in China, Berkeley: University of California Press, 1971, p. 147.

[27]Quoted by Lowell Dittmer, "Revolution and Reconstruction in Contemporary Chinese Bureaucracy," Journal of Comparative Administration (February 1974), p. 452.

[28]Maurice Meisner, Mao's China, New York: Free Press, 1977, p. 31.

[29]Ibid., p. 354.

[30] Ibid.

[31] Frederick C. Teiwes, "Before and After the Cultural Revolution," The China Quarterly (April-June, 1974).

[32] As quoted in Maurice Meisner,"The Moaist Legacy and Chinese Socialism." Asian Survey (November 1971), p. 1020.

[33] Renmin Ribao, October 25, 1977.

[34] The Hong Kong Ming Pao, quoted a Chinese official as admitting that it was a common practice in Peking for parents to bribe officials so that their children would be exempted from being sent to work in the countryside. Officials were also reported to have accepted bribes to arrange for changes in work assignments. See Ming Pao, June 28, 1977. (All dates for Ming Pao refer to its North America edition.) Another Renmin Ribao editorial exposed a former deputy secretary of the Honan Provincial Committee for embezzlement of public funds, a practice which appeared widespread at that time and had been euphemistically referred to in the Chinese press as "looseness in financial discipline." See Beijing Review, No. 50, December 15, 1978 p. 14, and Ming Pao, April 13, 1978.

[35] A Liberation Army Daily editorial reprinted in Ming Pao, January 12, 1978.

[36] Ibid. Also Ming Pao, June 19, 1978.

[37] Ming Pao, August 23, 1978.

[38] Ming Pao, June 19, 1978.

[39] Ibid.

[40] A Renmin Ribao editorial reported in Ming Pao, March 23, 1978.

[41] Ibid.

[42] Renmin Ribao, December 7, 1978.

[43] The Washington Post, March 12, 1979. Interviews conducted by Maria Chan Morgan in Guangzhou in the summer of 1980 also confirmed this report.

[44]One informant gave the figure of 10,000 Chinese killed during this war. Others confirmed that the casualties were large enough to discourage many young peasants from joining the PLA in the two years after the war.

[45]The Washington Post, May 3, 1979.

[46]The New China News Agency quoted Vice-Premier Kan Shi'en as saying that, "the four modernizations cannot be bought nor borrowed." The omnipotence of bonuses to the neglect of the role of political awareness was also criticized. See The Washington Post, March 17, 1979.

[47]The Washington Post, March 1, 1979.

[48]The Washington Post, May 3, 1979 and May 8, 1979. It was around this time that the Chinese brought back to the Politburo the aging economist Chen Yun who appeared to favor more cautious economic growth.

[49]Three high-level officials who were closely identified with the Cultural Revolution were ousted in March, 1979. They were Wang Dongxing, Ji Dengkui and Wu De. See The Washington Post, March 25, 1979.

[50]Jay Matthews of The Washington Post argued that there did not appear to be a major anti-war faction in the Peking leadership because few leaders who were shown evidence of suffering by Chinese living at the border area with Vietnam could argue against the invasion. The dispute among leaders was over other issues, such as the amount of freedom of expression allowed, but especially over political purges and economic priorities. See The Washington Post, March 13, 1979.

[51]Ibid.

[52]Beijing Review only reported part of Hua's speech. (See No. 25, June 22, 1979, p. 12.) But the Ming Pao reported his more severe criticism of bureaucratic shortcomings. See Ming Pao, June 26, 1979.

[53]Ming Pao, June 26, 1979.

[54]The text of this speech has not been officially published by the Chinese, but the Ming Pao published it in installments on March 2-5, 1980. Its authenticity

is beyond question.

[55]*Ming Pao*, March 4, 1980. Translation is by Maria C. Morgan.

[56]*Honggi*, No. 11, June 1, 1980, p. 8.

[57]*Ibid.*, p. 9. Translation is by Maria Chan Morgan.

[58]*Honggi*, No. 16, August 15, 1980.

[59]*The Washington Post*, August 31, 1980.

[60]*Beijing Review*, No. 43, October 21, 1977, p. 10.

[61]This important speech at an enlarged central work conference on January 20, 1962 had been circulating in the West since the Cultural Revolution as part of the unofficial red guard document called *Long Live The Thought of Mao Tse-tung*. It is included in Stuart Schram, ed., *Chairman Mao Talks To The People*, New York, Pantheon Asia Library, 1974. It was published in the *Beijing Review*, No. 27, July 7, 1978.

[62]*Renmin Ribao* editorial published in the Hong Kong *Ta Kung Pao*, November 28, 1978.

[63]*Ibid.*

[64]*Ming Pao*, June 26, 1979.

[65]*Beijing Review*, No. 28, July 14, 1980, p. 3.

[66]*Renmin Ribao*, December 7, 1978.

[67]*Beijing Review*, No. 26, June 30, 1980, p. 26.

[68]For an account of the educational changes after the death of Mao, see Suzanne Pepper, "Chinese Education After Mao: Two Steps Forward, Two Steps Back and Begin Again?" *The China Quarterly*, No. 81, March 1980, pp. 1-65.

[69]*Beijing Review*, No. 28, July 14, 1980, p. 3.

[70]*Ming Pao*, March 4, 1980. Translation is by Marcia C. Morgan.

[71]*Beijing Review*, No. 26, June 30, 1980, p. 7.

[72] Beijing Review, No. 32, August 11, 1980, p. 7.

[73] The Hong Kong Ta Kung Pao, August 4, 1980.

[74] Ming Pao, September 4, 1980.

[75] The Washington Post, September 8, 1980.

[76] Honggi, No. 16, August 15, 1980.

[77] Honggi, No. 11, August 15, 1980.

[78] This idea is explicated and the implications are examined in Chapter II, "The Organizational Heritage of the Chinese Communist Party", in Harry Harding Jr.'s forthcoming book, Organizational China, Stanford University Press, forthcoming.

[79] See for instance Richard Baum's explanation of the failure of the socialist education campaign in 1962-65 in Prelude to Revolution: Mao, the Party and the Peasant Question, 1962-1966, New York: Columbia University Press, 1975.

[80] Ming Pao, June 19, 1978.

[81] Deng's speech in January 1980 as reported in Ming Pao, March 4, 1980. Also Schram, op. cit., p. 179.

[82] Ming Pao, March 5, 1980. Translation is by Maria C. Morgan.

Chapter XI

THE ADMISTRATIVE SYSTEM IN TURKEY

1. Attilla Dicle

The first World War marked the end of the six-
century-old Ottoman Empire and the new Turkish Republic
emerged out of its ashes. In spite of all the efforts,
the new Turkish administrative system could not totally
break away from the traditional Ottoman institutions,
structures, and practices. The new system was, in a
sense, the product of the accumulated administrative
reforms of the last two centuries. Ataturk depended,
to a large extent, on the already existing small group
of young, western-educated and experienced bureaucrats
in achieving his large number of social, economic and
political reforms. Significant reforms such as the
adoption of "republic" as the new form of the state,
new administrative, civil and criminal codes borrowed
from Western Europe to replace the religious rules and
regulations, abandonment of theocracy, actualization of
secularization, laicism, etc., could not be achieved
without their help.

The development of the present-day Turkish administrative system has been evolutionary. The reorganization attempts of Selim III for a "New Order" and the
whole set of successful reforms of Mahmut II during the
first half of the 19th century, the well-known Tanzimat
or the Noble Rescript of the Rose Chamber (1839), the
Reform Edict (Islahat Fermani) of 1856, political associations of the late Ottoman period like the young
Ottomans (Yeni Osmanlilar) and the Ottoman Union and
Progress Association (Osmanli Ittihat ve Terakki Cemiyeti), the Young Turks movement (1889-1918), the
constitutional revolutions of 1876 and 1908, the independence war and the rebirth of the nation, the Constitutions of the First Republic (1921, 1924), the Kemalist
reforms, and other more recent developments as the
transition to the multiparty system and the change of
power from the Republican People's Party to the new
Democrat Party (1950), the military coup of 1960 and the
constitution of the Second Republic (1961), the military
intervention of 1971 and, finally, the military takeover of September 1980 all had their incremental effects
and footprints on the Turkish administrative system.
The history of the Ottoman-Turkish bureaucratic reforms
can really be considered to be the history of change

and modernization of Turkey.

An historical approach is, therefore, necessary for a thorough understanding of the Turkish bureaucracy and its role in the developmental process. Such an approach will also provide insights into the administrative systems of other Middle Eastern Countries, some of which were under the Ottoman rule for about four centuries.

In this study, after a brief structural overview of the Ottoman administrative system, we shall concentrate our discussions on the Ottoman-Turkish bureaucratic reforms, the evolution and the description of the existing system, and the role of the bureaucracy in the development of modern Turkey.

The Administrative Institutions of the Ottoman Empire:

The Ottoman Empire was started in Anatolia as a frontier principality and gradually transformed into the world's most powerful empire during the 15th and 16th centuries. It had a sovereign existence of more than six centuries (1299-1919). The Empire was composed of many nations with different cultures, covering large territories in three continents-Asia, Africa and Europe. It reached its territorial peak during the reign of Sultan Süleyman the Magnificent (1520-1566). The Turkish-Ottoman administrative system was perfected during the same period. In spite of some major changes over the years, the typical characteristics of the administrative system of this period remained more or less the same until the nineteenth century. Moreover, it was this bureaucracy which was responsible for the growth of the Empire and in reference to which later administrative reforms were carried out.

The origin of the Ottoman political and administrative philosophy can be traced back to the early Turkish culture in Central Asia. It was later amended, changed and shaped by Islam, the Seljuk Turks, the Persian, the Arab and the Byzantium cultures.

The Turkish political and administrative philosophy was influenced by Islam more than anything else, once the Turks were converted to Islam in the eighth century. The acceptance of the Gihad, the doctrine to extend Islam by force, was in accordance with the original Turkish philosophy of war and conquest. According to Karpat, "Islam gave the Turkish state a purpose, a

266

meaning, but at the same time it submerged the national characteristics of the Turks into its own, to the extent that 'Turk' became synonymous with 'Muslim', although Turks in general preserved such distinct characteristics as language and statehood."[1] Moreover, Islam gave the Ottomans a complete social system regulated by the religious Sacred Law Şeriat which was complete and unalterable and to which the Ottoman state was obliged to conform. The religious rules and regulations of Şeriat were extremely rigid and professed to provide for all relations of life.[2] It was under this influence that the Arabic alphabet was adopted, a large number of Arabic words were imported into Turkish language, and the Ottoman sultans, beginning with Selim I in 1517, acquired the title of Caliph (successor of the Prophet).

The power and authority of the Ottoman sultans rested essentially upon the old Turkish political and administrative philosophy, traditions, and the Sacred Law Şeriat. Although some of the sultans were well-trained, able persons and some others were natural leaders and respectively made extensive use of their knowledge, administrative skills and charismatic power, the dominant form of authority exercised by the rulers of the Empire was traditional and hereditary. The only significant limitation on the absolute power and authority of the sultans was Şeriat, the Islamic Sacred Law.

The old Turkish political-administrative philosophy, as formulated in the Kutadgu Bilik and analyzed in the writings of Nizam-ul Mülk (great Seljuk minister) and al-Ghazzala (the well-known Arab scholar) around the eleventh century, was obviously maintained by the Ottoman Turks without significant alterations. For example, according to the Ottoman statesman and historian of the fifteenth century Tursun Beg, harmony among men living in society could be achieved only by statecraft. Only statecraft, through the use of the power and authority of the ruler and the divine reason or Şeriat, could keep each individual in his proper place (as determined by his ability) in the society. Since the rules instituted by the ruler could not have a perpetual character, there would always be need for a ruler in a human society; he should always seek to strengthen his position by expanding his revenues and his armies; and should serve the society by providing public security and order.[3]

Similar arguments have been presented by another Ottoman chronicler, Mustafa Naima (1665-1716), more than a century later, as part of his model of "Circle of Equity." Naima argued that "(1) there could be no mülk (rule) or devlet (state) without the military; (2) maintaining the military required wealth; (3) wealth was garnered from the subjects; (4) the subjects could prosper only through justice; (5) without mülk and devlet there could be no justice."[4] In other words, creation of wealth by subjects, exploitation of such wealth by the ruler, and the provision of justice for the subjects have been the philosophical bases of the Ottoman political and administrative organization as well as the absolute power of the Ottoman sultans.

The Ottoman society was divided into two major classes: askeri (literally military) and reaya (subjects). Askeri class was the small group of rulers and was composed of those to whom the sultan had delegated executive and religious authority. These included the officers of the court and the army, the civil servants and the ulema (learned members of the Islamic community), all of whom were wholly tax-exempt. Reaya, on the other hand, was composed of all Muslim and non-Muslim subjects. Subjects paid taxes and did not participate in the government. They were divided into a number of subgroups each with different status and tax obligations. Those who were granted certain tax immunities in return for public service constituted an intermediate group between the military class and the peasantry or simple subjects.[5]

The Ottoman Empire was a theocratic monarchy with the sultan at the top exercising absolute power. His power was reinforced and its exercise over the whole Islamic community was legitimized after the sultan acquired the title of Caliph in 1517. The authority of the sultan-caliphs was thereafter based on both the traditional and religious grounds.

The political and administrative institutions of the Ottoman Empire have recently been studied along the career lines.[6] The careers or the institutions identified are (1) the palace institution (mülkiye), (2) the scribal institution (kalemiye), (3) the learned or ecclesiastical institution (ilmiye), and (4) the military institution (seyfiye).

1. The Palace Institution (Mülkiye)

The palace institution was the core of the ruling

class of the Ottoman society. It provided leadership, trained the rulers and the administrators, and produced qualified manpower for the government, the court and the army. It was "a school in which the pupils were enrolled for life." It was composed of the harem, the inner service, and the outer service. Before examining each of these, it will be useful to take a brief look at the systems of recruitment and training based on which the whole palace institution rested.

Recruitment: The members of the Ottoman ruling class, with the exception of the royal family, were recruited through such methods as capture, purchase, gift and tribute. All the members of the ruling institution were the slaves (kul) of the sultan. Slaves who were brought for the sultan or given him as gifts were boys from the Christian families. The system of periodic levying of tribute boys, which is known as devşirme, was essentially developed at the time of Bayezit I. The agents of the sultan were sent out every four years, more often after the sixteenth century, to conscript the brightest Christian children of ten to twenty years of age as slaves for the service to the sultan. The annual average of the tribute boys in the sixteenth century was estimated to be about three thousand —little less than one-half of the total recruits of the palace institution for each year.[7]

After careful registration, all the recruits for the sultan's slave-family were divided into two groups. Those who were judged to have exceptional qualities were chosen for special education and training. They were trained as Inner Service Boys (iç oğlan) for the imperial palace. The remainder (acem oğlan) were sent to the services of Turkish families, mainly in Anatolia, to be familiarized with the Turkish culture and to learn the Turkish language, faith, laws, and customs. Several years later they were re-evaluated and if found to be good Moslems, full Ottomans, and bodily well-developed, they were brought back to Istanbul and assigned services of the palace. The best of these became sipahis of the Porte, joined Janisarries, and subsequently rose to higher offices of government and military. The principles of "merit" and "promotion based on merit" were carefully observed in the ruling institution of the Empire.

Those who were selected for special training were further divided into two groups. A portion were dis-

269

tributed among the households of the provincial Governors and high officers of the central government and were educated and trained in almost the same way as the others in the palace. The second portion went through long years of education and training in the Palace School as pages. The most qualified pages were placed in the regular palace services while the others were assigned to military organizations as the sipahis of the Porte who could subsequently rise to the highest military and governmental positions in various parts of the Empire. Many members of the ruling class had their own slaves (gulâm) who were recruited through similar methods and were given similar training. Most of these could also become full members of the ruling class.[8]

Referring to the slave-family institution Albert Lybyer points out that "perhaps no more daring experiment has been tried on a large scale upon the face of the earth than that embodied in the Ottoman Ruling Institution." He continued:

> ...The Ottoman system deliberately took slaves and made them ministers of state; it took boys from the sheep-run and the plowtail and made them courtiers and the husbands of princesses; it took young men whose ancestors had borne the Christian name for centuries, and made them rulers in the greatest of Mohammedan states, and soldiers and generals in invincible armies whose chief joy was to beat down the Cross and elevate the Crescent. It never asked its novices, 'Who was your father?' or 'What do you know?' or even 'Can you speak our tongue?'; but it studied their faces and their frames and said, 'You shall be a soldier, and if you show yourself worthy, a general,' or 'You shall be a scholar and a gentleman, and if the ability lies in you, a governor and a prime minister.'[9]

With few exceptions all members of the Ottoman palace were the slaves of the sultan. The sultan had absolute power over their lives and property. He had the right to exact their absolute obedience. While "no disgrace was attached to the condition of being the sultan's slave," scholars agree that the title of kul or slave was felt to be an honor and the institutions they formed were considered to be noble institutions. Many Christian families were honored to see their children to be the members of the Ottoman ruling class and serve the sultan.10

The Palace School of Government (Enderun): The Ottoman Palace School of Grand Seraglio, one of the great and original institutions of the Empire, has not attracted sufficient attention from modern historians and students of political science and public administration. The school has been given a variety of names such as "college of pages," "military school of state," "Enderun," and more often "the Palace School." It has been considered by many scholars to be predominantly a military training institution. Thanks to past work of Western scholars, the true educational and administrative nature and the historical importance of this four-century-old Ottoman school for the field of public administration has been revealed.11

The Palace School was founded around 1450's by Muhammed the Conqueror essentially to educate and train the administrators of the state. The executive manpower needs of the palace, the government, the military, and the court were met by this school. The school was the first of its kind and unique in terms of its secular approach, comprehensiveness of its curriculum, and the length of its education. The school is referred as "the Palace School of Government" and is perhaps best described in the following passage:

> One of the most remarkable of their (Ottoman) institutions and at the same time one of the most remarkable educational institutions of its time, indeed of any time, was the Palace School (Enderun) ...The training covered an average period of about twelve to fourteen years and combined in almost equal proportions instruction in the humanities of Islam, in physical training and the arts of war and government, and in manual training; it was one of the most formal, systematic, and arduous courses ever devised in preparation for a public

271

career. As the keystone of the Turkish policy and one of the prime factors
which carried the Ottoman Empire to
its full flowering and helped to stay
its decline by the strength of the
traditions which were centered there,
the importance of this school can
hardly be overestimated.

Under Muhammad's enlightened
direction the Palace School expanded
and took on the definite character
of a school of government, and so
perfect an instrument did it prove
for the purpose for which it was
designed that its perpetuation and
development became one of the most
conscious policies and most powerful
traditions of his successors. Primarily and essentially secular in its
purpose-of which no better proof
exists than the fact that student
scholarships and the pay of the
entire personnel were distributed
from the Bureau of Infantry-the
Palace School of the Turkish sultans
was a greater departure from the
theological or medreseh type of
education than the medieval university was from the monastic and
cathedral schools.[12]

Harem: The imperial harem was a part of the Ottoman palace institution in which the women, the children
and the other female recruits of the palace lived. It
was, in a sense, a training school for the members of
the harem. The women were educated in reading and
writing, housework, embroidery, sewing, Islam, manners,
music, dancing, etc.

The harem was protected by black eunuchs. They were
led by kizlar ağasi who was ranked during the sixteenth
century only after the grand vezir and şeyhülislam. The
most influencial member of the harem, however, was the
sultan's mother (valide sultan). Among the women, next
in importance was the sultan's first son's mother and
then the mothers of other sons. Each wife had her own
court and staff, quarters and gardens. Below the wives
were the privileged women from whom the wives, later

concubines, were chosen.

The sons of the sultans lived with their mothers during the early years of their lives. After long years of elaborate education in the harem, they were sent out, accompanied by carefully selected courts, as governors of provinces.

The harem frequently exercised a powerful influence on the sultan and the affairs of the Empire. The importance of the valide sultan in the palace institution gradually increased as the number of able sultans decreased over the centuries.[13]

The Inner Service: The Inner Service of the palace was the domain of the pages and white eunuchs. It was composed of six departments or chambers: (1) the Privy Chamber (Has Oda), which was essentially responsible for the personal services of the sultan, (2) the Treasury Chamber (Hazine Odasi), which kept the financial archives, stored the valuables and handled the revenues and expenditures, (3) the Larder (Kiler Odasi), which provided the meals, (4) the Campaign Chamber (Seferli Oda), which carried on the campaign activities at the time of war, (5) the Falconry Chamber (Doganci Odasi), which took care of the hunting activities, and (6) the Large and Small Chambers (Büyük Oda, Küçuk Oda), which organized the training and the services of the pages.

The official meetings of the Imperial Council, receptions of ambassadors and similar activites were held in this section of the palace. The Inner Service was under the control of the Kapi Ağasi-the officer of the Gate. The pages could rise to such prestigious positions of the Privy Chamber as sultan's sword bearer, the head valet, and the confidential secretary. Depending on their ability, they could undertake important responsibilities in the Outside Service and could, furthermore, become military commanders, provincial Governors, vezirs, and grand vezirs.[14]

The Outer Service: This part of the palace was concerned with the conduct of the state affairs. It was composed of the officials who were responsible for the administration of the army, education, justice, architecture, etc. The outer palace included the members of the ulema (teachers, doctors, astrologers and religious leaders), the chief architect, the water supervisor, the commissioners of the mint, grains, and kitchen, the commanders of the military corps, the messengers, the gatekeepers, the gardeners, the artisans, etc. Some of these were responsible for the administration of the service throughout the Empire. At the time of war, each group formed a military force, accompanied the sultan and carried out specific military duties. They were organized into a complex hierarchy based on seniority and merit.[15]

2. The Scribal Institution (Kalemiye)

The scribal institution was the core of the Ottoman government. It was organized around both functional departments and guilds based on a rigid hierarchy. Each department was headed by a master who supervised the specialized foremen. The foremen, in turn, were responsible for directing and controlling the scribes, training the apprentices and examining the new candidates for membership in guild and department.

The highest-ranking government official was grand vezir. In addition to conducting government affairs, the grand vezir commanded the army in time of war and appointed some of the high level government officials. In the conduct of government affairs he was aided by the Imperial Council (Divan). The grand vezir carried on most of his duties at the Sublime Porte (Bab-i Ali) in Istanbul.

The Imperial Council was composed of the vezirs including the governors of important regions and provinces , the scribes (the defterdar or the chief treasurer and nişanci or the head of the grand vezir's chancery), the commanders of the armed forces (those of the Janissary and the navy) and the ulema (the two kazaskers or the judicial chiefs). The reis ul-küttap (the chief of the Council's scribes) and the chief translator, also attended the meetings. The vezirs were originally appointed to undertake some of the responsibilities of the grand vezir in his absence, particularly in time of war. Their number increased to nine during the sixteenth century. The Council passed on petitions, issued decisions, promulgated official orders, gave diplomas and made special pronouncements.

The regional, provincial and local governments were, in a sense, the extension of the scribal institution. The Empire was divided into two (later on more)

administrative regions called <u>beylerbeyliks</u>, one for
the administration of the properties of the Empire in
Anatolia and the other for Europe. Each region was
under the rule of a <u>beylerbeyi</u> or Governor-General
(later <u>vali</u> or <u>paşa</u>) who was appointed by an imperial
decree. He was granted one of the largest landed fiefs
(<u>has</u>) and enjoyed the title of <u>vezir</u>. The Governors-
General directed the military and civil affairs of
their regions with the help of their own staff and
assemblies (<u>divans</u>).

Each region was divided into provinces (<u>vilayets</u>),
which were further divided into towns (<u>kazas</u>), communes
and villages. Provinces were administered by centrally
appointed Governors (<u>sancak beys</u>). They also had their
own courts, carried the title of <u>paşa</u> and were responsible to the Governors-General.

3. The Learned Institution (Llmiye)

The learned institution was composed of the <u>ulema</u>
(the learned men). It was in charge of organizing and
maintaining a united community of Muslims interpreting,
applying and enforcing the religious law (şeriat),
teaching the religious sciences in the mosques and
schools, and training new learned men.16

Each province was divided into a number of judicial
districts and each judicial district was the domain of
a judge (<u>kadi</u>). The judicial system was headed by the
two <u>kadiaskers</u> (or <u>kazaskers</u>), one for Anatolia and the
other for Europe. In addition to their judicial work,
the judges supervised the mosques, religious endowments,
imperial land and the collection of taxes, appointed
instructors to schools, assessed special taxes, took
the census of animals, fixed the prices for grain and
handled the conflicts over the land ownership.

The <u>muftis</u>, another major group in the learned
institution, were the private practioners of law. They
helped the judges and other government officials in
interpreting the Sacred Law. They issued legal opinions
(<u>fetvas</u>) on specific questions. Suleyman the Magnificent organized this institution into a hierarchy similar
to that of the <u>kadis</u> and placed the <u>şeyhulislam</u> (chief
of Islam) in charge of it. From then on the <u>muftis</u> to
all major cities and districts were appointed by the
<u>şeyhulislam</u>.17

4. The Military Institution (Seyfiye or Askeriye)

All the members of the armed forces or the "men of sword" belonged to this institution. Their main duties were the protection and expansion of the Empire and the provision of order and security.

The armed force was divided into the land army and the navy. The two basic components of the land army were the kapikulu army (the slaves of the Porte) and the feudal army or the provincial forces. The kapikulu army included such units as the Janissary corps, the artillery corps, and the kapikulu cavalry The feudal forces, which provided the larger part of the armed forces, was composed of the landed sipahi calvary (the timarli sipahis) and the special or auxiliary forces such as the fortress guards, the derbent guards and the raiding forces.[18]

Decline and Reforms

The death of Suleyman the Magnificent was also the end of the Ottoman rise. Starting with the last quarter of the sixteenth century, the Empire first experienced a century of stagnation and then went through a long process of decline and reformation. The process of decline was gradual and the causes of decay were innumerable. Among the factors which brought an end to the expansion of the Empire, the political and military ones have attracted the greatest attention. However, a wide variety of social and economic problems and external developments also were responsible for the downfall of the Ottoman Empire.[19]

The Ottoman Empire was charactertized by the millet system which enabled the non-Moslem groups to maintain their cultural and national identities. The Ottomans failed to provide the necessary integration and sense of belongingness. Being more receptive to the Western nationalistic ideas, the economically well-developed Christian millets started to demand and fight for their independence.[20] Also, the rising prosperity of Western Europe and the increasing strength of Russia accelerated the independence movement and the deterioration of the Empire.[21]

The first ten sultans of the Ottoman Empire had been trained by the best teachers, had participated in government, ruled as provincial Governors, led

276

armies, and had risen to power through their abilities. They had used their slaves against the powerful Turkish aristocracy and had been able to provide the necessary balance in the society and control their subjects.

After Suleyman's death, however, weak sultans succeeded one another. They isolated themselves from the people. They were now educated and trained by the females and eunuchs of the palaces and sometimes became the puppets of the mothers or wives. Instead of the ablest, the eldest living male member of the dynasty or the one favored by the most powerful faction of the palace succeeded to the throne. The struggle for power and the conflicts among the members of the royal family were intensified.[22]

The order and discipline in the military corps gradually deteriorated. Most of their members left the barracks and military training and became landlords or merchants; but continued to enjoy their revenues and privileges. The Janissaries were granted to enroll their sons in the corps and started to receive regular salaries. Some of them were sent to provinces as garrison and became quite independent. They gradually became a part of palace politics and the determining force in the succession to the throne. They asked for bribes and/or salary increases in return for their support. Many local inhabitants entered the Janissary corps through the use of illegal means to enjoy privileged positions. The feudal army and the timar system (the distribution of imperial lands as fiefs for military service) also declined.

The devşirme system was abolished by mid-seventeenth century. Many devşirme boys, however, had already risen to the highest governmental positions. These members of the ruling class also participated in the palace politics and exploited their positions for personal gains. The government positions were sold to mostly unqualified people for large gifts and the position-holders, in turn, did their best to exploit their positions for material gains and political power. The widespread corruption and bribery practiced at the capital, soon became the dominant practice of the regional and local administrations as well.[23]

The political and military decay led to military and naval defeats. The income and capital accumulation based on war booty gradually decreased. Changes in international trade brought further economic difficulties. Capitulations (commerical privileges granted to foreigners, particularly to the French) were extended. Military fief-holders were replaced by absentee landlords and tax-farmers. Currency was devalued, taxes were raised and offices were sold. The attempt to extract more resources led to oppression and injustice.[24] The feudal exploitation became the greatest source of unrest and frequent internal uprisings and revolts.

The political, military, and socio-economic deterioration of the Empire was paralleled by the reform attempts. The early traditionalistic reform attempts of the seventeenth and eighteenth centuries were essentially based on the assumption that the Ottoman decline was the result of the failure to operate the original Ottoman system properly. It was believed that "reform could be achieved by making the system work as it had previously, eliminating those who stole, ending bribery and corruption, making appointment only according to ability, reforming and revitalizing the traditional military corps and throwing out all those who refused to perform the duties required of them."[25]

Among the early reformers of the Ottoman Empire, the Grand Vezir Sokullu Mehmet (1565-1579, who was a produce of the devsirme and also the Sultan's son-in-law), Sultan Osman II (1618-1622), Sultan Murat IV (1623-1640) and Grand Vezir Mehmet Köprülü (1656-1683, who also had entered the sultan's service as a devsirme youth), are well-known. Particularly the reforms of Murat IV deserve mentioning here. Following the advice of his adviser Koçu Bey, Murat IV eliminated all the Celali and Sipahi rebels. Thousands of bandits were sought by the Janissaries and executed on the spot. The timar system was completely reformed and once again became the financial and political basis of a strong army and administration. The timar holders who were either unable or unwilling to provide military service in return for their land were dismissed. The land was redistributed mostly among the Janissaries. Ability and honesty once again became the main criteria for appointments to government positions. All those who had attempted to use their positions for personal advantage and those who refused to conform were eliminated. Bribery and corruption was ended; order, security and military discipline was restored; the laws and regulations of the Empire were observed. In short,

Murat was quite successful in making old institutions work and set the pattern for the later traditionalist reformers.[26]

Nevertheless, the traditional reforms, although successful, lacked continuity. They were abandoned as soon as the immediate dangers were taken care of and, as a result, the decline of the Empire could not be stopped.

The failure of the Ottoman army to take Vienna (1683) gave Europe the opportunity to take the offensive. It also marked the beginning of a new era of internal disintegration and rapid decline. That was the first time that few people started to think that it was time to take a serious look at Europe, study their institutions and techniques and consider the possiblity of importing them.

The New Order of Selim III (1789-1807)

The most important and systematic reform attempt of the 18th century came from Selim III and his newly formed group of reformist administrators. Although most of his reforms were only partly successful, Selim III, was able to set the stage for the later more successful reforms and to open the Ottoman doors to Western technology. He attempted to reform all the existing military corps in accordance with the principle of separation of administrative and military functions, leaving the military commanders with only military duties. His reform attempts were largely resisted by the Janissaries and the Sipahis. This resistance pushed Selim into the development of an entirely new infantry force. This new military institution, Nizam-1 Cedit or "New Order," was created with the help of the European experts brought from France, England and Germany and was organized and trained in the European manner.

In addition to the military reforms, Selim also established many technical and engineering schools, changed the basic structure of the navy, reorganized the scribal service into an expanded administrative department, and dealt with some urgent economic and social problems. In his administrative reforms, Selim subjected the scribes to new standards of honesty and efficiency; inefficient ones were dismissed; nepotism and bribery was eliminated; appointments were based on

ability; appointment gifts required by Sultans was
reduced; and reis ul-küttap became adminstrative
assistant to the Grand Vezir and was put in charge of
the administrative system.

Although not too innovative, Selim's reforms
created lots of opposition and threatened the Janissaries who eventually revolted against him in May 1807,
first deposed and then executed him and secured a fetva
declaring his reforms illegal violations of religion
and tradition.

The Reforms of Mahmut II

Mahmut II (1808-1839), greatly influenced by his
cousin Selim III, emerged as one of the most sucessful
reformers of the Empire. He is sometimes referred to
as the Peter the Great of the Ottoman Empire. He
believed that no real progress towards reforms could be
made until all other sources of power in the Empire
were eliminated.

He successfully eliminated the Janissaries and
put an end to this centuries-old corrupt institution
in 1826. All the opposing forces, challenging sources
of power, provincial notables derebeys, dervishes, and
all armed forces other than the newly created army were
destroyed. During the last 13 years of his reign,
after having the main obstacles removed, Mahmut II
embarked on a whole series of large scale reforms in
all areas.[27] He put lots of emphasis on the education
and training by foreigners, sent students to European
military academies and, changed the titles, customs and
physical appearance in general. New schools (the
Imperial Music School and the School of Military
Sciences) were created; learning of foreign languages
by the Muslim Turks was emphasized.

The core of Mahmut II's administrative reforms
was the centralization of all powers in his hands,
elimination of all intermediate authorities, and
domination of the civilian government over the military.

To realize these ends, he abolished another major
institution of the Empire-namely the timar (military
fief) and the associated Ottoman type of feudalism.
The first Ottoman census and a land survey, for con-
scription and taxation purposes, were accomplished in
1831. Another category of lands and estates-the evkaf

(the pious foundations)-were brought together under
a new Directorate (later Ministry) of Evkaf with the
intention to centralize their revenues and expenditures and end the existing chaos in this old Islamic
institution. This reform helped him to weaken the
ulema and other religious powers and subject them to
the Sultan's control. In 1831 the first issue of the
Ottoman official gazette-Takvim-i Vekayi- was published.
New roads were built and a number of other measures
were taken to improve communication.

While extending and strengthening the authority
and control of the central government over the provinces, Mahmut II also subjected the central government
itself to a number of significant changes. Old institutions and traditions were replaced with new ones.
The new Serasker and his staff "became the nucleus of
the civilian Ministry of War which, until Young Turks
Revolution, was able to maintain the control of the
central government over the armed forces and prevent
the recurrence of anything like the constant janissary
uprisings that had terrorized the sultans of the
preceeding period."[28] For the first time, an office
was created for the Grand Mufti, which led to the
bureaucratization of the ulema, weakening their power
to resist changes. Some of the duties of the ulema
were transferred to the newly created Ministries of
Education and Justice.

In 1835, the office of the Grand Vezir- the sublime Porte- became the target of reforms. For the last
two centuries, the Sublime Porte had become an autonomous power center under the domination of the Grand
Vezir. Mahmut II changed the vezirs into ministers
and grand vezir into prime minister. The departments
of Kahya and the Reis Efendi were transferred into the
Ministry of Civil Affairs (later Ministry of Interior)
and the Ministry of Foreign Affairs respectively. The
office of the Defterdar became the Ministry of Finance.
A new Council of Ministers, presided over by the Prime
Minister, was created. This was followed by the creation of such new councils as the Council for Military
Affairs, the High Council for Judicial Ordinances, and
similar executive committees for agriculture, trade,
industry and public works. A new translation chamber
at the Sublime Porte was given the responsibility for
teaching Western languages and the training of public
servants for foreign service. The permanent embassies
in London, Paris, and Vienna, and resident missions in

other European capitals were reconstituted. And some of the early ambassadors became the major proponents of the later reforms. A whole new bureaucratic class, with a completely different background and with no aristocratic ties, came into existence.[29]

The Tanzimat Period (1839-1876)

Mahmut II died in 1839. His reforms were carried on by the bureaucrats under his sons Abdulmecid (1839-1861) and Abdulaziz (1861-1876). They promulgated a number of reforming edicts, which are collectively known as tanzimat or Reorganization. The first of these was formulated by Mustafa Resit Paşa, former ambassador to London, with the consent of the new sultan, and promulgated on the third of November 1839. This reform edict, known as the "Edict of Gülhane" or "Gülhane Hatt-i Humayunu" (sometimes referred to as the Noble Rescript of the Rose Chamber) was, in essence, the Ottoman "Bill of Rights." It proclaimed such principles as "the security of life, honour, and property of the subject, the abolition of tax-farming and all the abuses associated with it, regular and orderly recruitment into the armed forces, fair and public trial of persons accused of crime, and equality of all persons of all religions in the application of these laws".[30]

The Edict of Gülhane was followed by the "Reform Edict" or the Islahat Fermani, which was imposed upon the Porte by the European powers as a condition for participation in the Concert of Europe and the Paris Conference of 1856. This new rescript reaffirmed the principles and the promises of the 1839 edict, proclaimed complete equality of all Ottoman subjects and contained such provisions as adherence to the annual budget, codification of laws, a variety of judicial reforms, improvements of provincial and communal councils, etc.

These two reform edicts led to the development of the new concept of Ottomanism or the new theory of "one citizenship for all subjects of the Ottoman Empire" which remained valid until 1918. The newly formed Young Ottomans (Yeni Osmanlilar) Society (1865) was the first major political organization which aimed at achieving a constitutional monarchy. It was essentially under the influence of the Young Ottomans and the pressures of foreign powers that Abdulhamit II (1876-1909) promulgated the first Ottoman constitution of 1876.[31]

Equality of all Ottomans, inviolable personal
liberty, free exercise of all faiths, Islam as the
religion of the state, free press, free education,
equality of citizens in holding public offices, Turkish
as the official language, equitable taxation, right to
own property, a modern judicial system for provincial,
departmental and district councils, and a bicameral
legislature were some of the important provisions of
the constitution. The Parliament was composed of a
House of Deputies and a Senate. The deputies would
be elected by the people-one each for each 50,000 inhabitants; the members of the Senate would be appointed
by the Sultan for life.[32] The constitution, however,
preserved all the powers of the Sultan. Shortly after
its opening Abdulhamit II dissolved the parliament
suspended the constitution (1878), gradually abolished
the freedoms, and ruled despotically until 1908.

Young Turks Movement (1889-1919)

The suspension of the constitution led to the
establishment of a number of secret organizations aimed
at overthrowing the Sultan and reinforcing the constitution of 1876. It started with the revolutionary society
formed by a group of students at the Imperial Military
Medical School in 1889- the Ottoman Union and Progress
Association (Osmanli Ittihatve Terakki Cemiyeti) and
was followed by a number of similar associations established in Paris and other major European cities, led by
the intelligentsia who left the country because of police brutality. The members of the first association
called themselves the "Young Turks" and all other
organizations with the same purpose were named after
them. After some years of struggle over the leadership, tactics and strategies, the Young Turks Associations were able to get united in 1908. The same year,
the Young Turks, led by the intelligentsia of the lower
middle class background and supported by a number of
military leaders, revolted against Abdulhamit II's
despotism and forced him to restore the Constitution
of 1876. Abdulhamit was deposed; his brother Mehmet V
was brought to the throne; the Young Turks came to power
and with brief intervals remained in control of government until 1918.

As soon as in power, the Young Turks were divided
into several major groups with different ideologies and
reform strategies. Although they all shared the main
objective of saving the state, they struggled with one

another hoping to impose three different ideologies:
Ottomanism, pan-Islamism and Pan-Turkism. There were
conservatives who favored an Islamic Empire. Modern-
ists were further divided into liberals or Westernists
and nationalists. The liberals advocated Ottomanism,
decentralization, and some autonomy for the religious
and national minorities. The nationalists, on the other
hand were for central authority and Turkish domination.
A smaller group of the nationalists aimed at Pan-
Turkism or uniting all the Turks living abroad in one
single country.

Although the ideal of the Young Turks was to
establish a Western type of parliamentary democracy
their success in that direction remained quite limited.
Their success in controlling the parliament and the
powers of the sultan did not stop the growing opposition
which gradually pushed them into limiting the freedoms
and after 1913 led to a military dictatorship, dominated
by Enver, Talat and Cemal Paşas.

The Young Turks have been condemned for the intru-
sion of army into politics and militarization of government, denying the country a democratic government, the
practiced violence, repression and terror, their entry
into the first World War, and the subsequent defeat
which brought the end of the Ottoman Empire. However,
in spite of all the "plot and counterplot, repression
and sedition, tyranny, humiliation, and defeat," the
Young Turks tried to save the Empire through legislative and administrative action and prepared conditions
for the emergence of the new Turkish Republic.

The Young Turks introduced a new system of provincial and local administration which, with some minor
changes, remained in effect under the new Turkish
Republic. Police administration, transportation and
communication systems were improved. The military
police-gendamerie- was reorganized, extended and put
under the control of the Ministry of the Interior.
A policy of economic nationalism was adopted. Every
aspect of daily life was modernized and Westernization
movement gained momentum. During their first few years
there was an outburst of intellectual activity, political discussion and freedom to write and speak. Literature prospered; newspaper circulation increased, new
secondary schools were opened; the University of
Istanbul was reorganized and the status and education
of women were improved. A new Family Law, enacted

by emergency order, increased women's rights and imposed certain limitations on polygamy. Koran and certain prayers were translated into Turkish. Secularism gradually replaced traditionalism and the importance of the religious courts was minimized after the domestic legal cases were transferred to civilian courts.[33]

Emergence and Development of the Turkish Republic

At the end of the First World War, Sultan Vahdettin signed an armistice. The Committee of Union and Progress collapsed; the Young Turks ministers resigned; Enver, Ralat and Cemal Paşas left the country, and all other members were arrested. The allied forces occupied Istanbul. In 1919, a Greek army protected by the British, French and American warships landed in Izmir and advanced into the Anatolia. Various parts of the Empire were occupied by the French, British, and Italian forces. The Sultan and his government in Istanbul became mere puppets in the hands of the Allied forces.

Mustafa Kemal, the only successful war time military commander, was designated by the Sultan as Inspector General of the Third Army Headquarters to supervise the demobilization of the Turkish forces against the Allied occupation. Mustafa Kemal had departed from the Committee of Union and Progress in 1909 and could not be held responsible for defeat. He landed at Samsun, a few days after the Greek invasion of Izmir. There he immediately resigned from his military responsibilities and started to organize a movement and raise an army against the Sultan, his government and the Allied occupation.

Mustafa Kemal was already in touch with the resistance groups in Anatolia which were mostly in need of leadership. He joined with the Eastern Anatolian Society for the Defense of National Rights and later became its chairman. Under his charismatic leadership, the divided, hungry and exhausted people came together. He organized two Congresses, one in Erzurum (July 1919) and the other in Sivas (September 1919), where "a resolution for the defense of the integrity of national frontiers and the convocation of the National Assembly" was adopted and a free and independent Turkey was called for.

On the other hand, the Sultan had been convinced
to hold new elections; and the elections had resulted
in a parliament with a nationalist majority. However,
the nationalists were condemned by both the Sultan and
his government and the Allied forces in Istanbul. Some
nationalist members of the Parliament were arrested by
the British and some others were exiled to Anatolia.
Mustafa Kemal decided to hold a new election for the
Grand National Assembly which was opened in Ankara in
April 23, 1920 and was proclaimed as the only and
supreme power of the State. And Mustafa Kemal was
elected as its first President.[34]

After several years of continuous wars, struggle,
and negotiation, the Greeks were driven from Anatolia
and the Allies were obliged to negotiate a new armistice agreement with the new Turkish Government in
Ankara. All the foreign troops were removed from
Anatolia, Istanbul and Eastern Thrace. The Sultanate
was abolished in 1922. On July 23, 1923, the Treaty
of Lausanne was signed, and on October 29, 1923,
Turkey was proclaimed a Republic. Mustafa Kemal was
given the name "Atatürk" (father of the Turks) and
was elected as the first President of the Republic
by the Grand National Assembly.

The Reforms of Ataturk

As Mango points out, "Turkey has had many reformers. Among them Mustafa Kemal stands out as the most
radical and the most consistent.[35] During the independence war more than two and a half million people
had died. Foreign trade and state revenues had fallen
sharply; and the retail price index had skyrocketed.
The war had left leaving nothing but ruins and ashes
of the Ottoman Empire. Ataturk created a whole new and
modern nation out of those ruins. He used his Republican People's Party as the organized force to achieve his
reforms and made his reform program the official program of the Party. His ideas and policies expressed in
his speeches and practices came to be known as Kemalism.
The six principles of Kemalism which also provided the
ideological basis of Atatürk's reforms, were republicanism, nationalism, secularism, populism, etatism and
revolutionism.[36]

The Sultanate and the Caliphate were replaced by
the Republic. Republicanism was expressed in terms of
the sovereignty of the people and their right to rule
themselves. "Sovereignty Belongs to the Nation",

became the motto of the new Republic. The nation was to be governed by and for the people.

Nationalism focused attention on the Turkish nation inside the frontiers and excluded such ideas as "pan-Turkism", "Ottomanism", or "internationalism." Nationalism was institutionalized through the new Turkish Historical Society (1925), which developed nationalist theories of history and language (such as the Sun-Language theory), and the Turkish Language Society (1926) which was responsible for the Turkification of the language.

Secularism, according to Ataturk, meant total exclusion of religious influence from public life. This included both the separation of the state from religious institutions and the liberation of human mind from the religious restraints. To achieve this end, the caliphate, the Ministry of Religious Foundation, the office and the position of Şeyhulislam, and the entire system of religious schools (medrese) were abolished. In their place, two small departments (Religious Affairs and Religious Foundations) were created and placed directly under the prime minister's office. A unified system of secular education was created. Moreover, Şeriat courts were abolished and şeriat and mecelle were replaced by new secular civil, commerical, and criminal laws. All the dervish lodges, cells and religious tombs were closed and the use of religious titles was prohibited. Polygamy was eliminated. Divorce by court action and civil marriages were made compulsory. Women were liberated and were given the rights to vote and to be elected and to be employed in all fields on an equal basis. The international time, calendar and metric systems were adopted. All Turks were required to learn and use Latin Alphabets and adopt family names. Elementary education was made compulsory. The use of such titles as paşa, efendi, bey was prohibited. The Ottoman University (Dar ul-fünun) was reorganized as the University of Istanbul. The old Civil Service School (Mekteb-i Mülkiye) became the School of Political Science and was transferred to Ankara. Many technical and vocational schools and a faculty of Language, History and Geography were opended.

Populism emphasized the equality of all citizens before the law and necessitated the representative democracy or government by and for the people. This

principle was specified in the 1924 constitution and
was accomplished through the Grand National Assembly.
The Assembly had both legislative and executive powers.
The executive function was **delegated** to the President
and the Council of Ministers. Judicial functions were
carried out by the courts on behalf of the Assembly.

Etatism or statism referred to the role of the
state in economic development. The government supervised and participated in the economic activities.
Many new laws were passed to encourage and many new
banks were opened to support agriculture, industry
and business. State economic enterprises carried on
industrialization and played a major role in the overall economic development of the country.

Finally, revolutionism provided the philosophical
basis for reforms, change and transformation. The
reforms were carried on with a spirit of revolution,
through the use of radical and forced measures and
with the intention to achieve them in the shortest
period of time.

Recent Developments

Atatürk died in 1938. Ismet Inönü became the
second President of the Republic and remained in power
until 1950. During his presidency the public bureaucracy became a professional, prestigious and highly
protected institution with many prerogatives. It
gradually grew into a black-box, non-responsive to
the public needs and demands. The single-party rule
was maintained until 1946. In 1946 Inönü voluntarily
decided to extend and enlarge the political freedoms
and practice multi-party democracy.

The newly formed Democrat party won the elections
of 1950 and came into power with its free-enterprise
oriented economic policies. A period of fast growth
and prosperity was followed by high unemployment, debt
and inflation which, together with the revival of the
religious factions, led to the 1960 revolution. The
1961 Constitution created the Second Republic which was
based on social rights and freedoms, social responsibilities of the state, more sensitive balance of powers,
and a bi-cameral Parliament. The new election law based
on the system of proportional representation caused a
long period of unstable coalition governments. The new
State Planning Organization was eventually politicized

and was not able to develop the necessary economic
policies to prevent economic deterioration. The country was divided into ideological and religious camps.
The irresponsibility and inefficiency of governments
created an authority gap which was filled by the mili-
tant political groups. All these resulted in the 1971
military intervention and the September 12, 1980 military takeover.

The 1961 Constitution: Administrative Institutions of the Second Republic:

Although some new elements have been added to it,
the existing administrative system of Turkey is,
essentially, the continuation of the Ottoman administrative institutions. What follows is a brief description of the Turkish administrative system as formulated
by the 1961 Constitution. However, it should be noted
that some of these institutions may soon be changed or
reorganized by the National Security Council and the
recently formed Advisory Assembly (or the constituent
parliament.[37]

The provisions of the 1924 Constitution, which
were essentially based on the principles of the 1921
Constitution, can be summarized as follows: The
Turkish state is a republic; sovereignty belongs to
the Nation; the Grand National Assembly is the sole
representative of the Nation and exercises the right
of sovereignty; legislative and executive powers are
concentrated in the Grand National Assembly which
exercises its legislative power directly and its
executive power through the president of the Republic
elected by it and the Council of Ministers chosen by
him; the Assembly has the power to control and dismiss
the government; and the Judicial function is carried
on by the independent courts.

The concentration of both legislative and executive powers in a single Assembly later on became the
source of political misuses. The Democrat Party,
which came into power in 1950, started to limit the
autonomy of the universities, acquired the right to
oust civil servants without giving them the right of
appeal, restricted the freedoms, and threatened the
political opposition, the press and the Judiciary.
The Constitution contained no provisions to prevent a
government with the majority support in the legislative
body to abuse its power. This weakness of the 1924

Constitution, coupled with the inadequacy of the electoral system based on simple majority with multi-member districts, led to deviations from the democratic processes.

The 1961 Constitution, emerged out of the efforts to overcome the shortcomings of the 1924 Constitution, to prevent the legislative and the executive bodies from abusing power, to protect the independence of courts as well as individual rights and freedoms, and to recognize the modern social duties and responsibilities of the state. The "concentration of powers" was replaced by the "separation of powers" and a system of checks and balances.

The Constitution of the Second Republic (1961) brought such innovations as a bicameral legislature, presidential veto, Constitutional Court, State Planning Organization, "social state," autonomy for the universities, the news agencies, and the administration of radio and television, and more explicit and detailed spelling of individual rights and freedoms.

The Second Turkish Republic is characterized as a national, democratic, secular and social State under the rule of law and based on human rights. The legislative power is vested in the Turkish Grand National Assembly and cannot be delegated; the executive function is exercised by the President of the Republic and the Council of Ministers within the framework of the law; and the Judicial power is exercised by the independent courts on behalf of the Nation. Among the fundamental rights and duties, social and economic rights and obligations are emphasized. Some of these are the right to work, rest, equitable remuneration, to establish trade unions and employer's associations, to bargain collectively and to strike, social security, health and education. "It is the duty of the State to encourage economic, social and cultural development by democratic processes, and for this purpose to increase the volume of national savings, to accord priority to those investment projects which promote public welfare, and to formulate plans for development" (Article 41).

The Turkish Grand National Assembly is composed of the National Assembly and the Senate of the Republic. The Senate is one of the significant elements of checks and balances provided in the new Constitution.

Although the Cabinet is responsible only for the National Assembly and the principle of the supremacy of the lower chamber has been adopted, the Senate can play a significant role in Parliamentary control through questions, inquiries, general debate, and law-making process.

The President of the Republic is elected jointly by the National Assembly and the Senate for a term of seven years from among the members of either house. The President elect needs to dissociate himself from his party and other duties, and is not eligible for re-election. His duties relate to his dual roles as the head of the State and the head of the executive branch.

The Council of Ministers consists of the Prime Minister and the Ministers. The Prime Minister is appointed by the President from among the members of the Turkish Grand National Assembly. The ministers, in turn, are nominated by the Prime Minister either from within or from without the parliament and are appointed by the President. The Ministers of Justice, Interior, and Communications are required to resign prior to the elections for the National Assembly and be replaced by the new Ministers to be appointed from among the independent members of the Grand National Assembly.

Independence of Judiciary is another basic principle of the 1961 Constitution. It provides that the Judges and the courts be absolutely independent and free from interference in the performance of their duties. The decisions concerning the appointment, promotion, transfer, and/or removal of Judges are taken by a newly created autonomous Supreme Council of Judges.* A new Constitutional Court has been created for Judicial review of the legislative acts. No act or procedure of the administration is exempt from review by the courts.

The organization and functions of the administration are based on both centralization and decentralization. In terms of central administration, the country is divided into provinces, which are further divided into smaller administrative districts. The division is

---

*The Supreme Council of Judges has recently been abolished by the military administration.

based on geographical and economic factors and the requirements of public service. Provincial adminis-tration is based on the principle of self-government. Provinces can form regional self-governing organiza-tions to carry out specific public services. Local administrative bodies are public corporate entities. They are created to meet the needs of the local com-munities such as provinces, municipal districts, and villages. Their policy-making organs are elected by the people. The organization and functioning of the local administrative bodies and their relationships with the central government are regulated by law. Their sources of income need to be provided propor-tionate to their functions.

Public service functions are carried out by government officials as regulated by law. The civil servants, as well as all other government officials, are protected by the Constitution through detailed disciplinary procedures and subjecting disciplinary action to the review of the courts of justice. They are prohibited to join political parties and to discriminate between citizens on the basis of their political views.

The Role of the Civil Bureaucracy in the Modernization of Turkey

The civil bureaucracy has played a significant role in the modernization and development of Turkey. The reformers of the late nineteenth century emerged from among the bureaucrats. In fact, the bureaucrats dominate the whole Tanzimat period. They led the Young Ottomans movement and the Young Turks revolution. Ataturk depended, to a large extent, on bureaucrats in achieving his reforms. Thus, the bureaucracy has been the modernizing as well as the stabilizing force in the Ottoman-Turkish state. It has sometimes resisted but mostly supported change over the centuries.

The Ottoman-Turkish civil bureaucracy has its origin in the Ottoman Palace School of Administration (Enderun) and was developed, essentially, under the weak Sultans who succeeded Suleyman the Magnificent. The Grand Vezir gradually became the acting head of the state and the civil bureaucracy grew out of his head-quarters in the Sublime porte in Istanbul.

The growing civil bureaucracy had at least three

rivals: the military, the ecclesiastical institution, and the provincial nobles. Moreover, its strength was based on the power of its chief, the Grand Vezir, who was subject to the authority of the Sultan and whose power was quite insecure. The attempts of Selim III and Mahmut II toward political centralization, elimination of provincial notables and independent or rebellious paşas, and subordination of military and ecclesiastical (ulema) institutions to the civilian authority resulted in the domination of the civil bureaucracy over its rivals. The three basic developments of the nineteenth century which greatly influenced the growth of the Ottoman-Turkish civil bureaucracy are well summarized by Chambers thus:

> ...(1) The authority of the central
> government over the provinces was
> extended and regularized; (2) the
> military institution, itself bureau-
> cratized, was largely divorced from
> politics and subordinated to a
> government manned by civilians;
> and (3) the religious institution
> was so thoroughly subsumed into the
> civil bureaucracy that it ceased to
> exist as a separate entity.[38]

The central administration itself also was subject to reforms. As was discussed earlier, bribery and corruption had greatly reduced its efficiency. The central bureaucracy itself, just like the military and ecclesiastical institutions, had started to become a self-interested and independent source of power, a rival to the sultan's authority. While dealing with other problems, Mahmut did not neglect to reorganize the Sublime Porte. New offices, councils and ministries were created; new schools and training institutions were opened; and a number of other measures were taken to strengthen the civil bureaucracy and increase its efficiency.[39] The reform edicts of the Tanzimat period provided further job security, professionalization, specialization and rationalization of the Ottoman-Turkish bureaucracy. Red-tape, corruption, nepotism and favoritism were reduced.

It should be noted, however, that bureaucratic reforms of the Tanzimat period were different from many previous ones in the sense that they were led by the bureaucrats themselves rather than the reformist

Sultans. Although such Grand Vezirs as Sokullu and Köprülü had attempted in the past to reorganize the Ottoman government, this was the first systematic attempt on the part of the civil bureaucracy to reorganize and modernize itself, together with other institutions of the state, and undertake political leadership.

After the Turkish revolution, Atatürk and his associates regarded the bureaucracy as an instrument of nation-building. They were able to stimulate and rely heavily on the bureaucrats in carrying out their reform program. Their attempts to create a new and efficient bureaucracy and break away from the Ottoman tradition, however, were not enough to change the nature and structure of the Turkish bureaucracy.

During the first few decades of the Republic the bureaucracy grew in number and prestige. The etatist economic policy of the 1930's increased its role and importance. Civil bureaucracy was able to attract the ablest graduates of the universities. Bureaucrats willingly undertook the responsibility of achieving the goals of the revolution which had been identified in the program of the Republican People's Party as republicanism, nationalism, populism, revolutionism, secularism and etatism. They worked in close cooperation with the political leaders, and were supported in their efforts to achieve secularism and democracy by the academic intelligentsia. Some of them became political leaders and assumed the political responsibility of building and leading the Nation.

The etatism of 1930's created the necessary conditions for the emergence of a new middle class- the bourgeoisie. Under the Ottoman Empire economic activities had always been looked upon by the ruling class as something inferior and nonprestigious. Such activities were mostly carried on by the minorities and, as a result, an entrepreneurial group and an economic middle class had not risen. The transition to the multiparty system and the elections of 1946 and 1950 gave the new middle class the opportunity to rise to power.

As pointed out by Metin Heper, "the years 1950-60 witnessed a confrontation between a civil bureaucracy and the political representatives of the emerging bourgeoisie."[40]   The Democrat Party, with the promise and aim to open up the self-perpetuating bureaucracy to the people and subordinate it to their will, passed new laws which made it easier for them to dismiss and/ or retire the civil servants from their executive positions. Such attempts created resentment and antago- nistic attitudes against political leaders. The rising inflation which led to the loss of income for the bureaucrats, the unfulfilled promises and the dictator- ial tendencies of the Democrat Party- suppression of the opposition and the attempt to divide the people into different camps- brought the coup d'etat of May 27, 1960. It is believed by some that the 1960 Revolution, like many others before, had been engineered by the bureau- crats.[41]

After the 1960 Revolution, the civil bureaucracy started to regain some of its prestige lost under the Democrat Party. 1961 Constitution created a number of new autonomous institutions all of which were staffed by the bureaucrats. The State Planning Organization took the lead in the process of planned development. A new State Personnel Office was created and a new Personnel Law was passed (1965) which was a semi- successful attempt toward professionalization and rationalization of the civil service. Efficient admin- istration of the development programs gained importance. A major research project (METHAP) was initiated in 1962 to investigate the functions and the structure of the central government and make proposals and recommenda- tions for its reorganization. Similar projects were carried on on the local governments and the state economic enterprises. These projects, however, could not achieve much beyond several volumes of reports added to the earlier ones which embellish the shelves of these organization, essentially because of the coalition governments and the resulting political instability, economic difficulties and social unrest.

The indirect military intervention of March 12, 1971 put a new emphasis on bureaucracy and administra- tive reform. The high-level bureaucrats and techno- crats came to the forefront once again and played a significant role in politics. They could not, however, change much. The short-lived coalition or minority governments went on; the rising inflation and the ideological polarization, anarchy, chaos and terror could not be stopped until the bloodless military takeover of September 1980. Like all other institu- tions in the country, except the armed forces, the ministries and all government offices also were divided into the leftist and the rightist camps. The political parties, as partners of the coalition governments, changed a great number of civil servants in the ministries and the affiliated state economic enterprises, sometimes from the top executives down to the janitors, each time they came into power. This widely practiced partronage system, has significantly lowered the impartiality, professionalization, and efficiency of the civil service. The innovative and the reformist nature of the bureaucracy has greatly been suppressed by the political forces and their terrorist methods of power struggle.

It seems that the civil bureaucracy has once again been subdued to politics; but not opened to the people. However, the cost has been too high. The military has moved in and the bureaucracy has largely been crippled. Although the present military administration has stopped the deterioration process, it may take long years for the bureaucracy to regain its impartiality and efficiency and reassume its reformist role as the guardian of the state and the agent of change and development.

The recent developments in Turkey point out another interesting practice: the cooperation between the civil bureaucracy and the armed forces. The military has always played an important role in the Turkish politics. It has been in close cooperation with the civil bureaucracy in its power struggle against Sultans (after Mahmut II) and the political leaders of the Turkish Republic after 1950. It has supported the Young Turks Revolution, which was led by the bureaucrats and turned into a military dictatorship; has overthrown the anti-bureaucratic government in 1960; and has presently formed a government and an advisory council (constituent parliament) composed of senior civil and military bureaucrats. Like the bureaucrats, the military also has occupied an important place in the political leadership and has been another major modernizing force in Turkey.[42]

Although the Ottoman-Turkish civil bureaucracy has always been the main source of reforms and has undertaken a significant role in the development of modern Turkey, the number of reformers which it has generated has not been too impressive. There seem to be several reasons for that. Among them the authoritarian nature of the Turkish culture, the worsening reward system, the competition of the private sector, and the internal weaknesses of the bureaucracy itself are noteworthy.

The authoritarian nature of the Turkish society is well-reflected in the Turkish organization. It starts in the family, grows in schools, and practiced in organizations.[43] In the Ottoman Empire "the relations of government to people, man to woman, parent to child were hierachial and authoritarian." This paternalism, was maintained under the new Turkish Republic, although its basis was now secular rather than sacral. The prevalence of authoritarianism in Turkish culture has led to conformity, rigidity, obedience, stability, and lack of initiative.[44]

The salaries of the public servants have not kept pace with the rising costs of living. Their purchasing power dropped by fifty percent between 1950 and 1965. The Public Personnel Law of 1965 and the changes made in 1971 have not been able to fill the growing gap between the rising inflation and the income of the public personnel. This has been one of the major sources of low morale, dissatisfaction, bribery and inefficiency in the public organizations.

The situation is worsened by the new private sector competition. The competitive position of the government has rapidly declined since 1950's. The salaries, wages and perquisites paid to the executives in the private sector are much higher than those in the public sector. And the young and talented public executives thus are easily attracted to the private sector. The prestige of government jobs has declined and the high job security has not been incentive enough to attract the bright graduates to the public service and keep them there. During the last three decades the public organizations have served the private companies as training institutions. Many people have used the positions in the public service as stepping stones to obtain the necessary experience, and in-service training, and later transfer to the private sector as managers or executives.

The over-centralization, red tape, bribery, corruption, nepotism, favoritism, lack of open and lateral communication, rigid rules and regulations, legal emphasis put upon responsibility and accountability and similar weaknesses also have stifled the initiative of the public servants.

In conclusion, the Ottoman-Turkish civil bureaucracy which developed out of the "earlier scribal bureaucracy of the patrimonial Ottoman state," has gradually assumed the role of the modernizing elite. It has been able to perpetuate the Empire for more than six centuries and transform the new Turkish Republic into a modern state. It has been both the target and the agent of change. It has grown in size (more than a million) and prestige. Although it has been able to renew itself, it has not been free of weaknesses. It has lacked efficiency and rationalization. Its reformist nature has been stifled by its structural weaknesses, authoritarian nature and the external factors.

The National Security Council and the semi-military government, presently in power, have taken certain, mostly temporary, measures to stop the malpractices in the public service. They have already formed an Advisory Assembly essentially responsible for changing the constitution and appointed a large number of bureaucrats as its members. The civil bureaucracy has started to gain prominence, provide political leadership, and assume its role of reforming the state once again. As pointed out by Chambers, "the role of civil bureaucrats in the modernizing process will remain at least proportionate to their quantitative and qualitative strength within the national elite..."45

Footnotes

1. Kemal H. Karpat, Turkey's Politics: The Transition to a Multi-Party System, Princeton, NJ: Princeton University Press, 1959, p. 3.

2. C.H. Dodd, Politics and Government in Turkey, Berkeley: University of California Press, 1969, pp. 5-6.

3. Halil Inalick, "The Nature of Traditional Society: Turkey," in R.E. Ward and D.A. Rustow, eds., Political Modernization in Japan and Turkey, Princeton, NJ; Princeton University Press, 1968, pp. 42-63.

The readers will notice the great similarities between the views of the British philosopher Thomas Hobbes (1588-1679) and those of Tursun Beg who lived more than a century before Hobbes. For more information see Tursun Beg, The History of Mehmed the Conqueror, Translated by Halil Inalick and Rhoads Murphey, Chicago: Bibliotheca Islamica, 1978.

4. Stanford Shaw, History of the Ottoman Empire and Modern Turkey, Vol. I, Cambridge, Mass.: Cambridge University Press, 1976, p. 112.

5. Inalick, op. cit., p. 44.

6. Norman Itzkowitz, "Eighteenth Century Ottoman Realities," Studia Islamica XVI (1962), pp. 73-94; Richard L. Chambers, "The Civil Bureaucracy: Turkey," in Ward and Rustow, eds., op. cit., pp. 301-327; Shaw, op. cit., pp. 112-167.

7. Albert Howe Lybyer, The Government of the Ottoman Empire in the Time of Suleiman the Magnificent, Camridge, Mass.: Harvard University Press, 1913, p. 49.

8. Shaw, op. cit., pp. 113-115.

9. Lybyer, op. cit., p. 45.

10. Ibid, p. 114; Lawrence Ziring, <u>Iran, Turkey and Afganistan</u>, New York: Praeger, 1981, p. 15.

11. Lybyer, <u>op. cit.</u>; Barnette Miller, <u>The Palace School of Muhammad the Conqueror</u>, Cambridge Mass.: Harvard University Press, 1941.

12. Miller, <u>op. cit.</u>, pp. 3-4 and 32.

13. Shaw, <u>op. cit.</u>, p. 115; Lybyer, <u>op. cit.</u>, pp. 78-79 and 124-126; Wayne S. Vucinich, <u>The Ottoman Empire: Its Record and Legacy</u>, New York: D. Van Nostrand Company, Inc., 1965, pp. 25, 138-141.

14. Shaw, <u>op. cit.</u>, pp. 115-117.

15. Miller, <u>op. cit.</u>, pp. 137-156; Shaw, <u>op. cit.</u>, pp. 117-118.

16. Shaw, <u>op. cit.</u>, p. 132.

17. Vucinich, <u>op. cit.</u>, pp. 37-43.

18. Shaw, <u>op. cit.</u>, pp. 122-132; Lybyer, <u>op. cit.</u>, pp. 90-113; Vucinich, <u>op. cit.</u>, pp. 29-31.

19. Bernard Lewis, <u>The Emergence of Modern Turkey</u>, New York: Oxford University Press, 2nd. ed., 1979, pp. 22-39.

20. Karpat, <u>op. cit.</u>, p. 4; Hamilton A.R. Gibb and Harold Bowen, <u>Islamic Society and the West</u>, Vol. 1, Oxford: Oxford University Press, 1957, pp. 207-261.

21. Andrew Mango, <u>Turkey</u>, New York: Walker and Company, 1968, pp. 25-26.

22. Shaw, <u>op. cit.</u>, pp. 170-171.

23. Lewis, <u>op. cit.</u>, p. 22.

24. Mango, <u>op. cit.</u>, p. 25.

25. Shaw, <u>op. cit.</u>, p. 175.

26. <u>Ibid</u>, pp. 194-200.

27. Lewis, <u>op</u>. <u>cit</u>., pp. 76-105.

28. <u>Ibid</u>, p. 97.

29. For further information, see Carter V. Find-
ley, <u>Bureaucratic Reform in the Ottoman Empire: The
Sublime Porte</u>, <u>1789-1922</u>, Princeton, NJ; Princeton
University Press, 1980, pp. 70-150; Shaw, <u>op</u>. <u>cit</u>.,
pp. 280-284; Stanford J. Shaw and Ezel Kural Shaw,
<u>History of the Ottoman Empire and Modern Turkey</u>, Vol.
II, Cambridge, Mass.: Cambridge University Press,
1977, pp. 2-55.

30. Lewis, <u>op</u>. <u>cit</u>., p. 107.

31. Karpat, <u>op</u>. <u>cit</u>., pp. 11-13.

32. Vucinich, <u>op</u>. <u>cit</u>., pp. 102-103.

33. <u>Ibid</u>, pp. 110-111; Karpat, <u>op</u>. <u>cit</u>., pp. 15-
31; Lewis, <u>op</u>. <u>cit</u>., pp. 227-231; Shaw and Shaw, <u>op</u>.
<u>cit</u>., pp. 272-340.

34. Dodd, <u>op</u>. <u>cit</u>., pp. 20-22; Mango, <u>op</u>. <u>cit</u>.,
pp. 51-53.

35. Mango, <u>op</u>. <u>cit</u>., p. 51.

36. Walter F. Weiker, <u>The Turkish Revolution,
1960-61: Aspects of Military Politics</u>, Washington,
DC: The Brookings Institution, 1963, pp. 3-8; Lewis,
<u>op</u>. <u>cit</u>., pp. 242-293; Shaw and Shaw, <u>op</u>. <u>cit</u>., 375-
396.

37. For a full translation of the 1961 Constitution, see Ismet Gritli, <u>Fifty Years of Turkish Political Development</u>, <u>1919-1969</u>, Istanbul: Fakulteler
Mutbassi, 1969, pp. 167-224; Weiker, <u>op</u>. <u>cit</u>., pp. 77-
80, and <u>The Modernization of Turkey-From Ataturk to
the Present Day</u>, New York: Holmes & Meier Publishers,
Inc., 1981, pp. 221-240; Lewis, <u>op</u>. <u>cit</u>., 362-340;
Shaw and Shaw, <u>op</u>. <u>cit</u>., pp. 373-438.

38. Chambers, op. cit., p. 318.

39. Weiker, "The Ottoman Bureaucracy: Modernization and Reform," Administrative Science Quarterly
13, No. 3 (December 1968), pp. 455-457.

40. Metin Heper, "The Recalcitrance of the
Turkish Public Bureaucracy to Bourgeois Politics:
A Multi-Factor Political Stratification Analysis,"
Middle Eastern Journal 30, No. 4 (Autumn 1976), p. 489.

41. Frederick W. Frey, The Turkish Political
Elite, Cambridge, Mass.: The M.I.T. Press, 1965,
p. 38.

42. George S. Harris, "The Role of the Military
in Turkish Politics," Middle East Journal Part I,
Vol. 19, No. 1 (Winter 1965), pp. 54-66; Part II,
Vol. 19, No. 2 (Spring 1965), pp. 169-176; Roger P.
Nye, "Civil-Military Confrontation in Turkey: The
1973 Presidential Election," International Journal
of Middle East Studies 8 (1977), pp. 209-228; Ergun
Ozbudun, Social Change and Political Participation in
Turkey, Princeton, NJ: Princeton University Press,
1976.

43. Norman M. Bradburn, "Interpersonal Relations
Within Formal Organizations in Turkey," Journal of
Social Issues 19 (January 1963), pp. 61-67.

44. Frederick T. Bent, "The Turkish Bureaucracy
as an Agent of Change," Journal of Comparative Administration 1, No. 1 (May 1969), pp. 55-58.

45. Chambers, op. cit., p. 327.

## CHAPTER XII

BUREAUCRACY AND PUBLIC POLICY IN LATIN AMERICA

John W. Sloan

Introduction

Most Latin American policymakers believe that bureaucracy should be stressed over social mobilization in
order to promote an orderly process of modernization.
It is believed that the state, dominated by bureaucratic institutions, is necessary to promote both economic
growth and greater distributive justice. Whatever the
political leanings of a government, state intervention
has been an expanding part of the economic scene since
the depression. The paradox of this strategic choice
is that Latin Americans have placed the burden of promoting modernization in the hands of public officials-
both civilian and military-that they distrust. Indeed,
there is a mutual distrust between public officials
and the public that sets up enormous obstacles to this
strategy of modernization.

The purpose of this paper is to analyze Latin American bureaucracies in terms of their influence on
developmental policies. In succeeding sections we shall
examine, first, the reasons why Latin Americans have
become committed to a strategy of development that em-
phasizes bureaucracy; second, the structure and functions of modern bureaucracies; third, the weaknesses
of those bureaucracies; and, finally, the consequences
for public policy. The paper indicates that, while
policymakers have used the bureaucratic state as an
instrument of modernization, they have not been able to
modernize adequately the instrument itself.

Reasons for the Stress on Bureaucratic Development

Most Latin Americans have never been attracted to
the liberal state. The idea of the state playing the
role of referee among the competing interests of society
and concerning itself mainly with providing law and
order and a minimal level of public services is not
compatible with either the colonial heritage or the
developmental aspirations of most policymakers since the
1930's. Latin America endured 300 years of Spanish
and Portuguese colonialism, and this legacy still affects bureaucratic behavior today. The Spanish colonies

were considered the _personal_ property of the monarch. All laws were created in Spain by the Council of Indies which "set the stage for administration that was intensely personal at the same time it was intensely legalistic."1 The Iberian monarchies, in establishing and maintaining their rule over people thousands of miles away, institutionalized a paternalistic style of administration. The colonial legacy has inclined the nations of Latin America toward a top-down approach to modernization, whose characteristics are variously described as a patron-client system, a corporative tradition, or a patrimonial state. Solon Barraclough connects the colonial legacy with contemporary administration and policy when he writes that, "Outsiders are prone to regard the complicated labyrinth of price controls, production limitations, import and export subsidies, prohibitive tariffs, state-protected monopolies, exchange-rate manipulations, and special tax exemptions as a recent development imposed by misguided disciples of state intervention in the economy. Actually,the mercantilist systems of Spain and Portugal have much more to do with the present structures than is generally realized. The networks of regulations, licenses, official monopolies or concessions, quotas, and red tape were already largely formed in the 18th century."2 In the 20th century, the Latin American state has become the ultimate patron, from which citizens expect everything--except justice.

Proponents of a bureaucratic, state-centered style of development do not have to overcome a liberal heritage; there is no strong ideological limitation on statism in Latin America. Instead, there is an inherited belief system that holds that large numbers of people--Indians, peasants, workers, and urban squatters --do not have the capacity either to care for themselves or to influence the public policies designed to help them. The elites are inclined to stress that modernization is essentially an administrative problem rather than a political one. That is, public policy decisions should be made by elites with minimal political inputs from those who are considered least able to provide constructive influence and most likely, if autonomously mobilized, to promote violence and chaos. This attitude is nicely captured by Poitras' characterization of the Mexican elite: "Revolutionary leaders (the President, members of the party and government) believe that economic development and social change must be directed from the top by a fairly small group of public and private leaders. This preference has tinted the bureaucracy with a semiauthoritarian paternalism, even though the government party (the P.R.I.) officially represents workers, peasants, and the popular (middle) classes. This notion, which underlies the entire system--that economic and social change should be accomplished on behalf of the masses but without their meaningful participation--is closely related to the assumption that unmanaged economic growth would jeopardize the political stability that the country has maintained for decades."[3] In brief, Latin American elites are likely to reflect a low estimate of their citizens' ability to know what is best for them and a high estimate of their own capacity to decide what is best for the nation.

This belief in state-centered development is shared by practicing politicians of different political ideologies. The tradition of state-directed development is exemplified in the policies of Batlle y Ordoñez, Vargas, Cárdenas, Perón, Castro, Betancourt, Frei, and Allende. Each of these politicians substantially increased the role of the public bureaucracy in their nation's development. Vargas' view of the state reveals what the proponents of a bureaucratic directed style of modernization desire.

> Vargas struggled mightily to make the state the pivot and regulator of national socio-economic relations; as part of that strategy he sought to liberate the state from both internal and external pressures and to endow the state with as much autonomy as possible; finally, he instituted a process of modernization of social relationships which, at least after 1937, was based on a policy of industrialization. In a sense, the state became, under Vargas, both a means and an end; he sought to use the state to create a more coherent, modern and powerful nation which would express its power to the world in the form of a relatively autonomous and powerful state. One can argue it was a process of adapting the form of the traditional patrimonial state to the substance of the modern era.[4]

A second reason for the inclination of Latin American policymakers to pursue a bureaucratically-directed style of development is their critical view of the domestic bourgeoisie. Whereas the bourgeoisie in the Western industrialized countries are often viewed as having performed such progressive historical functions as promoting democracy, industrialization, and nationalism, in Latin America the belief has spread that the indigenous bourgeoisie needs help in state capitalist societies and should be eliminated as the major obstacle to development in state socialistic countries such as Castro's Cuba. In Latin America the bourgeoisie is criticized for not promoting democracy, for creating a process of industrialization that was too open to the exploitation of foreign capital, and for developing a self-indulgent consumerism that is inimical to both the rapid accumulation of capital and social justice. An Argentine social scientist justifies the dominant role for the state in promoting development by condemning the Argentine bourgeoisie for its lack of ascetism, for its inability to take risks, to innovate, to develop its own technology, and to export, and for its commitment to quick and speculative profits.[5] Under these circumstances, reformers call for the state to supplement the role of the native bourgeoisie, while radicals demand that the state replace and eliminate the bourgeoisie. With the bourgeoisie unable to accumulate capital or exhibit the necessary managerial talents, the state has tried to perform the role of economic advisor, regulator, planner and major entrepreneur in the process of modernization.

Structure and Function

Latin Americans have decided that they wish their future to be determined by the administrative state. According to Milton Esman, "The administrative state as an ideal type is one in which the state is the dominant institution in society, guiding and controlling more than it responds to societal pressures, and administrative (bureaucratic) institutions, personnel, and values and style are more important than political and participative organs in determining the behavior of the state and thus the course of public affairs."[6] Since the depression, and especially after World War II, virtually every Latin American government has shifted from a passive to an active role in promoting economic growth and involving itself in an expanding number of expensive distributive policies. Whether this type of regime is labelled paternalistic, corporatistic, or authoritarian, it is "typified by extensive state enterprises coexisting and supportive of the private economic sector, comprehensive responsibility for the provision of welfare services, . . .and functionally organized clientele groups dependent upon and even formally attached to the regime in power. Policymaking . . .is the exclusive prerogative of a small elite and is characterized by limited informational inputs, behind-the-scenes bargaining and accommodation and low levels of public discussion and debate. Not only does the government of such a state claim responsibility for a wide range of activities; it also tends to reserve important policymaking roles for public administrators."[7]

Latin American nations do not have free enterprise-capitalistic economies. At first, entrepreneurs relied upon the state to make the necessary infrastructural investments--but now they are dependent upon a vast array of public policies that provide them with protection, investment capital, water, electricity, cheap transportation for workers, and state controls over labor unions. With the exception of Cuba, most Latin American countries have state-capitalist economies where public investments and public enterprises play a far more significant role than in the United States.[8] Private enterprises are now more dependent upon state support than they ever were--or are--on foreign, private capital. Governments control or influence currency, credit, imports, public facilities, and labor, which means that the private sector operates in an environment where public decision-making can make or break any firm. Operating in this milieu, where all things are possible-from Castro's Cuba to Pinochet's Chile-the insecure bourgeoisie cannot perform the functions they perform in the Western democracies.

Latin America must now confront the problems that have emerged from import-substituting industrialization policies (ISI) and populist politics. These include: inflation, massive foreign debts, chronic balance of payments deficits, unemployment, skewed income distributions, inadequate economic growth (given population pressures), over-dependence on foreign technology, soaring rates of urbanization, and the insatiable demands for social justice as previous beneficiaries of selective welfare policies want more and potential beneficiaries agitate for universalization. Such problems create an atmosphere of painful uncertainty and mistrust which inhibits further development. For further development to take place--development compatible with the interests of the existing elites--many bureaucratic, military, and private enterprise elites believe that only a bureaucratic-authoritarian state can provide the social predictability necessary for what Guillermo O'Donnell labels "the deepening" of development. That is, for nations to move beyond the light industrial development nurtured by ISI, to attract foreign and domestic private capital, to raise public capital for infrastructural and heavy industrial investments, and to integrate and coordinate the unplanned industrialization that took place from the depression to the 1960's, the creation of the bureaucratic-authoritarian state is required. O'Donnell interprets such a political system to be a reaction to the growing activation of the popular sectors and to the need "to rebuild, perfect, and stabilize the mechanisms of capital accumulation."9 Based on the examples of Argentina, Brazil, Pinochet's Chile, Mexico, and Uruguay, O'Donnell claims the defining characteristics of the bureaucratic authoritarian state thus:

> (a) Higher governmental positions are occupied by persons who come to them after successful careers in complex and highly bureaucratized organizations--the armed forces, the public bureaucracy, and large private firms; (b) political exclusion, in that it aims at closing channels of political access to the popular sector and its allies so as to deactivate them politically, not only by means of repression but also through the imposition of vertical (corporatist) controls by the state on such organizations as labor unions; (c) economic exclusion, in that it reduces or postpones indefinitely the aspiration to economic participation of the popular sector; (d) de-politicization, in the sense that it pretends to reduce social and political issues to 'technical' problems to be resolved by means of interactions among the higher echelons of the above-mentioned organizations; and (e) it corresponds to a state of important transformations in the mechanisms of capital accumulation of its society, changes that are, in turn, a part of the 'deepening' process of peripheral

and dependent capitalism characterized by extensive industrialization.[10]

By giving priority to the development of their bureaucracies, the advanced nations of Latin America have created more complex administrative structures than exist in the United States. In the mid-1970s, for example, the Mexican federal bureaucracy was composed of 18 regular Ministries and Departments, 123 decentralized agencies, 292 public enterprises, 187 official commissions, and 160 development trusts.[11] In contrast, U.S. Government Manual, 1975-1976 lists 17 executive offices, boards, and councils, 11 departments, 59 agencies, 6 quasi-official agencies, and 64 other boards, committees, and commissions. More importantly, "By 1970 the Mexican government was involved in over 400 enterprises, either as the sole owner or as a partner with private interests. It has also invested heavily in economic infrastructure, accounting for 30 per cent of the gross domestic investment in the country since 1940."[12] The Mexican state now accounts for 22 per cent of the country's industrial activity. The irony of this situation is that the U.S. bureaucracy, although far below Weberian ideals, has greater administrative capabilities than any Latin American bureaucracy, and yet is asked to do less.

Studies of bureaucracies in different Latin American countries tell a similar story; they are generally growing in size and extending their influence over different sectors of society. In Venezuela, since the government nationalized the oil industry in 1976, the public sector now accounts for 60 percent of the Gross Domestic Product and directs over 200 agencies and companies. In Chile, the growth in the number of public employees from 1940 to 1970 increased nearly 400 percent to about 300,000 employees while the population increased only about 30 percent during the same period. One Chilean scholar comments, "The bureaucracy's activities permeated all of society. Almost everything had to be done with the aid or at least the concurrence of a public agency."[13] In Brazil, Schmitter writes,

> The role of the state apparatus in Brazil has grown from almost nothing before 1930 to include a vast variety of functions. Public authorities in Brazil currently own all, or at least a substantial proportion of the maritime, river, and railroad transport, petroleum,

steel and alkali production, mining of atomic
minerals, and electric power generation.
They intervene directly through institutes or
indirectly through the Bank of Brazil in the
commercialization of coffee, sugar, rubber,
cacao, rice, maté, pinewood, salt, cotton,
beans, corn, soybean, wheat, manioc flour,
and other products; they produce and export
most of the country's iron ore; they regulate
mining rights, communication and transport
concessions, exchange rates, and insurance;
they fix (or attempt to fix) prices on basic
goods, interest rates, minimum salaries, rents,
and minimum agricultural prices; they provide
much of the country's short-term and virtually
all of its long-term credit; they finance and
control directly port facilities, storage
areas for agricultural products and major housing projects. In addition, of course, they
have the usual sorts of government controls
over monetary, fiscal, investment, educational,
health, national security, and foreign policy.[14]

The increasing functions performed by Latin American governments are reflected in the increasing structural differentiation of both Ministries and decentralized agencies (analogous to the T.V.A. in the United
States). In many Latin American countries decentralized
state corporations (also called autonomous agencies) are
at least as important as Cabinet level Ministries. The
creation of such corporations is based upon the prevailing notion that regular line agencies cannot, or
will not, adapt to performing new functions (i.e., a
Ministry of Agriculture resisting efforts to carry out
an agrarian reform), and so a decentralized agency is
established in those policy areas where the political
elite is serious about implementing a particular program. In Columbia, for example, the traditional inefficiency of the Ministry of Education was countered
by the creation of three decentralized corporations to
build schools, to improve teaching methods, and to improve higher education.[15] Supposedly such decentralized
agencies can recruit a highly qualified staff, pay
higher salary schedules, and avoid ministerial red tape.
The attractiveness of such agencies is such that they
now number in the hundreds in several countries, with
larger budgets than line agencies. They regulate
prices, wages, and production quotas; they manage steel,
mining, electricity, railroad, utility, and petrochemical

corporations; they administer social programs; and they are involved in national planning, agrarian reform and regional development programs. The propensity of Latin Americans to create new autonomous agencies instead of making the regular Ministries adapt to performing new programs reminds one of their similar inclination to write new constitutions when the old one does not work or to create new political parties rather than reform the old ones.

Weaknesses in the Latin American Bureaucracies

The traditional Latin American bureaucracy performed the functions of (1) providing a channel for upward mobility for the educated middle class; (2) providing permanent incomes for that portion of the middle class which supported the regime; (3) providing a low level of certain services; and (4) providing opportunities for private entrepreneurship based on the powers attached to certain offices.[16] The traditional bureaucracy was not imbued with the spirit of public service; it served the personal and political needs of those who held public office. By emphasizing the bureaucratic approach to development, the Latin Americans are dependent upon their skills in creating a new, more development oriented bureaucracy, one that is contingent upon their administrators utilizing much greater rationality in making their public investment decisions, managing public enterprises, providing services to ever-expanding cities, and administering a complex variety of social policies. The success of this strategy is related to the speed by which a Weberian bureaucracy can replace the traditional bureaucracy and provide the efficiency to carry out the large scale administrative tasks associated with modernization. (See Figure I.) As Max Weber pointed out, such bureaucratization involves both structural and behavioral changes. The dilemma for Latin America is that it has encountered what Schmitter labels "structural overbureaucratization" and "behavioral underbureaucratization."[17] Structurally, the bureaucracy has differentiated itself into a proliferating number of departments, agencies, boards, and--especially --autonomous agencies. The result is the continuing rigidity of the old line departments and tremendous problems of administrative and policy coordination. Behaviorally, major segments of the bureaucracy also do not conform to Weber's ideal type. Varying proportions of Latin American bureaucracies are characterized by personalismo, nepotism, job insecurities, high

Figure I

Contrasting Characteristics of Bureaucratic
and Patrimonial Systems

Max Weber's Ideal Bureaucracy	Brazilian Patrimonialism
Specialization	Patron sponsorship
Division of Labor	Individualism
Hierarchy	Each case Personally handled
Standardization and routinization of work	Each case potentially an exception
Legal orientation	
Impersonality	Loyalties to the individual
Professionalization	

Over-all goals

Rationality	Employment
Economy	Employee Welfare
Efficiency	Preferential Treatment

Consequences

Strong capacity for goal achievement	Weak capacity for goal accomplishment

Source: Gilbert Siegel, The Vicissitudes of Governmental Reform in Brazil: A Study of DASP, Washington, DC: University Press of America, 1978, p. 29.

turnover rates, lack of expertise, inadequate use of expertise when it exists, lack of delegation of authority, formalism, stultifying legalism, unsatisfactory gathering and communication of information, use of the bureaucracy to relieve unemployment, self-aggrandizement (in terms of the benefits bureaucrats obtain for themselves), and lack of coordination.

Under these circumstances, the bureaucracy does not contribute what it should to increase the probability of rational developmental policymaking. This fact is widely know in Latin America. An advisor to the Colombian government complains that, "the country simply cannot hope to achieve the desired economic goals without modernizing its manner of conducting public business and making it much more efficient. . . . The whole system of multiple responsibility (in which no one is responsible), multiple signatures, endless shuffling about of papers, preaudit, and postaudit, . . .monthly budget allotments, archaic tax enforcement methods, and complete disregard for the convenience of the public, is costing the country heavily in unnecessary bureaucracy, unnecessary delays, and a great waste of time on the part of anyone who has anything to do with government, which includes practically everybody."[18] In Argentina one hears complaints about the inefficiencies of the state-run railroads; in Bolivia the nationalized tin mines lose money; in Brazil billions of dollars have not been able to alleviate the misery of the Northeast; in Venezuela billions of dollars have not achieved success in modernizing the agricultural system; and throughout Latin America the administrative costs of running social security programs are usually from 3 to 10 times higher than in the United States.[19] Perhaps the most discouraging case of bureaucratic greed and ineptness is displayed in Uruguay where Batille's democratic dream was turned into a fascist nightmare. Weinstein's study concludes, "The economic stasis experienced by Uruguay since the mid 1950's is in almost diametrical opposition to the growth statistics of the public sector."[20]

This is not to say that there are no bureaucratic success stories in Latin America. Such a list would include PEMEX in Mexico, PETROBRAS in Brazil, the Venezuelan Guayana Corporation, the Cauca Valley Corporation in Colombia, the Ministry of Hydraulic Resources in Mexico, and probably many others that have not yet been studied. Nonetheless, most studies of development administration in Latin America have concluded that

313

inefficient bureaucracies are a major bottleneck to moddernization and that efforts of administrative reform have proven to be inadequate.[21] Most bureaucracies are improving their administrative skills but not fast enough to keep pace with the accelerated demands that are being placed upon them by state-directed strategies of development.

One basic problem is that bureaucrats in Latin America operate in an environment that makes them feel vulnerable and insecure. Such an atmosphere inhibits rational decisionmaking from a developmental perspective. According to Victor Thompson, "Personal insecurity in an authority position is likely to create personal needs of such magnitude as to dominate over organizational needs. Resulting behavior, then, will be pathological from the standpoint of the organization and so has been called 'bureaupathic'. . . . Bureaupathic behavior stems from needs that can be generalized as the need to control. It is manifested in such things as close supervision; failure to delegate; heavy emphasis on regulations. . .precedents, and the accumulation of paper to prove compliance; cold aloofness; insistence on office protocol; fear of innovation; and restriction of communication. . . . In an extreme bureaupathic situation, it is difficult to see how development planning can take place."[22]

This situation is created because competition for governmental jobs is intense. In societies where there is high unemployment, public employment which offers adequate to good salaries, no chance of going out of business, extensive vacation time, and multiple fringe benefits--such as access to low cost housing, free medical care and drugs, periodic pay bonuses, and good pension programs--are very attractive. Administrative costs are exceptionally high in Latin America, which dilutes the ability of public agencies to fulfill their objectives. For good reason, one often hears the proverb, "He who divides and distributes keeps the lion's share for himself."

In the Mexican bureaucracy, employees are divided into two categories, base and confidence workers. Base workers are lower level employees who are fairly safe in their jobs from arbitrary dismissal. Confidence personnel are higher level employees who "are directly dependent upon their hierarchical superiors for continued employment although their salaries are now generally set by statute or regulation. A chief who wishes to dismiss a confidence worker simply informs him 'you have lost my confidence,' and after receiving indemnification, the employee must seek another job. At the change of administration, many confidence workers follow their chiefs to new appointments."23 Hanson estimates that "every six-year change in presidential administrations witnesses a turnover of 18,000 elective offices and more than 25,000 appointive posts. Of those positions about half provide good to excellent incomes, licit and otherwise."24 To be hired, promoted or fired for personal reasons rather than for merit is an obvious violation of the norms of a Weberian bureaucracy.

The system of rapid turnover in Mexico serves to remind both aspirants and incumbents that they are operating in a very precarious environment. High and middle level officials cope with this situation in a culturally legitimized manner; they develop patron-client relationships. Such relationships are based upon enduring personal bonds of reciprocity and personal loyalty between individuals in superior and subordinate positions. These bonds promote security and career mobility in a fragile environment. But such responses cannot alleviate the pressures generated in a scarce resource and job society. Competition for advancement is intense, so there are numerous patron-client networks competing through the upward channels for the limited number of top positions. If your patron advances and you maintain his confidence, you advance as well. If your patron loses the trust of his superior or you lose his confidence, then you may be fired. Bureuacrats are given the contradictory advice to be loyal to their patrons but to avoid factions that are falling out of favor with higher-level patrons. Personal loyalty must be constantly tested and proven in this environment since it is far more important for career advancement than expertise or commitment to public policy. It is safer for subordinates to communicate deference to their superior rather than accurate information or critical evaluations of public policy. Moreover, the turnover of high and middle level personnel means that bureaucrats must administer policies and establish a record in areas they know little about. In Grindle's words, "Unprepared for their responsibilities, they are nevertheless expected to take charge quickly, to plan new activities for the unit under their command, to revise operating procedures, and to implement rapidly the

directives of their superiors. These conditions place
a premium on the availability of trustworthy subordinates."[25] Subordinates are advised to: do things
fast; don't make mistakes; don't embarrass your super-
·iors. Such advice is a recipe for ulcers in a bureaucracy of competing factions and limited information
and expertise.

This insecure government has negative consequences
for the making and execution of rational public policy.
A bureaucrat improves his income and status through
vertical attachments rather than developing expertise
in particular policy areas. Hence, there is often a
divergence between career advancement and the needs of
the organization in carrying out its function. Rotation in office means that individuals do not develop
expertise or even responsibility for certain policy
areas since problems can be blamed on previous incumbents. Such conditions help create the "syndrome of
plazismo" for local governments in Mexico. In this
situation, officials support the creation of public
projects with low developmental importance. According
to Fagen and Touhy, ". . .these take the form of a
'beautification' effort: an improvement to the central
plaza, a new fountain, benches, paved areas, stalls,
or some other civic addition of marginal usefulness.
The attractions of such projects to cautious office-
holders are legion: they are physically and politically
visible; they can be completed in a relatively short
time and thus accrue wholly to the reputational capital
of the incumbent; they are for all the people and thus
require no hard choices as to what sector or project
should receive scarce resources; they are uncontrover-
sial in the tradition of 'good works;' they can often
be partially funded through the donations of others
eager to have their names associated with civic improvements."[26] Obviously, such attitudes are not conducive
to good maintenance procedures, which helps to explain
why so much of the capital stock in Latin America is
allowed to deteriorate.

Another irrationality of policymaking, identified
by Hirschman in Brazil and Grindle in Mexico, refers
to the lack of learning and serious evaluation of previous policies because of rotating personnel. In
Grindle's words, "Each new administration is concerned
with making its own impression on public programs quickly, and newly to preexisting plans. As a result, old
policies which have failed are reintroduced in the guise

of new solutions; old mistakes are repeated by the in-experienced cadres; and many programs which prove to be promising in one administration are shelved by the next. The experience which is accumulated by individual administrators as they move from agency to agency during their careers is the subtle capacity to persist through the management of human relations and politics; it generally has little relevance to the more specific tasks of designing and implementing policy."27

A second major problem of bureaucratic behavior concerns the issues of centralization and control. The overcentralization of Latin American bureaucracies has not brought about greater control; it has brought about less. Most agencies are organized like a monarchy in which little authority is delegated down the line and the chief administrative officer must sign everything. A recent Treasury Minister in Colombia complained that he had to sign between 200 and 300 documents a day concerning subjects ranging from millions of dollars for public works projects to a $200 travel allowance for a dentist in the Ministry of Health.28 Similarly, in Ecuador, a planning commission study of the Ministries of Development, Economy, Public Works, Education, and Social Welfare concluded: "The single person regime that channels all work and responsibility through the Minister himself, and the lack of technical agencies that could advise the Ministry on decisions that require co-ordination with the local economic policy of the government, has reduced those Ministries in practice to the fulfillment of routine administrative functions and has brought on an inertia to change that is not the fault of individuals, but the very weight of the system."29 Centralized control is impossible in complex governments short on legitimacy and rich in patron-client networks.

In analyzing the Venezuelan bureaucracy, Bill Stewart found that, the more authority is concentrated at the top, the less effective implementation of policy can be carried out by those below. With so little formal authority delegated downward, a tremendous number of requests for authorizations must flow upward. Few direct actions can be taken at intermediate levels. Bottlenecks inevitably occur as top executives find themselves inundated in details unimportant to specific cases but not to general policy. Formal communication becomes too slow and cumbersome. Top executives become increasingly dependent upon informal personal contacts to receive important information. Routine decisions,

317

unless lubricated by personal contacts, get bogged down in red tape. Top officials tend to become overly dependent on crisis management; lower officials tend to short-circuit official procedures by informally solving problems through the falsification of forms and reports. Stewart also found that, "The time and effort that must be expended in gaining the leaders' attention are so large that most bureaucratic exeuctives outside Caracas find it expedient to send a messenger with routing requests and to travel to Caracas whenever an important decision is needed. Within Caracas the same system is followed, although here the advantage of a messenger over the mail service is obvious and less time is lost in travelling. The drain upon subordinates' time and energy is great and its effect upon efficiency can only be negative."[30] In brief, the concentration of authority at the top in Venezuela does not result in the Venezuelan bureaucracy's performing developmental functions in a more efficient manner.

Weaver found similar problems in the Guatemalan bureaucracy. Again, the Guatemalan bureaucracy is highly centralized without effective control over its bureaucrats. Within agencies, directors are overwhelmed by being personally responsible to check and approve every petition, letter, and memorandum. Since top executives do not delegate authority, they cannot place responsibility. The administrative system lacks uniform procedures in collecting, integrating, and evaluating information. The high turnover of middle and top-level officials is not conducive to accumulating policy expertise and is detrimental to effective control and management. Rapid turnover is accompanied by procedural confusion. Moreover, the bureaucracy is stifled by legalism, a 'code fetish' which requires officials to be constantly consulting statutes, executive and legislative decrees, bulletins, and specific Ministerial orders. In Weaver's words, "where existing rules and regulations do not apply, long delays are incurred while a new circular or decree is prepared or a written opinion from the Minister's office. Consultants to the government of Guatemala have produced studies demonstrating that thousands of revenue dollars are lost each year because of spoilage, theft, and destruction of goods held by Customs while awaiting rulings on tariff rates. Similarly, all manner of development programs are delayed, clients angered and rebuffed, and business opportunities lost while bureaucrats search the code books or await rulings from their superiors."[31] In such a system, compliance with the code books becomes more important (and safer for insecure bureaucrats) than performance. Weaver's portrait of the Guatemalan bureaucracy suggests that one cannot expect a strong developmental performance from such an organization.

> We have a picture of top executives seated behind mounds of petitions, memos, and requests for rulings; beseiged by clients, friends, and subordinates begging for assistance or opinions; and occasionally and hastily scanning a report which is probably largely fictitious and almost inevitably devoid of critical analysis. But a basic condition of centralization--control--seems to be absent from this picture.[32]

A complaint frequently heard in Mexico, and in many other Latin American countries, is that the overcentralization of authority in the capital results in inefficient administration at the local level. In Mexico the federal government exercises enormous controls over the initiation, financing, and construction of most local development projects. Although this system results in long delays, as local officials must develop and maintain their personal contacts in Mexico City, it persists because it provides national officials with power, prestige, and patronage. Tuohy correctly argues that, ". . .whatever benefits accrue to rationalization and coordination of policy through the centralized organizational forms are lost owing to the corruption, inefficiencies, and careerism that are the other side of Mexican centralism. Thus, developmental planning gets sacrificed to system maintenance, and patronage takes precedence over expert performance."[33]

There is an administrative style in Latin America that assumes that intelligence only resides at the top of the bureaucratic hierarchy in the capital city, that lower officials--especially in the provinces--must be tightly controlled by regulations and cannot be trusted with discretionary authority, and that citizens are lying unless they have documentary proof or personal connections. Top officials are thus overwhelmed by trivia about which they complain, but it is part of their status to be deferentially besieged by subordinates. Middle and lower-level civil servants quickly learn that deference is far more likely to be rewarded than candor. Centralized authority may not mean effective centralized control, but it probably inhibits developmental innovations. The pathology of centralized authority and lack of effective control is nicely summarized by Mark Cannon: "A sense of exalted status accompanying a position of authority, a mistrust for peers and subordinates outside one's circle of personal influence, a sense of the inviolability of one's personal dignity, a readiness to take offense, a formalism emphasizing appearances--all these contribute to deference to authority and politeness which inhibit open communication of real feelings in Latin America. These features also contribute to a lack of skilful supervision which might help develop employees and mobilize their energy, skills, and commitment to institutional goals. Instead, supervisory situations sometimes become anarchic, partly because confrontation is avoided, or they become one-way authoritarian command relationships."[34]

The facade that obscured the personalistic realities of Latin American bureaucratic politics is a highly formalistic legalism. The combination of the Iberian heritage and a constant stream of lawyers graduating from the universities and being hired as civil servants has burdened the region with an "over-developed" legal system which stifles the bureaucracy. Just as the conquistadores brought along notaries to certify the legality of their behavior in subjugating Indians, contemporary bureaucrats display a meticulous and time-consuming concern with conforming the existence of formal legal authority for almost any decision. And discovering the operating law today is probably as difficult as it was for administrators in the colonial period. There is a lack of comprehensive digests, and the official gazettes are often not indexed. According to two legal scholars, "Instead of amending basic code provisions, Latin American practice is generally to adopt supplemental legislation, which, in turn, is amended and reamended. Frequently, one is forced to read a host of separate statutes and decrees regulating a given subject. . .and then undertake the jigsaw job of piecing together the provisions still in force to find the governing law. Hence, it is quite common to discover that the authorities charged with administering a particular body of law are unaware of significant changes in the statutory or case law. Inertia, ignorance, and inability to keep abreast of rapid-fire legislative change frequently combine to produce substantial differences between the formal norm and the law actually being applied."[35] But even in this situation a formalistic legalism is preserved through the concept of the "rightfulness of command." Morse explains that, ". . .in a patrimonial state, to which command and decree are so fundamental, the legitimacy of the command is determined by the legitimacy of the authority which issues it. Hence the importance of sheer legalism in Latin American administration as constant certification for the legitimacy, not of the act, but of him who executes it."[36]

A third major weakness of Latin American bureaucracies is their inability to coordinate their activities to effectively achieve developmental goals. As the modernizing state assumes more functions, there is a greater need for coordination and inter-agency cooperation. One would guess that centralized politics would be able to coordinate developmental policies but this is not true in Latin America. Part of the reason, as we have just discussed, is that centralized political systems do not exert effective centralized control through the administrative systems. Thus, the essential bureaucratic cooperation needed for state-directed development is lacking, and, the more bureaucratized a political system, the more costly this lack becomes.

This problem is no secret in Latin America. An ECLA study of social services in the region found that, "Despite. . .centralization, there is no real unification of standards of service. Each institution, program and unit functions with the minimum of communication, and while there may be some written regulations and procedures, implementation is on the basis of personal relationships. The very rigidity and complexity of administrative procedures and personnel policies contribute to this 'compartmentalization.' It prohibits free communication and mobility and favors the formation of cliques."[37] The study also concludes that there are too few inter-agency coordinating or consultative bodies, but even the few that do exist do not function effectively. Cannon claims that, "A committee meeting in Latin America is likely to turn into a monologue of some authority figure, or if it utilizes discussion, to evolve into a prolonged, somewhat random set of opportunities for individual expression rather than a serious and interrelated progressive elaboration of relevant data and analysis leading to a rational decision."[38] Sometimes a different type of problem prevails; in Colombia the Minister of Agriculture serves on 63 boards and commissions. Other studies refer to Ministries and decentralized agencies as independent empires and fuedalities in which consultation is kept to a mimimum and collaboration is almost nonexistent.[39] The areas where Latin American bureaucracies perform

321

most poorly because of lack of coordination are in administering distributive policies for the poor, agrarian reform, port facilities, and urban services.

The fourth problem of Latin American bureaucracies is corruption. The state-directed strategy of development increases the possibilities of corruption, and expanding corruption seriously dilutes the effectiveness of bureaucracies in bringing about modernization. There is some corruption in every society, but there is more of it in Latin America than in the Western industrial countries, and Latin American societies can afford it less.

Corruption means that officials take advantage of their public offices and decision making to obtain private gain. That is, they take bribes, they hand out privileged information to business partners, friends and relatives, they smuggle, they take advantage of disasters such as earthquakes and hurricanes, they speculate in currency and real estate, and they enforce the law in a particularistic manner to aid their friends and punish enemies. Such behavior is a continuation of the colonial legacy where a large number of laws were honored only in the breach. In Latin America, law continues to be extensive in its scope and particularistic in its application and thus invites corruption. Citizens cannot expect justice from public officials, and so those who can afford to do so attempt to buy special consideration and favors. The prevalence of corruption contributes to feelings of insecurity since so many officials and citizens have broken the law and could be exposed by enemies. According to Nye, a significant level of corruption is likely in Latin America because of "great inequality in distribution of wealth; political office as the primary means of gaining access to wealth; conflict between changing moral codes; the weakness of social and governmental enforcement mechanisms; and the absence of a strong sense of national community. . ."40 The dilemma for Latin America is that corruption has deep and constantly reinforced roots; the many who practice it do well; the few who get caught are not severely punished. In the absence of a public service tradition, the prevailing attitude is that "a smart man helps himself when he has the opportunity." In brief, too many bureaucrats exploit their positions for private gain; they "privatize" public decision-making.

The prevalence of corruption is reflected in

anecdotes, language and specific events. In Brazil,
the publicized scandals of 1954 caused President Getulio
Vargas to complain that he was drowning "in a sea of
mud." In Panama the joke is told concerning how the
President makes his budget decisions: a third for the
state and himself; a third for his friends and himself;
a third for himself. In Ecuador, the Finance Minister,
Luis Gomez Izquierdo states, "I understand why the business community does not want to pay taxes. . . . Aside
from the obvious, we have always believed that the government was corrupt, irresponsible and squandered whatever it got its hands on."[41] In Argentina, President
Juan Peron's Minister of Education in 1952 recalled
20 years later how he resigned when he saw that a man
with legitimate business with the President had to
bribe staff members to see him. "Look, Ivan," the
Minister remembered Peron as saying, "The British
Empire was built by good men and pirates, and I'm
going to build the Argentine empire with good men and
pirates."[42] In Colombia, "The term politiqueria refers to a type of selfish political maneuvering which
tends to subordinate all policymaking goals to the
personal rewards of the politician and his clique. Most
of those who are involved in politiqueria are individuals who participate in politics for no other reason
than for the materialistic rewards which flow from the
position obtained."[43] In Nicaragua, the corruption of
the Somoza government significantly contributed to the
eventual triumph of the Sandinistas in 1979. Many Nic-
araguans were particularly outraged by how Somoza and
his cronies took advantage of the 1976 earthquake which
devastated Managua.

But the best known corruption in Latin America
occurs in Mexico. Decades ago General Alvaro Obregon
announced that, "There is no general that can resist
a barrage of 50,000 pesos," and former President Emilio
Portes Gil complained that administrative corruption at
times "produced a climate of virtual asphyxiation."
Today President López Portillo proclaims that, "Corruption is the cancer of this country."[44] A certain level
of corruption is a norm of administrative behavior in
Mexico, from the customs official who accepts a routine
bribe (the mordida) to President Miguel Alemán (1946-
52) who became a millionaire developing Acapulco.
(Bribes at the top are called commissions.) Corruption
allows politicians and administrators to taste wealth,
and businessmen and labor union officials to buy favors.
Mexicans tell each other the cynical joke that their

country is one of the richest in the world; every six years it produces a new crop of millionaires. It is believed that, during the last year of each administration, corruption is particularly rampant because many officials cannot be sure they will have a job in the next regime. In Greenberg's words, ". . .the predicament of the bureaucrat, with no real union protection, no job security, and no guarantee of future income, causes him to turn to corrupt practices. Further, the life style expected of even middle-level bureaucrats demands an income well in excess of their formal salaries. The result is that these bureaucrats turn to extracting payments and kick-backs in order to attain a 'respectable level of living.'"[45] Controlling corruption is made difficult because two potential watchdogs of public morality--the press and the judiciary--are themselves part of the same system controlled by the PRI.

The style of state-directed development in Mexico provides too many tempting opportunities for bureaucrats to ignore. Agencies decide what can and cannot be imported and exported and which private firms will receive private loans for their expansion; they set price ceilings on a variety of products and services, and tax exemptions to individual plants. One well known example of corruption is that many filling stations in Mexico are owned by politicians, and PEMEX (the government oil corporation) assures them of a near monopoly in very profitable locations. Moreover, budgetary control of top officials is almost non-existent. Antonio Ugalde examined the State budget in Baja California in 1967 and found that under the heading "Personal Expenses of the Governor" there was an appropriation of a quarter-million pesos (12.5 pesos equal $1.00) for social research, but there was no publicly available record of just what kind of research was being conducted. The Governor's salary was 120,000 pesos, but over 700,000 pesos were earmarked for the Governor's expenses, plus 100,000 pesos for maintaining his residence.[46] Vernon correctly stresses that, "In a setting such as this, only mortal fear or an extraordinary elan could restrain some public officials from developing their liaisons with the private sector and exploiting their information."[47] Such fear and elan do not predominate in Mexican public administration.

In brief, without a strong public service tradition, a free press, and a strong independent judiciary, the strategy of bureaucratic development provides numerous and enticing opportunities for graft.

Conclusion: Bureaucracy and Public Policy in Latin America

The stress on bureaucratic development takes the Weberian bureaucracy several steps beyond its normal function. Not only is the bureaucracy expected to implement the policies of the political elite in a rational and efficient manner, but it is also expected to play a major role in the formulation of policies and the regulation of interest groups and social sectors. The role of bureaucracy in Latin American development has steadily expanded. Progress depends upon many variables, but most Latin American nations have placed themselves in a situation where the quality of their public sector will be the chief determinant of their success or failure in the foreseeable future. In many countries the rationality of public decision-making is the major determinant of the rationality of the economy and the political system. Many of the political, economic, and especially the military elites have decided that the kind of development they want requires "certainty," and that certainty can best be provided by subjecting major economic and political sectors of the society to bureaucratic control.

The problem in this strategy is that the growing bureaucratization of Latin America is not necessarily leading to the growing rationalization of these countries in terms of development. Latin America inherited a bureaucratic style from the 300-year colonial period, a style that was designed to maintain a stable and unchanging system. Grafted onto this traditional bureaucracy are modern kinds of agencies imbued with a greater commitment toward and capability of implementing rational public policy. Hence, the development of these countries is hindered by what Schmitter labels "structural overbureaucratization" and "behavioral underbureaucratization." Structurally, the bureaucracy differentiates itself continually, but behaviorally major segments of the bureaucracy still fall short of Weber's ideal type. Despite the efforts of administrative reformers, efficient bureaucratic agencies have frequently been isolated; great segments of the bureaucracy have been able to resist reform.

As the population of the countries of Latin America increases, as their cities rapidly expand and require coordinated services, as they nationalize important segments of their economies, and as they do not encourage local initiatives or mass mobilization, the governments are becoming increasingly dependent upon their public bureaucracies' developing greater administrative skill. But, with major segments of their bureaucracies performing at low levels of efficiency, a serious drag is placed upon the pace of development. Moreover, the bureaucratic capabilities of many countries are often stretched beyond the breaking point because they are being asked to administer the traditional aspects of government (internal order, finance, public works, and foreign policy), the infrastructure necessary for further modernization, an educational system to supply future human resource needs, a host of public enterprises, and a whole set of welfare policies.

Just how compatible a Weberian bureaucracy is with developmental administration is a matter of debate. Some have argued that in Europe the Weberian bureaucracy was related to the transfer of power from the aristocracy to the bourgeoisie and is therefore not applicable or progressive in Latin America where the bourgeoisie are already in power.[48] Critics claim that the Weberian bureaucracy is overly conservative with its career personnel, organized in a hierarchy, and performing routine functions. They contrast the routinization and predictability of a Weberian bureaucracy with the needs of the innovator and the entrepreneur of the developmental administrator. Critics also contend that bureaucrats overestimate their rationality and underestimate how much personal and class orientations affect their decision-making. Those who criticize the Weberian bureaucracy fail to see that it can be instrumental in changing the status quo under a reformist or revolutionary regime as well as maintaining it under a conservative regime. Critics underestimate how much constructive social change--as opposed to destructive change which relies on violence and mass mobilization--is dependent upon social predictability, rationality and efficiency. Increased productivity and distributive justice are contingent upon laborers showing up for work, students being taught, trains and buses running on time, electric power being available, taxes being collected, major public enterprises such as a nationalized oil industry or a copper mine showing profits, rational engineering practices, and efficient urban services. A more rationalized bureaucracy can mobilize resources, coordinate policies, and display the wisdom required to predict and choose which investments will

produce the optimum benefits for the economy and society.   Limited administrative skills mean limited
policy options in dealing with developmental problems.
Increasing administrative skills mean an increasing
number of policy options and the opportunity to select
more rational choices. Moreover, in the hands of an
incompetent bureaucracy, rational and irrational policy
may end up looking equally ineffective. For the bureaucrats to be able to administer the development of their
societies, the administrative isntruments itself must
be further developed. The blind cannot lead the blind.
Traditional bureaucracies, where public jobs are viewed
as sinecures and sources of employment, do not easily
lend themselves to the innovative behavior needed to
promote development.

The bureaucratic style of development chosen by
the Latin American elites had a number of consequences
for their societies. First, such a strategic choice is
not compatible with the democratization of these
nations. Neither the traditional nor the more modern
bureaucrats seek to encourage mass political participation. Mass participation interferes with the
personalistic style of the traditional bureaucrat and
the technocratic style of the modern bureaucrat.
Bureaucratic and technocratic means to resolve problems
appear to be more compatible with the authoritarian
traditions of Latin America than with democratic and
participatory methods.

Second, the state-centered style of development
has a strong tendency to concentrate bureaucrats in the
capital cities. Provincial areas are thus deprived of
the talented administrators they need for development.
This situation contributes to warped and uneven development. Moreover, decision-making in the provinces has
to be filtered through the clogged channels of the
capital city, which is a wasteful and time-consuming
activity.

Third, the bureaucratic development of the state
inevitably creates interests of its own that are partially separate from the social sectors in society.
The bureaucratic state does not merely reflect the interests of dominant social groups; neither does it have to
ignore the weaker social sectors (although it usually
does). The bureaucratic state aims to be the ultimate
patron. From this perspective, "the state does not

simply arbitrate among bickering factions; it proposes, disposes, and imposes its will."[49] The bureaucratic state is thus faced with a paradoxical task: it must have autonomy and it must sink roots. In Tony Smith's words, "It must have the autonomy of a unitary factor if it is to make long-term plans and to implement them despite some opposition. . . . Particularistic interests of every variety must be weaker than the state, which is competent to act on behalf of what it will call the collective good. At the same time, the state must sink roots, both as a precondition and as a result of this very effort at change. If some interests must be checked or broken, others must be mobilized and controlled if the state is to attain its ends."[50] This paradox is not likely to be overcome until a public service ethos is finally instilled in Latin American bureaucracies. The bureaucracy is both an instrument for goal accomplishment and a growing constituency that can devour enormous resources. There are still too many occasions where bureaucrats "privatize" the formulation and implementation of public policy.

Fourth, the growth of public bureaucracies has not yet sufficiently increased rationality in the making of public policy. Presidents, Ministers, and Governors like to link their administrations with a distinctive social and economic program. Consequently, the policies of one administration are rarely pursued by the next. With the lack of social mobilization in Latin America, programs do not build up the clienteles they do in the United States, which helps to account for zig-zag phenomena in the former and the greater policy continuity in the latter. Such personalistic styles of administration also help to explain why so little attention is paid to the problem of adequate maintenance. Why use scarce resources to maintain what was created by a predecessor and for which you will receive no credit? Wynia found in his study of policymaking in the five Central American republics that bureaucrats preferred to build longer roads with existing resources while outside consultants suggested shorter roads with higher standards which would require less maintenance work. Because highway maintenance does not bring the personal glory of highway construction, the former was seriously neglected with negative consequences for development.[51]

In Colombia, one advisor has complained that there are no decision-making units concerned with insuring that public expenditures yield the highest possible return to the economy in terms of well-being; feasibility studies are almost always positive; and original cost estimates are unrealistically low. In Currie's words: "Generally a large project seems to capture the imagination and receives preference over a number of smaller ones, regardless of their merits. . . . Slogans like 'opening up the country,' 'bringing new land into cultivation,' and 'eliminating the middlemen' are worth volumes of arguments and statistics."[52] Similarly, in Venezuela Levy concluded that, "in the allocation of public resources, there was no concept of priorities or considerations of alternatives. A project was judged on its engineering and political merits; economic criteria rarely entered into consideration. Consequently a project was often undertaken more as a monument to its engineer, to its Minister, or to the regime than as a contribution to national progress."[53] In Hanson's study of the educational bureaucracy in Venezuela, he found a typical Latin American bureaucratic problem.

> Many of the administrative processes in Venezuela seem to be formulated for ideal conditions that do not exist in the real world. Under ideal conditions everything is predictable and controllable. The highly rule-oriented system guides the actors through their prepared steps. Unfortunately, there is little provision made for the unanticipated. Thus, when maps wear out, or windows are broken, or a typewriter stolen, or a teacher wants to introduce a new way to teach reading, the administrative system is not equipped to deal rapidly with these unanticipated developments. That is to say, if the administrative process does not go according to plan, there is no built-in correction device (i.e., low level supervisor with authority) which can resolve the problem where it happens when it happens.[54]

In some ways the Latin Americans have chosen a style of development that they are not culturally prepared to pursue (which is just another manifestation of the vicious circle of underdevelopment). The Weberian bureaucracy is antithetical to the dominant social values in Latin America. But despite this problem and others we have discussed, the elites in Latin America appear committed to this strategy because it appears to be the one most compatible with their interests.

Footnotes

[1]Bill Stewart, Change and Bureaucracy: Public Administration in Venezuela, Chapel Hill: The University of North Carolina Press, 1978, p. 11.

[2]Solon L. Barraclough, "Agricultural Policy and Strategies of Land Reform," in Irving Louis Horowitz, ed., Masses in Latin America, N.Y.: Oxford University Press, 1970, p. 109. See also John Leddy Phelan, "Authority and Flexibility in the Spanish Imperial Bureaucracy," Administrative Science Quarterly V (June 1960), p. 51.

[3]Guy Poitras, "Welfare Bureaucracy and Clientele Politics in Mexico," Administrative Science Quarterly, 18 (March 1973), p. 19.

[4]James M. Malloy, "Social Security Policy and the Working Class in Twentieth-Century Brazil," Journal of Inter-American Studies and World Affairs 19, (February 1977), p. 45.

[5]Marcos Kaplan, "El Estado Empresarial en al Argentina," El Trimestre Economico 36 (enero-marzo 1969), p. 74.

[6]Milton J. Esman, Administration and Development in Malaysia, Ithaca, N.Y.: Cornell University Press, 1972, p. 62.

[7]Merilee S. Grindle, Bureaucrats, Politicians, and Peasants in Mexico: A Case Study in Public Policy, Berkeley: University of California Press, 1977, p. 4.

[8]John M. Hunter and James W. Foley, Economic Problems of Latin America, Boston: Houghton Mifflin Co., 1975, pp. 236-237.

[9]Guillermo O'Donnell, "Reflections on the Patterns of Change in the Bureaucratic-Authoritarian State," Latin American Research Review XIII, o. 1 (1978), p. 12.

[10]Ibid., p. 6

[11]Grindle, op. cit., p. 3.

[12]Gary W. Wynia, The Politics of Latin American Development, N.Y.: Cambridge University Press, 1978,

p. 293.

[13]Arturo Valenzuela, "Political Constraints to the Establishment of Socialism in Chile," in Arturo Valenzuela and J. Samuel Valenzuela, eds., Chile: Politics and Society, New Brunswick, N.J.: Transaction Books, 1976, p. 18. See also Charles J. Parrish, "Bureaucracy, Democracy, and Development: Some Considerations Based on the Chilean Case," in Clarence E. Thurber and Lawrence S. Grahm, eds., Development Administration in Latin America, Durham, N.C.: Duke University Press, 1973, p. 241.

[14]Philippe C. Schmitter, Interest Conflict and Political Change in Brazil, Stanford, California: Stanford University Press, 1971, p. 247.

[15]Alan Gilbert, Latin American Development: A Geographical Perspective, Baltimore, Maryland: Penguin Books, 1974, p. 265.

[16]Gilbert B. Siegel, "Brazil: Diffusion and Centralization of Power," in Thurber and Grahm, op. cit., p. 373.

[17]Schmitter, op. cit., p. 34.

[18]Lauchlin Currie, Accelerating Development: The Necessity and the Means, N.Y.: McGraw Hill, 1966, p. 236.

[19]Charles J. Parrish and Jorge I. Tapia-Videla, "Welfare Policy and Administration in Chile," Journal of Comparative Administration 1 (February 1970), pp. 455-476.

[20]Martin Weinstein, Uruguay: The Politics of Failure, Westport, Conn.: Greenwood Press, 1975, p. 109.

[21]For example, see, Gilbert B. Siegel, "The Politics of Administrative Reform: The Case of Brazil," Public Administration Review XXVI, No. 1 (March 1966), pp. 45-55. Lawrence S. Grahm, Civil Service Reform in Brazil, Austin: University of Texas Press, 1968; Robert T. Groves, "Administrative Reform and the Politics of Reform: The Case of Venezuela," Public Administration Review XXVII, No. 5 (December 1967), pp. 436-445; Roderick Groves, "The Colombian National Front and Administrative Reform," Administration and Society 6, (November 1974), pp. 316-337; and Thurber and Grahm, op. cit.

[22]Victor A. Thompson, "Bureaucracy and Innovation," Administrative Science Quarterly 10, (March 1965), p. 10.

[23]Grindle, op. cit., p. 43.

[24]Roger D. Hanson, The Politics of Mexican Development, Baltimore: The Johns Hopkins Press, 1971, p. 178.

[25]Grindle, op. cit., p. 57.

[26]Richard R. Fagen and William S. Tuohy, Politics and Privilege in a Mexican City, Stanford: Stanford University Press, 1972, pp. 28-29.

[27]Grindle, op. cit., p. 167.

[28]El Tiempo, Bogotá, Colombia, 28 de julio 1974.

[29]Republica del Ecuador, Junta Nacional de Planificacion, Plan inmediata de desarrollo (Quito: mimeo, 1961), pp. 79-80.

[30]Stewart, op. cit., p. 9.

[31]Jerry L. Weaver, "Bureaucracy During A Period of Social Change: The Case of Guatemala," in Thurber and Grahm, op. cit., p. 329.

[32]Ibid., p. 335.

[33]William S. Tuohy, "Centralism and Political Elite Behavior in Mexico," in Thurber and Grahm, op. cit., p. 279; see also Antonio Ugaldo, Power and Conflict in a Mexican Community: A Study of Political Integration, Albuquerque, N.M.: University of New Mexico Press, 1970, p. 122.

[34]Mark W. Cannon, "Interactive Training Techniques for Improving Public Service in Latin America," in Thurber and Grahm, op. cit., p. 173.

[35]Kenneth L. Karst and Keith S. Rosenn, Law and Development in Latin America: A Case Book, Berkeley: University of California Press, 1975, p. 65.

[36]Richard M. Morse, "The Heritage of Latin America," in Louis Hartz, ed., The Founding of New Societies, N.Y.: Harcourt, Brace and World, 1964, p. 174.

[37]Virginia A. Paraiso, "Social Service in Latin America: Functions and Relationships to Development," Economic Bulletin for Latin America,Vol XI (April 1966), p. 84.

[38]Cannon, op. cit., p. 159.

[39]Fred Lerry, "Economic Planning in Venezuela," in Thurber and Grahm, op. cit., p. 83; Herbert Emmerick, "Administrative Roadblocks to Co-Ordinated Development," in Egbert De Vries and Jose Medina Echavarria, eds., Social Aspects of Economic Development in Latin America, Belgium: UNESCO, 1963, p. 350; Leopoldo Solia, La reali realidad economica mexicana: retrovision y perspectivas (Mexica: Siglo Veintinuno Editores, SA, 1970), p. 227

[40]Joseph S. Nye, "Corruption and Political Development: A Cost Analysis," American Political Science Review 61 (June 1967), p. 418.

[41]The New York Times, June 29, 1970.

[42]The New York Times, November 18, 1972.

[43]David W. Dent, "Urban Development and Governmental Response: The Case of Medellin," in Wayne Cornelius and Robert V. Kemper, eds., Metropolitan Latin America: The Challenge and Response: Beverly Hills: Sage Publications, 1978, p. 138.

[44]Hansen, op. cit., p. 125; The New York Times, June 29, 1976.

[45]Martin H. Greenberg, Bureaucracy and Development: A Mexican Case Study, Lexington, Mass. Health, 1970, p. 71.

[46]Ugalde, op. cit., pp. 120-121.

[47]Raymond Vernon, The Dilemma of Mexico's Development, Cambridge, Mass.: Harvard University Press, 1963, p. 150.

[48]Alberto Guereiro-Ramos, "The New Ignorance and The Future of Public Administration in Latin America," in Thurber and Grahm, op. cit., p. 399.

[49]Peter S. Cleaves, "Policymaking in Peru Since 1968," paper presented to the Latin American Studies Association, Houston, Texas, Novermber 1977, p. 2.

[50]Tony Smith, "The Underdevelopment of Development Literature: The Case of Dependency Theory," _World Politics_ XXXI (January 1979), p. 280.

[51]Gary W. Wynia, _Politics and Planners: Economic Development Policy in Central America_, Madison: Univeristy of Wisconsin Press, pp. 150 and 173.

[52]Currie, _op. cit._, p. 201.

[53]Levy, _op. cit._, p. 83.

[54]Mark Hanson, "Characteristics of Centralized Education in Latin America: The Case of Venezuela," _Comparative Education_ 6 (March 1970), p. 56.

CHAPTER XIII

BUREAUCRATIC STRUCTURE AND NATIONAL
DEVELOPMENT PROGRAMS: THE INDONESIAN
OFFICE OF THE JUNIOR MINISTER

Garth N. Jones

Introduction

Few developing countries have given as much
attention to establishing an organizational structure
to facilitate the execution of planned   development
programs as Indonesia. One of the first actions of the
Orde Baru (New Order) was to rationalize the cumbersome
organizational structure which evolved during the
Sukarno regime. At one time there were over 100 ministries with overlapping tasks, duties, responsibilities,
and authority. A complete organizational overhaul was
necessary to bring about administrative order and
responsibility.[1]

In carrying out the reorganization, classical
concepts of organizational design were followed. Careful attention was given to rational division of labor,
departmentalization of functional activities, establishment of workable spans of control, and clear cut delegation of authority. Organizational goals and objectives were systematically structured into meaningful
programmatic operations. Unity of command and of
communication patterns were to be followed. Organization by product or purpose was to take precedence over
organization by function. Territorial jurisdiction
for each major central government agency was specified.
Introduced was an unusual degree of uniformity in both
organizational structure and operational procedure.

Intent of reorganization was for the executive to
function in a highly integrated and systematic fashion.
The organizational work force was to be utilized
intelligently and coordinated effectively, interpersonal relations directed to coincide with organizational
goals and objectives, and internal control patterns
established to discourage dysfunctional interpersonal
behavior. Sanctions and rewards for employee performance were developed.

The executive function was organized to insure attainment of national development goals. Highest priority of the government was accelerated development to meet the "basic needs" of the people--adequate food, clothing, shelter, safety, health, education. Although authors of the reorganization stressed uniformity in structure and procedure, they were very much aware of the potential constraints of bureaucratic rigidity. Nevertheless, they evidenced confidence the executive bureaucracy could perform as an equitable and responsive problem-solving mechanism. Built-in capacity to adapt to change in an orderly and steady fashion would be possible to avoid system overload. Because of mounting social problems, many of which are traceable to excessive population pressures particularly on the island of Java,[2] the possiblilities of reducing pent up social forces are minimal. The New Order was faced with a surge of environmental turbulence. The future of the nation rested almost soley upon the capacity of the executive bureaucracy to deliver meaningful "development packages."

An innovative feature introduced into the new executive organization was the establishment of formal boundary spanning units in the President's cabinet, the most important of which were six junior ministers who were assigned responsibility to insure systematic implementation of carefully prescribed development programs.[3] These ministerial positions were created in 1978, as part of further refinement of the newly established structure, to insure top-level executives, including the President, will have direct access to accurate and relevant data concerning (1) the implementation of development programs and (2) the context of change forces at work in the operational environment of plan implementation. They also were vested with facilitative capacity to "coordinate, integrate and synchronize" development programs. During the years 1980 and 1981 operational details were being formulated as to how each of these six ministerial offices will function. However, to date there are encouraging evidences these ministerial offices are carrying out meaningful activities in facilitating and expediting the implementation of development programs.

On the other hand, a perplexing issue continues as to the capacities of the managers at the operational levels to utilize effectively this introduced organizational device which necessitates the employment of

extraordinary managerial skill and application of
sophisticated management technology--especially in
data and information processing and dissemination.
The remainder of this discussion will address especially
this issue. In this regards, two broad aspects will
be discussed. First will be a description and analysis
of the executive branch within which the offices of the
six junior ministers function. The second will examine
the management system and behavioral factors and processes necessary for these offices to function effectively as facilitators and expeditors of priority
development programs. In discussing these two aspects,
primary attention will be given to constraints, initiatives, and intents in operationalizing the executive
bureaucracy. Included will be preliminary comments on
the bureaucratic response to the innovative feature of
the office of the junior minister. A summary and general conclusion will be drawn.

Executive Organization

Underlying Premises of the Executive Structure:
The executive organization is structured around rank-in-
person rather than rank-in-position. Each rank determines the office structure and complex which is carefully specified by law.[4] Provincial and regional/local
governments operate mainly as subnational entities,
although in recent years increased autonomy has been
granted to them.[5] Administrative authority of the
Governors of the 27 provinces has markedly increased.
This organizational factor coupled with strengthened
local interest articulation makes the Governors significant actors in Indonesian political-administrative
affairs.

Structural and Non-Structural Agencies: Although
apparently not specified in the law, there has arisen
out of current administrative usage a useful organizational differentiation between what is termed a structural agency (instansi strukturil) and a non-structural
agency (instansi non-strukturil/bukan (not) strukturil).
Possibly, better terms could have been utilized to desig-
nate the differences between these two kinds of agencies
since all have organization structure. Nevertheless,
the underlying concept is sound.

Structural agencies are those established to carry
out activities of an indefinite and permanent nature
essential to the conduct of government affairs.

Included are such activities as defense, foreign affairs, and public health. Non-structural agencies are those established to carry out activities of a definite and temporary nature essential to the achievement of development goals as determined by the Cabinet. Once the goals are achieved or the Cabinet sets new goal priorities such agencies are to be quickly abolished. Thus, this legal concept provides an administrative means for both insuring continuity as well as change in the structure of the executive organization.

Operating procedures take into account the fundamental differences in organizational purpose. Structural agencies must follow the standard operating procedures (SOP) such as pertain to appointment, promotion, and removal of personnel. Special laws or regulations cannot be enacted to place one structural agency in a preferential position against the others. On the other hand, the law establishing a non-structural agency may contain operating procedures different from the SOP. This applies as well to the organization structures of such agencies.

Executive Structure

A fuller understanding of the underlying premises may be gained from a brief examination of the executive structure. The present Cabinet which was established on March 31, 1978, and termed the Development Cabinet, consists of 17 departments and 13 offices of state Ministries. The former are all deemed structural agencies and the latter non-structural agencies. This is reflected in the differences of authority enjoyed by the classes of ministers who head these two kinds of agencies. All of the ministers may attend Cabinet meetings. However, ministers heading 17 departments constitute the "core" cabinet. The state ministers are placed into three catagories which specifies their differing rank and status in the Cabinet.

Two Presidential Decrees, Numbers 44 and 48, issued in 1978 with amendments thereto, provide for the basic structure and procedures of the 17 executive departments.[6] Presidential Decree Number 44/1974 specifies the basic principles for the organization of these departments. This Decree is based on Chapter V, Article 17, of the Constitution which follows:

The Cabinet

(1) The President shall be assisted by Ministers of State.
(2) These Ministers shall be appointed and discharged by the President.
(3) These Ministers shall head governmental departments.

Elucidation to Article 17 explains that Ministers of State are responsible to the President only, not to the Legislature. They are not ordinary senior civil servants because it is the "Ministers who primarily carry out the Government's authority (pouvoir executif)."[7] They are also "state leaders" and fully responsible for their particular "charge".

Presidential Decree Number 45/1974 and amendments thereto specify the organizational detail of each of the 17 departments. Included as well in the Presidential decrees is the organizational structure for special kinds of institutes and non-departments such as the National Institute of Administration which is located in the Office of the President.

For the purposes of this discussion, it is not necessary to detail the organizational structure of the 17 departments. Generally, they constitute three major divisions of labor: the inspector general, the secretary general, and two to five directorates-general. In addition, within each department there may be established centers and bodies empowered to carry out specialized tasks and responsibilities such as operation of an agricultural training center. Each directorate is divided into subdirectorates and further into sections. The maximum number of each subunit is also limited by law. The secretary general follows a similar structural breakdown except the descending order is bureau, division, and subdivision.

The inspector general is responsible to insure governmental affairs and matters assigned in his department are conducted according to the purposes and procedures as laid down in the law. The secretary general is assigned the administrative-management function--personnel, budgeting, housekeeping activities. The director general is given specific executive functions, mainly of a line nature.

The consequence of the reorganization is the establishment of a highly compartmentalized and uniform organizational structure, based on standard operating
procedures. Each department has a clear-cut mandate
which may logically be reduced to specific organizational tasks. The structure is designed to assure expedi-
tiously the execution of the tasks much like the maneu-
vres of a well trained "military formation."

Each Minister is the chief administrator of his
assigned department. There is nothing comparable in
the Indonesian government to the position of the British
permanent secretary or the former position of the secretary general who assumed the principal administrative
authority. As the Constitution specifies, Ministers
heading departments must be fully capable of and respo-
nisble for administering details in their assigned
departments and in faithfully executing their assigned
public policies. The structure of reorganization is
designed to carry out the intent of this constitutional
mandate.

Articulation by Rank-in-Person: By structuring the
execuitve organization around rank in persons, the
administrative premise is that dynamic, strategically
placed managers will articulate the executive system
operations into an effective super-organization--provi-
ding a unifying perspective for administrative action.

The intent of the reorganization was that authority
should be commensurate with responsibility. In large
scale complex organization this is not entirely possible
especially at the higher levels of management. Nevertheless, each top manager would fully be responsible for
the execution of the development program tasks and
responsibilities assigned to him. Rank-in-person would
be the principal means by which to deal with this organizational difficulty, since in concept it cuts across
all organizational boundaries. Directors-General, who
are responsible for the major development programs are
all of equal rank and thus should be able to relate to
each other in organizational sets. For a specific
illustration, should the government's policy be increased production of food within the next five years, with
the goal of achieving self-sufficiency in rice supplies
within a five year period, then logically this is the
program responsibility of the Minister for Agriculture.
Under the present organizational arrangement, he does
not have authority commensurate with this responsibility

since irrigation is located in the Department of Public Works. Regardless, he must develop an organizational spanning capability where the Irrigation Directorate of the Department of Public Works will fully participate in his area of assigned program responsibility. Increased rice production in Indonesia can only be acheived by expansion of the irrigated agriculture and the better utilization of irrigation water supplies. Full support of the Directorate of Irrigation is required. This requires forging of close interpersonal linkages which is deemed to be possible by utilization of commensurate "rank".

High Level Coordination: The boundary spanning construct as instituted for the implementation of development programs, places a premium on performance of "hard hitting" public managers who effectively cooperate with each other to move forward priority development activities set by the President and his Cabinet. In spite of zeal and good intentions, Indonesian top decisionmakers were early faced with the classic problem of functional/technical versus product/program organization. Since Indonesia opted for a functional/technical form of management efficiency, the organizational requirement of coordination become critically important in carrying out activities of development programs such as the example for increased food production. Securing the kind of inter-agency cooperation and support did not readily occur, with each agency head ascribing higher priority to his own permanently assigned tasks and responsibilities rather than to those temporarily assigned to him as part of an interagency development program. The Cabinet may accord increased food production the highest priority in its policy directive of planned development, but this does not translate into the same meaning for a harassed director of public works who is responsible for a number of competing construction projects-- building roads and highways, hydro-electric sites and buildings.

To remedy this organizational situation, the President introduced a specific measure to insure high level coordination in the implementation of development programs. Included were the appointment in his "Third Development Cabinet" three state Ministers with the task to coordinate specific sectors of development activities, commonly termed Menko (Ministers of Cooperation). In order to facilitate the implementation of selected priority development programs as determined by the

Cabinet, six junior Ministers were subsequently appointed. These two Presidential actions in 1978 essentially completed the organizational arrangement of the present Cabinet.

Office of Junior Minister: In design, the organizational structure gave emphasis to the execution of development program but yet it provided at the same time the advantages of functional/technical efficiency. The principal means in achieving this high level of organizational performance would be through effective vertical "coordination, integration, and synchronization" of selected development programs. The offices of the junior Minister would be given this primary responsibility by providing a boundary spanning role which encompassed the necessary development activities of two or more departments as well as the provincial/regional governments.[8]

Under the present development priorities, the six junior Ministers provided under Presidential Decree are attached to a relevant departmental (core) Minister except in one case to a specific coordinating entity. They are as follows: (1) Food Crops to Agriculture, (2) Cooperatives to Trade and Cooperatives, (3) Transmigration to Manpower and Transmigration, (4) Community Housing to Public Works, (5) Youth to Education and Culture, and (6) Women Affairs to Coordinator Minister for People Welfare.

Each junior Minister has his own secretariat. Nevertheless, major administrative support is provided by the Ministerial department to which his office is attached. The junior Minister has no independent budget or administrative authority. For example, the junior Minister may propose the nomination of a person to fill a vacant position in his organization but the actual appointment is made by the secretary-general on behalf of the appropriate Minister.

Administratively, it appears no unusual problems have arisen under this complex arrangement. The standard operating procedures apply. The junior Minister holds higher rank than any of the top bureaucrats--mainly secretary-general, and directorates-general. By law, he has direct communication to the President. In addition, he is accorded other powers by law which place him in a strong organizational position.

Beyond these administrative similarities, each junior Minister's office has developed different kinds of boundary spanning approaches and networks and implementation strategies to carry out the assigned development program responsibilities.

Operationalizing Executive Bureaucracy

Operationalizing the executive bureaucracy has proven to be a more difficult task than the design of organizational structure. Although progress under the New Order has been made in narrowing the gap between planning and producing of meaningful goods and services for the public's benefit, the distance remains unsatisfactory. It should be recognized under the best of circumstances that this is not an easy matter. Indonesia is an exceedingly complex society, from 200 to 300 distinct ethnic groups, most of which have strong identity and competing rivalries. Bhinneka Tunnggal Ika (Diversity Becoming Unity) is the national motto that both describes reality and a goal yet to be achieved. Infuse into this complex social milieux aggressive Communism and revivalistic Islam, the political situation becomes tenuous at the best and too frequently volatile.[9]

Institutionalizing the Bureaucratic Polity

Constructive political development has been a difficult process in Indonesia. In 1957 parliamentary democracy ended with the declaration of martial law. For eight or so years thereafter the bureaucracy was torn by bitter factional rivalries which culminated in the abortive Communist coup in September 1965.

To achieve political stability, the Suharto New Order administration instituted a bureaucratic polity that in style and function has a strong resemblance to the former Dutch colonial practice. One Dutch scholar suggests "that the period from 1942-65...characterized by instability and turmoil, was an intermezzo in the pattern of continuity in Indonesia's social and political system." In contrasting the New Order and colonial administration, he observes:

Now as well as then, economics and technocratic decisionmaking dominate the style of govern-

343

ment and material development to the detriment
of political development; mechanisms of control
originate at the top and are forcefully implemented; the Indonesian military has taken over the
tasks and the positions of the pre-war Binnenlands
Bestuur (Ducth internal administration) that
guaranteed the political and administrative
integrity of the territory; the second echelon
of adminstrators is strongly tied to the local
and regional levels; the military style of
internal administration, the circulation of
personnel through the ranks and administrative
units, and the emphasis on esprit de corps are
similar to the style of the Dutch; altogether
this style has revived the adminsitrative
dualism of the colonial period. The regime
has been and is primarily interested in guara-
nteeing law and order with the purpose of
favouring an economic-capitalistic style of
development; the regime is political and technocratic, and very suspicious of revolutionary
ambitions; social radicalism is suspect and
forbidden in its organized forms; risks are to
be avoided and social unrest needs to be
suppressed immediately.[10]

Other observers of Indonesian politics have reached
a similar conclusion. [11] Power and participation in
national decisionmaking are restricted almost entirely
to the civil servants and particularly to those at the
highest levels of the bureaucracy. Highly trained
specialists known as the technocrats exercise great
power. The core of the bureaucracy, comprising the
bureaucratic, military and technocratic elite of the
nation, numbers less than one thousand persons.

Participation in government is limited and tends
to be restricted to the local levels. In practice it
consists largely of seeking individual relief from
government regulations and extractions. Its pattern
generally follows the traditional hierarchy of authority
and patron-client groupings. Mass mobilization is strongly discouraged by the government, and when they occur
the initiative usually has come from the elite to demonstrate public support for a particular government
purpose.

The antecedents for the Indonesian bureaucratic

polity are traceable to the Javanese culture which sees
human life and the socio-political order as a reflection
of the cosmic order. Order and harmony are the main
objectives in Javanese life. These goals can be achieved
by persons seeking to reach a state of rasa (inner harmony) in perfecting such personal qualities as self-
control, asceticism, and etiquette. Order is conceived
in a hierarchical pattern of the traditional Javanese
state which centers around the autocratic, divine king
residing in his kraton (palace) "from which the life
blood of the state emanated, permeating all ranks of
society."[12] This sort of traditional Javanese thought
profoundly influences the political affairs in Indonesia.
As the eminent Indonesian scholar Sudjatmoko explains,
this provides:

> ...the tendency toward paternalistic authorita-
> rianism, the inclination to seek employment in
> the civil service the preoccupation with prestige
> and status rather than function and performance,
> the unquestioning obedience to authority, the
> almost exclusive concentration of politics in
> the capital and the emphasis on strengthening
> the national will through indoctrination and
> revolutionary fervor rather than the solving
> of practical problems.[13]

Politically, the age-old cleavage underlying
Indonesian politics still remains with sharp division
between Javanese traditionalism and neo-traditionalism
and the Muslim orthodoxy (the santri Muslim). At this
time, the mystic-oriented officer corps apparently
dominate the political situation--affecting a detent-
like relationship with the orthodox Muslim. Thus, the
Javanese orientation underpinning the executive bureaucracy evidences substantial acceptance and strength.

Transforming the Bureaucratic Polity

Indonesia lacks nearly all of the factors necessary
to transform its present bureaucratic polity into a more
open and democratic state of affairs. The vast majority
of the people are very poor, with annual per capita
incomes below one hundred dollars. Although educational
progress is remarkable, the maintenance of this human
investment is daily eroded by a weak infrastructure for
disseminating mass information and creating new learning
opportunities. Communications and transportation faci-

lities are gorssly inadequate to service this largest of all island nations. Its social patterns are under great stress, with accommodations between the old and the new not smoothly integrating into new social wholes. The political rationale for the state remains contested by powerful segments of society, although progress is being made in gaining acceptance of Pancasila idealism.

The political decisionmakers are caught in a difficult position. They understand that governing the far flung archipelago demands wholesale decentralization and devolution of government activities, yet they realize each time this has occurred in the past inimical interests have managed to take these opportunities to control local regions for advancing their own political purposes. even in plotting the overthrow of the central government.

Presently, the Indonesian bureaucratic polity is stable but weak. Nevertheless, it can easily rule the nation. There are few indications that it will modernize itself. Political reform along the lines of constitutional democracy is unlikely to emerge in the foreseeable future. However, this does not mean that the situation is stagnant. Quite the contrary; progressive measures are being taken to enhance the capacity of the bureaucracy to perform mainly by introducing professionalism into the executive bureaucracy.

Professionalizing the Executive Bureaucracy

The New Order authors of the administrative reform understood well the state of the nation's political maturity. Although evidencing confidence in the bureaucracy to rule, they recognized the need for establishing responsible bureaucratic behavior. Fortunately, a number of favorable social factors existed which would facilitate the renewal of bureaucratic responsibility.[14] Throughout the island nation strong commitment to national ideals continued. Civil servants were accorded respect. The values of halus (sophisticated/refine) deportment and commitment to dinas (official service) remained paramount. The position of being a civil servant was prestigious even though they receive incredibly low salaries.[15] Especially on the island of Java, the bureaucrat was as much a dignitary as a functionary.

Enhanced performance became the principal strategy initiated by Indonesia's administrative reforms to bring about bureaucratic change. Indonesians are highly people oriented. They attach great significance to l'esprit de corp (semangat) to accomplish organizational needs and ends. For this reason, features of Javanese social behavior and practice are especially attractive. It would be extremely difficult to infuse into their socio-culutral milieu machine bureaucracy characterized by "standardization of work processes as the prime coordinating mechanism, the technostructure (the process of standardization) as its most crucial part, and limited horizontal decentralization."[16] This smells too much of a factory which the Indonesian bureaucracy is not prepared to accept nor possibly is appropriate for their situation. Machine bureaucracy operates well in simple and stable environments which are relatively mature in both size and age. This is not the present world of the Indonesian civil servant.

Nevertheless, there has been considerable effort on the parts of external forces, mainly those providing economic assistance, to introduce characteristics of machine bureaucracy into Indonesian administrative practice. This has been skillfully resisted, although this fact is not well documented.[17]

Indonesia, on the other hand, has sought to professionalize the bureaucracy--giving particular attention to strengthening its key managers. A large number of specialized training institutions have been established and advanced degree educational programs initiated. The premier institution is the National Institute of Administration which is located in the Office of the President and over the last 25 years has been instrumental in bringing about major administrative change and reform. Thus, there are at work forces changing the ascriptive-formalistic oriented bureaucracy into a dynamic-professional oriented bureaucracy.

Indonesia does not yet have a professional bureaucracy. Progress in this direction is discernable where standardization of skills as the prime coordinating mechanism is utilized, the operating core (where the work is actually done) as the most important part of the organization is stressed, and decentralization along both vertical and horizontal dimensions is sought.[18] Increasingly, attention is being focused on horizontal task specialization among skilled professionals. An acute shortage of skilled and trained talent has forced this kind of organizational experimentation.[19]

A word of caution is necessary, however. Indonesia is still a long way from developing a professional bureaucracy, and may be it will never do so except in selected instances. Nevertheless, forces are at work in this direction. This is especially evidenced in technical agencies such as public health, medical care, public works and higher education. The rationale for establishing the offices of junior Ministers supports the operational aspects of mobilizing a bureaucracy which in design is professional in nature. The consequence of external donors in attempting to introduce "machine bureaucracy" through their technical assistance efforts have resulted in the infusion of sizeable number of well educated and trained professionals/technocrats into the executive bureaucracy. While still structured around rank-in-person, expertise to perform in position is increasingly being given importance. Indonesian bureaucracy is rapidly becoming a collectivity of professionals.

Operationalizing Priority Development Programs

The new bureaucratic structure based on a formal system of communication, rigid patterns of authority, and a high level of division of labor introduced a kind of military order into the government required to systematically execute centrally planned development programs but it also created a number of perplex organizational problems and exacerbated several chronic ones stemming from the nation's social complexities. Finally, this form of organization tends to breed a relatively high level of conflict. The director generals in the executive bureaucracy have become extremely powerful, jealously guarding their jurisdictional domains. Some Indonesians called them "warlords". A Governor of East Java once "remarked that his two greatest enemies were the Solo River (which floods) and the poor coordination among these 'vertical agencies'(instansi vertikal) in his province."[20] In too many instances, the lack of joint planning between the vertical agencies reduced the potential benefit of priority development programs. Central government agencies almost at will carry on their activities, by-passing provincial and local authorities and seldom taking time to coordinate their activities within a larger program context. The chronic problem of social equity in the conduct of government affairs still continued.

Indonesian leadership attempted to correct this overall situation through centralized planning and financial control, and with some measure of success. Development programs were carefully formulated and financial resources allocated according to development priority. Nevertheless, implementation problems became increasingly prevalent as Indonesian planners undertook larger scale development programs which required the combined capabilities of several vertical agencies such as the greatly expanded transmigration effort. Resettling two and a half million landless and near landless persons, for example, over a five year period requires an unusual organizational capability, apart from the question of social equity. Involved are six of the seventeen vertical (line) departments, including therein over 50 directorates and subdirectorates.

Operationalizing the executive bureaucracy for systematically carrying out such large scale development programs soon became a major concern of Indonesia's top leadership. Fresh and innovative approaches were necessary, since nothing in Indonesia's past organizational repertoire seemed applicable.

The central need in the implementation of these large centrally planned undertaking was administratively identified as that of enhanced project integration, coordination and synchronization. The task was to secure an optimum of organizational technical efficiency, i.e., capturing a combination of technical capabilities of each specialized agency for achieving goals of priority development programs. More specifically, would it be possible to direct systematically the specialist/technical capabilities of each of the appropriately identified directorates-general into carefully prescribed large scale development efforts but yet at the same time preserve each of their legally defined purpose and organizational integrity? For instance, engineering talent is in critical short supply. Would it not be best to concentrate this talent in the Directorate of Public Works and establish therein appropriately designed task groups to function within the larger development program efforts? Basically, there was no other organizational alternative. There was no question that those agencies assigned responsibility for priority development programs would rather have their own engineering staff complements, but this is not possible since there are not enough engineering personnel to service all the various agency projects. The administrative task then is to

organize in a systematic manner a number of separate and
discrete project activities based in the vertical agencies of both the central and provincial governments
within a larger context of program development. Bluntly
stated, how does the top executive leadership get the
directors-general, the Warlords, to work in unison to
carry out inter-agency development programs? The solution to this organizational problem was the establishment of the six offices of junior Ministers.

Institutionalizing Optimum Technical Efficiency

The newly created offices of junior Ministers will
operate from some position of management strength, with
the importance of management optimum technical efficiency understood. Sophisticated central planning, information processing, and resource allocating measures
within a program context have been introduced to facilitate the achievement of national development goals.
The term program is used in the typical meaning associated with program budgeting as conceived within national
plans. Program is defined as a set of interrelated activities, which usually cut across departmental organization, to support a national objective. Program budgeting is a link between budgeting and planning, since programs are the means by which planning objectives are
advanced. Sometimes in Indonesian planning/budgeting
practice, there may be confusion between the technical definition of program and sector. However, this has
not contributed to any implementation problems. Basically, the terms program and sector are used interchange-
ably.

With targets and goals clearly specified in five
year plan documents and within a well conceived program
context, the task of establishing the appropriate kind
of temporary organizational structure to achieve development ends becomes administratively feasible. Both the
enabling law creating the offices of junior Minister
and the executive intent is that each junior Minister
will take the initiative in designing the necessary
administrative machinery to expedite the development
program under his purview. This includes both the structure as well as the operational procedures and details.
Using Indonesian military terminology which is incorporated into the law, each junior Minister is invested
with "command" authority to carry out his mission. The
expression command has special meaning in the Indonesian

context.[21] This does not discount the fact that the
process of decisionmaking is nationally based mufakat
(unanimous consent of all), reached by way of musyawarah
(extensive deliberation). Each office of junior Minister has established a centralzing line of command which
in effect makes it a super-directorate-general for program implementation purposes. In intent when the junior
Minister speaks the appropriate directors-general listen.

Powerful bureaucratic measures within the Indonesian context are available to give the office of junior
Minister implementation capability beyond that of simple
persuasion. Included are political means such as enhanced organizational rank, direct lines of communication
to the Cabinet and to the President, and Ministerial
status conferred on the junior Minister. The later is
particularly important, since under Article 17 of the
Constitution, Ministers of state exercise "pouvior
executif." They are "state leaders," with a fully
mandated "charge".

Introduce into this temporary organizational arrangement which is clothed with command authority, enhanced
administrative capabilities in the various forms of
matrix/project management, cost accounting, controlled
financial allocation, and performance auditing and evaluation, it becomes a powerful factor in the bureaucratic process. Its temporary organizational nature further enhances the agency's power base since the self-
serving propensities of bureaucratic interests become
minimized. For the occupants it becomes a "sink or
swim" proposition.

On the other hand, it must be acknowledged that the
perceived strengths of this organizational innovation
may also become basically a severe organizational deficiency. Possibly, the most difficult aspect will be the
recruitment of competent middle managers. Inter-agency
deputation is not a common practice in Indonesia except
for the military providing personnel to the civil bureaucracy. Job security is a strong personal need. Undou-
tedly, it will be difficult to recruit competent persons
to fill these temporary positions.

Furthermore, in Indonesian bureaucratic practice
authority is rarely delegated. It could be that the very
purpose for which the offices of junior Minister were
established in dealing with the problem is undermined
with excessive concentration of authority at top levels

of the executive organization. On the other hand, this could possibly be avoided if the top executive appoints the right persons to these positions. The Javanese concept of power (kasekten) has charismatic qualities which makes it indivisible and adhering to a person rather than being a manifestation of particular relationships between people.[22] The person in charge is indisputably in charge. Thus, the right person in the office of junior Minister has the legitimate power to perform while not being fully invested with the formal authority to carry out a program mission which cuts across several vertical agencies.

Although cultural strengths are evident supporting the organizational innovation of the junior Minister, further reorientation in attitudes and outlook of the bureaucracy is required--replacing several of the premises upon which recent administrative reforms were based. For example, if the notions of collegial teams, horizontal and vertical integration, role exchange, interim problem-solving undertakings, utilization of temporary organizational forms, and sustaining self-actualized projects groups are to be introduced, then the conventional bureaucratic predilections toward rank, status, prerequisites, power, chain of command, line versus staff, planning/policy versus project implementation, must be modified. The imposed mechanistic approach, with its order and response characteristics, must be supplanted by a more organic oriented approach, with its diffused order and response characteristics.[23] It is too early to judge whether or not this is possible. However, again cultural values enunciated in such forms as mufakat and musjawarah provide a favourable milieu for this to occur.

Summary and Conclusions

Few of the problems that developing nations have proven to be as complex and intractable as finding effective means of implementing planned development programs. This will undoubtedly become more complex in the ensuing years as these countries embark on larger development programs designed to promote equitable growth and extend benefits to poorer and neglected social groups.

Although in recent years considerable comment has occurred concerning the inadequacies of centralized planning and the capacities of executive bureaucracies to perform, nevertheless other development alternatives have not shown any greater promise. Large scale undertakings require large scale organizations. The central problem becomes effective inter-agency program implementation. Recent tendencies toward stressing decentralization of planning and adminsitration and of widespread participation by intended beneficiaries in the design and implementation of development programs are no guarantees that systematic development will occur. Adam Smith's "unseen hand" does not work in the "development game," either for the grand schemes of 1950s and the 1960s or the modest schemes of the 1970s. Both schemes encountered pervasive and intransigent social obstacles and in both instances a lack of attention to organizational and management detail occurred which quickly destroyed any credibility.

The lesson to be learned from the last three decades of planned development effort is that the administration is the critical factor for success; and in this regard, the most important aspect is the administrative capability of the executive bureaucracy to perform. This matter is not simply going to "wither away".

Agreed, decentralization and devolution along with increased popular participation are requisites for constructive development. At the same time there must be in-place a centralized bureaucratic mechanism which holds together everything in proper balance. Following the organizational maxim of General Motors, one of the world's largest and successful private corporations, large scale organization requires decentralization with centralized control. The missing element making this possible in the planned development efforts of many developing nations is that centralized control becomes just that--control and not technical service. Suggested in the Indonesian experience is the need for enhanced facilitative administration starting at center and spreading throughout carefully selected and identified development programs as determined by the highest executive authority in consultation with public constituents and needs. The principal organizational mechanism in Indonesia to insure this has been the introduction of the offices of junior Minister which are clothed with command authority to facilitate program execution through the process of systematic coordination, synchronization, and integration of project activities vested mainly in selected vertical (line) agencies of

353

central and provincial governments. Should this organizational experiment prove successful, it will be one of the most important organizational contributions in recent years to the implementation of centrally planned development.

Footnotes

^{1}A sizeable body of literature largely in the Indonesian language exists on this subject which is synthe-
sized in the following: Bintoro Tjokroamidjojo, Pengan-
tar Administrasi Pembangunan, Jakarta: Lembaga, Peneli-
tian, Pendidikan dan Penerangan Ekonomi dan Sosial, 1978.
Title is Introduction to the Administration of Development. For an excellent discussion in the English language, although slightly dated, see Sondang P. Siagian,
"Improving Indonesia's Administrative Infrastructure:
A Case Study," in Hahn Been Lee and Abelardo G. Samanto,
ed., Administrative Reforms in Asia, Manila: Philippines:
Eastern Regional Organization for Public Administration,
1970, pp. 95-126.

^{2}Java is approximately the size of the state of
Louisiana with a population from 85 to 90 million.
Although there has been a decrease in the rate of population growth, each year one and a half million or more
people are added to the total population.

^{3}This is literal but possibly misleading translation. Some persons have used the term associate minister.
However, this does not convey the proper context, since
the Menteri Muda (Junior Ministers) are positions with
Ministerial rank and status. They are junior only in
the sense that Ministers in the present Cabinet are
ranked into three categories.

^{4}Information on the legal and organizational arrangements of the Indonesian government is found in the
following: Landasan dan Pedoman Induk Penyempurnaan
Administrasi Negara, Republic Indonesia, Jakarta: Lembaga Administrasi Negars, 1979. Title is Basis and Guidelines for Perfecting State Administration, Republic
of Indonesia.

^{5}The central and provincial/local autonomy has been
a problem dating back to the Dutch colonial period for
which to date a satisfactory solution had not been
found. The present legal/institutional arrangement is
contained in Statutory Law No. 5, 1974.

^{6}The pattern of law in Indonesia is complex because since 1945 three different Constitutions have been
in effect and each provided for different types of law-

making and law-enforcing procedures. Under the present 1945 Constitution which was reinstated in 1959, a Presidential Decree (Keptusan Presiden) is promulgated by the President to give effect to an Article of the Constitution or to implement a law of the legislature. As such a Presidential Decree constitutes a high form of law.

[7]J. C. T. Simorangkir and B. Mang Reng Say, Around and About the Indonesian Constitution of 1945, Jakarta: Djambatan, 1980, p. 21. This is a translation from the Indonesian language. The elucidation under Indonesian practice has legal import.

[8]The term office is used as found in Daniel Katz and Robert L. Kahn, The Social Psychology of Organization, 2nd ed., New York: John Wiley & Sons, 1978. See particularly p. 168, "...in any organization we can locate each individual in the total set of ongoing relationships and behaviors comprised by a particular point in organizational space; space is in turn defined as terms of a structure of interrelated office and a pattern of activities associated with them. Office is essentially a relational concept, defining each position in terms of its relationship to others and to the system as a whole..."

[9]The literature on Indonesian politics is overwhelming. For succinct summaries within the context of this discussion, see Guy J. Parker, "Indonesia 1979: The Record of Three Decades," Asian Survey 20 (February 1980), pp. 123-124, and Sidney R. Jones, " 'It Can't Happen Here' : A Post-Khomeini Look at Indonesian Islam," Asian Survey 20 (March 1980), pp. 311-323.

[10]Taken from Niels Mulder, Mysticism and Everyday Life in Contemporary Java, Singapore: University of Singapore, 1978, p. 97. Mulder references J. A. A. Van Door, Orde-Opstand-Orde: Nolities oven Indonesie, Boom Mappel, 1973, pp. 76-77.

[11]For a fuller discussion, see Karl D. Jackson, "Bureaucratic Polity: A Theoretical Framework for the Analysis of Power and Communications in Indonesia," in Karl D. Jackson and Lucian W. Pye, eds., Political Power and Communication in Indonesia, Berkeley: University of California Press, 1978, pp. 3-22.

[12]For an interesting discussion, see C. L. M. Penders, _The Life and Times of Sukarno_, Singapore: Oxford University Press, 1975, especially p. 138 et seq.

[13]_Ibid_, p. 139.

[14]See James L Peacock, _Indonesia: An Anthropoligical Perspective_, Pacific Palisades, CA.: Goodyear Publishing Co., 1973, pp. 141-142.

[15]For an excellent discussion, see Cline Gray, with a note by H. W. Arndt and R. M. Sundrum, "Civil Service Compensation in Indonesia," _Bulletin of Indonesian Economic Studies_ 15 (March 1979), pp. 85-124.

[16]See Ricky W. Griffin, _Task Design: An Integrative Approach_, Dallas, Texas: Scott, Foresman and Co., 1982, p. 136.

[17]This conclusion is based on 25 years of study and observation of economic assistance to Indonesia. In the 1950s and early 1960s US/AID, United Nations Agencies and other external donors provided extensive assistance in public administration which on reflection was heavily designed within the scientific management approach. When I returned to Indonesia for seven months in 1980, I surprisingly noted that again a number of external donors were involved in technical assistance activities not unlike those 20 years ago. In a polite manner Indonesia had rejected the model of machine bureaucracy.

[18]See Griffin, _op. cit._, pp. 130-131.

[19]See my "Boundary Spanning and Organizational Structure in National Development Programs: Indonesian Office of Junior Minister Transmigration," _The Chinese Journal of Administration_ 33 (May 1982), pp. 75-116.

[20]See Donald K. Emmerson, "The Bureaucracy in Political Context: Weakness in Strength, " in Karl D. Jackson and Lucian Pye, eds., _op. cit._, p. 127.

[21]See for instance, U. L. F. Sundhaussen, "The Military: Structure, Procedures and Effects on Indone-

sian Society," in Jackson and Pye, eds., op. cit.,
pp. 45-81.

[22]Emmerson, op. cit., p. 124.

[23]These terms are basically used as advanced by
Thomas Burns and G. M. Stalker, in The Impact of Innovation, London: Tavistock Publications, 1961.

CHAPTER XIV

STATE SOCIALIST ADMINISTRATION IN THE U.S.S.R.

Michael E. Urban

For those who are not too familiar with the formal structure of the Union of Soviet Socialist Republics (USSR), a few words of introduction might be handy in comprehending its size, complexity and uniqueness. The Soviet Union is a federal system. At the highest level are the 15 Union Republics, which collectively make-up the Union. Below those are the 20 Autonomous Republics, 8 Autonomous Regions and 10 National Areas. The various levels of political organization, which include others, could be shown graphically thus:

```
┌--Soviet of USSR

├--Union Republican Soviets

├--Soviet Autonomous Republics, Territories
│       (kray), Regions (oblast) and
│       certain major cities

├--Soviets of Autonomous Regions and National
│       Areas (okrug)

├--District (rayon) Soviets, certain towns
│       outside of District jurisdiction

└--Soviet of Towns, settlements and villages
        (or rural soviets)


        Source: David Lane, Politics and Society in
                the USSR, New York: Random House,
                1970, p. 145.
```

Articles 86 and 88 of the Soviet Constitution provide for formal autonomy of these levels, thus reflecting the diverse national and ethnic make-up of the USSR, which contains well over 100 national and ethnic groups in addition to larger nationalities that enjoy republican status. Following the federal principle, the Supreme Soviet is divided into two chambers: the Soviet of Nationalities and the Soviet of the Union. Inasmuch as it is in session for about two weeks per year, the great bulk of its business is carried on by its Presidium, a sort of "collective president" whose Chairman at the present time is also the Party leader, Yuri Andropov. The most important task performed by the Presidium of the Supreme Soviet is monitoring the behavior of the administrative apparatus, the Ministries and state committees, who collectively make-up the Council of Ministers.

The Communist Party of the Soviet Union (CPSU) is unique in that the hierarchical chain of command from Ministry to performing units is parallelled by the organization of the Communist Party's own apparatus of administration. Graphically it may be shown thus:

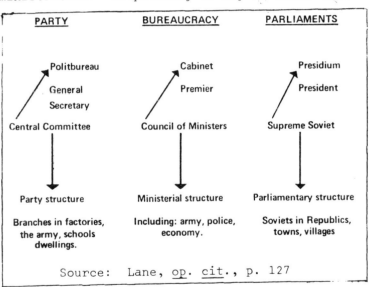

PARTY	BUREAUCRACY	PARLIAMENTS
Politbureau	Cabinet	Presidium
General Secretary	Premier	President
Central Committee	Council of Ministers	Supreme Soviet
Party structure	Ministerial structure	Parliamentary structure
Branches in factories, the army, schools dwellings.	Including: army, police, economy.	Soviets in Republics, towns, villages

Source: Lane, op. cit., p. 127

The Party monopolizes authority in the sense that "the party's values are dominant and solely legitimate: i.e., in Soviet terminology, only the party safeguards the interests of the working class. It decides the social, economic and political goals of the society: it fixes the relationship between men and property, shapes the dominant economic and political mores, and exercises control over the selection of the leading personnel in the government of the country."[1]

In state socialist societies, among which the USSR is the leading example, the political state has to all intents and purposes displaced what can be regarded as "civil society" in other modern systems. With the exception of purely personal, mainly family-based relations, all that exists is either directly or indirectly a manifestation of the political system. This seminal fact complicates the study of Soviet administration in a number of ways. First, the object of analysis, governmental administration, is enoromous. What is non-governmental? We can recognize numerous areas of governmental intervention in, say, Western administrative systems. Yet, in so doing, we simultaneously recognize a non-governmental sphere which, despite the scope of governmental regulations, subsidies, licenses, despite the fact that an entire industry might exist because of government, remains <u>analytically</u> distinct from the political state. Such distinctions are all but impossible to draw in the Soviet context. The closest approximation to a non-governmental entity would be the category of "social organizations" which includes everything from chess clubs and sports organizations to trade unions and the Communist Party.[2] There may be juridical grounds for distinguishing between the state and such social organizations.[3] From a political perspective, however, the distinction comes to nothing. Most "social organizations" are extensions of the state and are created by it for some specific purpose, whether enlisting volunteers to assist in the maintenance of public order or to organize some activity which the state has approved (eg., sports).[4] The exceptions to this rule are the Communist Party and its offspring, the Communist Youth League. As we shall see below, these are the exceptions that prove the rule. A comprehensive account of Soviet administration, then, would perforce include all organized activity in the USSR. Consequently, some organizing ideas are required in order to sort out what is of central concern to students of amdinistration from what is secondary or derivative.

Second, and related to the need for organizing ideas, is the question of "bureaucracy" within the circumstances of state socialism. As a concept, bureaucracy is commonly associated with, if not equate to, administration. I wish to avoid conflation of these terms, however, for in state socialist systems the concept of "bureaucracy" has little application. Following Max Weber, we can think of bureaucracy as above all a form of life, a mode of social action, which is governed by certain principles. Indeed, as an "ideal type", the concept refers to human organization and action as no more than the physical manifestation of these principles. Bureaucracy is a 'rationalized" mode of human interaction, rationalized in the sense that behavior is subject to evaluation on the basis of technical rules and the rules, themselves, are subject to evaluation on the criteria of organizational efficiency and effectiveness.[5] As Weber pointed out long ago, bureaucracy in the sense described here is unthinkable outside of a market society.[6] At a minimum, the rationalization of social action implies calculated evaluations, measured behavior. Hence, a unit of measurement, a standard equivalent against which all things can be evaluated, is presupposed by the bureaucratic mode of organization. This standard equivalent is money, understood not as a thing, of course, but as expression of a relation among things. As such, money tells us how much something costs and, therefore, whether it is rational to organize in one way or the other, to produce one thing or another, to substitute one thing in the production process for another and so on. Inasmuch as state socialist societies are organized on the basis of a central plan and not a market, money is not in these societies a standard equivalent. Bureaucracy in the sense of rationalized social action does not exist, although hierarchically administered organizations certainly do. This point may seem at first to be no more than splitting hairs. I intend to show, however, that drawing such a distinction between bureaucracy and administration is essential to an explanation of the dynamics of a state socialist system.

Third, markets involve not only means of calculation (money), but an orientation around which such calculations occur, namely, profit. Units of the political state in capitalist societies do not usually have profit as a goal, but this is a detail. State activity is integrally connected to the generation of profits in capitalist systems if for no other reason than that state revenues depend upon profit-making by capitalist firms.

What represents the analogue to a profit orientation for state socialist systems? The argument which I shall develop below suggests that control of positions or offices to which resources belong is the primary desideratum for all actors in the administrative system. Here we might only note that such is above all a political consideration and that our "exception" among social organizations in the USSR is the Communist Party. The Communist Party is the organizational vortex of the struggle within the Soviet system for control of positions and their attendant resources. The Communist Party exercises what is officially described as its "leading role" in the Soviet system in three ways. It holds the power of appointment to all important posts in the state apparatus, so all important office holders directly owe their positions to the Party[8]; all occupants of important state positions are themselves Party members and subject to Party policy and Party discipline in their capacities as state officials[9]; the Party apparatus (i.e., the full-time, paid Party officials and subalterns) frequently intervene directly in state matters to insure that Party objectives are bieng met by the state.[10]

While calling attention to these general relations between Party and state hierarchies, we would do well to avoid reifying either the Party or the state as some monolithic thing which has its own goals and acts in an unified, coherent manner to secure them. Behind the formal appearances of unanimity, discipline and the like, each hierarchy reveals a bewildering set of particular interests, cliques and informal alliances which not only may run counter to centrally established Party policy but equally can involve segments of the state administration working with counterparts in the Party apparatus against groupings composed of other state organizations and their Party allies.[11]

Finally, by way of introduction, I would like to link together some of the points thus far made and to put forward a general idea which will serve as an approach to analyzing Soviet administration in what follows. Inasmuch as all things of value in the Soviet system—whether housing, education, goods, services information, or travel—are allocated by the state. Those who occupy state positions (or, in the case of the Party apparatus, those who control appointments to these positions) control access to things desired by others. Action is structured around particularistic (non-market) exchange among those who control access to desirable things. Exchange relationships tend to become quite "long", they involve a great many actors and span a variety of institutions. In a word, they amount to "networks".[12] Such networks are not unfamiliar to students of traditional or developing nations. What marks state socialism, a social formation built on this type of exchange, as sui generis is the fact that we are neither dealing with

363

the simple form of production common to a traditional, agrarian village, nor are we speaking merely of political cliques who exchange among themselves within the larger context of a market-oriented society.[13] Rather, we are dealing with a gigantic industrial economy where no market mechanism is at work. We can offer two propositions, then, which will orient our understanding of state socialist administration. On the quantitative side, whatever is done, prevented, changed, produced, etc., is a function of some exchange between the holders of resources. And, on the qualitative side, the nature of what is done is always a value established by the parties to a particular exchange; or, to put it another way, value neither resides in things themselves nor is it established by an impersonal market. Value is what is identified as valuable by the relevant parties. This may mean, for instance, that the production of quality goods might appear in one situation as a preferred activity or that in another, owing to different circumstances, the production of shoddy goods or for that matter sheer waste assumes a definite value for those in the exchange relation. We shall develop these ideas at greater length, below. Before doing so, however, some background on the Russian experience and the emergence and development of the state socialist system is in order.

The Foundations of Soviet State Socialism

Although the advent of state socialism roughly corresponds to the inauguration of the first Five Year Plan (1929), this new and theretofore historically unique social formation neither emerged from thin air nor came into existence in some ready made form. Much of the administrative pattern and style visible in the thirties can be traced to the pre-revolutionary Tsarist bureaucracy.[14] Indeed, as the first Five Year Plan went into effect, enoromous numbers of former Tsarist officials still populated the state administration.[15] Much of their habits, attitudes and manner seem not only to have remained[16] but to have rubbed off on Communists who took up posts in the governmental apparatus.[17] Additionally, we should bear in mind that the outlines of state socialism which we can discuss in retrospect did not leap from the architect's blueprint into reality. The decision reached by the ruling Stalinist faction to embark on a crash program of industrialization, blanket nationalization and the forced collectivization of the peasantry emerged from a long and bitter struggle within the Communist Party and owed a great deal to Stalin's efforts to defeat his opponents and to his fear of impending war.[18] The enoromous shocks experienced by the Soviet society in the wake of these measures, the dislocations and conflicts which resulted from them, became yet more objects for the state to contain. As Nicholas Lampert observes, the "particular forms of state domination which developed were an effect of the continuous effort to respond to activities that were out of 'control', and to confront the unintended consequences of previous political decisions.[19] Schematically, the following aspects of emergent state socialism in the thirties are indispensable to an understanding of the administrative order which over time congealed in the Soviet Union.

1. Class relations and rapid industrialization:

The politically directed industrialization of the Soviet Union changed fundamentally the character of Soviet society. Limitations of space prohibit a discussion of the quantitative changes which this involved-- the transformation of much of the peasantry into the new industrial working class, the growth of industry and of industrial centers etc. The qualitative side of the changes, however--the replacement of one set of social relations by another, merits consideration. We might begin by contrasting the quantitative and qualitative dimensions of rapid industrialization. Regarding the former, there is no doubt that physical output and plant expanded rapidly during the First Plan.[20] In a qualitative sense, however, the opposite appears to be true. As Christian Rakovsky, a leading member of the Party's Left Opposition, was able to show as early as 1931, the onset of the First Plan brought about a reduction in the productive forces of the economy.[21] Industrial output rose in sheer physical quantity but declined in quality so precipitously that the net result was a set back in real growth. Steel production, for instance, registered a sharp incline on paper, but the quality of the steel dropped to the point that its useful life was reduced at a rate exceeding production increases. There would be more bridges, more rails and so forth, but these would wear out the faster. Rather than growth in the proper sense, the industrialization of the thirties simply transferred enoromous resources from one sector to another; the industrial plant was thereby physically increased in proportion to a 50 per cent drop in the (already low) standard of living of the working class.[22]

The industrial working class of the thirties witnessed its collective situation deteriorate sharply even while individual workers often experienced unprecendented upward mobility. As industrial expansion continued and, more, successive purges removed wave on wave of engineers plant directors and administrators who served as scapegoats for the accidents, mistakes and failures which accompanied the breakneck pace of industrialization, the opportunities for advancement from the shop floor to the director's office were considerable. During the years 1929-1936, for instance, approximately two of every three new top managers was a former worker. [23] In 1936 the Great Purge began. By the time it ran its course (1936-1938), every hierarchy in the Soviet system--the Party, the army, the state apparatus, the economy, even the secret police--was literally savaged. [24] The innumerable positions vacated by those who were packed off to the labor camps, prisons or simply shot were filled in the main by a mass of hastily educated young men drawn primarily from the ranks of the working class, the so-called men of '38. [25]

The other side of the good fortune befalling those individuals who advanced rapidly during the purges from the working class into administrative positions was, of course, the misery which befell the working class as a whole. As living standards plummeted and production targets rose astronomically, workers' interests, especially with trade unions recently gutted by the government, [26] were increasingly oriented toward resistance. [27] Equally, the immediate labor shortages introduced as part and parcel of ambitious targets for industrial expansion increased in some respects the capacity of the working class to offer resistance. There are some elements of class compromise involved here. On the one hand, unemployment was abolished, thus altering the relations between classes at the point of production in favor of working. On the other, more and more punitive labor legislation emerged which severely punished breaches of labor discipline, culminating in the 1940 law which enserfed the worker to his factory and included the death penalty for relatively minor offenses. This punitive legislation was almost impossible to enforce. Already shorthanded, factory directors were exceedingly reluctant to lose additional workers and run the risk of failure to meet planned output targets. But alongside these aspects of compromise, the dominant mode of class relations seem to be that of struggle; and active resistance from the side of the working class was met by unprecedented coercion from the police or, more aptly, the police state.

If police repression and, ultimately, the terror and labor camps system broke the active resistance of the working class, then how might the resolution of this phase of class struggle be described? The term "social atomization", as used by Hillel Ticktin, seems an apt one for summing up at least one aspect of social relations under state socialism.[28] Atomization, in short, refers to the severing of all "natural" relations among the people in society or, alternatively, it amounts to a prohibition against all social communication which deviates from the official, and thoroughly prepostorous, definition of reality. As an ideal-type, an atomized society would be one in which each individual found himself an isolated and helpless "atom" before the Leviathan. In certain respects (for instance, the capacity of workers to offer organized resistance to the authorities), social relations in the USSR approximate this ideal type. In other regards, however, they do not. Class-based collective resistance, always spontaneous and sometimes violent in nature, is not altogether absent in the contemporary Soviet Union.[29] More to the point, however, resistance to the authorities is on-going and has assumed a form congruent with the organizational landscape of state socialism. That is, a more or less passive resistance of the working class--absenteeism, alcoholism, shoddy work, negotiated work norms (low ones or none at all)[30]--is as much a feature of the Soviet system as is its opposite and (spurious) reflection in the official reality--newspaper celebrations of labor victories, "socialist competition", national days of "voluntary" (unpaid) labor etc. It seems to me that this relationship between classes constitutes the substratum from which spring the more or less surface phenomena which are familiar to all observers of the Soviet Union: the poor performance, the extra-legal exchange systems, and the conflicting incentives. Mindful of these class relations, we are in a better position to comprehend the nature of administration in its state socialist variants and to see in these seeming "dysfunctions" the expression of class relations as they appear through the medium of formal organizations.

2. Organizational and administrative changes:

In calling attention to the progressive expansion of the state apparatus as a series of ad hoc attempts to contain the social dislocations and tensions which accompanied the rapid industrialization of the thirties,

we are also bringing into focus another feature of Soviet
state socialism which is central to an understanding of
Soviet administration. As the administrative apparatus
expanded, the central political leadership progressively
lost control of it. The apparatus of repression clearly
expanded the abilities of the center to prevent certain
things from occuring. The police state smashed all
forms of political opposition. Strikes, critical publications, even parlor conversations about politics among
close friends seemed to belong to the past. Yet the
authorities were more and more at a loss to make things
happen, that is, to secure patterns of performance congruent with the center's directives. The brutal coercion of the Stalin regime met its limit in the very industrial order which the regime brought about.[31] To take
one example, engineers and technical specialists bore
the brunt of numerous political campaigns in the thirties
which the regime concocted to affix blame when plans were
not fulfilled or to further discredit the remnants of
the older opposition groups and their alternative programs which held a definite attraction for powerful figures in the leadership who came to an appreciation of
the irrationality involved with continuing to puruse the
course which Stalin had charted.[32] The ensuing arrests
of engineers and specialists depleted their already thin
ranks. Acute shortages of technical personnel developed
and hindered continued, not to mention expanded, industrial production. The arrests continued, but the rules
had to be changed. Instead of drawing a sentence to be
served in a labor camp, the convicted engineer would be
sentenced to work in his regular work.[33]

     This conscious bow to reality was replicated innu-
merable times in manifold ways throughout the emerging
state socialist order. The production targets handed
down by the center were so ambitious and the resources
available to performing units so strained that all manner
of informal and illegal activity was resorted to by the
administrators in order to meet the production goals.
This tendency to secure results by whatever means necessary more and more took on systematic features. Those
who controlled resources parlayed their positions into
veritable administrative "empires". Each hierarchy,
whether an industrial Ministry, the secret police, or
the writers' union, sought to free itself from the uncertainty of depending on others for inputs. Each, that
is, developed an economy in miniature within itself
complete with its own construction units, social services, housing, educational insitutions, holiday resorts,
and so on. The duplication and waste stemming from such

practices is not really as important for our purposes as the centrifugal forces which this unleashed throughout the entire state organization. The central planners and political directorate watched all but helplessly as performing units deviated from the spirit if not the letter of central instructions and those who were to monitor and control the behavior of these units began, very early on, to find their interest in colluding with them.[34] A recent study of Timothy Dunmore thrown this matter into sharp relief. Dunmore, examining the experience of the Fourth Five Year Plan, found that central direction of the Soviet economy, given the organizational pattern of this economy itself, is largely fictitious. "The leadership's priorities", he writes, "were only fulfilled if and when they were the priorities of the relevant parts of the bureaucracy."[35]

As the economy continued to expand after Stalin's passing, as organizations were enlarged and became more complex, these centrifugal forces in Soviet administration only increased. Containing them has been a prime objective of the political leadership in the post-Stalin period. A look at the reforms attempted to regain central direction over the sprawling and unmanageable apparatus and the successive failures of these attempts, will enable us to develop the simple ideas on particularistic exchange networks with which we began and bring into focus the peculiarity of administration under state socialism.

The structure and Dynamics of Relations Within the Administrative Apparatus

Although more responsible for the creation of a state socialist system than any other single individual, Stalin, while still alive, represented the main obstacle to the fruition of its tendencies. On the side of the political, the elite rapidly moved, following the dictator's death, to ensure its "collective security". That is, the terror was rapidly decommissioned and the ensuing state of affairs seems to be permanent. As Seweryn Bialer puts it, this concern with personal security among the elite "was the key reason why the system of Stalinism could not survive its creator. The leadership as a whole, and the elites as a whole, wanted a new deal."[36]

The stick, as it were, was rapidly whittled down to a relative stub in the post-Stalin period. Tha actors in the administrative apparatus were quick enough in locating for themselves the carrots. A Soviet official, writing under the psuedonym of Leo Timofeev, has provocatively captured the essence of contemporary Soviet state socialism thus:

> The longer the relatively peaceful period without war, revolution or mass repression lasts, the more the Soviet socio-economic system takes on the appearance of a colossal black market...The black market is not just the loophole, not just the secret doorway we surreptitiously cut in the wall. The black market is both the loophole and the wall itself...(it is) the very essence of our economic system. [37]

Timofeev's metaphor is suggestive and, I think, particularly useful for piercing the facade of formal organizational relations in the USSR and locating an internal dynamic behind the appearances. His "wall" might be understood as the formal system--the national Ministries and state committees which sit atop massive, hierarchical administrative chains through their counterparts in each of the country's constituent republics, through regional-level subordinates (trusts, associations, field offices, corresponding departments in regional government and so on), to the units of activity at the ends of these chains (factories, firms, retail stores, schools, etc.). The Communist Party and other auxiliary organizations, such as "people's control" (which involves ordinary citizens in the inspection and monitoring of performing units) trade unions (which play a role in labor relations and the provision of social services to their members) and the procuracy (which is responsible for detecting and prosecuting legal violations), are part of this formal system, the "wall" too. The "hole", of course, refers to behavior which transgresses the formal rules of these hierarchies. The utility of the metaphor resides in the fact that it invites us to think about the "hole" as something more than an aberration, a defect, a departure from the norm. Both the wall and the hole are integral parts of the stat socialist system. The essential difference between them refers to the question of position and perspective. That is, were we to take the position of, say, General Secretary of the Communist Party, it seems rather obvious that his incentives and activities would be structured primarily along those of the formal system. He resides at the top and his efforts are therefore bent toward insuring that all those below perform in the prescribed

ways. In a word, he is the chief administrator and his
success, like those of all administrators, is closely
connected with the matter of how well he is able to get
others--through the use of the incentives which he
controls--to work. As soon as we move down the hierarchy, however, we encounter a complication. Not only
does the occupant of a given office has a superior who
controls certain incentives which he might employ to
induce a certain behavior on the part of this subordinate,
but the subrodinate encounters others outside of the
hierarchy of which he is a part who also command resources which might be used as incentives. These incentives
would induce him to act in ways at variance with those
prescribed by his formal superiors.

A recent newspaper account might illustrate this
second side of the Soviet system, the "hole", whereby
resources are exchanged <u>outside</u> of the official hierarchical chains of command and behavior departs from
what might be preferred by the top officials. According
to the deputy director of a construction organization,
his firm, which relies upon steel girders supplied by
another firm in order to carry out their assigned task,
construction, was shorted by their supplier during the
second half of the previous year by 100 per cent. No
girders were delivered; construction ground to a complete
halt. This presented a certain problem for those in the
construction firm vis-a-vis their superiors. If no
construction is carried out, no plan is fulfilled;
negative incentives (sacking the firm's management or,
at least, depriving them of the customary bonuses) are
the likely result. Anticipating these consequences, the
firm began to fire off reminders, requests and complaints
to those concerned. But to no avail. The steel girders
did not arrive. The author of the article reports how
he then paid a visit to his reluctant supplier. On
arrival he found a crowd outside the director's office,
a crowd composed of emissaries ("<u>tolkachi</u>", or "<u>expedi-
ters</u>") from numerous other firms which had also been
shorted. These emissaries would disappear one at a time
into the director's office. They wore looks of humiliation as they exited and made room for the next in line,
hat in hand, who stepped in to see the director. The
director together with the top Party official in the
plant was choosing among the inducements offered by these
emissaries. The fact that the central plan specified
a certain allottment of steel girders for most if not
all of the respective (or "prospective") clients in no
way diminished the fact that additional incentives--
bribes, favors and so forth--were required in this case

for the plan actually to go forward.[38]

This episode is something of a representative illustration of behavior which deviates from the intentions of the top leadership. There is every indication that such behavior is not only widespread, but becoming more so.[39] Some observers suggest that this pattern has everything to do with the post-Stalin political accommodation reached by the elite, principally, with the end of the terror. The accommodation, while it insured the physical safety of the top authorities themselves, also deprived these same authorities of perhaps their most powerful (negative) incentive to control their respective hierarchies. The post-Stalin pattern involves a greater differentiation among the various elites and a concomitant weakening of the leadership to control these elites.[40] Much the same can be said with respect to relations between elites and non-elites.

A second important implication in the post-Stalin accommodation involves politics and policy. Unable to liquidate its opponents, any dominant group in the political leadership must be prepared to bargain with as well as maneuver against its rivals. Zdeněk Mylnár, a former leading official in the Czekoslovakian Communist Party, describes a pattern which he noticed on his route to the top, a pattern present within apparently all state socialist political systems:

> The struggle for genuine influence in the decisionmaking process...involves a jockeying for position in the lower, apparently less important, sections of the apparatus. Even secretaries of the Central Committee try to have their own personal "agencies"--that is, a a group of people--in the various departments of the apparatus...The genuine influence enjoyed individual secretaries, department heads, and other higher functionaries depended on how many people loyal to them or in their personal debt they had in the various lower-level departments. And there too, are various informal and, to the uninitiated eye, invisible groups and cliques united by a shared outlook.[41]

As a consequence of this arrangement, bold new policy initiatives on the part of the top leaders are rather unlikely. Instead, compromises and ambiguity in policy seems the order of the day.

Yet another implication within the post-Stalin pattern should not be missed in this regard. This involves tenure and is expressed in the Soviet shibboleth as "trust in cadres". When officials are sacked for incompetence or illegal activities more than a mere personnel change is involved. Someone's group, someone's clique has come under attack. The top leaders are, no doubt, quite mindful of this for their individual influence within the leadership depends in part on their supporters at lower levels. To oversimplify, but only slightly, the end of the terroe meant that informal groupings within the Party and state apparatus, networks extending from Moscow to the villages, would exist and flourish; the existence of such groups ties together the interests of patrons and their client/supporters; turnover (excepting death and voluntary departure) more or less ended with the terror.[42]

An example or two might serve to illustrate this matter of tenure in office within Soviet administration. The task of policing the members of the Communist Party falls on the Committee for Party Control organized under the Party's Central Committee. The chairman of this Committee for Party Control is A. Ya. Pel'she, who is also a member of the Politburo. In describing the work of Party Control in a booklet published in part as a set of instructions to officials working in this area, Pel'she relates the importance of understanding and counselling for those who have violated Party and state discipline. Expulsions from the Party for such offenses are not necessary. One must show understanding, he contends, and take into account the full set of circumstances surrounding violations.[43] Equally, G. V. Romanov, who heads the Leningrad Regional Party Committee and is also a member of the Politburo, refers in this same booklet to the importance of "trust and respect for cadres". He relates a case involving the director of a certain institute who is described as an administrative disaster. He takes all decisions without any consultation with others in the institute and shows a knack for regularly doing the wrong things. Moreover, this individual, while director, paid no attention to plan fulfillment except systematically to falsify data to give the appearance that the plan targets were being met. As a result, the guilty party ended up losing his directorship. He was not, however, expelled from the Party and the implication seems clear that he remained in the institute or was imply reassigned to another administrative position.[44] With the reader's indulgence,

373

these examples are taken from the writings of the Party's interal policemen and are intended as instructions to subalterns as to how to approach cases invloving serious transgressions of the rules.

The Experience of Reforms

The post-Stalin period has witnessed numerous attempts by the political leadership to reform and to improve thereby the performance of the state administrative apparatus. All of the reform measures to be discussed here were explicitly directed at improving economic results. As might be expected from our discussion so far, new inducements and organizational modifications have been the hallmarks of the various reform efforts. So far, at least, compulsion and coercion have not been resorted to in either an intensive or systematic way. This too, in light of our foregoing discussion regarding the sort of "collective security" which seems to obtain among rival groupings and cliques and the relations between patrons and client/supporters within such, should be unusurping. Turning to the question of administrative practice, this relative political stalemate among rival groups finds its results in a policy stalemate. To be cure, a great number of new policy initiatives have been attempted in the post Stalin period. A review of these might highlight their essential shortcomings, viz., reforms which intend to alter relations and behavior within the administrative apparatus threaten various power centers and groups within it. The resistance of those who stand to lose something as a result of reform has been stiff and the reformers, so far at least, have proven no match for this resistance.

1. Kruschev's Sovnarkhozy:

The most radical of the reforms inaugurated was begun by Nikita Kruschev in the late fifties. By the time it had run its course it had dismantled the central apparatus of some two-thirds of the Soviet administrative state. A new pattern of organization was installed, the sovnarkhozy, or "councils of the national economy". In brief, Kruschev's efforts were aimed at decentralizing the administrative apparatus and locating decisionmaking and responsibility in regional units which resembled miniature national economies. In the language employed by the Soviets, the reform attempted to overcome "departmentalism"--a term signifying a long, verticle administrative chain of command and associated with the display

374

of narrow self-interest on the part of central "departments" and their subordinate units, waste, duplication
of effort, poor coordination, inertia and so forth.
"Departmentalism" seems closely associated with the
centralized or "branch" principle of organization. Its
opposite, the "territorial" principle, refers to the
links among performing units in a given region and,
although it too has a tendency toward vice ("localism"),
it was upgraded by Kruschev as the antidote to the
heavily centralized system which he was attempting to
manage.

The territorial principle of administration aims
at producing proportional and balanced growth within
the economic regions of the USSR.[45] Firms are coordinated by a more proximate decision center. Local economies
of scale develop. Potential advantages for producers,
suppliers, customers on a mutual basis are easier to
locate and realize than is true under circumstances
wherein chains of command run all the way to Moscow.

Inasmuchas the sovnarkhozy decentralized the
administrative state, they also, willy nilly, decentralized the Party. The "actions", so to speak, had
largely moved from Moscow to the economic regions.
Kruschev further decentralized the Party in 1962 by
creating separate and co-equal Party organizations
in the regions, one with responsibility for agriculture,
the other with responsibility for industry.

In retrospect, it appears that these reforms succeeded in uniting both the state and Party apparatus in political opposition to Kruschev. If we reflect for a
moment on the matter of power and privilege, the reforms
meant at a minimum that many or perhaps most of those
who had risen to the top of their respective hierarchies
were packed off to the provinces to adminster a
sovnarkhoz. No longer did their positions enable them
to maintain and extend the network of relations which
they had entered and developed en route to the top.
Needless to say, life in Kaluga or Krasnodar is not life
in Moscow. Not only are the amenities much leaner but
Moscow under the centralized pattern is the hub of all
activity. For example, a high official confronting a
certain difficulty (say a supply shortage in his department), might solve his problem by calling on other officials in question; perhaps he met them at a dinner party
or has worked with them on some commission. They may
even be his friends. Such situations would expedite his

375

business enoromously. At the least, sould the potential helpers be complete strangers, he can still ask them for a "favor", one which would be granted in reciprocity for some consideration he or a member of his particular clique or network might provide in future. Kruschev's reforms radically changed this pattern and this time-honored method of problem-solving largely disapperaed during his leadership. No sooner was he ousted from office than his successors immediately restored the old pattern or organization.

2. The Kosygin Reform:

Within a year of Kruschev's departure a new reform effort was launched. It has commonly become known as the "Kosygin reform", after its chief architect and political sponsor, Alexei Kosygin who replaced Kruschev as Chairman of the Council of Ministers. The essence of this reform, too involved decentralization. Its aim was to devolve more decisionmaking responsibility upon performing units by decreasing the number of plan indicators which performing units were required to meet and raising the importance of economic incentives such that a firm's success would be measured in saleable output and registered a "profit" for the firm itself. The watchword was "cost-accounting" (khozraschet), a notion which relied upon quasi-market devices such as "sold" as opposed to simply produced output and profitability for performing units in order to link the self-interest of the individual units with innovations and cost-saving improvements intended to raise the level of performance in the economy as a whole.

The cost-accounting method has not only been introduced very slowly (by 1978, only four Ministries were operating fully on the principle[46]) but has been rolled back in many respects. The various funds within the jurisdiction of enterprises were growing in many cases quite rapidly as a result of the reform: enterprises were making profits and their financial means expanded proportionately. By 1971, according to George Feiwel, these funds had become so large that the control of central authorities over investment decisions was being eclipsed by the enterprises. In 1973, limits were imposed on the size of the profit-fed funds which enterprises could retain. In 1977, investment funds reverted to the Ministries, investment decisions were re-centralized, profit was confiscated by the Ministries if not spent within one year.[47] And these reassertions of central authority over the economy, control of which seemed to be slipping more and more into the hands of enterprise managers, were only the tip of an administrative iceberg which wrecked the Kosygin reform[48] and other experiments which grew out of its general orientation.[49]

3. Production Associations (ob"edinenie):

Whereas the two reforms just discussed aimed at decentralizing decisionmaking and seem to have met major resistance from central authorities who suffered a diminution of power as a result of them, the logic of the "production associations" (ob"edineniya), an economic reorganization begun in 1973, seems to work largely in the opposite direction and remove autonomy from individual enterprises which are grouped by product line and territorial location into larger administrative units. The ob'edineniya, as Brezhnev made clear in his speech to the Twenty-Fourth Party Congress in 1971, are intended to achieve economies of scale, reduce duplication and improve economic coordination.

With respect to their formation, much of this appears to be cosmetic. Getrude E. Schroeder reports that

in many cases, their formation merely amounts to "changing the names on the doors"; most of them seem still to be located in Moscow, and even in the same buildings; (for example 8 of the 9 industrial associations created by the Ministry of Tractor and Agricultural Machinery are located in Moscow, where there are no tractor plants); many of them manage the same enterprises as before, now amalgamated into associations, and their behavior continues as of old.[50]

Yet this reform, which ostensibly seeks to expand the control of middle levels in the economic mechanism has met resistance from below as well as from above. At stake for enterprise directors and factory level Party officials is, again, the question of control of resources. If enterprises are grouped into associations, the directors become little more than clerks. The firms which they manage carry out decisions made by those who direct the association. Enterprises do not keep separate financial accounts; their status is reduced from that of a unit, to that of a sub-unit. Equally so for Party organizations within the enterprises. Consequently, after the initial wave of reforms and the consequent resistance which mounted within Ministries, enterprises and Party organizations, some compromises appear to have been reached. Most importantly, by the mid-seventies, ob"edineniya would be formed on, effectivly, a nominal basis. Their constituent units would, contrary to the logic of the reform, retain their own financial accounts and effectively all of their previous operational autonomy.[51] This compromise appears to be a firmly ensconced undertanding in Soviet administration today. In December 1982 a new round of associations was begun which summoned into being agro-industrial associations at both district and regional levels. Neither do these new associations deprive their constituent units of their previous legal status and autonomy, nor do they have the authority to take measures without the approval of the units' superiors at the center.[52]

4. Attempts at Improving Performance Through Raising Living Standards:

Another strategy emanating from the center and designed to promote performance is anchored in the hierarchy of soviets which extend from the Supreme Soviet of the USSR through the republics, regions, major cities, districts and villages. The soviet structure was largely moribund by the time of Stalin's passing and its revival, beginning in the late fifties, can be interpreted as an effort by the central Party leadership to use the soviets as a counterweight to the recalcitrant Ministries.[53] By equipping through a series of legislative acts these organs of self-government with certain authorities and responsibilities in the economy (principally, with increased soviet control over the local consumer economy, housing and the right to supervise construction projects and to make recommendations to superiors regarding the behavior of enterprises located on their respective territories) and by encouraging citizen participation within their own soviets (whether volunteering for soviet work, instructing their deputies as to what constituents would like to see accomplished, or simply registering complaints) the regime has wagered on the ability of these institutions to reduce economic waste and, more importantly, to stimulate a pattern of economic rationality (from the point of view of the center, at least) whereby workers have an incentive to work well inasmuch as an improved living standard can be gained thereby. On the surface, these efforts seem intended to complement the trust of the reforms discussed above. Their focus however, is less on redesigning the administrative system

and more on securing energy, initiative, performance--
what are called "final results"--from the workforce
through the use of material incentives.

The strategy is multi-faceted and involves too many
individual measures to be treated here in much detail.
But a look at the focal point of these efforts--improving
performance via an increase in material incentives--will
shed considerable light on the thrust of this regime
strategy and why so little has come of it.

For some time now, the Soviet leadership has
acknowledged that continued emphasis on growth in
"sector A" (i.e., heavy industry or producers' goods)
is self defeating. As Leonid Brezhnev maintained before
the Party's Central Committee in November 1978, "the
entire course of economic development confirms again
and again that sector B industries,..constitute an
important condition in the effective functioning of the
economy as a whole, in improving material incentives."[54]
Intent upon pursuing a policy favoring "sector B" (light
industry and agriculture, the consumer sector) in the
short run in order to improve the performance of both
sectors A and B in the long term, the leadership had
already adopted targets for the Eighth Five Year Plan
(1966-1971) which called for a reversal of the long-
standing pattern favoring sector A. For the first time,
sector B would be the priority; growth in consumption
would outstrip growth in heavy industry. With respect
to this objective, however, the plan failed. The same
objectives were repeated for the Ninth Plan (1971-1976).
It failed.[55] The Tenth Plan abandoned this strategy,
but the current Plan (1981-1986) has returned to it.
Prospects for success appear to be rather dim at the
moment (eg., since 1981, the regime has ceased to publish
comprehensive statistics for agriculture, which would
probably indicate exceptionally poor harvests).

How is it that in a centrally planned economy, the
central planners are unable to control a variable as
elementary as the relative rate of growth in these two
sectors? The answer goes to the heart of state socialism
as a system of power wherein control of offices and their
attendant resources is all-important. The first fact of
import in this regard is that over one half of the
consumer goods produced in the USSR are turned out by
large firms which are oganizatinnally grouped in sector
A.[56] These enterprises are primarily engaged in the
production of producers' goods and look upon their
consumer goods lines as secondary and, in a sense,

residual. That is, when resources are short and given enterprise is experiencing difficulty in meeting its primary targets, it is able to shift resources from its secondary lines in order to close the gap.[57] But why would a firm sabotage its own plan for consumer goods in this way? More, why would it be countenanced by the firm's superiors, especially if the Party and the Plan have given priority to consumer goods production? The concept of particualristic exchange, developed above, provides an answer. Producer goods are more valuable, that is, to the parties involved in exchange at or near the top of the various hierarchies. To illustrate, suppose our firm produces drill presses and toasters. What advantages accrue to us for fulfilling our plan of toaster production? Not many. We meet the plan, we receive bonuses, perhaps, for turning our high quality toasters, and that is the end of it. The toasters go to the retailers where they are sold to consumers. Consider, however, the drill presses. Another firm or group of firms are in need of these. Their production will suffer; they miss their targets and lose their bonuses should there be a deficit of drill presses. This too worries their superiors in the hierarchy. These superiors have contacted our superiors and have explained the urgency of their need for our product. The relevant Party officials have also been informed. We decide to honor their request and we divert resources from our toaster line; we do them a "favor". Is it unreasonable to expect that this favor will not be returned directly or indirectly to us? Next year, for instance, we may run short of some resource. Would not one of the above groups--firms, their supreriors, Party officials in the region--be in a position to help us? Action would seem to hinge on the relative advantage of exchanges avaialable to the actors, and this relative advantage, in turn, would depend upon the relative access to resources and contacts available to the parties in question.

With respect to the consumer goods sector proper, i.e., enterprises producing only consumer goods, a similar difficulty obtains. Such enterprises are typically the "poor relations" of the Soviet political economy. As the above illustration might suggest, they are not usually in a position to compete effectively for scarce material resources. The creation of the State Committee for Supply (Gossnab) in 1957 was on the surface at least, designed to equalize this relative disadvantage by locating the supply function in a single agency more proximate to and, assumably, more responsive to the

380

center. Since its inception, however, Gossnab has not
altered the supply problem. In fact, seventy-seven of
the industrial Ministries have their own autonomous
supply system. Gossnab functions, in the words of a
Soviet observer, only "for those who are ill", not for
those who are healthy so far as supply is concerned.[58]
Nationally, Gossnab allocates some 14,500 products
while the "healthy" among the Ministries account for
over 40,000 products.[59]

Another shortage which is particularly acute among
firms in sector B involves the work force. Sector B
enterprises are not only shorthanded, they also experience higher rates of labor turnover than do their
counter-parts in sector A, something which further hampers
their efficiency.[60] Turnover in this sector seems a
direct result of "poverty". Sector "B" enterprises are
as a group unable to offer their employees the amenities
available to workers in sector "A"--housing, day care
facilities, clubs, clinics and so on. The result is
that workers in sector "B", having been trained, having
compiled a good work record, etc., are likely to leave
for a job in sector "A".

Housing is of principal import among those amenities
which enterprises utilize in order to attract and retain
labor. The policy of the regime speaks to offsetting
the advantage of sector "A" in competing for labor, and
to rationalizing the entire housing economy of the USSR
by transferring housing stock from enterprises to the
organs of local government, the soviets. Housing managed
by local government is generally better and more economically maintained than that which belongs to the enterprises.[61] Beginning in 1967, a series of decrees has
been issued by the government which instructs that all
housing be transferred to soviets.[62] The results in the
Russian Republic are instructive: transfers have occurred,
but such involve housing formerly in the possession of
smaller enterprises in sector "B"[63] or dilapidated and
out-of-repair units which sector"A" enterprises unload
on local soviets.[64] The housing reform, then, serves
to further handicap sector "B".

Finally, a word on the overall affect of these
abortive measures as they regard the primary policy
objective, namely, increasing the motivation of the work
force to work well by raising living standards and increasing material incentives. Consumer goods production
has fallen short of its projected mark, but there has
been a rather consistent increase in wages since the

mid-fifties.[65] The purchasing power, in other words, of the population has expanded considerably and out of all proportion to available articles of consumption. Igor Birman, an emigre Soviet economist, has put this matter into sharp relief. The combination of wage increases and consumer goods shortfalls results in "saving" (although, as he points out, "not spending" would be more accurate description under Soviet circumstances) on an unprecedented scale.[66] In 1960, savings were equal to 10 per cent of the entire national income; in 1970, they equalled 43 per cent of the national income. By 1980, Birman estimates, this figure exceeds 70 per cent.[67] The implications should be clear. Soviet workers face neither the negative incentive of unemployment/poverty nor the positive incentive of increased consumption.[68] And the regime continues to face the question: How to get the workers to work?

Prospects

This question of labor productivity was on the mind of Yuri Andropov when he delivered his first address as General Secretary to the Central Committee of the Party on November 22, 1983. Labor productivity, he told his audience, has fallen below plan targets over the first two years of the current (Eleventh) Five Year Plan. This, plus the irrational use of resources by management, were singled out as the main problems which he intends to tackle.[69]

It would be premature to offer now any firm prediction, much less, assessment, of how policy under Adropov might differ from that of his predecessor. Two things, however, might bear mention. First, there has been a renewed emphasis on labor discipline and stricter observation of legality.[70] Some measure of compulsion and the threat of it seem intended to deter people from being absent from or late to work. This is not the first time that such campaigns have been launched,[71] nor is it likely to be the last. Results are, however, another question entirely, and while we have not at this time any firm results to judge as to the effectiveness of renewed compulsion, the past indicates that this policy is not terribly fruitful, especially over the long term.

Second, Andropov referred in his speech to the need to place "people with a sense of the new" in decision-making positions. This portends a far greater change than merely resorting to compulsion. It implies personnel changes at the top and a few of these have already been made.[72] Yet, according to the analysis presented here, a full scale purge of the Party and/or state hierarchies would amount to a frontal assault on the sinews of the state socialist system--the groups, cliques and networks which have established their respective niches and which are the organic forms inhabiting its lifeless formal structures. It is unlikely that this system's chief administrator would initiate such a frontal assault and unlikelier still that, were he to do so, he would succeed.

Footnotes

[1]David Lane, Politics and Society in the USSR, New York: Random House, 1970, pp. 128-129.

[2]Ts. A. Yampolskaya, Obshchestennye organizatsii v SSSR, Moscow: Nauka, 1972.

[3]G. V. Barabashev and K. F. Sheremet, Sovetskoe stroitel'stvo, 2nd ed., Moscow: Yuridicheskaya litera-tura, 1981, pp. 521-555.

[4]During an interview with the secretary of the executive committee of a district soviet in Moscow in October 1979, I received a detailed description of how the state creates and manages such "social organizations". Working through its deputies and pensioners who have been active in the Party, executive committees of soviets enlist people to organize "public" or "social" work. The social organizations thereby created are directly super-vised by various standing commissions of the soviet which are in turn directly supervised by the soviet's executive committee.

[5]See my Ideology of Administration: American and Soviet Cases, Albany, NY: State University of New York Press, 1982, esp. Chapters 2 and 3.

[6]Max Weber, From Max Weber: Essays in Sociology, ed., by H. H. Gerth and C. W. Mills, New York: Oxford University Press, 1946, esp. pp. 212-216, 233.

[7]James O'Conner, The Fiscal Crisis of the State, New York: St. Martin's Press, 1973; Clause Offe and Volke Rónge, "Theses on the Theory of the State," New German Critique 6 (Fall 1975), pp. 139-147.

[8]Inter alia, Bohdan Harasymiw, "Nomenklatura: The Soviet Communist Party's Leadership Recruitment System," Canadian Journal of Political Science 2 (December 1969), pp. 493-512.

[9]Party members in any state institution form a Primary Party Organization (the basic unit of the Party structure) within the state body. This Primary Party Organization is expected to act as a "guiding nucleus"

for within the state institution, direct from within
the state machine on the basis of Party directives. The
role of "guiding nucleus" for Primary Party Organization
was adopted at the Communist Party's Eighth Congress,
in 1919.

[10]Jerry F. Hough, The Soviet Prefects, Cambridge,
Mass.: Harvard University Press, 1969; George Fischer,
The Soviet System and Modern Society, New York: Ather-
ton Press, 1968.

[11]Mary McAuley describes this situation in her
Politics and the Soviet Union, Harmondsworth: Penguin,
1977.

[12]On the idea of exchange relations and networks,
see David Willer and Bo Anderson, eds., Networks Exchange and Coercion: The Elementary Theory and Its
Applications, New York: Elsevier, 1981.

[13]Carl H. Lande, "Networks and Groups in Southeast
Asia: Some Observations on the Group Theory of Politics,"
American Political Science Review 67 (March 1973), pp.
103-127.

[14]See the essays in Russian Officialdom: The
Bureaucratization of Russian Society from the Seventeenth
to the Twentieth Century, ed. by W. M. Pintner and D. K.
Rouney, Chapel Hill, NC: University of North Carolina
Press, 1980.

[15]E. H. Carr, Socialism in One Country, Vol. 1,
Harmondsworth: Penguin, 1970, p. 130.

[16]Before his death, Lenin lamented that "we now
have a vast army of government employees but lack
sufficiently educated forces to exercise real control
over them...Down below...there are hundreds of thousands
of old officials whom we got from the tsars and from
bourgeois society and who, partly deliberately and
partly unwittingly, work against us." See his Problems
of Building Socialism and Communism in the USSR, Moscow:
Progress Publishers, 1969, p. 15.

[17]The chief of the secret police, Felix Dzerzhinsky
remarked at the Twelfth Party Congress (1923) that the
Soviet administrative machinery "has preserved all the

features of the old apparatus, the previously ownership-in-the-office (chastnovladetel'skii) apparatus, has become the state apparatus." He went on to refer to the transmission of old habits, procedures, patterns of superior-subordinate relations, etc., from the former Tsarist officials to the new Communist recruits. His observations are quoted by B. D. Lebin and M. N. Perfil'ev in their Kadry apparata upravleniya v SSSR, Leningrad: Nauka, 1970, p. 209.

[18]Stephen Cohen, Bukharin and the Bolshevik Revolution, New York: Alfred A. Knopf, 1973.

[19]Nicholas Lampert, The Technical Intelligentsia and the Soviet State, New York: Holmes and Meier, 1979, p. 6.

[20]Anatole G. Mazour, Soviet Economic Development, Princeton, NJ: D. Van Nostrand, 1967.

[21]Christian Rakovsky, "At the Congress and in the Country," 1931, republished as "The First Five Year Plan in Crisis," Critique 13 (Spring 1981), pp. 13-54.

[22]Blair A. Ruble, Soviet Trade Unions, New York: Cambridge University Press, 1981, p. 18.

[23]Lampert, op. cit., p. 64.

[24]Roy Medvedev, Let History Judge, New York: Vintage Books, 1973.

[25]A. L. Unger, "Stalin's Reviewal of the Leading Stratum: A Note on the Great Purge," Soviet Studies 20 (January 1969), pp. 321-330.

[26]Ruble, op. cit., pp. 13-23.

[27]These remarks draw heavily on recent conversations with Don Filtzer who is currently preparing a book on the development of social relations in the USSR in the thirties.

[28]See in particular Hillel Ticktin's essay, "Soviet Society and Professor Bettelheim," Critique 6 (1976),

pp. 17-44.

[29]M. Holubenko, "Soveit Working Class Opposition," Critique 4 (1975), pp. 5-26; Vadim Belotserkovsky, "Workers' Struggles in the USSR in the Sixties," Critique 10/11 (1980), pp. 37-50.

[30]On the question of the scope of managerial control in the work place and the necessity for management to offer enoromous concessions to the work force in order to secure some measure of performance, see Vladimir Anderle, Managerial Power in the Soviet Union, Westmead, U.K.: Saxon House, 1976.

[31]See for instance, the essays in Chalmers Johnson, ed., Change in Communist Systems, Stanford: Stanford University Press, 1970.

[32]Boris Nicolaevsky, in J. D. Zagoria ed., Power and the Soviet Elite, Ann Arbor: University of Michigan Press, 1965.

[33]Lampert, op. cit., pp. 92-94.

[34]Ibid., p. 87; James H. Oliver, "Turnover and Family Circles in Soviet Administration," Slavic Review 32, No. 3 (September 1973), pp. 527-545.

[35]Timothy Dunmore, The Stalinist Command Economy: The Soviet Apparatus and Economic Policy 1945-53, New York: St. Martin's Press, 1980), pp. 146-147.

[36]Seweryn Bialer, Stalin's Successors, Cambridge: Cambridge University Press, 1980, p. 46.

[37]Leo Timofeev, "Black Market Technology in the USSR: Or, The Peasants' Art Starving," Telos 51 (Spring 1982), p. 5.

[38]A. Ashlov, "Kak ya stal tolkachom," Izvestia (January 8, 1983), p. 3.

[39]Gregory Grossman, "Notes on the Illegal Private Economy and Corruption," in Soviet Economy in a Time of Change, Vol. 1, Washingotn, DC: Government Printing Office, 1979, pp. 834-855; Dennis O'Hearn, "The Second Economy in Consumer Goods and Services," Critique 15

(1981), pp. 93-109; George Feifer, "Russian Disorders," Harper's (February 1981), pp. 41-55; Konstantin Simis, USSR: The Corrupt Society, New York: Simon and Schuster, 1982.

[40]See Alexander Yanov, Detente After Brezhnev: The Domestic Roots of Soviet Foreign Policy, Berkeley, CA: Institute of International Studies, University of California, 1977.

[41]Zdnek Mlynar, Nightfrost in Prague, New York: Karz, 1980, pp. 55-56. See also, T. H. Rigby, "The Soviet Leadership: Towards a Self-Stabilizing Oligarchy?" Soviet Studies 22 (October 1970), pp. 166-192; Idem, "How the Obkom Secretary Was Tempered," Problems of Communism 29, No. 2 (March-April 1980), pp. 57-63.

[42]The work of George Breslauer on this subject is very instructive. See his "On the Adapatibility of Soviet Welfare State Authoritarianism," in Karl Ryavec, ed., Soviet Society and the Communist Party, Amherst: University of Massachusetts Press, 1978, pp. 4-21; Idem, "The Twenty-Fifth Congress: Domestic Issues," in Alexander Dallin, ed., The Twenty-Fifth Congress of the CPSU, Stanford: Hoover Institute Press, 1977, esp., pp. 8-13.

[43]A. Ya. Pel'she, "Po-Leninski trebovatel'no i chutko, in A. N. Bezotvetnykh et al, eds,, Aktivnye pomoshchniki partiinykh komitetov, Moscow: Politizdat, 1974, pp. 5-22.

[44]G. V. Romanov, "Rabote partiinykh komissii povsednevnoe vnimanie, " in Bezotvetnykh et al, op. cit., pp. 23-28.

[45]N. Nekrasov, The Territorial Organization of the Soviet Economy, Moscow: Progress, 1974.

[46]Gertrude E Schroeder, "The Soviet Economy on a Treadmill of 'Refomrs'," in The Soviet Economy in a Time of Change, p. 314.

[47]George Feiwel, "Economic Performance and Reforms in the Soviet Union," in David R. Kelly ed., Soviet Politics in the Brezhnev Era, New York: Praeger, 1980, pp. 70-103, esp., 83.

[48]Schroeder, "Soviet Economic Reform at an Impasse" Problems of Communism 20, No. 4 (July-August 1971), pp. 36-46.

[49]The best known and most critical of these is the Shchekino experiment which took its name from the chemical firm where it was first introduced. The Shchekino method relies on unemployment and wage incentives for workers (that is, management discharges as many workers as it likes,, retains the wage fund it would have used to pay them and distributes this surplus as incentive among the employees who remain) as the fulcrum for boosting performance. Obviously, were this method introduced across the board, massive levels of unemployment would result. It has been extended to some 1000 firms so far and the results are revealing. After an initial period of great economic success, results taper off and performance plummets. On the Shchekino attempt and its failure, see Bob Arnot, "Soviet Labor Productivity and the Failure of the Shchekino Experiment," Critique 15 (1981), pp. 31-56.

[50]Schroeder, "The Soviet Economy on a Treadmill of 'Reforms'," op. cit., p. 317.

[51]Dunmore, "Local Party Organs in Industrial Administration: The Case of the Ob"edinenie Reform," Soviet Studies 31 (April 1980), pp. 195-217.

[52]Tipovoe polozhenie, Council of Ministers of the USSR, "O raionnom agropromyshlennom ob"edinenii," and Tipovoe polozhenie, Council of Minsiters of the USSR, "O oblastnom agropromyshlennom ob"edininii," in Izvestia (December 9 and 10, respectively, 1982).

[53]Peter Vanneman, The Supreme Soviet, Durham: Duke University Press, 1977, p. 14.

[54]Quoted by Jane Shapiro in her "Soviet Consumer Policy in the 1970's," in Kelley, ed., op. cit., p. 106.

[55]See Antonio Carlo, "The Crisis of Bureaucratic Collectivism," Telos 43 (Spring 1980), pp. 3-31.

[56]Izvestia, (February 4, 1983), p. 1.

[57]G. V. Barabashev, "Na novom etap," Sovety narodnykh deputatov (June 1981), pp. 15-16; P. Shamonov, "Rastut etazhi Sverdlovska," Izvestia (June 17, 1982), p. 2.

[58]Yu. Panchencko, "Organizator ili 'dostavala'," Izvestia (February 12, 1983), p. 2.

[59]Scroeder, in The Soviet Economy in a Time of Change, p. 323.

[60]A. Sokolov, "Vozmozhnosti est', nado umelo ikh ispol'zovat," Izvestia (October 18, 1981), p. 2.

[61]N. Polozhenko, "Chto prinimat' na balans," Sovety narodnykh deputatov, (August 1980), pp. 54-58; I. Bogdanov, "Esli vzat'cya po-khozyaiski," Sovety narodnykh deputatov (April 1981), pp. 39-41.

[62]Postanovlenie No. 807 of the Council of Ministers of the USSR, April 26, 1967. The most recent repetition of this decree was "O razvitiizhilishchnogo khozyaistva, uluchshenii ispol'zovaniya i sokhannosti zhilishchnogo fonda," postnovlenie of the Supreme Soviet of the USSR, June 15, 1981.

[63]M. N. Tarachenkó, "Vzaimodeistvie mestnykh Sovetov i ministerstv," Sovetskow gosudarstvo i pravo (August 1980), p. 76.

[64]Polozhenko, op. cit., pp. 54-56.

[65]Janet G. Chapman, "Recent Trends in the Soviet Industrial Wage Structure," in A. Kahan and B.Ruble eds., Industrial Labor in the USSR, New York: Pergamon Press, 1979, pp. 151-183.

[66]Igor Birman, "The Financial Crisis in the USSR," Soviet Studies 32 (January 1980), pp. 84-105.

[67]Idem, "A Reply to Professor Pickersgill," Soviet Studies 32 (October 1980), pp. 586-591.

[68]It should be clear that I am not considering the intrinsic rewards (the pleasure taken in performing work)

390

as a positive incentive for workers in the Soviet Union.

[69]_Izvestia_ (November 23, 1982).

[70]See for instance the references to a flood of letters from "ordinary workers" complaining about these problems as described in _Izvestia_ (December 11, 1982).

[71] For example, Joel C. Moses, _Regional Party Leadership and Policymaking in the USSR_, New York: Praeger, 1974, P. 1.

[72]Roy Medvedev discusses these in his "The First 100 Days of Yuri Andropov," _In These Times_ (March 30-April 5, 1983), pp. 11-12.

CHAPTER XV

EPILOGUE:
THE POLITICS OF BUREAUCRATIC ADMINISTRATION[*]

Fred W. Riggs

The case studies contained in this volume provide material for a number of interesting and important comparative analyses. The book might as well have been titled, "The Politics of Bureaucracy in Certain Countries of the Third World." Indeed nine of the chapters use the word 'bureaucracy' in their titles. The fact is, of course, that public bureaucracies—provided the term is used to include military officers as well as civil servants—play a major role (often a dominant role) in the politics of most Third World countries.

This point needs to be stressed because writers in "comparative politics" consistently play down, if they do not ignore, the political activities and influences of public officials (military and civil). Sometimes, of course, they do write about the "military" as though it were a political institution apart from or outside the state bureaucracy—a practice bound to distort any understanding of either the political or the administrative systems of the countries concerned.

By contrast, in the study of "comparative administration" it has become clear that one cannot explain public administration anywhere without taking into account not only the activities of appointed public

---

[*]The editor, Krishna Tummala, invited me to prepare this epilogue after the country studies presented in this book (excepting those on Indonesia and the Soviet Union, which were added subsequently) had been completed, suggesting that I try to relate them to my own experience and to the history of the Comparative Administration Group (CAG) and its aftermath. In accepting the invitation, I find myself obliged to offer remarks that are rather personal in style. For the last decade, I have become preoccupied with different problems, but I have also written a few things relevant to comparative administration. References to them are given so as to provide a few links to the small tradition of comparative administration that at times, seems to have become lost.

officials, but also the roles of elected officials (if any) both as they impinge on bureaucratic behavior, and as they themselves engage in administrative functions. The myth of the separation of "politics" and "administration"--never more than a myth in Western countries-is clearly a misleading shibboleth in non-Western societies. Here, indeed, the roles of appointed officials (military and civil) are so patently political that if one were to analyze only the administrative functions they perform, one would have very little of interest to say. At least the evidence contained in these chapters tends to support this proposition. This is not to say, of course, that the normative goal of distinguishing administrative from political functions is unimportant; but this leads us to a different level of analysis.

Variations in Bureaucratic Performance

Once one becomes conscious of the political roles public officials can play, one immediately discovers their wide range of variation. In the countries selected for scrutiny here this range is vividly illustrated. Consider for example, the following statement in the report on Bnagladesh by Khan and Zafarullah:

> The bureaucratic machinery is top heavy, elitist, decadent, inefficient and expensive. It can no longer justify its existence in its present form except on the selfish ground of self preservation...It is difficult to perceive any end to this bureaucratic rot and the consequent citizens' nightmare unless there is radical reform in the socio-political and economic spheres in the country.[1]

At the other extreme, by contrast, we find in Quah's report on the public bureaucracy in Singapore that it has been remarkably effective in carrying out the developmental goals of the state in an efficient manner with minimal corruption and abuse of office: "...it plays an important and effective role in national development..."[2]

How can we account for this striking difference? No doubt one can think of many differences between the culture, social structure, geography and history of Bangladesh and Singapore which might account for their contrasting administrative records, but there is one obvious and dramatic political difference, namely the relative power position of appointive officials.

The situation in Singapore is characterized by the domination of an extra-bureaucratic political system centered on the People's Action Party (PAP) and its charismatic leader, Lee Kuan Yew. But let Quah make the point in his own words:

> ...the most important reason for the effectiveness of the public bureaucracy in natinoal development is the ability of the PAP government to change the attitudes and behavior of the civil servants...the PAP government (also) provided them with the necessary legal powers, financial resources and equipment to perform their tasks.[3]

The inability of the Bangladesh polity to sustain a viable extra-bureaucratic power structure has, by contrast, left the full responsibility for public decisionmaking in the hands of the bureaucracy (military and civil). Lacking the means to hold officials accountable, is it any wonder that their performance should be governed by selfish motives of "self preservation", generating a structure that is "top heavy, elitist, decadent, inefficient and expensive"?

It is tempting to oversimplify the dichotomy drawn above. Moreover, the countries selected for analysis in this book include only two good examples of clear cut bureaucratic domination--Bangladesh and Pakistan. Yet throughout Asia, Africa, the Middle East and Latin America this kind of political system is, surely, the most prevalent. A sure sign of bureaucratic domination, of course, is the phenomenon of coup politics. Whenever the electoral system cannot be counted on to generate authoritative political leadership (as distinct from the mere legitimizing of the rule of those who have seized power by violence) and if the monarchic system of hereditary office-holding has disappeared or been reduced to impotence, what alternative modes for the recruitment of a country's top political leaders remain?

In such circumstances, where the powers of government are monopolized by military and civil officials, I contend that the only road to power lies through intra-bureaucratic struggle. In such struggles it would indeed be surprising if civil servants could ever seize power. Conspiratorial coup groups and ruling juntas (admittedly sometimes including civil servants as members) are most likely to succeed, typically overthrowing, not a civilian regime composed of elected politicians but, rather, a ruling circle consisting of career bureaucrats (military and civil) who had themselves come to power by a similar route.[4]

Bureaucratic politics in regimes dominated by coup groups should not be expected to resemble that found in the United States or other politics where public officials can advance both their self interest and policy goals by "lobbying" with private interest groups and legislative committees in order to gain support for the laws and budgets required to maintain their bureaucratic interests. In such polities the price that public officials must pay for political support is surely at least moderately effective administrative performance.

By contrast, in a bureaucratic polity, we should expect the conduct of bureaucratic politics at intermediate and lower levels to consist of behind the scenes maneuvering or even passive conformism designed to safeguard one's position in the event of a regime change. After all, any coup group after scizing power, while seeking to displace its obvious enemies, will also want to retain enough public officials to carry out the minimal functions of public administration.[5] Attempts to upgrade the administrative competence and integrity of public officials in a bureaucratic polity by means of internally generated and monitored reforms seem to have few prospects for success. We must, instead, ask ourselves what rewards are offered, by whom, to officials who perform services with exceptional merit, if we want to understand the process or propsects of administrative reform.

Variations in Constitutive Politics

If the explanation of variations in the administrative capabilities of public bureaucracies hinges on the exercise of countervailing power by extra-bureaucratic political institutions, then we need, in order to understand administrative systems, to pay close attention to variations in the way such extra-bureaucratic systems are organized and how they impose constraints or rewards on public officials.

When we try to do this, however, we find that we are handicapped by a curious terminological deficiency. Although electoral and party systems are surely part and parcel of a larger complex in which elected assemblies play (in theory) a central role, we have no generally accepted term for this more comprehensive configuration of political elements. To call it a "political system" is utterly misleading because it appears to categorize bureaucracies as "non-political". As we have seen, however, in many if not all polities, bureaucratic politics are important even when they are not decisive. The "political system" in any country, therefore, must include its bureaucracy--and surely this is even more true in the Third World than it is in the First or Second.

I have previously referred to the total complex of institutions revolving, in principle, around an elective assembly as a "constitutive system".[6] Pending the discovery of a better term, let me suggest here that there are great variations in the design of constitutive systems and these surely affect bureaucratic behavior--including both the administrative and the political functions performed by public officials.

As a first break, let us distinguish, at their polar extremes, between the most effective and the most ineffective constitutive systems. In many Third World countries we do find quite ineffective constitutive systems, where official parties, dominated by appointed officials, manipulate elections to seats in a rubber-stamp and legitimizing but impotent elected assembly. Many examples could be cited, but analysts typically disregard them, recognizing their virtual irrelevance to the political process.

Thailand provides a classic case where bureaucratic (military) domination has prevailed most of the time since the revolution of 1932.[7] The various coup groups have, nevertheless, after coming to power, promulgated formal constitutions and established constitutive systems centering on an elected (or partially elected) but pliant and ineffectual assembly. Among the countries reported in this volume, the Philippines currently offers another example of a powerless constitutive system. This situation may, of course, be exceptional because the Philippines have, in the past, experienced vigorous constitutive politics, and President Ferdinand Marcos originally came to power by an authentic electoral process, even though he has subsequently imposed a personal autocracy via martial law and manipulated re-elections.

The result, according to Richter's account in this volume is: "The Congress, independent judiciary, party system, press, and people through the election or interest group process have been rendered impotent." "The new controls," she adds, "come in the form of the expanded and greatly enriched military,...a new group of technical and political experts,...and an international group of donor organizations..."[8] Note that all three of the new "controlling" groups are essentially bureaucratic, consisting of appointed office holders. Note also that the autonomy of the press, interest groups, and the judiciary are everywhere contingent on the existence of a viable constitutive system--or, more precisely, a certain kind of constitutive system. But in the absence of such a system, we cannot expect the press, interest groups, and courts to be vigorously self-assertive and politically influential.

Curiously, in her list of extra-bureaucratic institutions, Richter fails to mention parties or a party system. Lacking the notion of a "constitutive system," it is easy enough to overlook its existence--its strengths and weaknesses, and its decisive role--and to place in a single list both the parts of such a system and the institutions that lie outside its boundaries. So ineffective and inconspicuous is this system in the contemporary Philippines that Richter does not even bother to tell us that there is today an "Interim National Assembly" in the country, about four-fifths of whose members were elected as candidates of the Marcos-dominated New Society Movement. Moreover, without the protection of a viable constitutive system, how could one expect such autonomous institutions as private interest groups, the press, and the judiciary to exercise any real power or influence over the bureaucracy?

Relatively effective constitutive systems are, by contrast, typical of most if not all of the polities of the First and Second World, and they are found also in some countries of the Third World--including at least half of those described in this volume. The explanation of differences in administrative performance among polities hinges, for them, upon variations in the structures of their constitutive systems.

397

Consider the differences, now, between the constitutive systems that contain one-party systems, and those in which multi-party competition for seats in the elected assembly is politically decisive. No doubt both types of constitutive systems can impose more or less effective constraints on the administrative performance of public officials, but in different ways, and with variable results. A single party system can easily dominate its elected assembly, rendering it impotent to perform any important political functions. As a result, the dynamics of bureaucratic performance hinge on relations between the ruling party and official agencies-- a fact well reflected in the analysis of the contemporary Chinese polity, as described by Freedman and Morgan's chapter. It is no doubt true that most one-party systems are Communist in ideology, but that is not necessarily the case--Singapore providing an excellent example.

The efforts of the Communist party to dominate and restrain the rampant growth of Chinese bureaucracy have no doubt, been less successful than those of the PAP in Singapore. Although the causes of the so-called "Cultural Revolution" were no doubt highly complex, an undercurrent was surely the urgent pressure of Mao Zedong and his supporters to curtail the growth of bureaucratic power and privileges, and the excesses committed in the name of this cause reflected widespread dissatisfaction with the emerging establishment, as documented in the Freedman/Morgan chapter.

Students of comparative politics typically emphasize the importance of multi-party systems in relation to open (democratic) politics by contrast with the authoritarianism more typical of one-party systems. Here we may focus, instead, on their relation to public administration. But first it is necessary to point out not only that elected assemblies play an important role in all multi-party systems lodged in politically effective constitutive system, but having such assemblies is a requisite for the survival of any multi-party system.[9] As a corollary we may assume that it is the party-system-in-the-assembly that affects public administration in polities with an effective multi-party constitutive system, whereas it is the party alone that seeks to control bureaucracy in the one-party system.

In a complete analysis one would have to add a further distinction bewteen presidential and parliamentary systems: the administrative impact of parties being much less in the former than the latter. However, apart from the United States and one or two other equally exceptional cases, the presidential system of government leads to military dictatorships and autocracy. We can, therefore, ignore the completely atypical pattern of relationships between public bureaucracies and the constitutive systems that exist in the United States, where many "sub-governments" built on a trioka that includes government agency, interest group, and legislative committee have been widely studied and reported. For our purposes the more typical parliamentary structure of government is exemplified not only in Europe, but in several of the country-studies offered in this book. Here political parties, through the elected assembly, play a larger role, and public officials, while active, have to play politics in a more secretive way.

Or, in the case of highly polarized party system, they become openly politicized in a partisan sense.[10] This occurs when, in a multi-party system, the cabinet can be formed only by a multi-party coalition. One consequence may be the colonization of government ministries by partisan appointees (i.e., a "spoils system"). The Israeli case, as described by Rosenbloom and Mahler in this book, provides an excellent example.

It is important here to distinguish between different kinds of bureaucratic politics--notably between more and less partisan varieties. In the American system, after career services based on the merit principle had been institutionalized, bureaucratic politics tended to revolve around programmatic and policy issues because party discipline in the assembly (Congress) does not determine the policy line of a popularly elected president. The more legislation depended on cross-party alliances, the less partisan became the struggles of bureaucratic politics.

But in a polarized multi-party system, by contrast, partisanship plays a decisive role in public administration--as it did, of course, in the American presidential system before the introduction of civil service reforms, and as it still does in many American state and local jurisdictions. But even a well institutionalized merit system can scarcely resist the partisan pressures that prevail in a highly polarized parliamentary

system. Bureaucratic partisanship is, no doubt, reduced
in public administration in parliamentary sytems that
are not polarized, where a single party can rule, and
where its rule may extend over long periods of time.
England and Japan provide good examples--but we do not
find any systems of this kind in the chapters presented
in this book. Nor shall we find them, I think, in any
Third World countries.

The Pendulum Effect

To speak of constitutive systems as "effective"
or "ineffective" can, unintentionally, imply that they
are necessarily and permanently cast in one or the other
mold. In fact, of course, if we think of the relative
power exercised by constitutive systems as a variable,
we can easily see that it may wax and wane. Indeed, in
some polities there may be a more or less regular pendulum swing in which periods of bureaucratic domination
are succeeded by the rise of constitutive politics.
However, the results of this pendulum effect may well
be quite skewed: in some countries (Greece, for example)
we find bureaucratic domination having a limited life-
expectancy, whereas in countries like Thailand, the
exercise of power by a constitutive system tends to be
short-lived.

In Koehn's report on Nigeria we find, perhaps, an
example of a polity in which the tendency to bureaucratic rule is more evenly balanced against periods of
constitutionalism. The Turkish system, as described
by Dicle, might be another such example.

To explain the pendulum effect it is more important to examine the dynamics of bureaucratic domination
than it is to study the inner workings of constitutive
systems. To oversimplify, when a constitutive system
bankrupts (perhaps for reasons beyond its control) and
fails to find acceptable solutions for a wide range of
fundamental public problems, a mood of public despair
provokes a crisis in which some public (typically military) officials find themselves propelled to seize
power--as much from a spirit of public service as private ambition. Having come to power on a pledge to
eliminate corruption and incompetence in public office,
and to promulgate effective solutions to major public
issues, the new bureaucratic rulers may soon find themselves confronted with difficulties beyond their control.

At this point they face the increasing likelihood of being replaced by a new (secretly organized and hence invisible) coup group. To forestall such an anticipated disaster--and perhaps to save their own lives--a ruling group may well declare itself in favor of democratic reforms, sponsor a new constitution, hold elections, and promulgate an elected assembly. Normally such groups try to coexist with a dominated constitutive system, typically offering themselves as candidates. But sometimes they also miscalculate and find themselves displaced. In exceptional cases, having been sufficiently discredited by misfortune, a ruling junta may even turn power over to elected officials with gracious self-abdicating gestures, perhaps thereby hoping to avoid a worse fate than the fall from power.

The analysis of the pendulum effect can raise interesting questions for the study of political development--whether or not a dialectical process may come into existence which could eventually generate a stable political system, perhaps one dominated by elected politicians rather than by appointed public officials.

For students of public administration, however, an equally interesting question involves the effect of pendulum swings on the execution of public policies. I suspect that in many cases at least--and Nigeria as reported by Koehn, seems to offer an example--the residual power of entrenched bureaucracies tends to defy the efforts of newly instituted constitutive systems to bring them under effective control. Eventually the efforts of popularly based governments to dominate their bureaucracies can lead to increasingly severe frustrations and the return, in due course, to bureaucratic rule. Such at least, was the history of Thailand in 1976. Whether or not a similar reversal will occur in Nigeria remains to be seen. For public administration, however, this means that newly established constitutive systems may not survive long enough to succeed in bringing their public bureaucracies (civil and military) under effective control.

The Importance of Political Ecology

Anyone interested in administrative reform and impatient to improve bureaucratic performance may regard the foregoing discussion as "academic" in a pejorative sense. Yet, if such propositions as those offered above are valid, then administrative reform must be contingent on changes in the extra-bureaucratic environment of bureaucratized politics. But such changes, in turn, depend on forces which may be thought of as external to the "political system"--using this term to embrace both the constitutive and the bureaucratic subsystems as they interlock with each other.

Let me suggest three such sets of forces--there may well be others. I have in mind the <u>historical</u>, <u>technological</u> and the <u>world-system</u> contexts (or environment) of any political system as underlying determinants of its politico-administrative performance.

A good deal of <u>historical</u> information is, no doubt, contained in our case studies, but their focus is blurred by the way that historical influences are ordinarily perceived. We find a good deal of emphasis on the colonial or semi-colonial background of most of the countries included in our sample. The systems of bureaucratic organization created by imperial powers to dominate and administer conquered dependencies have tended to persist, by sheer inertia, into the post-independence period. Thus the colonial heritage and persisting neo-imperialist forces are blamed for what could, instead, be explained better if a different model of historical dynamics were used.

The colonial period, after all, had no reason to institutionalize representative institutions during their time of dominance. In India, exceptionally, the British Raj retreated step by step from the pressures generated by an insurgent Congress Party, granting at each stage some of the rights and institutions of parliamentary self-government. In the Philippines, also exceptionally, the ambivalence of the American Congress toward the conquest of the Philippines was reflected in the early establishment of a Philippine Congress.

Generally speaking, however, it was only when imperialism confronted its own demise that a ruling power would consent to or even facilitate the creation of political institutions for representative government--i.e., a constitutive system. In the post-independence struggle for power, long entrenched and large bureaucracies (including the armed forces) easily dominated or suppressed nascent parliamentary institutions and political parties.[11] This tended to be true also in new states that never experienced full-scale imperial rule, such as Thailand, Turkey, and China. In Japan, exceptionally, the Western-type constitutive system established during the Meiji Restoration evolved _pari passu_ with the modern bureaucracy so that, after a narrow escape and the American occupation, it has become a well-established institution.

The technological factors affecting bureaucratic power have attracted less attention in the literatures of comparative politics and administration. Yet, I would argue, the growth of modern high-energy technology, and the spread of organizational methods--the skills necessary to create and operate large scale bureaucracies--contributed both to the need for modern types of governmental administration and to the possibility of creating them. By contrast, although elected assemblies, electoral systems, and party systems could utilize modern technology, it is quite possible to utilize industrialism and promote its growth without creating a constitutive system--Saudi Arabia is a conspicuous example. While the Saudi state continuously expands its bureaucratic machinery, it easily blocks the emergence of any kind of representative political structures.[12]

A third aspect of the phenomenon of bureaucratic power has, by contrast, attracted a great deal of attention, including some references in case studies presented here. I have in mind the world system of interdependency in which countries of the Third World find themselves. The relevance of this system to the emergence of bureaucratic power, however, has scarcely been noted. My basic argument would be that this world system contributes greatly and continuously to the growth and strengthening of bureaucratic power at the same time that it does nothing to strengthen the growth of extra-bureaucratic institutions (especially of constitutive systems). Most of the attention of writers on the world system is directed to "political economy," especially the pernicious role of multi-national corporations in national development. An additional consequence of the impact of MNCs, however, that needs to be studied is its effect on administrative performance in host countries. I suspect that bureaucracies are expanded in order to cope with new problems generated by the operations of international firms, and at the same time bureaucratic corruption is increased by reason of the pressures or inducements offered by agents of these same firms.

We should not, however, ignore the direct impact of government-to-government relations. Two aspects or levels should be mentioned. In an atmosphere of intergovernmental conflict and domestic insecurity, almost every country has been induced to dedicate more and more of its resources to military ("defense"!) preparations. The growing size of the armed forces and the increasing investment in military hardware--all of which requires the services of highly trained specialists--surely contributes to the growth of bureaucracy, especially the part of the bureaucracy (the military) that is most capable of seizing power in any intra-bureaucratic struggle for political supremacy.

Non-military inter-governmental relations, however, also generate pressures that contribute to the growth of bureaucratic size and power, including the most well-intentioned efforts to help developing countries by means of technical and economic assistance programs. Virtually all substantive aid programs are directed to and implemented by direct relations between appointed officials of the aiding and the aided countries. By contrast, virtually no external aid programs are directed--nor could they be so directed--toward the strengthening of constitutive systems. When, exceptionally, elections are fostered by external pressures--as they were in South Vietnam--the predictable ineffectiveness of the results tended to discredit any serious study of the conditions under which external influences could prove effective in support of an emergent and viable constitutive system. Ironically, technical assistance programs in the field of public administration no doubt also contributed--though in a very small way-- to the enhancement of the power position of public bureaucracies, and hence indirectly served to undermine their administrative capabilities. Although I doubt that many (if any) administrative advisers saw the connection, they were surely worried by their own ineffectivenss, a fact that contributed in an indirect way to the rise of interest in comparative administration in the United States.

The Fate of Comparative Administration

The culture shock experiment by Americans who engaged in overseas programs to offer advice in public administration contributed directly to the rise of interest in "comparative" or "development" administration in the U.S. This phenomenon helps explain the comments about the fate of comparative administration offered in the Prologue to this book by Tummala. He asserts that the field "found its place in the sun" during my steward-ship of CAG in the 1960's, but that during the 1970's it "floundered" and suffered a "self-imposed failure." He nevertheless acknowledges the "dissensus" that exi-sted from the very beginning among those professing an interest in comparative administration.

How could it, indeed, have been otherwise? The field came into being only as a result of a series of anxious questions raised by returning expatriates whose efforts to help foreign governments and universities launch administrative development or reform programs had proven unsuccessful and painful. Most of those who initially associated themselves with CAG were scholars who, after several years of teaching and research in American Universities, found themselves involved in overseas technical assistance projects, chiefly to establish counterpart educational or training programs in countries of the Third World. We all shared a perce-ption that American administrative experience and theory needed serious revision if it was to be made relevant and useful to scholars and public officials working in developing countries. In that context of shared concern it is scarcely surprising that a wide diversity of opi-nions flourished as we struggled together to find use-ful answers in a new and chaotic field of study. Altho-ugh the answers we proposed diverged widely from each other, we shared a common sense of the importance of the questions that needed to be answered. Moreover, we supported each other in our efforts, even when our posi-tions on the possible answers diverged widely--in fact we may have reveled in what we thought to be creative diversity of opinions.

During the 1970's the freshness of overseas expe-rience dimmed as the number of specialists in public administration returning from overseas radically decli-ned. Meanwhile a new generation of American scholars came on the scene: persons who had, indeed, studied comparative politics as well as comparative administra-tion. This was also a generation impressed with the need for phiolosophical and methodological sophistica-tion, or for systematic exposure to the interdiscipli-nary study of selected world areas and their languages, or they were dedicated to new epistemologies, such as phenomenology, critical theory, hermeneutics, and the radical perspectives that writers on the world system

405

and interdependency had generated. Others were also elated by the quest for a "new public administration" that radically challenged conventional assumptions made in the teaching of American public administration.

In various ways these new academic or scholarly perspectives provided amunition for attacks on whatever had gone before, including several stereotypes of what had been done in the 1960's under the heading of "comparative" or "development" administration. Meanwhile the freshness of concern based on direct experience abroad had waned. The sense of adventure or discovery was lost. In its place came a mood of disillusionment and discontent--what promised to be an important new field of research and teaching seemed to have collapsed unceremoniously. Yet the new critics of comparative administration had no answers of their own, nor did their attacks reflect a shared paradigm.[13] They helped to undermine what had been done without offering something new in its place.

Now, in the first years of the 1980's, I anticipate that a new wave will arise, putting the experiences of the 1960's and the 1970's into a fresh perspective. This will result, I think, from two opposite tendencies: the increasing parochialization of American scholarship on the one hand, and the nascent universalization of administrative study overseas on the other.

Increasingly American scholarship has become re-directed to domestic issues and experiences. Even some of those who, following their return from overseas assignments in the 1960's, became leaders in comparative administration, found these efforts to be insufficiently rewarding and they returned to their original preoccupations with American administrative problems and solutions. Meanwhile a new generation of specialists in public administration found fewer opportunities for international experience at a time when the Western-inspired institutes and schools of public administration in the Third World had begun to supply their own personnel and to establish their own research programs. The resulting parochialism generated a widespread feeling that the important issues in public administration are those to be confronted at home, while the study of administration overseas is either exotic, unsound, or fruitless.

Meanwhile, a process of universalization has been

occurring abroad. The new institutes, schools, and departments of public administration have matured, and their faculties are now offering their own advanced degrees. For better or worse, these scholars are necessarily comparativists for two important reasons. First, much of the available literature does not concern their own countries and so, using these materials, they must expose students to the administrative experience of countries other than their own. Second, in many countries it is scarcely wise or expedient to probe too deeply into the realities of governments plagued by arbitrary and corrupt administration--where bureaucratic domination in fact marks the political system. For this very reason, also, in some countries departments of public administration can flourish while departments of political science wither because they appear to be too threatening to those in power. The study of "admistration" appears, instead, to be not only safe but useful. As a result, the resources dedicated to administrative as compared with political studies have tended to increase.

Even so, teachers concerned about domestic conditions find it more expedient to focus on foreign experience--perhaps some of its lessons will not be lost on their own students. At least the graduates of administrative study programs in the Third World are typically far more sophisticated in their perception of cross-national experience and theory than are the graduates of most American universities.

In such a setting labels change. What was originally viewed as new and surprising when "comparative administration" emerged in the 1960's is now seen to be routine and necessary. No one can claim to understand "public administration" when all that she or he knows is the administrative experience of one country. As a result what was once thought of as "public administration" in the United States must now be re-categorized as merely "American public administration." What we used to think of as "comparative public administration" must now be viewed, in most countries, and surely so outside the U.S., as nothing more than ordinary "public administration." In short, public administration today, in a global sense, is essentially and necessarily comparative.

Fortunately for Americans, therefore, there is

Hope in the Pandora's Box of woes that I have described. This hope arises from the reverse flow of schoalrs that is now occurring. Instead of Americans going abroad, we have a growing number of foreign scholars coming to the United States. Although we may well lament the adverse effects of this "brain drain" on the countries that lose some of their talented scholars, we must also acknowledge that Americans (or the Western world) are the main beneficiaries. Foreign scholars, knowing well their native languages, are also able to bring us better analyses based on fuller coverage of information sources still opaque to most American analysts.

This book gives us a good example of the consequences. At least a third of the authors of the country studies reported here are foreign scholars living and writing outside of their homelands. I expect this trend to continue. The study of foreign areas in the United States has already come to be almost monopolized, in a few instances, by expatriate scholars teaching at American universities. If this book may be seen as a harbinger of the 1980's, may we not look forward to a time in the 1990's when artificial distinctions will have vanished, when the study of public administration will, indeed, have become a universalized subject of study? A future symposium on "administrative systems of the world" will then contain, not just chapters on India, China, and Nigeria, but also companion chapters on an equal footing, devoted to administration in England, the U.S.S.R. and, of course, the United States. Let us hope, at least, that this volume is only the first intimation of even better things to come.

Footnotes

¹Khan and Zafarullah, *supra*, p. 181.

²Quah, *supra*, p. 63.

³*Ibid*, p. 65.

⁴The dynamics of coup politics in a bureaucratic polity are analyzed in more detail in Riggs, "Cabinet Ministers and Coup Groups: The Case of Thailand," *International Political Science Review* 2, No. 2 (1981), pp. 15-188.

⁵The argument for political passivity of intermediate and lower level officials in a bureaucratic polity is elaborated in Riggs, "Three Dubious Hypothesis," *Administration & Society* 12, No. 3 (November 1980), pp. 301-326.

⁶See, for example, Riggs, "The Context of Development Administration," in Riggs, ed., *Frontiers of Development Administration*, Durham,NC: Duke University Press, 1970, pp. 72-108, esp. pp. 72-83.

⁷For further details, see Riggs, *Thailand: The Modernization of a Bureaucratic Polity*, Honolulu: East-West Center Press, 1966.

⁸Richter, *supra*, p. 90.

⁹The argument for this opinion is given in Riggs, "Legislative Structures: Some Thoughts on Elected National Assemblies," Allan Kornberg, ed., *Legislatures in Comparative Perspective*, New York: McKay, 1973, pp. 39-93.

¹⁰The concept of a polarized party system is elaborated in Giovanni Sartori, "European Political Parties: The Case of Polarized Pluralism," Jospeh LaPalombara and Myron Weiner, eds., *Political Parties and Political Development*, Princeton, NJ: Princeton University Press, 1966, pp. 137-176.

[11]Historical evidence based on Southeast Asian case studies is given in Riggs, _Legislative Origins: A Comparative and Contextual Approach_, Pittsburgh,PA: International Studies Association, 1975; Occasionl paper No. 7.

[12]The link between spreading industrial technology and the rise of modern bureaucracy is suggested in Riggs, "Prismatic Societies in Public Administration," _Administrative Change_ 1, No. 2 (December 1973), pp. 12-24.

[13]The diversity of views held by contemporary critics of comparative administration are presented in the symposium on this topic contained in _Public Administration Review_ 36, No. 6 (November-December 1976). See also the rejoinder by Riggs, "The Group and the Movement: Notes on Comaparative and Development Administration," in the same issue, pp. 648-654.

About the Contributing Editor

     Krishna K. Tummala is an expatriate from India.
After initial gradaute training in Political Science
and Public Administration, he taught College in his
native land, before coming to the United States in
1968. He attended the State University of New York at
Albany, and the University of Missouri, Columbia, and
obtained the Ph. D. degree from the latter. Since
then, he taught at Murray State University, Murray,
Kentucky, Ball State University, Muncie, Indiana, and
the University of Wyoming, Laramie, Wyoming. He is
currently Associate Professor and Director, M. P. A.
program, Department of Political Science, Montana
State Univeristy, Bozeman, Montana.

     His teaching and research interests are in the
areas of personnel management, public budgeting and
comparative public administration, besides American
public policy. His last book, The Ambiguity of Ideology
and Administrative Reform (1979) was published by
Allied Publishers, New Delhi, India, and is being now
distributed in the U. S. by South Asia Books, Columbia,
Missouri. It was a comparative study of administrative
reforms in India, United States and Britain. He was a
Research Fellow (1973) and Senior Research Fellow (1978)
of the Indian Council of Social Science Research, New
Delhi, India.

     His research project, "Affirmative Action Programs:
A Cross-National Experience," is the recipient of a
MONTS-NSF grant (1982). As an outcome of this, he is
currently serving as the Contributing Editor of the
proposed volume, Equity in Public Service Across Nations.
He is also working on another volume, Public Budgeting
in the United States.

411